Anthropological Papers

Museum of Anthropology, University of Michigan
No. 75

Prehistoric Food Production
in North America

Edited by Richard I. Ford

Ann Arbor, Michigan
1985

Printed in the
United States of America

ISBN 0-915703-01-7

Dedicated to the Memory of

Volney Hurt Jones
(1903–1982)

He led us out of the darkness

Contents

Illustrations

Tables

Preface

Richard I. Ford

The decade of the 1980s is witnessing the most productive period in the history of archaeobotany. Several major research programs (discussed in this volume) and numerous cultural resource management projects have yielded an unprecedented quantity of plant remains from archaeological sites throughout the United States. Added to this expanding data base are the research tools provided by the scanning electron microscope (SEM) and by accelerator radiocarbon dating and an increased number of the best trained archaeobotanists ever to handle prehistoric plant fragments. The result is an explosive expansion of our knowledge about the variety of cultivated and domesticated plants and their history in aboriginal America.

The purpose of this volume is to present the cultural contexts into which fully domesticated plants were introduced from Mexico or the conditions under which indigenous plants were genetically altered by prehistoric people. Hopefully, the book provides the necessary framework for understanding the exciting discoveries we anticipate throughout the remainder of the decade. The papers were originally prepared in 1980 but all have undergone extensive revision since 1983 and in some cases as recently as November, 1984. Future research questions are also posited for the benefit of students and professionals, but for all, the papers are written to present a cultural and historical structure for integrating the new information and interpretations we eagerly anticipate from our archaeobotanical colleagues in the years ahead.

The inception of this volume was a modest conference sponsored by the School of American Research. Human interaction and interrelationships with plants was central because insufficient new information was available to discuss the dog or the turkey. Little did those in attendance realize that from 1980 to 1984 a new domesticated chenopod and an amaranth cultigen from Mexico would be identified; 2000-year-old tobacco and a second species would appear in the East; two grasses in the Southwest would suggest local domestication; and new evidence would indicate squash cultivation in the East to be so very old and corn-growing in the Southwest so young. These important developments are discussed in the revised papers but were unknown at the time of the conference.

An Advanced Seminar convened at the School of American Research in Santa Fe, New Mexico, on March 2–8, 1980, to discuss the topic, "The Origins of Plant Husbandry in North America." A fertile tone of spirited debate was established the first day when the objective of the conference itself was questioned. It was contended that "husbandry" implies a skewed division of labor in favor of men and arbitrarily narrows the multitude of relationships between people and their biological environment. Furthermore, the term customarily is applied to the management of animals, but since in North America north of Mexico the only domesticated animals, the turkey and the dog, were not widely used subsistence items, it would be better to employ a term befitting the many plants that were manipulated to some degree by prehistoric Indians. Following the lead of Braidwood in the Near East, the term "food production" was advanced and quickly adopted to convey the breadth of the conference. The title of this volume preserves the intention of the participants.

The conferees were botanists, ethnobotanists, and archaeologists. It was mandatory for the success of the Seminar that some participants know the plant biology of the taxa under discussion and at the same time that the archaeologists have insightful and first-hand knowledge of the subsistence patterns of the geographic areas under discussion. Throughout the Seminar comparisons were made between cultural developments and processes of food production in the eastern and southwestern United States. The organization of this volume reflects the logical progress of the discussion.

Before the Seminar convened, it was certain that domesticated plants had entered the eastern United States millennia before they did the Southwest. Consequently, it was essential that the archaeological basis of eastern Texas was familiar to at least one participant since that area would be discussed frequently. Dr. Dee Ann Story, who is the leading authority on the prehistoric cultures of eastern Texas and Professor of Anthropology at the University of Texas, Austin, provided the necessary background and clarified the ecological and cultural problems that any plants would face as they diffused northward from eastern Mexico.

The first domesticates were hard-shell cucurbits. Dr. Charles B. Heiser, Jr., Distinguished Professor of Botany at Indiana University, has been investigating the gourds for some time. His contribution was essential for understanding the basic botany and evolutionary problems of these garden plants. He is also the botanical authority on the sunflower, and that annual flower demanded discussion as well. His botanical knowledge is so extensive that his contribution to the success of the Seminar was far more important than his excellent paper alone.

Frances B. King is a paleoethnobotanist at the Illinois State Museum with extensive experience in the Midwest. More significantly, at the time of the Seminar she was researching the squash and bottle gourd remains from Phillips Springs and making comparisons with the same species from other sites. Her experience with these archaeobotanical remains was invaluable.

The prehistory of the Archaic and Woodland periods in the East must be understood before the introduction of these tropical cultigens into existing cultures can be assessed. Furthermore, the subsequent manipulation of native plants can only be appreciated by knowing the cultural changes over this long period of time. Dr. Patty Jo Watson, who is an archaeologist at Washington University in St. Louis, has unparalleled experience excavating open sites and caves in the East that have yielded a wealth of plant remains. Each and every plant discussed she associated with its cultural context.

Archaeological investigations in the lower Illinois River valley have produced an abundance of archeological plants. These have been studied and identified by David L. Asch and Nancy B. Asch, who are both staff members of the Center for American Archeology at Northwestern University. Both of these paleobotanists are knowledgeable about the taxonomic and botanical history of several native plant taxa. David Asch participated in the Seminar.

Rockshelters, where they have not been pillaged, are an invaluable source of desiccated plant fragments. Dr. C. Wesley Cowan of the Cincinnati Museum of Natural History had recently excavated several of these sites and reexamined the floral contents of many more. He is also a paleoethnobotanist who has studied prehistoric maygrass and the ecological associations of economic seed plants. The experience of the Asches and Dr. Cowan was indispensable for an appreciation of indigenous plant cultivation and their eventual domestication.

In the Southwest the problems are different and the domesticated plants are more numerous than elsewhere. The premiere issue, of course, is the origin of maize. Dr. Walton C. Galinat, who is a maize geneticist and anatomist at the University of Massachusetts Agricultural Experiment Station, has worked with archaeological maize throughout his professional career. His ideas about the origin of maize in Mexico are presented in his published paper. However, during the Seminar we benefited from his knowledge of the spread and further breeding of corn within the continental United States.

The date for the introduction of maize into the Southwest has been controversial for three decades. Dr. Michael Berry, a cultural resource management archaeologist, has reanalyzed all the radiocarbon dates for maize and presents a radical evaluation in his chapter. Since the Seminar, a number of accelerator radiocarbon dates have been obtained. They are included in this volume and those for maize substantiate his conclusions.

Dr. Paul E. Minnis, who is a paleoethnobotanist and archaeologist at the University of Oklahoma, has examined in detail the role of domesticated plants in the prehistoric economies of the Pueblo areas of New Mexico and Arizona. He provided the cultural context for food production in the Southwest.

The historical background and dynamic interactions by humans to manage the production of food were summarized by Richard I. Ford. Dr. Ford is Director of the Ethnobotanical Laboratory at the University of Michigan.

The results of the Seminar are incorporated into individual papers as well as the summary chapter by Ford. That chapter also contains brief reference to unresolved issues requiring further research that were proposed by the participants.

Each participant focused on the following issues during the Seminar:

1) What were the human demographic situation, subsistence and settlement systems, and intra-regional social relations in the East and Southwest when domesticated plants were introduced from Mexico?

2) By what means or processes were they introduced to both areas?

3) What were the genetic or phenotypic characteristics of these plants?

4) How were they integrated into existing economies?

5) What cultural, nutritional, and ecological changes resulted, and when?

6) What was the nature of the food production technology? Was it intensified over time?

7) What, if any, cultural or ecological limits restricted expansion of the new technology?

8) How did plant food production relate to sedentarism in both areas?

9) How and when was obvious plant breeding manifested?

10) What genetic changes followed initial cultivation in terms of new varieties of domesticated plants? When were they recognizable in the archaeobotanical record?

The Seminar succeeded because of the steadfast interest, extensive experience, and authoritative knowledge of the participants. The opportunity to participate so intensely with such scholarly colleagues changed our individual minds about many issues and opened new vistas for understanding food production. We left Santa Fe most grateful to the School of American Research for the unique interaction we experienced, and we hope this volume conveys the excitement we experienced debating the critical issues of plant food production.

The Processes of Plant Food Production in Prehistoric North America

Richard I. Ford
Museum of Anthropology, University of Michigan

Domesticated plants and animals have long been recognized as the font of civilization. When Childe (1936) popularized the concept of the "Neolithic Revolution," he was merely highlighting recognition by historians, social philosophers and archaeologists that food production brought surplus, security, and civilization to human society. Since he wrote, however, excavation of prehistoric archaeological sites and the recovery of subsistence remains have placed food production in a new perspective. The botanical changes and prehistoric dissemination of most major domesticated plants and animals are now well documented, but the cultural processes leading to the genetic changes that characterize these domesticates remain in the realm of speculation.

Certainly this is the situation for understanding food production in prehistoric North America north of Mexico. Except for tobacco, all plants produced here were consumed even if their primary usage was for other purposes such as gourd containers and cotton textiles. Most of the domesticated plants were introduced from Mexico, but several indigenous plants were grown for subsistence purposes. The attention these indigenous species have garnered within the past decade now permits this continental area to be viewed as a laboratory for understanding the origins of domestication elsewhere. But the processes involved in the transformation from wild to domesticated plants and from foraging to farming techniques must be explained.

PLANT PRODUCTION

Plant production is the deliberate manipulation of specific floral species by humans for domestic use or consumption. In other words, the term subsumes a number of activities affecting biological growth by means of cultural practices and volition through which humans intervene in the life cycle of a plant to assure the availability of some useful part, either edible or utilitarian. Agriculture as we know it in Western culture is but one in an array of techniques employed to propagate plants.

The methods to control the quantity and to increase the probability of the availability of plant resources for cultural purposes may assume many forms (Bronson 1977). The emphasis in this chapter is the many types of interaction that constitute plant food production. The inadvertent consequences of manipulating a seemingly wild plant or the complexity of procedures followed to raise a crop plant makes it difficult to bound with precision where one form of extraction ends and another begins. When they are viewed along a continuum of categories of interaction or as several types of behavior toward plants, then our understanding is enhanced. Figure 1.1 illustrates some of these cultural activities which range, left to right, from least disruptive, even

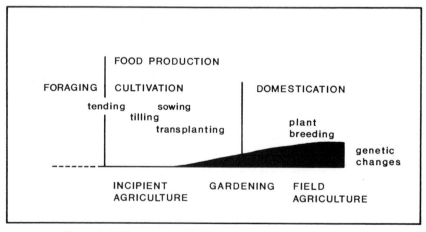

Figure 1.1. The stages and methods of plant food production.

outside the realm of deliberate production, to complete domestication resulting in a plant's total dependence on humans for its existence. These types of interaction were not discrete over time but became cumulative as new ones were discovered. By the time plant breeding was practiced, a series of methods for maintaining plants known to the ancestors were also used.

For several millennia following their arrival the dominant mode of subsistence for prehistoric Native Americans was hunting and gathering or plant foraging. How much their procurement methods changed the biology of the utilized plants is debatable. Undoubtedly plant reproduction was understood by the first Americans but whether any deliberate actions were undertaken to assist the growth of a plant species in a particular location, a sure sign of food production, is unknown.

Certainly *unintentional* tending may occur as a consequence of collecting a useful plant part. The very act of gathering a plant resource at a particular time with accompanying trampling and accidental seed dispersal may benefit the plant population, albeit for unanticipated or unplanned reasons. The intensive gathering of a particular plant may have unexpected genetic consequences that are unrecognized by human foragers. On Figure 1.1 the dashed bottom line indicates this possibility. Humans may be choosing larger seeds or another morphological feature that selects against less desirable traits. Over time these changes may be genetically maintained even if the humans are no longer collecting in that locality. The initial collection of teosinte, the ancestor of corn, and the condensation of its lateral branches with their tiny cobs that were dispersed by humans may represent such an accidental genetic change (Galinat, this volume).

Perhaps fire, as Lewis (1972) has suggested, was employed to increase vegetative growth or to regenerate annual seed or fruit reproduction. Whether this "tool" was an early means of plant production remains untested from a perspective of origins although fire certainly was useful for such purposes ethnographically (cf. Stewart 1956). Wild fire will select for certain species. Deliberately set fires of course will do the same, but the people can determine its timing and direct its benefit toward certain species. The use of fire both to eliminate competitors under edible acorn oak trees and to encourage the sprouts of *Corylus* for baskets by California Indians may have had early prehistoric antecedents that were precursors to food plant production.

Food production begins with deliberate care afforded the propagation of a species. Generically these varied activities are subsumed under plant *cultivation* (Fig. 1.1). The cultivation of plants does not imply that they are domesticated, but it does mean that humans have disrupted a life cycle for the benefit of some plant or plant population. The ultimate goal of this activity is for humans to obtain with greater ease or in larger quantity a particular plant product. There are many ways to cultivate plants.

Tending encourages plant growth by means of weeding, pruning, and other methods to limit competition or to care for the plant. Removing by hand competing vegetation surrounding a particularly useful plant or population of a single species is commonly observed throughout the world. Patches of famine tubers are treated in this manner in the Pacific and medicinal plants often receive this beneficial attention in the Pueblo Southwest. An archaeological demonstration of this technique is another matter, however. It is such a casual activity that it leaves no material correlates and the response from the plant is either a quantitative increase in yield or a prolonged presence in a particular locality, neither of which are discernible by archaeobotanical methods. Nonetheless, in evolutionary terms deliberate tending must be regarded as a common means of aiding food production.

A more obvious cultivation procedure is the mechanical *tilling* of the soil by means of a digging stick or hoe in order to encourage the appearance or germination of certain species of plants. Tillage may prepare a nursery bed for naturally dispersed seeds or it may have positive biochemical results by increasing the moisture holding capacity of the soil, by aerating it to assist root gas exchange, or by oxidizing allelopaths in the soil. The common sunflower, *Helianthus annuus*, produces chemicals that are detrimental to its own seedlings (Wilson and Rice 1968). Perhaps an initial stage in its eventual domestication was the digging of the soil by Archaic people to assure the growth of sunflowers the next year, even though it is doubtful that people knew the biological bases of their behavior. Moreover, using a digging stick to obtain bulbs and tubers may increase the size of a species' population by detaching bulblets or lateral tubers. This is a common result in areas where wild onions or Jerusalem artichokes are intensively harvested: the more one gathers, the more one gets. Again, archaeobotanical evidence for this cultivation method is tenuous, despite the possible discovery of appropriate implements.

Another type of cultivation is *transplanting*. Literally this cultural technique involves excavating a plant from one locality and replanting it elsewhere, usually for convenience of its use or to assure its availability. If its new habitat conditions are markedly changed, then protection and concomitant interference in its growth cycle are necessary for its survival where it is relocated. The long-term care required by these plants may in fact lead to the selection for new genetic characters or to hybridization with closely related but not necessarily economically significant plants. Theoretically, transplanting may be quite casual or it may be the beginning of a designated space where a variety of plants from various habitats are assembled and nurtured in a garden-like habitat. Ethnographically, of course, we know that transplanting of medicinal and ceremonial plants is quite common and the maintenance of multispecies gardens exist even in the presence of large scale field agriculture.

Transplanting as recorded ethnographically usually entails the relocation of small perennial herbs or shrubs. When true arboriculture began in North America is unknown. Trees have been noted growing outside their accepted range of distribution (cf. Black 1978) but most appear to be a consequence of seedlings begun from the accidental dispersal of seeds and then subsequent protection in some form. Planting trees in anticipation of a future harvest appears to come later in the evolutionary history of cultivation. For the most part ethnobotanists have shown that such trees are allocated to a culturally defined space as an edge plant, as a garden border, or as an orchard. Orchards were not part of prehistoric food production in North America until Europeans introduced the technology early in the contact period both in the East and the Southwest.

A common type of cultivation is the *sowing* of seed. In its simplest form this technique includes the deliberate dispersal or broadcasting of ripened seeds at the time they are harvested. Beyond this "casual" form of husbandry, there are more complex procedures for storing the seed through a period of dormancy and tilling the soil in preparation for planting them. Considering the number of points in the life cycle of the plant when human selection occurs, it is little wonder that this procedure can result in the selection for most obvious useful genetic changes. For example, larger seeds may be selected for simply by using a shallow tray basket to winnow seeds. Similarly, by synchronizing the sowing of seeds, they germinate simultaneously and are ready for harvest at once. This scheduling procedure selects against seeds with germination delay mechanisms. Sowing also allows seeds from one habitat to be planted in another. All aspects of harvesting, storing, and sowing wild seeds are best exemplified ethnographically by Yuman people living along the lower Colorado River (Castetter and Bell 1951). The prehistoric sowing of maygrass (Cowan 1978) and Archaic sumpweed (Asch and Asch, this volume) are comparable examples.

The cultivation by whatever means of wild plants or plants which are undergoing the first few genetic changes resulting from human selection of useful characters does not necessarily produce a staple crop.

Most likely a seasonal supplement to an already varied diet was the goal of the first prehistoric food producers with the significant difference being that the probability of a harvest was increased and the need for any reconnaissance to locate a viable plant population as foragers must do was eliminated. Because these benefits of the initial stages of plant production have potential evolutionary importance for cultural development, they have been regarded as examples of incipient agriculture (Steward 1949:10). From the perspective of economic activity these otherwise descriptive forms of crop manipulation do constitute a series of stages covering long periods of time until new plants are created by human selection and human-made plant communities become the dominant source of human subsistence.

As mentioned above, gardening is an economic activity related to the creation of a culturally defined spatial area where plant production occurs. It always entails the protection and harvesting of many species of plants, but they need not be domesticated in the genetic sense of the term. In fact, even today gardens consist of weedy species, annuals, biennials, and perennials maintained for food, medicine, utilitarian, or simply aesthetic appeal. Undoubtedly multipurpose gardens prevailed prehistorically as well (cf. Ford 1979).

Domestication is the final stage of plant food production. Cultural selection for useful phenotypic characters resulted in new plants dependent upon humans for their existence. Domesticated plants are cultural artifacts. They do not exist naturally in nature; they cannot normally survive without human assistance. Because the genetic changes leading to true domestication are cumulative, it is difficult to identify an absolute distinction between wild and domesticated plants. The domestication of plants is a continuous process, and is only one of several plant propagation practices occurring simultaneously in any culture. Domesticates, too, may only be seasonal supplements in a diet, or because of cultural selective forces, may actually constitute the yearly staple for the culture.

As a domesticated species becomes more important in the subsistence economy, more space may be allotted to its production. Despite certain disadvantages, the singular important characteristic of domesticated plants is that their production can be increased significantly by clearing one habitat and in its place creating an environment conducive to the maximal growth of the favored crop. When geographical space is devoted to a plant in this manner, then field agriculture (horticulture) results with the reduction in the number of species grown and with primary attention focused on only one or at most a few species, e.g., corn fields with beans and squash.

Plant breeding probably had an accidental beginning and most likely did not have cultural significance for the creation of special varieties and the maintenance of certain constellations of genetic features until prehistoric economies were dependent upon domesticated plant food staples and their successful production, despite environmental perturbations. In fact, plant breeding may be viewed as a cultural attempt to replace a generalize domesticate by creating varieties attuned to different environmental circumstances and to increase yield as insurance against crop losses. Viewed from the perspective of a particular plant species, its phenotypic appearance changes step-wise as some of its mutations are selected by human techniques to satisfy specific cultural needs. Consequently, even though a plant may be domesticated, it may be changed if its importance changes from a garden food supplement to a large field crop and finally with further breeding to a number of environmentally sensitive varieties. In evolutionary perspective each agricultural technique, it should be noted, results from cultural changes and then the new plants serve to maintain the increased cultural complexity and co-occurring larger human populations.

BRIEF HISTORY OF PLANT FOOD PRODUCTION

The scientific investigation of the origin of agriculture began little more than a century ago. Alphonse de Candolle assembled existing knowledge from numerous sources with the publication of *Géographic Botanique Raisonnée* (1855) and he followed this remarkable book with an even more encyclopedic inventory of cultivated plants, *Origine des Plantes Cultivées* (1886). In this monumental work he proposed a series of steps from gathering to regular cultivation and recognized that archaeology provided the direct proof of ancient forms and the distribution of the earliest cultivated plants (1959:1–16).

Darwin (1875) also considered the question of the evolution of domesticated plants under the conditions of natural selection. Unfortunately, an understanding of ethnology and cultural selection is absent from his work as is an appreciation of archaeological evidence.

The contribution that expanded the geographical concepts of de Candolle was made by Vavilov (cf. 1951). He accepted de Candolle's idea of centers of domestication and developed a number of world areas, including one for Mexico and Central America (Vavilov 1931). These were based upon genetic diversity of varieties found in each area. This criterion becomes the key for locating the geographical area in which a domesticated plant arose. Although some of the specifics of his study are incorrect based upon subsequent research (cf. Smith

1969), his ideas are still applicable in any attempt to locate where humans and particular species first interacted (cf. Harlan 1971).

Discussions about the origins of agriculture in the New World were more speculative than those of the pioneer economic botanists in Europe. Morgan (1877), for example, viewed the stages leading to agriculture from a general evolutionary perspective as a threefold process: tillage of open alluvial land, gardens, and plowed fields. Archaeological evidence from the continent was not available to him but for his purposes it was unnecessary.

With the exception of a few attempts to save plants from archaeological sites (e.g., Mills 1901 and Kidder and Guernsey 1919) and recognition that they would be helpful for understanding agricultural origins (Harshberger 1896), little was done with archaeobotanical materials for the first three decades of this century beyond providing a botanical identification. Spinden (1917) proposed his "Archaic Hypothesis" to account for the development of New World cultures by means of the diffusion of a maize, beans, and squash complex out of the Mexican Highlands. He believed that agriculture was invented only once, and without archaeobotanical evidence to refute his position it was generally acceptable, at least by his anthropological contemporaries working north of Mexico.

His idea was challenged by Sauer (1952) who argued for a more tropical lowland source of agriculture, and at the same time he proposed a hypothesis to account for the beginnings of New World agriculture. He envisioned that it began with sedentary fishermen living in a seasonal environment in northwest South America. This agriculture was based upon vegetable cuttings which were bred as part of the leisure time afforded by fishing for experimentation with plants to solve problems caused by seasonal variation in food availability.

An additional series of seminal ideas were presented by Anderson (1952) who saw "dump heaps" as an enriched habitat for the evolution of new plant forms based on recognition of gigantism by prehistoric people and by hybrid vigor caused by human disturbance to the landscape. His work stimulated considerable research for understanding domesticated plants and plant breeding by Native Americans north of Mexico (e.g., Anderson and Cutler 1942).

The beginnings of modern archaeology in the United States fostered the recovery of floral macroremains. In the Southwest the origin of agriculture was not viewed as a significant problem since it diffused from Mexico. Kidder (1924) ignored the question in his summary of the archaeology of this culture area. Nonetheless, with the accumulation of desiccated plant remains from cliff shelters and pueblo ruins it was inevitable that some order was needed to explain the variation.

Carter (1945) set forth such a scheme which depended upon diffusion of plants along two corridors from Mexico. One came up the west coast of Mexico while a second came up the east coast into the eastern United States before diffusing across the Plains into the Southwest. Amsden (1949) set forth an argument about the importance of considering the diffusion of maize itself. However, with the discovery of seemingly primitive maize in Bat Cave (Mangelsdorf and Smith 1949), the issue of agriculture in the Southwest became far more complex and the still unresolved question about its initial acceptance and impact on prehistoric cultures was reopened (Amsden 1949).

The archaeological plants examined by Gilmore and Jones introduced a revolutionary concept into the discussion of prehistoric North American agriculture. Based upon Gilmore's (1931) identifications and size of seeds from the Ozark bluff shelters, he concluded that the achenes of giant ragweed, pigweed, lamb's-quarters, sunflower, and marsh elder were domesticates. Jones (1936) carried this interpretation further following his analysis of plant materials from Newt Kash Hollow. To the group of indigenous plants proposed by Gilmore as cultivars, Jones added maygrass, and elaborated the hypothesis for a native Eastern Agricultural Complex by suggesting its origin centered in the central Mississippi Valley at a time prior to the introduction of any tropical agricultural plant from Mexico.

Quimby (1946), however, questioned some aspects of this hypothesis based upon his assessment of the archaeology of the dry shelters in the Ozarks and Kentucky. Without rejecting the idea of an indigenous group of domesticated plants, he did argue that it could not be established that their domestication occurred before maize became established.

The previously mentioned theoretical ideas developed by Anderson (1952) were combined with those of Gilmore and Jones by Fowler in 1957 (1971) when he expanded upon the central Mississippi Valley as an area for aboriginal plant domestication. He pointed out that a number of significant prerequisites for domestication were met in the area: the plants prefer open habitats, the prehistoric people reoccupied sites with the accumulation of rubbish in a midden, they were highly dependent upon plant foods, and these occurred in the Archaic time period. When these observations were combined with the evidence for cultivated plants from the East, he concluded that it was reasonable for local domestication to have its beginnings in the Archaic.

The most significant unresolved problem was whether the Eastern Agricultural Complex began before or after tropical cultigens came into the East. Nelson (1917) had found what he regarded as domesticated sunflowers in Mammoth Cave in the absence of maize. A similar lack of maize was discovered in the material from Newt Kash Hollow examined by Jones (the maize remains were never sent to him and he only discovered their existence with the publication of the shelter by Webb and Funkhouser [1936]). Griffin (1952), however, tentatively suggested that the Southwest rather than Mexico was the source of the idea for domestication. Only additional excavation and radiocarbon dates would resolve this issue.

By returning to the Mammoth Cave area Watson (1969, 1974) and her co-workers felt that this issue could be resolved. Indeed, they found further evidence for domesticated sumpweed (marsh elder) and sunflower as well as the other Eastern Agricultural Complex plants. None was present without squash (*Cucurbita pepo*) or the bottle gourd (*Lagenaria siceraria*) and none predated the Early Woodland. What was most significant was that maize was not present. Yarnell's participation as part of this research team resulted in an important series of papers updating knowledge of plant husbandry in the East (Yarnell 1969, 1972, 1976, 1977, 1978).

Only within the past decade has the priority of tropical cultivation been resolved. Work at Phillips Springs (Chomko and Crawford 1978) and the Little Tennessee (Chapman 1978) has shown that gourd and squash preceded the domestication and perhaps even the cultivation of indigenous disturbed habitat plant species in the East.

Despite resolution of the chronological debate in favor of a Mexican origin for domesticated plants, the actual processes associated with eastern Archaic beginnings of indigenous plant food production north of Mexico have defied solution. In the East the presence of squash and gourd suggest a garden horticulture but how this technology was transmitted and the process related to its botanical amplification must be addressed. Similarly, the role these gourds had in the diet and for later cultural development remains unknown. And finally the question related to further breeding and replacement of gathered wild plants cannot be ignored.

In the Southwest maize and squash remain the initial and foremost introduced species from Mexico but their integration into a pre-ceramic, semi-nomadic lifeway is not understood. The geographical, biological, and cultural reasons to explain why these cultivars arrived so late in the Southwest, at least relative to the eastern gourds, need research. Likewise, the late appearance of the cultivation of indigenous southwestern plants must certainly be contrasted with events in the East.

With this number of significant but unanswered questions about the origins of plant manipulation and genetic control in prehistory, the area north of Mexico can be viewed as an incomparable laboratory for explaining the many forms of plant food production that will enlighten our knowledge of the processes of agricultural beginnings throughout the world.

THEORETICAL CONTRIBUTIONS

Perhaps no other question in science has fostered as much cooperation among practitioners from a diversity of disciplines as has the origin of agriculture. For the past 100 years archaeologists and botanists, geographers and zoologists together have tried to solve the most salient problem for understanding the rise of civilization. Although the sequence of events or processes are still not completely recognized for any single geographical area and the ultimate "why" is unanswered, this multidisciplinary research has advanced the frontier of knowledge about prehistoric cultural relations with plants and animals much farther than is commonly recognized (cf. Reed 1977).

Biological Contributions

Botanists have laid an indispensable foundation to further research (cf. Heiser and Galinat, this volume). They have examined potential ancestors of domesticated plants and have described their behavior and distribution. They have also recognized the mutational steps to domestication and have specified the necessary phenotypic changes. They have reconstructed prehistoric environments and have suggested the habitats where potential domesticates should have been found. And they have provided the technical identifications of the plant remains recovered by archaeologists.

Ancestors of Domesticated Plants

De Candolle directed attention to the homelands of domesticated plants with his concepts of geographical botany. Vavilov (1926) inaugurated field research to confirm ideas about ancestral plants of the major domesticated plants, and in the course of his worldwide collecting trips, he argued for a number of independent centers of domestication. The adaptive characteristics of these species identified them as annual weeds (Ames 1939) and with only a few families of plants, particularly the grasses and legumes, contributing the staple economic cultivars (Harlan and de Wet 1965). Moreover, the natural productivity of these plants has been studied for understanding both annual variability and their subsistence potential (cf. Harlan and Zohary 1966). Detailed biological studies related to North American taxa are now proceeding with excellent studies of maygrass (Cowan 1978), lamb's-quarters (Asch and Asch 1977), sunflower (Yarnell 1978), and Sonoran panic grass (Nabhan and de Wet 1984).

Genetic Changes

New species arising from environmental and cultural selection have formed the basis of plant evolutionary study for the past century, but the speed of genetic changes which resulted in domesticated plants is still a source of wonder. The general genetic mechanisms underlying mutation and genotypic variability in domesticated plants have been discussed in many sources (cf. Brewbaker 1964; Hutchinson 1965; Schwanitz 1966; and Pickersgill and Heiser 1976). Schwanitz (1966) has emphasized that since selection was for useful plant parts, the basic genetic question is one of the causes of gigantism. However, this phenotypic character is most apparent from one generation to the next if the species is more mutable than others, a feature believed by some geneticists to be an important prerequisite for domestication of corn (Mangelsdorf 1974). For grasses large seeds, a nonbrittle rachis, and loss of mechanical means of protection are but several of the most conspicuous of the many genetic changes that brought them into a dependent relationship with humans. How they were selected for remains a critical question. Burkhill (1953) felt that genetic isolation by removing a newly domesticated plant from its wild ancestors was important. On the other hand, not all wild elements were eliminated at once, and for some, hybrid vigor with ancestors is important for preventing loss of genetic diversity (cf. maize, Galinat, this volume).

Whether or not the cultural selection of specific phenotypic characters was a result of deliberate experimentation is debatable. Sauer (1952) and other botanists argue this human behavior led to domestication, but experimentation in a Western scientific sense is rarely observed among band and tribal level cultures. Other conditions leading to recognition of valued genetic traits must be considered before experimentation is asserted as the efficient cause.

Paleoenvironmental Conditions

The habitats of the ancestral forms of domesticated plants have been examined from the perspective of the general climate and biome where they evolved (cf. Wright 1977) and the habitat preferences of the species themselves. Again Vavilov (1926) following de Candolle argued for mountainous areas for the beginnings of domestication because of the habitat diversity they afford and the number of varieties they produce. The habitat preference of the nutritionally significant North American species is any form of geographic or cultural disturbance— "dump heap", fire scar, wind throw, floodplain—and the more of such habitats, the larger the stands of these pioneering ruderal species (Heiser 1969). Ultimately, food production overcomes environmental limitations of scattered patches by increasing accessibility and reducing search time (Bronson 1977).

Archaeobotany

Botanists have benefited from the recovery of archaeological plant parts for testing their hypotheses about crop evolution. Long ago de Candolle (1886) acknowledged the significance of this form of evidence after he saw the remains from Swiss Lake Dwellings identified by Heer (1865). A similar symbiosis between botany and archaeology was proposed by Harshberger (1896) in the United States. Without botanically trained specialists to recognize the plant parts and to provide taxonomic identification, much invaluable information which forms the bases of all explanations of prehistoric plant production and its beginnings would be lost. The papers in this volume demonstrate the range of archaeological plant evidence from North America.

Social Science Contributions

Interestingly, despite the importance of agriculture in human affairs, very few of the social sciences have contributed any useful insights for understanding agricultural origins. Basically, geography and archaeology as a branch of anthropology have made important discoveries or advanced new ideas. Through the decades psychological arguments appealing to individual genius, human nature, or cultural superiority have been found wanting and untestable.

Explanations in biology have been more concerned with answering "how" anatomical changes and speciation occurred. In contrast, the social sciences entertain "why" questions. This results from emphasis in the disciplines on the complexity of human behavior and in a search for cause in human history.

Material Prerequisites

If any one conclusion has conditioned the explanation for the beginnings of plant husbandry and excluded consideration of exceptional intelligence (or extraterrestrial contacts), it is that the technological items required to process plant foods were used millennia before recognizable alterations in genotypes occurred. Archaeologists have uncovered a long record of grinding stones, collection equipment, and storage facilities which were needed for the preparation of seed plants for consumption (Flannery 1969, 1973). The exploitable technology for processing plants must be identified for each cultural area and related both to the plant's anatomical and biological constraints imposed on their prehistoric collectors and to the nutritional consequences of different methods of cooking and storage.

Socioeconomic Conditions

Hahn (1909), a pioneering geographer, was one of the first scientists to suggest that the origin of agriculture might relate to the intellectual interest of humans, or more specifically women whom he credits with beginning domestication of plants, rather than material need. Although some of his ideas were quite fanciful, if not utterly ridiculous, nonetheless, he directed research toward broader cultural context. Childe (1936) brought this perspective into archaeology, and from his lead a number of significant generalizations have emerged. First, agriculture arose in areas where plants were extensively collected by hunters and gatherers (Braidwood 1960). Second, they relied on a number of different species, or "broad spectum" collecting in Flannery's terms (1969). Third, sedentarism was not a precondition for agriculture, and the earliest domestication is found in remains associated with nonsedentary or semisedentary people. Fourth, no complex form of social organization was necessary for the advancement of food production or its diffusion from one culture to another.

Environmental Explanations

For most of the past century, the single most common explanation for the invention of agriculture has been environmental stress on availability of food. Childe (1952) in his "propinquity theory" hypothesized extreme climatic change following the last glaciation forced humans and plant species together into oases where domestication followed for the continued maintenance of these plants. The role of the environmental change in arguments related to food production have not disappeared. Instead, they either have focused on those climatic and biotic factors affecting a particular species or have been combined with other explanatory factors to become parts of a dynamic disequilibrium model.

Population Growth

Binford (1968) introduced an extremely important variable into the discussion of agricultural origins: human demography. In anthropological studies of ecology and evolution, human biology was viewed apart from cultural adaptation. Consequently, biology followed different laws and could be regarded as responsive to rather than a cause of cultural changes. Binford argued that population growth could disrupt local population density leading to emigration from regions favoring population growth, such as coastal areas, to areas which were marginal where domestication would develop in order to provide food necessary to maintain the increased population. Agriculture, then, is a response to a reduced carrying capacity caused by environmental stress on food procurement or by an increase in the human population. His contribution to this historical discussion has been adapted and modified by others (Meyers 1973; Flannery 1973) or has been amplified with discussions surrounding Boserup's (1963) ideas of population growth as an independent variable (cf. Spooner 1972).

Ecological Interaction

Flannery (1968, 1969) and Harris (1969) have approached the problem as an ecological system composed of interrelated species and feedback loops to assure continuity of a complex ecological system. For Flannery (1968) scheduling of seasonal resources and other cultural practices preserved a system in dynamic equilibrium; that is, if one resource was lacking or inefficient, others could be sought in its place in the economy. On the other hand, if this system is disrupted for one or more of several possible reasons—local population density, sedentarism, climatic stress, socioculture changes, etc.—then one resource may be favored through direct manipulation leading to economic dependency and eventual domestication (Flannery 1973). The point of this argument is, of course, that causality is complex, that agriculture can occur numerous times and in many places, and that the mechanisms or processes may not be the same in every situation.

A THEORETICAL MODEL

When a systemic perspective is accepted and the variables include those derived from botanical investigation, geographical studies, and archaeological research, theoretical considerations have priority over disciplinary identities. Such is the situation with current explanations for the development of food production. For Latin America several outstanding summaries place the domesticated plants in their tax-onomic, ecological, and prehistoric cultural context (cf. Flannery 1973; Pickersgill 1977; Heiser 1979; Pickersgill and Heiser 1977; Cut-ler 1968). North America lacks similar synthetic treatment.

Building on the ideas of Binford (1968), Flannery (1968, 1973), Har-ris (1977) and Ford (1977) we can begin to appreciate the initiation of food plant production techniques and the integration of domesticated plants into the prehistoric cultures in the eastern United States and the Southwest. Both regions are characterized by marked seasonal climatic patterns and the cessation of most plant growth in winter; thus *avail-ability* of edible resources is a critical problem. At the same time, dur-ing periods of active vegetative growth and reproduction, unexpected annual variation in productivity occurs, and *predictability* becomes a problem. A human population has nutritional needs that must be met in both quality and quantity. These may be satisfied with a few prime resources. Lacking these it may be necessary to resort to a number of secondary resources if sufficient diversity exists.

The subsistence problems posed by an inadequate food supply and unpredictability can be solved if a large foraging space (territory) is available to assure access to *alternative* patches for collecting plant food of the *same* species. Thus if a particular species fails to reproduce sufficient for human needs in one area, another patch can be visited to collect the necessary food product. In this circumstance the human population may be moving over large distances but food stress is not necessarily a serious concern. Hickory nut collecting by Archaic peo-ple of the Eastern Woodlands or, at the same cultural stage, foraging for pinyons in the Upper Sonoran areas of the Southwest present this possibility. This strategy depends upon knowledge of food potential of the territory throughout the year.

Ideally, a group would like to have adequate foodstuff available in season throughout the year. This would satisfy both their nutritional needs and any social obligations. Rarely is this possible, however. For-agers may find alternative collecting areas unavailable for several rea-sons. First, the distribution of a critical food resource may be inadequate from patch to patch to meet the population's needs. Sec-ond, human population distribution in a region may change as a con-sequence of increase, emigration, or social division of a group leading to the reduction in the original territory. Third, social conflict may limit access to alternative areas. Under these circumstances alternatives to moving from one patch to another for the same species must be considered.

The solutions are all cultural and may entail one or a combination of cognitive, social, or technological means to deal with food shortages. One is to concentrate on an available food of lower cultural preference. Another is to collect a wider variety of plant resources classified as food, even if they are secondary and require more time to gather and/ or to process and to prepare. Perennial climax or sub-climax forest and grassland products like nuts or seeds vary in yield from one year to the next. Thus if an option to foraging for these species is to intensify the collection of annual fugitive species, that is, those in pioneer disturbed habitats but that are quickly succeeded by perennial species if disturbance does not continue, then some form of cultivation may be necessary. The deliberate disturbance of the habitat to maintain the annual availability of such ruderal species may range from burning, to tilling, to sowing seed. For example, in the Eastern Woodlands an inadequate supply of forest nuts may lead to intensified harvest of small starchy seeds from river floodplains. The latter have fewer calories by weight than hard-shell nuts and consume more time to harvest but can satisfy human nutritional requirements without the need for access to an ever larger territory. In the face of changing patterns of availability, these may have been the first steps to effective food production.

To extend this logic further, as territories become smaller, effectively eliminating alternative collecting areas, or more marginal relative to culturally preferred resources, then additional strategies may be implemented. Two social solutions are to exchange for food with another human population or to take up residence with affines elsewhere in order to obtain the desired plant food. On the other hand, several technological alternatives are also available. One is to cache surplus food for those times of the year when it will be unavailable; storage then is a way to overcome unpredictable or inadequate harvests. Still another is to allocate space for the cultivation of several species and the collection of still other plants that colonize these anthropogenic habitats. Certainly the gardens of the Late Archaic and Woodland period in the East and the first cornfields in the Southwest afforded this possibility. A final one is to modify the landscape to maximize the environmental requirements of a single plant species. Clearing large tracts of forest to eliminate competitors and to increase sunlight, building irrigation canals to carry a regular supply of water, and constructing terraces to hold deeper fertile soil are notable examples. Under these conditions, for example, as an annual plant, corn production could be expanded at the expense of the yield from replaced plant communities and its cultivation selected for specific colonizing plants which often had not occupied the area under natural conditions.

In North America two contrasting "initial kicks" were given to the subsistence base in the East and Southwest with very different results. In the East the idea of agriculture came from Mexico many millennia before even native plants were obviously cultivated, much less domesticated. By way of contrast in the Southwest the relatively late arrival of maize agriculture quite rapidly changed the subsistence pattern and cultural orientation of these prehistoric societies. Again, the contrasting history of these parallel developments gives the processes of plant food production in the United States a unique position for a theoretical as well as a practical understanding of the origins of agriculture elsewhere in the world.

Adaptive Strategies of Archaic Cultures of the West Gulf Coastal Plain

Dee Ann Story
The University of Texas at Austin

General interest in the archaeology of the southern half of Texas and northeastern Mexico has long centered on the question of whether or not cultigens and other Mexican traits diffused across the West Gulf Coastal Plain into the eastern United States. In one of the more comprehensive reviews of this issue, Alex Krieger (1948) concluded that the inland route through Texas proposed by Melvin Gilmore (Thone 1935) provided an easy and logical avenue for diffusion from Mesoamerica, but that there was no direct archaeological evidence of contact. The apparent absence of native agriculture in much of the area traversed by the "Gilmore Corridor" has led, over the years since Krieger's article, to its being discredited in favor of a route through the American Southwest.

A reassessment of this position is called for by new archaeological data that establish Mexican species of squash and, less clearly, bottle gourd as appearing at least 1000 years earlier in the eastern United States than in the Southwest (Chomko and Crawford 1978:407). This paper, then, is in many ways an updating of Krieger's 1948 article. It focuses on Archaic patterns of adaptation between about 6000 B.C. and A.D. 100. This paper first describes the natural environments of the West Gulf Coastal Plain, and then it synthesizes archaeological data pertaining to economic and related cultural systems in these environments.

THE AREA

Definition

As used in this paper, the West Gulf Coastal Plain is an arbitrarily delineated section of the Coastal Plain physiographic province (Fenneman 1938:1). It extends from northeastern Mexico through the southern and eastern portions of Texas (Fig. 2.1). In Mexico, the southern boundary is formed by the Sierra Madre Oriental and the Coahuila Folded Belt (West 1964a:Fig. 3). The delineation of the other boundaries follows Fenneman (1938:100–102) who draws his line at the southern and eastern margins of the Edwards Plateau, then north along the western edge of the Grand Prairie to the Ouachita Mountains, and east to the lower Mississippi alluvial valley.

While the West Gulf Coastal Plain serves as a convenient geographic unit for a synthesis of archaeological remains potentially pertinent to the origin of early plant husbandry in the eastern United States, it should not be viewed as a cultural area. Nor has it received much systematic attention from archaeologists. Thus, where there is relevant information from sites nearby, but outside the area, these data have been incorporated into this study. In particular, extensive use has been made of information from the Lower Pecos and southern Edwards Plateau regions in Texas, mainly because the Archaic cultures in these regions are far better documented than any on the West Gulf Coastal Plain. And in general there is a bias in favor of the archaeology of Texas because it is more familiar to me than the archaeology of other portions of the study area.

Modern Environments

Within the West Gulf Coastal Plain there are many differences in topography, climate, soils, and biota that form almost innumerable local environments. Broad patterns and relationships can be discerned, but these do not realistically constitute well defined or uniformly agreed upon natural regions (cf. Johnson 1931; Arbingast et al. 1973). The area is consequently summarized here in terms of selected environmental characteristics that provide a background for the subsequent discussion of Archaic cultures.

The most unifying feature of the area is its geologic history which has given rise to a series of relatively young and undeformed (except in

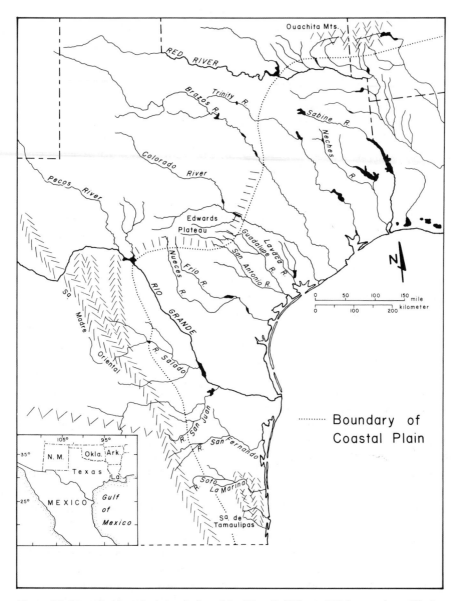

Figure 2.l. Map showing the boundaries of the West Gulf Coastal Plain, nearby uplifted physiographic regions, and major rivers.

portions of northeastern Mexico) surface formations arranged in belts roughly parallel to the Gulf of Mexico. Together with climate these formations have greatly influenced many other elements in the environment. For the most part, the topography north of the Rio Grande is a gently rolling, seaward-sloping plain (Fenneman 1938:104). To the south, in northeastern Mexico, the topography is more varied (MacNeish 1958:10; West 1964a; Bonnie et al. 1970:6–7) in that, from east to west, there is first a narrow strip of coastal lowlands characterized by littoral sand and clay dunes, muddy lakes, and flatlands; next, a gently rolling plain that widens as it approaches the Rio Grande; and finally, abutting the mountains, a much-dissected plain.

Adjacent to most of the West Gulf Coastal Plain are uplifted physiographic regions—the Sierra Madre Oriental, Coahuila Folded Belt, Edwards Plateau, and Ouachita Mountains—that offer striking contrasts in topography. And, extending high above the coastal plain in northeastern Mexico are the San Carlos Mountains and the Sierra de Tamaulipas. More than providing contrasts in relief, these uplands are sources of different mineral, floral, and faunal resources. In some areas they contain caves and rockshelters which have yielded perishable artifacts and invaluable data on aboriginal plant utilization. They also have an important orographic effect on rainfall patterns (Vivo 1964:189; Carr 1967:20–21). In the more drought-prone portions of the area it is the windward (gulf) facing escarpments that usually receive more moisture and that may have served as refugium for human populations during dry periods.

To a large extent, the relationship between climate and culture is via the influence that climate exerts on the nature and distribution of flora and fauna. Other factors, of course, are also involved. For example, in Figure 2.2 which shows the main modern vegetation regions within the West Gulf Coastal Plain, the effects of the mountains of northeastern Mexico and the soils that have formed on the belt-like geologic formation in Texas are particularly evident (Gould 1962; West 1964b; Bonnie et al. 1970; Arbingast et al. 1973).

The eastern part of the study area is dominated by forests which have two main expressions, oak-hickory-pine (region 1) and longleaf pine (region 2). To the south and west, these forests gradually give way to prairies (regions 4 and 6) and subhumid deciduous savannas (regions 3 and 5). A large expanse of mesquite-chaparral savanna (region 7) occupies south Texas and northeastern Mexico. In the isolated San Carlos and Tamaulipas mountains scrub oak and pine (region 8) occur sporadically in the higher elevations, and about the lower elevations of the latter range there is a deciduous thorny tropical forest (region 9).

Not shown in Figure 2.2, but significant to prehistoric subsistence, are the gallery forests along many of the rivers and streams. Particularly notable and widespread economic species in these riparian environments are the pecan and oak.

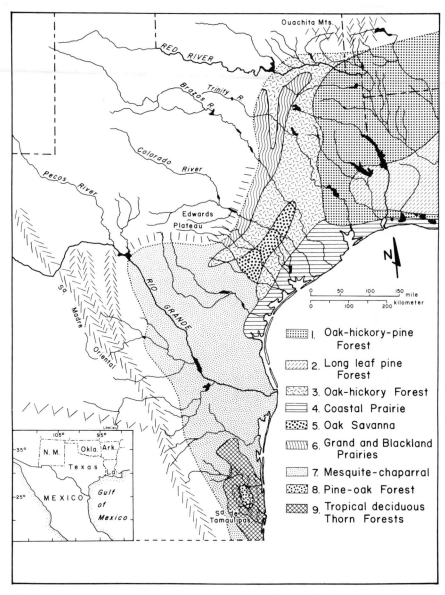

Figure 2.2 Main contemporary vegetation regions within the West Gulf Coastal Plain.

The zoogeography of the vertebrate fauna of the area has been summarized by Blair (1950, 1952) and Stuart (1964) in terms of three biotic provinces: Tamaulipan, Texan, and Austroriparian. The Tamaulipan coincides with vegetation region 7 and is the only one of the three provinces that is confined to the West Gulf Coastal Plain. It also has the most heterogeneous assemblage, as subtropical, southwest desert, Great Plains, and eastern forest species occur in this province. The Austroriparian occupies the eastern timberlands (vegetation regions 1 and 2) and is the western limit of many species widely distributed in the southeastern United States. In fauna, as in vegetation (regions 3–6), the Texan province is an ecotonal area.

Past Environments

Holocene environments of the study area are poorly known and are vulnerable to interpretation in terms of overly simple models of climatic change. Table 2.1 summarizes the evidence accumulated to date on paleoenvironments and correlates it with the major climatic episodes proposed for North America by Bryson and others (Bryson et al. 1970; Wendland and Bryson 1974; Wendland 1978; see also climatic models for central Texas proposed by Gunn and Weir 1976; Gunn and Mahula 1977; Gunn 1979).

There are obvious problems in interpretation of these data, partly because they are skimpy and partly because they are not entirely consistent. The vegetation records from the Lower Pecos region and from the bogs in south-central and east-central Texas show only gradual changes. These Bryant and Shafer (1977:15–19) see as representing a slow, but continual, warming and drying trend. On the other hand, the pollen records from southeastern Oklahoma, the long-term fluctuations in the distribution of the bison and the brocket (*Mazama* or red deer), and the depositional units and stream geomorphology in Texas (Trinity, Brazos, and Colorado rivers) and the Sierra de Tamaulipas suggest that the mid-Holocene was a time of major climatic change. This MacNeish (1958:199) and Aten (1979:528–29, 1983:136) have identified as a dry Altithermal period.

Since the step-like, quasi-stable climatic models, such as those proposed by Bryson and others, seem more heuristic than a gradual progression to modern conditions, the paleoenvironmental data are synthesized in terms of three provisional climatic intervals:

(1) During the early part of the Holocene, between approximately 7000 and 5000 B.C. (and roughly equivalent to the Boreal climatic episode of Bryson et al. 1970), the climate was generally cooler, and/or more humid, perhaps with weakly differentiated seasonal changes.

Most modern vegetation elements were present in each region of the West Gulf Coastal Plain, but probably were not fully differentiated into the communities of recent times. In locally favorable environments, there survived some floral and faunal species more characteristic of the Pleistocene than of the later Holocene.

(2) Between about 5000 and 3000 or 2500 B.C. (roughly equivalent to the Atlantic climatic episode of Bryson et al. 1970 and to what others [e.g., Aten 1979, 1983; Benedict 1979] prefer to identify as either the Altithermal or postglacial thermal optimum), droughts became more frequent and often extended over a large geographic area. Wendland's (1978:279) hypothesis of strong, dry westerlies in the Great Plains during this period seems consistent with more recent experiences, since such winds have been the cause of many modern droughts in Texas (Carr 1967:11–14). Indeed, the recent Texas droughts which culminated in 1910, 1917, and 1956 perhaps serve as useful analogs of the dry conditions that appear to have prevailed during long portions of this interval. Some researchers working in central Texas (e.g., Gunn and Weir 1976; Gunn and Mahula 1977) and in western North America (e.g., Benedict 1979) have proposed two episodes of drought separated by a period of increased effective moisture. Dates suggested for the dry intervals vary from between 5000–4500 B.C. and 4000–3500 B.C. (Benedict 1979:1) to between 6000–4000 B.C. and 3000 to 2000 B.C. (Gunn and Weir 1976:32). Although there is as yet no paleoclimatic evidence from the West Gulf Coastal Plain to support the two-drought model, it is probably a more useful working hypothesis than the one long drought proposed by Antevs (1955).

Except perhaps in a few favorable niches, relict Pleistocene biota disappeared. In general, the extent and density of mesophytic flora appears to have declined in many regions while the more xerophytic species expanded their distributions. Large bison herds evidently did not often frequent the coastal plain and the brocket retreated from the Sierra de Tamaulipas into more tropical parts of Mexico. Other changes in the vertebrate fauna are not evident, although the sample for this time period comes mostly from the southern and eastern edges of the Edwards Plateau and may not be representative of the coastal plain (Lundelius 1967:20).

(3) Beginning about 3000 or 2500 B.C. the dry conditions ameliorated and by at least 1500 B.C. essentially modern regional patterns of biota were established. Present-day stillstand was reached sometime between 2000 and 1000 B.C., and the barrier islands along the coast began to form. Climatic oscillations and the biotic responses to them no doubt continued. The best evidence for this comes from pollen

TABLE 2.1
SUMMARY OF PALEONENVIRONMENTAL DATA FROM OR NEAR THE WEST
GULF COASTAL PLAIN

Dates	South & East-Central Texas		Central Texas	S.E. Oklahoma		Lower Pecos
	Phytoliths *(Robinson 1979)*	Pollen *(Bryant 1977)*	Colorado River Alluvial Phases *(Baker & Penteado-Orellana 1977)*	Pollen Ferndale Bog *(Albert 1981)*	Pollen Jenkins Rilley Slough *(Albert 1981)*	Vegetation *(Dering 1979)*
A.D. 300		Establishment of modern vegetation communities	Phase 3 — Drier			Modern grasslands; scattered shrubs, juniper/oaks; decline of pine
0						
B.C. 400			Phase 4 — High sinuosity; Mesic			———?———
800	——?—— Tall grasses; dense riverine forests ——?——			Oak-hickory forests	Return of forest— oak, hickory and pine	Resurgence of pine
1200						———?———
1600	Short grasses; reduction in riverine forests					Continued slow drying and warming trends; grasslands, juniper/oaks
2000						
2400	——?——			Grassland and oak savanna		Grasslands in uplands with scattered xerophytic shrubs and semi-succulents
2800	Tall grasses; dense riverine forests		Continued dry		——?—— Grasses and other non-arboreal elements dominate	
3200						
3600						Juniper/oaks
4000	?		Fine sediments			
4400						
4800						
5200					———?———	Increase in herbaceous species
5600			Colorado Channel Phase 5 — Low sinuosity			
6000						Some reduction in oaks and juniper
6400						Decline of pines
6800			Coarse sediments			
7200			Increased seasonality of rainfall and temperature			
7600						South: juniper/oak parkland; grassland with xerophytic species
8000						North: pinyon/pine (parkland?)

(Vertical text in Pollen/Bryant column: Gradual loss of arboreal elements (except oak); increase in grasses and herbs*)*

(Vertical text in Jenkins Rilley Slough column: Arboreal pollen dominant; possibly pre-Altithermal oak-hickory forest*)*

TABLE 2.1 CONTINUED

Southern Plains	Coast		Sierra de Tamaulipas		Major Climate Episodes of Holocene
Bison *(Dillehay 1974)*	Upper Texas Coast *(Aten 1979, 1983)*	Sea Level *(Gagliano & Smith 1971)*	Fauna *(MacNeish 1958)*	Geomorphology	Episodes *(Bryson et al. 1970)* *(Wendland 1978)*
Bison present	Seasonal patterns of precipitation and temperature; stabilized sea level	Modern stillstand; barrier islands develop	Brocket present but frequencies fluctuate	Moist to wet development of new terrace	SUB-ATLANTIC
		—?—			SUB-BOREAL
Bison absent	Further reduction in stream flow; formation of caliche	Sea level rise	Brocket absent	Dry dissection of middle terrace in Diablo Canyon	
	Reversal of sea level: erratic stream flow; drying of wet lands in Louisiana and east Texas		Brocket present		ATLANTIC
Bison present	Reduced rates of flow in Trinity and Brazos rivers	Sea level rise	Brocket and beaver	Wet development of middle terrace	BOREAL

studies in southeastern Oklahoma (Albert 1981), the brief presence of bison herds in the Lower Pecos region (Dibble and Lorrain 1968; Dillehay 1974), and changes in the geomorphology of the lower Colorado River (Baker and Penteado-Orellana 1977). On the whole, however, the cumulative effects of the climatic changes during this interval were less than in the previous interval. In the light of modern climatic patterns, it seems reasonable to hypothesize that since about 2500 B.C. the environments of the more humid portion of the study area were more stable (i.e., less subject to yearly variations) than those of the semiarid regions to the west (for a fuller discussion of this see Gunn 1979).

To summarize, there is marked diversity in the modern environments of the West Gulf Coastal Plain. Short-term changes, mostly droughts, are well documented in historic times, and in general, they have been more frequent and more intense in the semiarid portions of the area. Paleoenvironments are not yet well understood, but it is probable that significant climatic fluctuations occurred throughout the Holocene. Although provisionally delineated, these changes should be considered as potential influencing, though not determining, factors in the patterns of adaptation that developed in the area between ca. 6000 B.C. and A.D. 100.

THE ARCHAEOLOGY

Over the past decade there has been a notable increase in archaeological investigations in the West Gulf Coastal Plain, at least north of the Rio Grande. Regional summaries (Shafer 1981; Hester 1981; Lynott 1981; Prewitt 1981; Story 1981; Schambach and Early 1982; Aten 1983; Bell 1984) are beginning to appear and process oriented research is winning favor over cultural-historical reconstructions. The most impressive gains in information have concerned the later cultural developments. Research on early hunters and gatherers, which are referred to throughout the area as Archaic period cultures, has progressed slowly. Archaic remains in large regions, such as the coastal plains of northeastern Mexico, are almost totally unknown. Cultural sequences within the Archaic period are, with few exceptions, weakly defined and largely dependent upon projectile point stratigraphy and cross-dating with complexes outside the area.

Because so much of the information pertaining to the Archaic is spotty and poorly controlled, it can be integrated and discussed in only a very general and provisional way. The chronological framework chosen for this purpose is three periods: Early, Middle, and Late

Archaic. This scheme has been frequently used in the area but with marked differences among researchers in how the periods are defined and dated. Since local and regional developments have not been synthesized into a widely agreed upon, comprehensive framework, it has been necessary here to make some alignments that are at variance with the schemes used in some regional studies. In doing so, I have relied heavily on the best established projectile point sequences and have assumed that they are applicable wherever comparable point styles are found.

The Early Archaic is here dated from approximately 6000 to 3500 or 3000 B.C., the Middle Archaic from ca. 3500 or 3000 to 1000 B.C., and the Late Archaic from 1000 B.C. to 200 B.C. in some regions to as late as A.D. 1200 in other regions. Over much of the area hunting and gathering societies survived into historic times, and the end of the Archaic is not marked by any notable economic or social changes. For convenience and consistency with other researchers, the Late Archaic is terminated with the first appearance of pottery and/or the bow and arrow. The distinction between the Early Archaic and Paleo-Indian periods is also arbitrary and has been more variably defined than the end of Late Archaic. I have begun the Early Archaic at the approximate time when early lanceolate-style dart points largely disappear from the archaeological record.

The constructs of Early, Middle, and Late Archaic are admittedly crude, but in view of the poor quality of the data, they are useful for organizing an overview of early hunting and gathering cultural systems. Within this framework I have attempted to identify and discuss major cultural elements and to suggest possible explanations for the spatial and temporal patterning of these elements. Of most interest here are the livelihoods, adaptive strategies, and settlement systems.

Early Archaic
(ca. 6000 to 3500 or 3000 B.C.)

The best evidence for human occupation during this interval comes from the inner margins of the coastal plain and the adjacent physiographic regions (Fig. 2.3). Along the southern and southeastern edges of the Edwards Plateau and in the Lower Pecos region are found relatively high site densities and the most tightly controlled temporal and contextual data (Sollberger and Hester 1972; Weir 1976a; McKinney 1981; Prewitt 1981). Apparently contemporaneous occupations have been identified in southeastern Oklahoma, especially in the Ouachita Mountain region. Few of these occupations, however, are contained in well stratified deposits and none has been ^{14}C dated to

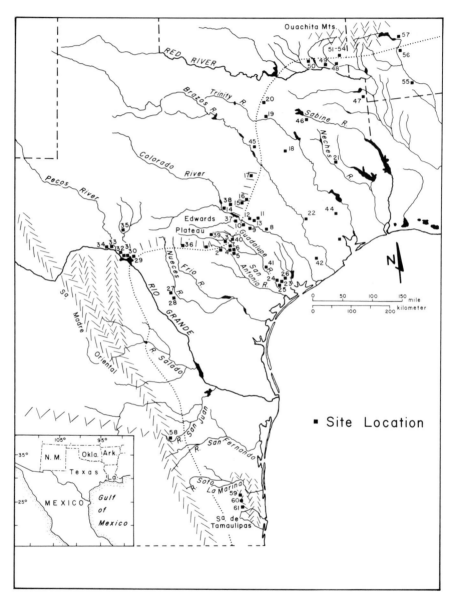

Figure 2.3. Distribution of Early Archaic sites in or near the West Gulf Coastal Plain. See Table 2.2 for a listing of site names.

this period (Wyckoff 1984:127–45, Table 6.1). In southwestern Arkansas, most of the sites with components believed to date at least in part to this period have been related to the Tom's Brook culture (Schambach and Early 1982:48–53). Some of these components, including that at the Paw Paw site on the Ouachita River, are associated with rich, but as yet largely unexcavated, midden deposits.

Elsewhere the archaeological record is meager. In eastern Texas and western Louisiana the highly disturbed nature of most sites and the general lack of interest in the Archaic have combined to create a lacuna in a region that may have been extensively occupied between ca. 6000 and 3000 B.C. An even larger information gap exists in northeastern Mexico and extreme south Texas. Long sequences have been defined by MacNeish (1958) for the Sierra Madre, Sierra de Tamaulipas, and northern Tamaulipas with the Nogales phase and the early part of the Ocampo phase falling in Early Archaic times. Both Epstein (1969, 1972) and Nance (1971, 1972), however, have disputed the ages assigned these phases and have argued that they are more reasonably dated later, perhaps after about 3500 B.C. If the latter placement is accepted, the only certain Early Archaic component in northeastern Mexico is at the site of La Calsada, 30 km west of Montemorelos, Nuevo Leon (Nance 1971, 1980). There are no data from south Texas that are helpful to establishing the ages of the Nogales and Ocampo phases or that can be related to much of the La Calsada sequence. Farther to the west, in Coahuila, the Cienegas Complex (Taylor 1966) is dated primarily to the Early Archaic but is still very poorly defined.

The striking geographical concentrations of Early Archaic sites (Fig. 2.3) can be attributed largely to unevenness in archaeological investigations. In the less well studied regions of northeastern Mexico and extreme south Texas, the sample may be further biased by an inability to define artifacts distinctive to Early Archaic times. While it is plausible that these two factors alone could account for the observed site distributions, it also is conceivable that Early Archaic remains are archaeologically more visible along and near the inner margins of the West Gulf Coastal Plain because these regions were in fact more intensively utilized than other regions.

The hypothesis that all the study area was occupied during this period, but that some regions were frequented more often and/or by larger groups, merits serious consideration (cf. Epstein 1972; Nance 1972). Both Paleo-Indian and Middle Archaic sites seem to be more evenly distributed throughout the area—a possible indication that sample bias alone does not adequately account for the apparent Early Archaic site concentrations. Paleoenvironmental data (Table 2.1) further suggest that the interval between ca. 5000 and 3000 B.C. may

TABLE 2.2
EARLY ARCHAIC SITES IN OR NEAR THE WEST GULF COASTAL PLAIN

No. on Fig. 2.3	Site	Reference
	Texas	
1	Strohacker (41KR29)	Sollberger and Hester 1972
2	San Geronimo (41BX196)	Weir 1976a
3	41KE49	Kelly and Hester 1976
4	Camp Bullis (41BX376, 402, 403, 409)	Gerstle et al. 1978
5	Granberg II (41BX271)	Hester and Kohnitz 1975; Hester 1980
6	Waterhole (41BX300)	McGraw and Valdez 1978
7	41BX36	Gerstle et al. 1978
8	Thunderbird (41BP78)	Duke 1977
9	Jetta Court (41TV151)	Wesolowsky et al. 1976
10	Millican's Bench #8 (41TV163)	Kelly 1971
11	Cervenka (41WM267)	Prewitt 1974a; Hays 1982
12	Merrell (41WM2)	Campbell 1948
13	Tombstone (41WM165)	Prewitt 1974a; Hays 1982
14	Granite Beach (41LL2)	Crawford 1965
15	Youngsport (41BL78)	Shafer 1963
16	Landslide (41BL85)	Sorrow et al. 1967
17	Baylor (41ML35)	Story and Shafer 1965
18	Old Union Bridge (41LT12)	Prewitt and Mallouf 1977)
19	Wheeler	Crook and Harris 1952
20	Old Dallas Dam (41DN6)	Crook and Harris 1952
21	George C. Davis (41CE19)	Newell and Krieger 1949
22	Thurmond	Shafer 1977
23	41VT17	Fox and Hester 1976
24	Willeke (41VT16)	Fox and Hester 1976
25	41VT20	Fox and Hester 1976
26	J-2 Ranch (41VT6)	Fox et al. 1978
27	Chaparrosa Ranch	Hester 1976
28	Chaparrosa Ranch	Hester 1976
29	Devil's Rock Shelter (41VV264)	Prewitt 1966
30	Devil's Mouth (41VV188)	Johnson 1964; Sorrow 1968
31	Arenosa (41VV99)	Dibble ms
32	Hinds Cave (41VV456)	Shafer and Bryant 1977
33	Eagle Cave (41VV167)	Ross 1965
34	Conejo (41VV162)	Alexander 1974

TABLE 2.2
CONTINUED

No. on Fig. 2.3	Site	Reference
	Texas	
35	Baker Cave (41VV213)	Word and Douglas 1970
36	La Jita (41UV21)	Hester 1971
37	Greenhaw (41HY29)	Weir 1979
38	McCann	Preston 1969
39	Wounded Eye and Shep (41KR107, 109)	Luke 1980
40	Panther Springs Creek (41BX228)	McKinney 1981
41	41DW98	Fox et al. 1974
42	41WH19	Patterson and Hudgins 1981, 1983
43	Doering (41HR5)	Wheat 1953
44	Scott's Ridge (41MQ41)	Shafer and Stearns 1975
45	Ballew and Francis	Watt and Agogino 1968
46	Yarbrough (41VN6)	Johnson 1962
47	Mothershed Spring (41CS43)	Henderson 1979
	Oklahoma	
48	Mahaffey (34Ch-1)	Rohrbaugh et al. 1971; Perino and Bennett 1978
49	Burroughs (34Ch-43)	Rohrbaugh et al. 1971
50	Houchins (34Ch-75)	Rohrbaugh et al. 1971
51	Biggham Creek (34Mc-105)	Wyckoff 1965a
52	E. Johnson (34Mc-54)	Wyckoff 1967b
53	Hughes (34Mc-21)	Wyckoff 1965b
54	Woods Mound (34Mc-104)	Wyckoff 1967c
	Arkansas	
55	Paw Paw (30U22)	Schambach and Early 1982
56	Cooper (3HS1)	Schambach 1970
57	Gulpha (3GN20)	Harrington 1920
	Mexico	
58	La Calsada	Nance 1971, 1980
59	Diablo Cave	MacNeish 1958
60	Nogales Cave	MacNeish 1958
61	Armadillo Cave	MacNeish 1958

have been a time of prolonged periods of aridity. It is significant in this regard that the regions of highest Early Archaic site density are ecotonal in character and are elevated enough to have an orographic effect on rainfall. In times of environmental stress, these regions may have provided somewhat more abundant resources for hunters and gatherers.

However, to judge from what information is available (see especially summaries by Wyckoff 1967a, 1970, 1984; Sollberger and Hester 1972; Weir 1976a), Early Archaic population densities were everywhere low. With the possible exception of the Paw Paw site and other components of the Tom's Brook culture (Schambach 1970; Schambach and Early 1982), most sites are small, widely distributed, and nonspecialized. They are often surface or slightly buried scatters of lithic tools and debitage on knolls and fossil floodplains, many times mixed with later materials. When buried components are found, they usually underlie larger Middle and Late Archaic occupations. In the Lower Pecos region and the mountainous portion of northeastern Mexico, rockshelters were sometimes utilized as campsites. Shelters also occur in the Edwards Plateau, but they were either very rarely used during Early Archaic times, or the deposits containing early occupations have been subsequently removed. In this region, as well as elsewhere, open sites prevail.

There is little in the existing literature that permits a meaningful classification of sites beyond the gross functional categories of camps and lithic procurement stations. Few burials can be attributed to this period and the most commonly reported cultural features are hearths. The distribution of the lithic procurement sites is dictated, of course, by the natural distribution of cherts. On the Edwards Plateau and in the Ouachita Mountains are numerous upland flint outcrops as well as alluvial gravel deposits. On the coastal plain, siliceous stones occur in gravel deposits, except along the immediate coastal zone where pebbles and cobbles are for all practical purposes absent. In general, then, the lithic procurement stations are found in upland areas, either on old terraces or at flint outcrops.

Proximity to water, wood, and food resources that aggregate near streams and rivers seems to have been the most important factor determining the specific location of encampments. An analysis of settlement patterns in a small area north of San Antonio, Texas (Gerstle et al. 1978:175–213) has observed that Early Archaic (called pre-Archaic in that study) campsites are found mostly on higher elevation above the modern drainages and that later Archaic sites are more often on or near modern floodplains. Subsistence changes may be indicated by these distributions, but, in the absence of detailed study of possible changes in the floodplain and channel morphology, the case is weak. In another settlement study (Nance 1972:172–73) it was argued that Early Archaic populations in the Lower Pecos region were largely confined to the major rivers (Rio Grande and Pecos) in response to dry Altithermal conditions. This has not been substantiated by additional research in that region or elsewhere. Indeed, with the major exception of the coastal zone (where any early occupation would now be submerged), the locations of sites dating between ca. 6000 and 3000 B.C. do not seem to differ appreciably from those of later Archaic times. Put another way, multicomponent Archaic sites are common while isolated Early Archaic occupations are infrequent.

Many of the Early Archaic artifact types are widely distributed, perhaps reflecting high group mobility, frequent changes in group composition, and a lack of well defined territories. While the more distinct regional patterns of later times cannot be recognized, there are some indications of several broad areal artifact clusters. Since these extend across different ecological zones, it is unlikely that they represent specific adaptive strategies. Perhaps they are simply areas within which there were frequent intergroup contacts and information exchanges; in a sense, spheres of interaction.

The most readily defined of the clusters occurs in the central part of the study area and in the adjacent Lower Pecos and Edwards Plateau regions. Sollberger and Hester (1972) have described this material under the term "pre-Archaic," and Weir (1976a, 1976b) has defined it as the San Geronimo phase. The most distinctive of the artifact forms are a number of dart point styles: corner-notched expanded stem forms, concave base stemmed forms, well made triangular forms, and heavily barbed forms. Specific types, including Gower, Uvalde, Bell, and Martindale have been recognized but are not precisely defined, and designations such as "Early Barbed" and "Early Triangular" are often used instead. There is some support for a provisional sequence within this array of point styles (see especially Sollberger and Hester 1972:336–38; Prewitt 1981). The earliest forms seem to be Martindale, Gower, and Uvalde, which possibly overlap in time with Angostura and other, as yet untyped, lanceolate styles. Apparently later styles include Bell and "Early Triangular" as the most widely distributed types and Wells and Morrill as more geographically limited forms. Less temporally distinctive artifacts include Clear Fork and Guadalupe gouges; lanceolate, thick-ovate, and irregular bifaces; burins and burin spalls; circular scrapers and other unifacially trimmed flakes; and, rarely, grinding implements. In a provocative comparative study of Archaic tool assemblages in the Edwards Plateau region, Weir (1976a:47–105; see also Gunn and Weir 1976) found that Early Archaic chipped stone tools were relatively diverse and nonspecialized. This, he hypothesized, reflected a diffuse economy and a need for a large technological inventory to exploit a wide variety of resources (Weir 1976a:122).

A second, but perhaps more heterogeneous, areal cluster can be discerned to the north, in southeastern Oklahoma (Wyckoff 1967a, 1970, 1984; Rohrbaugh et al. 1971; Perino and Bennett 1978) and adjacent portions of Arkansas (Hoffman 1969, 1970; Schambach and Early 1982), Texas, and probably Louisiana. Although many of the artifacts, especially the dart points, found in these regions differ from those in the central cluster, precise comparisons do not come easily. In the northeastern part of the study area the chronologic controls are poor and artifacts have been analyzed in terms of broadly defined periods that do not align well with the temporal frameworks used in much of Texas. Thus, Early Archaic in this study equates in part with what in Oklahoma and Arkansas is usually identified as Middle Archaic. More serious, a number of the dart point types defined in central and western Texas are recognized and, inadvertently, redefined in Oklahoma and nearby areas. Other point styles—such as Calf Creek in Oklahoma and Arkansas, and Bell or "Early Barbed" in Texas— which appear to be morphologically the same, of comparable age, and continuous in distribution have not been typologically related to one another. The need for a comprehensive, integrated framework and for typologies that recognize both regionally distinct and areally-shared forms is obvious but beyond the scope of this study. Tentatively, then, a northern cluster is recognized principally on the basis of such types as Johnson and Big Sandy. These appear to date after the Dalton and San Patrice types, and thus probably after 6000 B.C. Also occurring, and evidently dating even later, are Carrollton, Dallas, and Calf Creek points. Hafted-end scrapers and side-notched pebbles are found at sites attributed to the Tom's Brook culture in southwestern Arkansas (Schambach and Early 1982:51), but not at what Wyckoff (1984:136–40) has identified in eastern Oklahoma as the Tom's Brook complex. Other associated tools appear to be relatively few in number and to include nonspecialized scrapers, knives, and occasional grinding implements. In general, the cultural ties are with the Archaic of the eastern United States.

In between the northern and central clusters, in the central part of eastern Texas and along the eastern edge of the Edwards Plateau, occur assemblages similar to those found both to the north and to the southwest. The Youngsport site (Shafer 1963) in Bell County and the George C. Davis site (Newell and Krieger 1949) in Cherokee County are good examples. Youngsport is exceptionally well stratified and contains in the deepest cultural-bearing deposits Gower points, a few knives and scrapers, and a Clear Fork gouge. In a zone immediately above were recovered Wells, Morrill, and Carrollton-like points as well as a Clear Fork gouge, and two scrapers. Higher zones had an excellent sequence of Middle and Late Archaic material. At the Davis site Early Archaic artifacts are not stratigraphically separated from a Caddoan component, but they are confined to the eastern and southern portions of the site. Types present are Morrill, Wells, and Bell or Calf Creek, all of which possibly date after ca. 4000 B.C. Not found at either Davis or Youngsport but occurring at some nearby sites are rounded stones with notches and sometimes grooves. Known as Waco sinkers (Watt 1938), these and the side-notched ones in the Arkansas sites may have functioned as net sinkers. If this inference is correct, they may be one of the few more specialized Early Archaic implements.

Much farther to the south, in northeastern Mexico and extreme south Texas, Early Archaic and later phases in the three sequences defined by MacNeish (1958, 1964) have been synthesized under the inclusive concept of Abasolo (also termed Repelo) tradition (MacNeish et al. 1967:240–44). The main artifacts linked to this tradition are triangular and leaf-shaped dart points, gouges, mullers, and small scrapers. However, the Archaic sequence (Nogales phase, Repelo complex, and Abasolo complex) defined for the coastal plain is based on very limited excavation data and it may be that Nogales phase dates largely to the Middle rather than the Early Archaic, as these periods are defined herein.

Along the immediate littoral zone of Mexico and Texas no site dating between 6000 and 3000 B.C. has yet been recognized. It can, nonetheless, be predicted with reasonable confidence that any Early Archaic artifacts that might eventually be found will relate closely to nearby inland assemblages. Evidence of a marine subsistence pattern, if it did exist during Early Archaic times, would now be submerged offshore.

Occupational residues that can be related directly to Early Archaic subsistence practices are extremely limited. However, just beyond the coastal plain, dry shelter deposits in the Lower Pecos region and in the mountains of northeastern Mexico have contained well preserved faunal and floral remains. The northeastern Mexico data (MacNeish 1958, 1964) indicate that, in general, subsistence was based on wild plant collecting, hunting, and incipient cultivation, in that order of importance. The earliest evidence for cultigens, which include squash (*Cucurbita pepo*) and, less certainly, gourd (*Lagenaria*), and chili pepper (*Capsicum annuum* or *C. frutesceus*), comes from the Infiernillo phase in southwestern Tamaulipas and dated to 7000–5000 B.C. Wild plants utilized during this phase are not detailed but apparently include agave, opuntia, and runner bean (*Phaseolus coccineus*). During the later (5000–3000 B.C.) Ocampo phase squash, gourd, and beans (*Phaseolus vulgaris*) were added to the species cultivated, although wild plant foods (unspecified) continued to make up the greater part of the diet. Information pertaining to animal exploitation has been published (MacNeish 1958:139–40) only for the sites in the Sierra de Tamaulipas. Here, during the Nogales phase (5000–3000 B.C.?), hunting is estimated to have contributed between 15% and 20% of the food bulk. The species exploited were whitetailed deer, peccary, and coatimundi.

Much of the Lower Pecos subsistence data, like that from northeastern Mexico, has been only partially analyzed and incompletely reported. The most thorough of the Lower Pecos studies is Alexander's (1974) analysis of Conejo Shelter. Other sources of information are: several poorly quantified floral (Irving 1966) and faunal (Raun 1966) inventories; an analysis of animal bones (Word and Douglas 1970) from the first of three excavations (Hester 1979) at Baker Cave; a study of the macroplant residue from Hinds Cave (Dering 1979); and an intensive analysis (Williams-Dean 1978) of 100 coprolites dating to ca. 4000 B.C. and representing one of a number such lenses in a well defined latrine area at Hinds Cave.

Early Archaic economies in the Lower Pecos region relied heavily on plants and secondarily on animals. Mainstays of the diet were semidesert succulents: Prickly pear (*Opuntia*), lechuguilla (*Agave lecheguilla*), and sotol (*Dasylirion*). Frequently, but perhaps less regularly, utilized were walnut (*Juglans microcarpa*), persimmon (*Diospyros texana*), onion (*Allium ?drummondii*), mesquite (*Prosopis*), guajillo (*Acacia berlanderi*), dropseed (*Sporobolus*), and yucca (*Yucca*). Less commonly consumed plant species included grape (*Vitis*), hackberry (*Celtis*), *Chenopodium*, *Amaranthus*, oak (*Quercus*), and unidentified grasses. Rarely found, but of interest, are buffalo gourd (*Cucurbita foetidissima*) seeds. Rodents and lagomorphs are by far numerically the most common species in the faunal samples. Whitetailed deer and fish also occur, although they are notably less frequent than in later Archaic deposits. Minor faunal elements include land snails, mussels, coyote, fox, skunk, reptiles, and birds.

Despite the number of different species utilized by the inhabitants of the Lower Pecos region, efforts to define seasonality and duration of occupation (Alexander 1974) have been frustrated by a paucity of reliable indicators (Dering and Shafer 1976:222–26; Williams-Dean 1978:248–54). Many of the fruit-bearing species respond more to rainfall patterns than to temperature changes, so that at best a long, warm season and a short, cool season can be discerned. This and the extensive use of succulents available year-round has led Shafer (1981:134) to doubt that a strict seasonal schedule was followed by hunters and gatherers in the Lower Pecos region.

From Early Archaic sites on the coastal plain, there is nothing more than small collections of animal bones and we can only speculate on the nature of the subsistence practices. Perhaps they were non-specialized, as Weir (1976a:122–23) has suggested for the San Geronimo phase, and did not concentrate on any particular resources, or did not utilize any to the maximum possible extent. The lack of large midden accumulations seems compatible with extensive rather than intensive resource exploitation.

To summarize, during most or all of the Early Archaic, population densities were apparently low. The inner margins of the coastal plain and adjacent uplands may have been more frequently utilized than other regions, or else supported slightly higher population densities, perhaps because during periods of aridity the higher elevations provided relatively more productive habitats for hunters and gatherers. Since most sites are small and widely scattered, it is probable that throughout the area populations were organized into small social groups, perhaps family units, which were reasonably stable, as well as bands which were more fluid in composition. Territorial boundaries may not have been maintained and constraints on mobility were probably few. Economic systems are hypothesized to have been diffuse, utilizing a variety of resources and frequently shifting the loci of subsistence activities rather than intensifying the use of any specified resource.

Middle Archaic
(ca. 3500 or 3000 to 1000 B.C.)

Middle Archaic sites are more numerous and varied than those of the Early Archaic. The evidence is often quite abundant and comes from all regions within the West Gulf Coastal Plain, although along the coast sites are infrequent and probably date after 2000 B.C. The Edwards Plateau and Lower Pecos regions continue to be major sources of well controlled information, and the mountains of northeastern Mexico provide invaluable data on cultigens.

A number of important changes can be discerned during this period. They are an apparent increase in population, the development of regionally distinct cultural patterns, changes in settlement patterns, technology, economic and social systems, and, possibly, the formation of territorial boundaries.

The increase in the number of sites (they are far too numerous to plot on a small scale map) and the amount of occupational debris at many of them are indicators of an increase in population. Although it is impossible to quantify the demographic change or to compare precisely one region with another, it is possible that population growth was considerable and widespread. Researchers working mainly in the central part of Texas (Sollberger and Hester 1972:338; Weir 1976a:124; Gunn and Weir 1976:32) see the increase as having been sudden. But since the lack of tight temporal controls forces the use of gross units of time, it may be that the abruptness of the demographic jump is more apparent than real.

Possible reasons for the implied change in the vital reproduction and/or survival rates are not well understood. Sollberger and Hester (ibid.) have looked to an amelioration of dry conditions and, presumably, increased habitat productivity. Referring only to central Texas, Weir (1976a:124–30) suggests an expansion of oaks which in turn led to the development of an economic system focused mainly on acorns and deer. Weir goes on to hypothesize that

> with an increased abundance of food a natural response is an expanded population. With an expanded population the means of communication are enhanced and possibly new political systems arise (Sahlins and Service 1960). The local group equilibrium system for this [Clear Fork] phase shifted from one [during the San Geronimo phase] of widely scattered self-sufficient nomadic bands to one with an expanded number of bands who probably participated in sharing seasonal activities. [1976a:126]

A systematic explanation—wherein, after an initial "kick," population density, mechanisms for social integration, technology, and environment have interacting, deviation-amplifying effects—has much appeal. Moreover, the "kick" need not be the same in all regions. An expansion of nut-bearing hardwoods is plausible (Table 2.1) for the eastern portion of the coastal plain but not for the more southerly regions. It may even be that diffusion of early cultigens associated with the Eastern Mexico agricultural complex provided the initial impetus in some regions. As yet there is no archaeological support for this hypothesis.

With the greater number of sites and inferred higher population densities more regionally distinct cultural patterns emerge. These patterns generally coincide with major ecological regions and apparently represent broadly similar strategies of adaptation as well as spheres of intensive intergroup information exchange. Certainly, the traits that serve to delineate these patterns are much too widespread to be correlated with specific social entities.

In the heavily-wooded eastern part of the coastal plain, remains believed to date to Middle Archaic times have been grouped under the early LaHarpe aspect (Johnson 1962:268–80). There is much uncertainty about these data, mostly because the sites are characteristically multicomponent and severely mixed (Story 1976, 1981). To complicate the matter further, preservation of organic residue is usually poor and dense vegetation cover makes site recognition and definition difficult. Speculating on the basis of the scanty information available (see summaries by Johnson 1962; Wyckoff 1970; Hoffman 1970; Shafer, Baxter, Stearns, and Dering 1975), Middle Archaic subsistence practices centered on hardwood nuts and deer. The balance of the diet was probably obtained from mussels, fish, bear, small mammals, birds, berries, a variety of herbaceous annuals, and woody species such as plums, honey locust, persimmons, and haws. Since these food resources today are widely and fairly equitably distributed over much of the region, it seems reasonable to hypothesize that there should be a great deal of redundancy in the settlement systems. This is not to suggest that there were no differences between systems, or between the elements comprising a specific system, but rather that these differences were probably less than in a region such as south Texas (Hester 1981) where food resources are far less regularly spaced and perhaps more subjected to variations caused by short-term climatic fluctuations. I would also expect the resources of the eastern portion of the coastal plain to have supported fairly high, evenly distributed population densities and to have favored the development of mutually exclusive territorial rights.

Farther to the west, where the forests give way to grasslands except along the streams, there have been only cultural assessment surveys and limited excavations (Duffield 1963; Sorrow 1966; Prewitt 1974b; Shafer, Dering, and Baxter 1975; Prewitt and Mallouf 1977; Lynott and Peter 1977; Skinner 1981; Mallouf 1979). Here occupation appears to have occurred mostly along the main stream valleys and at the margins of the grasslands. To judge from the relative frequencies of point types, population densities were lower or the intensity of exploitation was less in the Middle Archaic than in later times. Perhaps, as Shafer and others (ibid.) have suggested, much of the use of this region was intermittent and by groups who mostly lived to the west and east. The occurrence of both central and east Texas point styles (Prewitt 1974b:11–14) tends to support this interpretation. In addition, Lynott (1979:92) has pointed out that the tall grasses would not have supported large bison herds. If such grasses were well established by Middle Archaic period, it is possible that sparse food resources in the uplands was a factor in keeping population densities low. Limited bison hunting may have been practiced, but plants and animals in the floodplain and immediately surrounding environs were probably far more important to aboriginal subsistence practices.

In the central portion of the coastal plain, Middle Archaic sites are more numerous and are found mostly in or near the stream and river valleys. Present evidence (Fox et al. 1974; Prewitt 1974a; Fox and Hester 1976; Campbell 1976; McGuff 1978; Hall 1981) indicates that occupation was primarily along the Brazos, Colorado, Lavaca-Navidad, and Guadalupe rivers, and their main tributaries. Knolls and bluff edges provided favored locations for habitation, doubtless because they are often strategically situated for exploitation of both riverine and upland habitats. It is also possible that in portions of some drainages the floodplains were not very suitable for habitation (Baker and Penteado-Orellana 1977; Fox et al. 1974:213–14). Occupational sites vary in size and suggest that the size of exploitative groups changed with seasonal and spatial variations in food resources. Terrestrial and aquatic faunal remains are often well preserved and indicate that riverine resources were more intensively used than upland resources. At the Venom Hill site in Palmetto Bend Reservoir on the Navidad River, sea trout and marine shellfish remains possibly reflect excursions to the coast (McGuff 1978:160). However, since the barrier island system had not yet formed, the presence of these fauna more probably indicate that saline and brackish waters extended much farther inland than they do now (ibid.). Direct evidence of plant utilization is lacking, for even at sites such as Venom Hill (McGuff 1978:54) and Loeve-Fox (E.R. Prewitt, personal communication), where large volumes of earth have been fine-screened, few or no charred floral remains were recovered.

Many of the artifacts found in the central coastal plain, especially the projectile point styles, are of types which occur more abundantly in adjacent regions. In general, the typological similarities are closest with the Edwards Plateau region to the north and northwest. South Texas forms extend eastward to at least the lower reaches of the Guadalupe, and specimens resembling east Texas types have been found in the lower Brazos drainage. The implications of these interregional similarities have been little explored, but it may be that they reflect extensive subsistence ranges (Fox et al. 1974:210). Some groups ranged very widely in search of foods to judge from the early sixteenth century descriptions of the Mariame Indians left by Cabeza de Vaca and his fellow Europeans (Kelley 1952; Campbell and Campbell 1981). The Mariames spent the fall, winter, and spring on the lower Guadalupe, living mostly on pecans, fish, and other riverine resources. Then, with the onset of summer, they journeyed en masse some 130 km southwest (Campbell and Campbell 1981:13–15), where for about three months they exploited primarily the prickly pear. The great prickly pear fields of south Texas were also extensively utilized by more local hunters and gatherers, as the Cabeza de Vaca account makes clear.

The sixteenth century sharing of highly aggregated resources is a pattern that might well date back to Middle Archaic times in south Texas. Hester (1981) has emphasized the environmental diversity of this region, calling attention to high and low density food resource areas. High densities of resources occur along the major rivers (San Antonio, Frio, Nueces, and Rio Grande) and their permanently flowing tributaries, about large inland bodies of standing water (such as La Sal Vieja), on the Rio Grande delta, and in the immediate coastal zone. Low density resource areas include much of the Sand Plain and other uplands, as well as small, intermittent streams. Two broad models of adaptation, savanna and maritime, have been proposed by Hester (ibid.). The savanna adaptation can probably be traced back to the Middle Archaic, but the maritime adaptation may not have emerged until Late Archaic times. Within the savanna pattern Hester (1981; see also Mallouf et al. 1977) has noted a number of variations in sites and artifacts which seem to reflect both cultural and adaptive differences. In general, small sites prevail in the low density areas and probably represent short-term hunting and/or gathering forays. Large occupation sites are associated mostly with the better watered environments where the number and variety of plants and animals are greater. In these areas the stays were longer and/or by larger groups. We should expect to find a series of rather closely-spaced and fairly large sites that can be related to the congregation of different groups at prickly pear fields; but such sites have not yet been reported. In this regard, it is probably significant that Edwards Plateau and Lower Pecos projectile point styles occur in the northern part of south Texas while stemless forms such as Tortugas and Abasolo prevail in the southern sector (Nunley and Hester 1966). Although these styles cannot be linked with any specific group, they do suggest that some peoples from the north at times ventured south, perhaps to the nearest concentrations of prickly pear.

The stemless dart point forms found in south Texas extend into northeastern Mexico (MacNeish 1947, 1958; Hughes 1947), but because of the limited amount of archaeological research in this region, we do not know whether or not similar patterns of adaptation are also represented. Middle Archaic sites are certainly present and correspond to MacNeish's Repelo and early Abasolo complexes. It seems possible that the marked environmental variations in this region, especially the central and southern sections, favored a foraging round that ranged from east to west, from the mountain fronts to the coastal lowlands.

Beyond the coastal plain, in the Sierra de Tamaulipas, La Perra phase sites have yielded primitive forms of corn and squash (*Cucurbita pepo*). Nonetheless, hunting and wild plant collecting continued to provide the bulk of the foodstuffs (MacNeish 1958:154–56). In southwest Tamaulipas, there is a greater variety of cultigens, for by the time of the Guerra phase (ca. 1800 B.C.) corn, squash, gourds, pepper, common beans, small runner beans, and cotton were grown. By about 1500 B.C. pottery was being manufactured.

Much farther to the north, in the Lower Pecos region, numerous wild plant remains have been recovered from Middle Archaic sites (e.g., Alexander 1974; Dering 1979). The number of plant species utilized increased somewhat over Early Archaic times, and deer as well as fish were being more extensively exploited. On the Edwards Plateau to the east, Middle Archaic sites (especially those of the Round Rock phase) are abundant. These include large accumulations of burned rock—the famous Texas burned rock middens—which may represent prolonged stays at favored locales. Specifically, Weir (1976a:128–219) believes that these middens are associated with the exploitation of acorns.

The increase in site size and the intermittent nature of site use suggest that during the Middle Archaic bands may have been the prevailing social group. Since regional subsistence resources vary in kind and density, the inferred bands should have varied in size and structure from one region to another. In regions such as south Texas, where the food resources are both spatially and seasonally very concentrated, there may have been macrobands which dispersed into smaller foraging groups during lean times. Other regions, such as east Texas and the Edwards Plateau, may have supported a number of small local groups who utilized relatively small territories and who constituted dialectical tribes (Weir 1976a:130–32).

Regardless of the social arrangements, it is quite probable, because of apparent increased population, that group mobility was more circumscribed than in Early Archaic times. Not only would movement be reduced, but territorial boundaries and group claims to resources should begin to emerge. Good evidence for the existence of territory-specific groups comes from cemeteries, since they imply that a group had frequent and repeated access to a locale. Cemeteries could also have served to make known, perhaps even sanctify, a group's rights to resources. Reference to the remains of ancestors, especially if these represent a number of generations, provide an easily-understood, awe-associated means for the living to communicate their title to valued resources of an area (Saxe 1971:51). At least two, and possibly three, cemeteries can be related to the Middle Archaic period (Fig. 2.4).

Two of the cemeteries, the Ernest Witte and Morhiss sites, occur in the central coastal plain. The third, the Mason burial cave, is near the southern edge of the Edwards Plateau. The best dated and documented is the Ernest Witte site on the lower Brazos River, ca. 70 km west of Houston (Hall 1981). Here, four temporally distinct burial groups were uncovered. The earliest of these, Group 1, consisted of 50 burials (representing a total of 61 individuals) which are ^{14}C dated, when corrected, to between 2610 ± 140 B.C. (Tx–2453) and 1530 ± 90 B.C. (Tx–2127). Group 2 contained 145 burials and is related to Late Archaic times; Groups 3 and 4 are post-Archaic in age and are comprised of 10 and 13 burials, respectively. The Mason site is a 30 foot deep vertical cave that contained the remains of an estimated 80 individuals (Benfer and Benfer 1962). The four identifiable projectile points (two Nolans, a Travis, and a Tortugas) found among the jumbled human bones in the cave suggest a Middle Archaic date. Because the site was not systematically excavated, little is known about the mode of burial disposal. Indeed, it is perhaps questionable whether or not this site should be considered as analogous to cemeteries such as Ernest Witte. The Morhiss site with 250 burials (Campbell 1976) is clearly a cemetery but is poorly dated. Middle Archaic point styles occur at Morhiss and it is possible that some of the interments date to this period. However, until the site has been analyzed in detail, the burials are best regarded as being of uncertain age.

At both Ernest Witte and Morhiss there are variations in grave good associations and mortuary treatment which probably symbolize different statuses within an egalitarian social system. Even though the more common Middle Archaic burial is a single interment in or near a camp, these cemeteries are by no means aberrant. They reveal that in Middle Archaic times social identities and organizations were becoming increasingly important elements in the adaptive strategies. The greater number (Fig. 2.4), and in some cases greater complexity, of Late Archaic cemeteries reinforces this view.

Late Archaic
(ca. 1000 B.C. to between 200 B.C. and A.D. 1200)

During the Late Archaic there was both an intensification of previously existing cultural patterns and the emergence of new ones. The most striking cultural changes occurred in the eastern portion of the coastal plain, and for the first time there is good evidence of exploitation of the coastal zone. Pottery appears about 200 B.C., or earlier, in

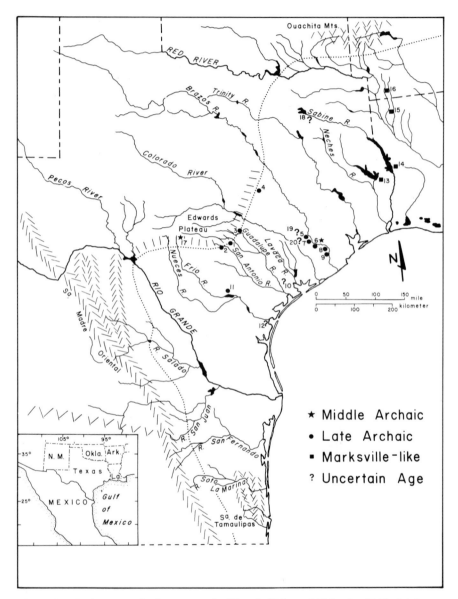

Figure 2.4. Early cemeteries in or near the West Gulf Coastal Plain. See Table 2.3 for a listing of site names.

TABLE 2.3
EARLY CEMETERIES IN OR ADJACENT TO THE WEST GULF COASTAL
PLAIN

No. in Fig. 2.4	Site	Reference
1	Hitzfelder (41BX26)*	Givens 1968
2	Orchard (41BX1)	Grant Hall, personal communication
3	Locke Farm (41CM25)	Texas Archeological Research Laboratory (TARL) files, University of Texas at Austin
4	Owl Hollow (41BL3)	TARL files
5	Goebel (41AU1)	TARL files
6	Ernest Witte (41AU36)	Hall 1981
7	Leonard K (41AU37)	Hall 1981
8	Albert George (41FB13)	Walley 1955
9	Big Creek (41FB2)	TARL files
10	Morhiss (41VT1)	Campbell 1976
11	Loma Sandia (41LK28)	Charles Johnson, III, personal communication
12	Oso Creek (41NU2)	TARL files
13	Jonas Short (41SA101)	Jelks 1965; McClurkan et al. 1980
14	Coral Snake (16SA48)	McClurkan et al. 1966; Jensen 1968; McClurkan et al. 1980
15	Bellevue	Fulton and Webb 1953
16	Shane's Mound (3LA6); Cicero Yound (3LA7)	Hoffman 1970 Schambach 1982
17	Mason Burial Cave (41UV4)*	Benfer and Benfer 1962
18	Yarbrough	Johnson 1962
19	Piekert (41WH14)	Kindall 1980
20	41WH39	Fabac ms.

*Cave with a vertical shaft entrance. Another burial cave, 41VV620, has recently been discovered in the Lower Pecos region, but the findings have not been analyzed.

some parts of the eastern region, while in south Texas Late Archaic (preceramic and/or pre–bow and arrow) components are dated as late as ca. A.D. 1200.

During the Late Archaic all portions of the coastal zone were occupied at least to some extent. The temporal controls are very poor, and it is not known how quickly the coastal adaptation developed. There are hints that in the early part of the period the use of the coast may have been largely intermittent and by groups who focused more on inland resources. Later, perhaps with the formation of the barrier islands (Dolan et al. 1980) and the resultant rich variety of estuarine habitats (Parker 1960), utilization of the strand line seems to have increased. By historic times (Aten 1979, 1983; Campbell and Campbell 1981), groups were confined to a relatively narrow strip along the coast.

They did not range very far inland, nor did inland groups usually have access to the coast. Delineation of coastal territories could well date back to sometime in the Late Archaic. A number of cemeteries have been reported, particularly in the central and southern sections (Hester 1969a; Hester and Corbin 1975), but unfortunately, many are of uncertain age.

Despite the still meager nature of the archaeological sample, several broad patterns can be discerned. Most important, marine resources—fish and shellfish—were utilized primarily, perhaps entirely, on a seasonal basis. A fulltime maritime economy supplemented by inland foods obtained through exchange, did not develop. The best indications of seasonality come from the highly patterned growth rings of the brackish water clam, *Rangia cuneata*, which is abundant in the humid portions of the coast (Aten 1972, 1981; Skelton 1978). Although much of the relevant data have not been made available, it seems that coastal species were usually exploited during the warm portions of the year (Aten et al. 1976:14; Skelton 1978; Aten 1983:158–59). The balance of the subsistence round was evidently spent a short distance inland, where the main economic activities were hunting and plant collecting. Significant differences should exist between these seasonal settlements, but the site sample is too small to define any pattern. More generally, it can be observed that the density of the marine resources greatly influenced the subsistence and settlement systems. For example, along the highly productive bays in the upper and central parts of the Texas coast, shell middens were common and often extensive (Campbell 1960; Story 1968; Corbin 1974; Aten 1983). Farther down the Texas shoreline, where the molluscan fauna is comprised mostly of small sized individuals (Parker 1960), the sites are fewer and smaller (Hester 1969b).

Another pattern which becomes evident in Late Archaic times, is the exchange inland of marine shell ornaments, or raw material for ornaments, probably in return for siliceous stones or finished stone tools. Never very numerous, shell ornaments are widespread in Texas and are usually found as burial offerings. With the exception of the Group 2 burials at the Ernest Witte site, there is no evidence that the exchange system was well organized. Trade seems to have been sporadic and probably dictated largely by convenience and immediate need.

Most Late Archaic inland habitation sites in south Texas, and perhaps also in adjacent parts of northeastern Mexico, appear to be similar to those of the Middle Archaic period. However, the data are very limited. Hester (1981) has observed that Late Archaic sites are more numerous but does not say whether or not this increase is associated with any subsistence or other cultural change. Research currently underway in the Choke Canyon Reservoir on the Frio River (Grant Hall, personal communication) will no doubt help clarify these and other problems. A particularly important site in the Choke Canyon area is a very large Late Archaic cemetery, Loma Sandia. Excavated by the Texas Department of Highways and Public Transportation under the supervision of Charles Johnson III, this site contained habitation debris from several different occupations, as well as some 200 burials. The analysis of this site has not been completed, but apparently the occupations and the cemetery are of different ages. Offerings are common in the cemetery and, significantly, include projectile point types often found on the Edwards Plateau to the north and, to a lesser extent, the Guadalupe River to the east. Since these are made from locally available stone (Johnson, personal communication), they do not seem to represent exchange. The size of the cemetery, moreover, implies that: (1) the territorial range of the group or groups represented was not extensive, or (2) that there was a well established seasonal round wherein related groups, possibly a macroband, gathered in the vicinity of the cemetery. If the latter were the case, perhaps during other parts of the yearly round the macroband dispersed into small, more widely ranging groups.

A possibly related cemetery, the Orchard site, farther to the northeast, in San Antonio, was recently excavated by The University of Texas at San Antonio. This site, like Loma Sandia, has evidence of a burial ritual which involved the placement of deer antlers over the body of the deceased (Grant Hall, personal communication). And, like the Group 2 cemetery at Ernest Witte, large conch shell gorgets were included as offerings. Until more information is available, the significance of these similarities is uncertain, except that the three cemeteries seem to reflect the establishment of territories and subsistence schedules.

At the risk of overextending the available information and oversimplifying the situation, it may be suggested that by the end of Late Archaic times the hunters and gatherers of south Texas had developed an efficient and stable subsistence-settlement system. This is not to imply that there were no subsequent cultural changes, but rather that the general patterns of adaptation and ways of life remained much the same until disrupted by Europeans and Apaches. Perhaps most important, group size may have been partly maintained by cultural practices such as marriage regulations and infanticide. Certainly, the lifestyles in south Texas did not subsequently change nearly as much as those in the eastern region. The one possible exception is in the Rio Grande delta where in late prehistoric times there is evidence of a specialized shell industry and extensive trade which involved, among others, Huastecan groups to the south (MacNeish 1947; Hester 1969a; Prewitt 1974c; Mallouf et al. 1977).

In some portions of the study area there are suggestions of changes which could possibly be linked to more mesic conditions between ca. 1000 B.C. and A.D. 1 (Table 2.1) and/or the presence of bison herds. Dillehay (1974) has postulated that the latter had returned to the southern plains ca. 2500 B.C. and remained in the area until ca. A.D. 500. Bison bones do occur occasionally in Middle Archaic sites, but there is some evidence, mostly indirect, that the impact of these herds may have been more significant between ca. 1000 and 500 B.C. The nearest reported kill site is in the Lower Pecos region, at Bonfire Shelter (Dibble and Lorrain 1968). Here a massive bison drive, or a series of drives over a very brief period, has been ^{14}C dated to ca. 700–800 B.C. The dart point forms associated with this kill (Montell, Castroville, and Lange) are infrequent in the area and suggest to Dibble (ibid.:72) that it ". . . was the of knowledgeable bison hunters who had followed an unusual southward migration of large herds." Although the presence of bison and possibly of intrusive bison-hunters appears to have had little impact on the local Lower Pecos groups and their subsistence practice, this may not have been the case elsewhere. To the east, on the Edwards Plateau, Weir (1976a:131–36) has noted that these same point forms are associated with what he sees as a period (the San Marcos phase) of economic change, probable population decline, and perhaps the presence of new peoples. Farther east, in and near the grasslands, Late Archaic sites are more common than those of earlier periods, and even on the eastern fringe have yielded Montell, Castroville, and Lange points, along with a number of east Texas types (Sorrow 1966). It is, thus, attractive to relate the widespread occurrence of these point forms to more mesic conditions and an increase in bison herds. However, there is conflicting evidence. No bison kill sites other than Bonfire have been reported on or near the coastal plains, and bison bones are not commonly recovered from habitation loci (Dillehay 1974:Fig. 4; Lynott 1979). Perhaps it is the mesic conditions that are more important. Conceivably, they might in part explain the large size of the cemetery at Loma Sandia and the increase in number of interments (145 Late Archaic burials versus 61 Middle Archaic) at the Ernest Witte site.

A mesic interval and a larger cemetery at Ernest Witte seem consistent with the high visibility of Late Archaic habitation sites over much of the central portion of the coastal plain (e.g., Fox et al. 1974; Skelton 1977). Of the several explanations that could account for the prominence of these sites, the most reasonable is either an overall increase in population, or a reduction in group mobility. No obvious changes in subsistence behavior have been reported, although a survey of the proposed Cuero Phase I Reservoir on the Guadalupe River (Fox et al. 1974) did find that the Late Archaic sites were more concentrated on the floodplain. This shift may reflect more intensive exploitation of riverine resources, or simply geomorphological changes which made the floodplain more habitable than in earlier times.

Farther east, on the lower Brazos and in the vicinity of the Ernest Witte site, Late Archaic sites are also fairly common. Most are near gullies which have cut into bluff edges overlooking the Brazos floodplain (Hall 1981). The one excavated site with a Late Archaic habitational component (AU37) yielded a number of faunal remains but no charred plant parts. Many riverine species, including fish, mussels, frogs, turtle, and raccoon, were present, as were more widely ranging animals such as deer, opossum, terrapin, and rabbit. While the data from this site do not suggest a highly localized population, the Ernest Witte cemetery does. Moreover, the Group 2 mortuary at Ernest Witte differs markedly from the much earlier Group 1 burials. The former is larger, contains more offerings, and displays more variations in modes of interment.

The several radiocarbon dates obtained from Group 2 skeletal remains at the Ernest Witte site extend from ca. 650 B.C. to A.D. 450. On the basis of typological similarities with neighboring regions, however, the more probable span is ca. 300 B.C. and A.D. 450. In part, the Group 2 burials are contemporaneous with the post-Archaic, Marksville-like burial mounds such as Jonas Short, Coral Snake, Shane's, Cicero Young, and Bellevue to the east (Fig. 2.4), and the very Late Archaic Twin Sisters phase to the west. Some of the grave inclusions—especially the corner tang knives of central Texas flint, the boatstones and gorgets made of igneous and metamorphic stone from the Ouachita Mountains, and the numerous marine shell ornaments (including the so-called sandal-sole gorget form)—indicate that the people responsible for Group 2 burials were participants in an exchange network which reached to the east, north and, less certainly, the southwest. The marine shell items are the most numerous and may have come from the nearby Texas coast. But, as Hall (1981:306) points out, a source much farther east cannot be excluded. The relatively low incidence of the other exotic items suggest that the flow of goods may have been infrequent, perhaps reflecting an intermittent, down-the-line exchange system. Nonetheless, it seems to have been fairly well established and to have had a regional impact. Very nearby (Fig. 2.4) are comparable, though less well sampled cemeteries—Albert George (Walley 1955), Goebel, Big Creek (Hall 1981), Piekert (Kindall 1980), and 41WH39 (Fabac n.d.)—which have yielded comparable specimens. At Ernest Witte the differences which exist in the modes of disposal of the corpses and the distribution of offerings do not follow easily defined social patterns. In general, the variability within Group 2 burials is very similar to what Winters (1968) has described for the Indian Knoll culture in the Midwest.

One set of Burial Group 2 associations is clear and important: five adults, three males and two females, were found with projectile points so positioned as to indicate violent death. These dart points are of nonlocal styles and sufficiently variable in form to suggest to Hall that more than one enemy group may be represented. Another report of possible violence comes from the Piekert site (Kindall 1980), a small Late(?) Archaic cemetery to the west of Ernest Witte. At Piekert, two of the 11 individuals recovered may have died from point wounds. One was an adult female, the other an infant.

Combined, the Witte and Piekert sites provide good evidence for intergroup conflicts. These hostilities may have stemmed from competition over resources which were becoming scarce because of habitat changes or overexploitation. The relatively small size of the post-Archaic Burial Groups 3 and 4 at Witte (10 and 13 individuals, respectively, versus 145 in Group 2) and the absence of luxury goods in these two later cemeteries also point to significant cultural changes after about A.D. 500.

The most striking of the cultural manifestations dating perhaps as early as 1000 B.C. are to be found in the heavily-forested northeastern portion of the West Gulf Coastal Plain. Here there are a large number of sites which contain Gary type dart points and other artifacts attributable to Late Archaic and early post-Archaic times. This apparent increase in sites could reflect either (1) better preservation and, hence, higher archaeological visibility, or (2) changes in the subsistence-settlement system. The appearance by about 500 B.C. of what Schambach (1982) has characterized as early Fourche Maline culture and, then later, the construction of Middle Woodland–like burial mounds argue in favor of the latter of these two possibilities. While these and other apparent changes may not have been uniform or even contemporaneous throughout the northeastern sector, they very well may have set into motion the processes that ultimately culminated in the widespread Caddoan tradition. These developments parallel, and closely relate to, those farther to the east. Nonetheless, it is doubtful that they can ever be understood if regarded simply as westward extensions of either people or ideas.

Tightly controlled data to test alternative explanations are lacking, or have not found their way into the literature. Thus, what role, if any, was played by tropical and other cultigens is not known. No remains of a cultivated species have been reported and, in general, information on subsistence practices is sparse. A chipped stone tool sometimes identified as a gardening hoe (e.g., Wyckoff 1967a:83) occurs at some sites, especially in southeastern Oklahoma and southwestern Arkansas. These implements, however, have not been carefully studied for use-wear and it may be, as Schambach (1982:179) has suggested, that they served instead as wood-working tools.

It also is very difficult to define meaningful settlement patterns or to characterize the structure of individual components. With the possible exception of the Yarbrough site on the Sabine River (Johnson 1962) and, more tenuously, the Arnold site on the South Sulphur drainage (Doehner and Larson n.d.:92–93), no cemeteries have been reported for a preceramic Late Archaic site in the northeastern portion of the coastal plain proper.

Perhaps several centuries after pottery-making became fairly widespread, burial mounds appear in southwestern Arkansas, northeastern Louisiana, and east-central Texas. Few of these mounds have been carefully investigated, and it is not easy to make an accurate count of them. Including two possible such mounds at the Poole site in the Ouachita Mountains, Schambach (1982:179–80) estimates that there were at least 13 in southwestern Arkansas. In northeastern Louisiana, there is Coral Snake in the Toledo Bend area (McClurkan et al. 1966; Jensen 1968) and, farther to the north, Bellevue (Fulton and Webb 1953) and six apparently related mound sites (Webb and Gregory 1978:2). Jonas Short (Jelks 1965; McClurkan et al. 1980) in the Angelina drainage is the only certain example in Texas.

Each of the more systematically excavated of these burial mounds (Shane, Cicero Young, Bellevue, Coral Snake, and Jonas Short) had a central feature which contained the cremated, or partly cremated, remains of one or more individuals. Since these features lie below, or very near the base of, the mound, they appear to represent trigger events, perhaps the death of one or more prominent individuals. While there is a good deal of variation from site to site, other features—such as artifact caches and/or additional burials—often occur in the mound fill. Associated offering are not numerous (none at Bellevue), but many of those recovered are notable as they include such items as copper ornaments, large and well made bifaces, and Marksville pottery. Although there are similarities to Marksville mounds to the east, many of these resemblances are superficial (see discussion in Schambach 1982:180) and provide no basis for postulating any population intrusion. Rather, these mounds more probably reflect the emergence of more complexly organized local groups with more specialized roles and ranked statuses which perhaps included a headman as the most important position. For reasons not understood, these societies seem to have been unstable, for by ca. A.D. 400 or 500, the burial mounds have disappeared and with them the evidence for the maintenance of ranked statuses. Then sometime during the eighth or ninth century A.D. villages, and even more complex social systems, known as Caddoan, emerge. With these groups come the first direct evidence of cultigens—eight-rowed corn—in the West Gulf Coastal Plain.

From at least Late Archaic times on, the adaptive strategies in the southern part of the coastal plain and those in the eastern section became increasingly divergent. This suggests to me a model which relates many of the major cultural differences to ecological factors (see Gunn 1979:265 for a model which refers many of the differences within the Texas Archaic to climatic zones). In the southern reaches of the area, in south Texas and perhaps adjacent portions of north-eastern Mexico, food resources are unevenly distributed and droughts are frequent, sometimes intense. At the Archaic technological level these conditions selectively favored the development of: (1) relatively high group mobility and low population densities; (2) well defined, but often shared, rights to seasonally and/or spatially abundant resources such as prickly pear, maguey, mesquite, and pecan; (3) social units which were not integrated beyond the exogamous band level; and (4) social roles which were largely determined by sex and age. Intergroup social and economic exchange mostly took place when groups aggregated at the rich resources. Exchange was based on reciprocity between individuals and families and served to provide valuable ties in times of need.

Farther east, in the predominantly hardwood forest region, food resources are more evenly distributed and chances of loss due to long-term droughts were much less than in the southern sector. Even at a fairly simple technological level, the selective pressures were lower than to the southwest and there developed: (1) higher population densities; (2) more limited group mobility and mutually exclusive territorial and resource rights; and (3) more complex social systems which featured greater role definition, sodalities, and the like for maintaining intra-group harmony, organizing task groups, and obtaining resources beyond a group's territory. In brief, social solutions were more varied and more energy was spent preserving these solutions, particularly in legitimatizing statuses and group identities. This, in turn, created a sociocultural environment in which cultigens and other energy-capturing innovations should have been readily accepted.

The central portion of the coastal plain as well as the littoral zone fall in between the easily contrasted extremes of the model. At times, and mostly in the southwestern part of the central region, the trend would be to the southern strategy. At other times, and especially in the eastern parts of the central region, the trend is toward the eastern strategy. Cabeza de Vaca's account of the Mariames, for example, portrays the southern strategy, while the Ernest Witte site relates more to the eastern strategy.

CONCLUSIONS

Whether or not cultigens were grown on the West Gulf Coastal Plain prior to the ninth century A.D. remains an unanswered question. Nevertheless, the Gilmore Corridor should not be rejected as a possible route for the early spread of squash and bottle gourd from northeastern Mexico into the eastern United States. It is easily traversed and is the most direct avenue for such diffusion. In addition, there are archaeological indications that prior to 2500 B.C.—by which time early Eastern Mexican cultigens were well established in the eastern United States—human populations on the coastal plain were very mobile and were probably interacting over large geographical expanses. These conditions were perhaps optimal for the dispersal of squash and gourd whose primary use was as containers rather than food (see Watson, this volume). J. Charles Kelley's (1952) hypothesis that the gathering of groups at the south Texas prickly pear fields was a vehicle for the northeastward spread of cultigens, however, does not seem probable because the archaeological evidence suggests that this pattern did not develop until after 2500 B.C. Indeed, it may even be that the establishment of regular subsistence schedules and territorially-constrained rounds acted as deterrents to later diffusion of traits from Mexico.

The main conclusion to come from this study, then, is that there is presently insufficient data to prove or disprove the Gilmore Corridor hypothesis, but that this hypothesis merits rigorous testing. This, I believe, could be effectively and most economically accomplished by intensive investigation of Early Archaic sites in the central portion of the coastal plain. The Guadalupe drainage in particular should be closely studied. Here there are appropriate age and well stratified, but very poorly sampled, sites. Moreover, it is primarily along the Guadalupe that the enigmatic *Cucurbita texana* Gray (Heiser, this volume) occurs. If cultigens did in fact diffuse across the coastal plain of Texas, they should be archaeologically recoverable by massive flotation. That this has not been done at strategically situated, sufficiently early sites is why we cannot at this time properly assess the Gilmore Corridor.

ACKNOWLEDGMENTS

Many individuals have been of assistance to me during the course of my researching and writing of this paper. In particular, I am indebted to E. Mott Davis who patiently listened to my evolving ideas and who offered many constructive suggestions; to Nancy Kenmotsu who checked my bibliographic citations and plotted site locations; to Thomas R. Hester, Grant D. Hall, Charles Johnson III, Elton R. Prewitt, Robert J. Mallouf, Thomas N. Campbell, Glen L. Evans, and David S. Dibble who made available to me unpublished manuscripts and other useful information; to Terrisa Lazicki who typed the manuscript; and to the other seminar participants who provided five days of stimulating discussion.

Some Botanical Considerations of the Early Domesticated Plants North of Mexico[1]

Charles B. Heiser, Jr.
Indiana University

Whether there was an independent origin of agriculture north of Mexico has been a subject of some interest for a number of years. A study of the sunflower originally aroused my interest in this problem, and I propose to discuss the sunflower as well as several other species that bear on the subject. Unfortunately, more questions may be raised than are answered.

SUNFLOWER (*Helianthus annuus*)

As a wild plant the sunflower is widely distributed in the United States extending into southern Canada and northern Mexico (Heiser et al. 1969). Its distribution before humans appeared on the scene must remain a matter of conjecture. It may have originated in the Southwest where today small-headed forms of the species are found that are probably the nearest to the ancestral type. The greatest concentration of annual species of *Helianthus* presently occurs in the Southwest and the nearest relative of the sunflower, *H. argophyllus*, is found in southeastern Texas. The sunflower thrives in areas receiving less than 35 inches of rain a year. The large weedy form of sunflower

57

found in the central and eastern United States probably originated from the introduction of the wild sunflower from the West in prehistoric times. East of the Mississippi River the sunflower occurs sporadically, only rarely forming large populations, and generally grows in highly disturbed areas near cities. These weedy sunflowers for the most part do not appear to be escapes from cultivation, but there may have been an introduction of genes into them from the domesticated sunflower through hybridization.

Shortly after the Discovery the sunflower was seen in cultivation in eastern North America and Mexico (Heiser 1951). Not until the late nineteenth century was it observed in cultivation in the southwestern United States, and how old it is as a domesticate in this area must remain in doubt. The archaeological record reveals the domesticated sunflower from central and eastern North America (Heiser 1955; Yarnell 1977, 1978). There are very few archaeological records from the Southwest, and the material that has been found falls into the size range of wild sunflowers. No archaeological reports are known from Mexico.

Several accounts indicate that the wild sunflower was an important food in the West (Heiser 1951). It has been hypothesized that the western wild sunflower became a camp following weed and was introduced eastward by humans. Then somewhere in what is now the central United States it became a domesticated plant. From there it went back to the Southwest as a domesticated plant and eventually it reached Mexico (Heiser 1955, 1978). Other interpretations are, of course, possible. Donald Lathrap (oral communication, 1973), for example, supposes that the wild sunflower was cultivated in the Southwest and went eastward as a cultivated plant where in time the domesticated form appeared. The present distribution of the wild sunflower does not rule out a domestication in northern Mexico; its absence from the archaeological record in Mexico does not, of course, eliminate the possibility of its domestication there. MacNeish (1965) considers that it was domesticated in the Southwest between 3600 and 2000 B.C. and spread to Mexico around 2000 B.C. However, we have no knowledge of how old the domesticated sunflower is in the Southwest, and as Richard Ford pointed out (oral communication, 1979) it might have been introduced by the Spanish. If this is true, it would mean that the domesticated sunflower went directly to Mexico from central or eastern North America or was the result of an independent domestication.

The possibility that the domesticated sunflower had more than one origin deserves consideration. Although the idea that a domesticated plant had a single origin was widely held in the past, it is now known that there may be exceptions. A wide ranging wild plant could have been domesticated at different places and at different times (Carter 1945; Heiser 1965; Whitaker and Carter 1946). One might then suggest that there were independent domestications of the sunflower in the Southwest and in the central area and perhaps even in Mexico.[2] The hypothesis that the domesticated sunflower originated in the central United States and then diffused to the Southwest and Mexico, however, seems more reasonable. The evidence supporting it comes from the archaeological record. Moreover, the Indian varieties of sunflowers from the eastern United States, the Southwest and Mexico are so similar that it is rather difficult to visualize more than a single original domestication.

With domestication came several changes in the sunflower. The domesticated sunflower is unbranched and bears a single massive head whereas the wild sunflower is much branched and bears many small heads. Originally it was postulated that the change from the branched to the unbranched condition resulted from a single mutation, but it is now considered more likely that it involved more than a single step. More than one gene is now known to control branching (Putt 1964). Evidence for a transitional type may perhaps be indicated by the material from Newt Kash Hollow where heads of various sizes are found. This could mean that the people there had a branched sunflower bearing a large terminal head and smaller lateral heads. The alternatives are that they had two kinds of sunflowers or that growing conditions influenced the size of the heads.[3] In addition to the larger heads, there was also an increase in size of other parts of the plant with domestication. The much larger achenes of the domesticated plant showed increased variability in shape and color patterns. The achenes tended to remain in the head rather than falling from the plant at maturity. The last change is hardly unexpected, for most plants domesticated for their fruits or seeds usually lose the dispersal mechanism of their wild progenitor.

Finally there is another change that commonly occurs when a wild plant becomes domesticated. Seeds of the domesticated sunflower germinate rapidly and uniformly whereas those of the wild and weedy types germinate very slowly and unevenly. Seeds of the previous year will give little or no germination when planted in the spring. To overcome this I ordinarily plant the achenes in pots in the late winter, water them and place them outside for a month or six weeks where they are subjected to alternate freezing and thawing. Then when they are brought into the greenhouse the seeds germinate fairly evenly but still not as rapidly as those of the domesticated sunflower. Experiments have not been conducted to explain why seeds of wild sunflowers behave as they do, but it may have something to do with the armor layer present in the achenes of the wild and weedy types which is generally lacking in the cultivated types. Freezing and thawing would break the armor layer allowing water to reach the seed.

Seed germination has been discussed for it raises an interesting question. If when humans began to cultivate the sunflower the planting were done in the late spring, it is likely that they would have obtained a very poor stand until mutants were selected that gave rapid and even germination. Planting possibly could have been done in the very early spring with better results, but planting in the fall would be even better. Would they not have tried to imitate nature by planting seeds when the wild achenes fall from the head? However, planting would have to have been transferred to the spring at some point in order to allow selection for rapid and evenly germinating seeds.

How long did it take to develop a domesticated sunflower? This question is impossible to answer for several reasons. It was a gradual development, and the time required would depend on a number of factors, including the size of the gene pool, the mutation rate and the intensity of selection. If intentional selection were exercised it is likely that some changes could have been fairly rapid. Fifty generations involving both conscious and unconscious selection might have been sufficient to have produced rather dramatic results. The archaeological record tells us far less about the evolution of the domesticated sunflower than it does for corn, for usually the only part of the sunflower preserved is the achene, and the increase in the size of the achene was probably much slower than the change for certain other characters. With increasing numbers of achenes that are securely dated coming from archaeological sites we may be able to say more about the development of the achene in the future, remembering, of course, that some caution must be exercised.[2] It is likely that any achene over 7 mm long should be interpreted as coming from a domesticated plant.

Where did the domestication take place? As pointed out previously it probably occurred in the central United States. To narrow it down more precisely is impossible at this time. Although it is conceivable that the domestication took place in one locality, it is perhaps more likely that people began to "experiment" with the plant in several places over a rather broad area at about the same time. While some changes were occurring in one place, others were arising in other places. From time to time the plant was carried to new places and there may also have been an exchange of seed between the groups growing the sunflower. Thus the best that can be hoped for is to point to a rather broad area as the place of domestication.

This brings us to another question. Why were sunflowers ever planted deliberately in the first place? If sunflowers grew well as weeds, why plant them? One might suggest demographic pressure, or for that matter, that the first plantings were simply a sacrifice to the gods as a token offering. More likely groups of people found themselves in an area where sunflowers didn't grow naturally and desired them as a food source, or planted them simply because they desired more of them at a given place. Although sunflowers grow abundantly as weeds in many places, Wilson and Rice (1968) have shown an alleopathic effect in the sunflowers in Oklahoma that includes a self-toxicity. Thus wild sunflowers would tend to disappear in a given plot in time and might have been planted deliberately in other plots to maintain the plants. The idea of planting, of course, need not have been an indigenous development. Even if the sunflowers were domesticated before other domesticated plants had come up from Mexico, the idea of planting could have resulted from stimulus diffusion. It is probably futile to look for a single factor to explain why humans started planting, for as Niederberger (1979) has suggested it was probably a combination of factors that led to the origin of agriculture.

Some years ago one might have asked why people domesticated the sunflower if they already had maize, bean and squash, but now we know that the sunflower was probably domesticated before maize and beans appeared in eastern North America. When the Europeans arrived, the sunflower was fairly widely cultivated but it appears to have been a minor crop, grown chiefly for its oil. Thus it served a purpose that the other plants did not.

JERUSALEM ARTICHOKE (*Helianthus tuberosus*)

Today the Jerusalem artichoke is widely distributed as a wild plant or weed in the eastern half of the United States. The idea that it was a cultivated plant of the Indians rests primarily on Champlain's observations in what is now eastern Massachusetts in 1603 (Salaman 1940). As a weed the plant sometimes grows in almost pure stands, and if Champlain had observed such near the Indian village and found the tubers being used for food he might have concluded that it was cultivated when actually it was not. To learn whether or not it was actually domesticated an attempt was made, without too much success (Heiser 1976), to learn more about the plants that first appeared in Europe. However, the tubers that first reached Europe may have been larger than those of the wild plants which suggests that the Indians may have selected for larger tuber size. It is also possible that Massachusetts was outside of the natural range of the species which would suggest human introduction. Plants do occur naturally in Massachusetts today but these appear largely to be escapes from cultivation. Thus all that we can say at present is that it is likely that the Jerusalem artichoke was being cultivated at the time of the arrival of Europeans and that it may have been domesticated. There is as yet no archaeological report of the Jerusalem artichoke, so it can contribute little to our understanding of the origin of agriculture in the eastern United States. That the domesticated plant is little changed from the wild plant might suggest that it is a late domesticate. On the other hand, if propagation took place vegetatively by tubers, as it probably did, one might expect less rapid change than in a sexually-propagated species.

SUMPWEED OR MARSH ELDER (*Iva annua*)

Sumpweed has been thoroughly reviewed in several papers (Asch and Asch 1978; Yarnell 1972, 1978), and there is little to add. It remains one of the most interesting of domesticated plants for its failure to survive into historical times. From the increase in the size of the achene we can reason that it was a domesticated plant. It is rather difficult to imagine its having been domesticated as a food plant after other food plants had been acquired from Mexico.

Today sumpweed is widely distributed in the central United States where it is generally found in moist soils near streams or lakes. However, it grows well in ordinary upland gardens. I have grown it for several years at Bloomington, and the plants are as vigorous, or more so, than in natural sites. Moreover, it reseeds itself as Asch and Asch (1978) found. The seeds, like those of the sunflower, require cold treatment in order to give good germination.

Asch and Asch (1978) suggest that if sumpweed were grown in upland sites by the Indians it would provide the isolation necessary for differentiation to occur. However, if disruptive selection were to operate, as postulated for sorghum (Doggett and Majisu 1968), differentiation of a domesticate might occur even if the cultivated plants were grown adjacent to the wild plants.

Yarnell (1978) mentions an autoploid sumpweed that I grew which had achenes considerably larger than those of the diploid plant. Some explanation is in order. Some years ago when I was growing both sumpweed and various *Helianthus* species I had occasion to treat the latter with colchicine so I also treated sumpweed seedlings at the same time. The few autoploids secured were vigorous and showed the typical *gigas* characters associated with a raw polyploid. However, the plants produced very few filled achenes. It is known that selection can improve fertility in autoploid maize (Gilles and Randolph 1951), and the same might be true of sumpweed, but such experiments have not yet been carried out. An interracial hybrid giving rise to an autoploid might conceivably have better fertility than an interracial autoploid. Such might have occurred had people carried seeds from some distance to an area where sumpweed already occurred naturally.

There is, however, no reason to suspect that the domesticated sumpweed was either an auto- or alloploid. The increase in achene size could well have come about through selection just as it did in the sunflower and many other plants without a doubling of chromosomes.

In 1983 I planted seeds in the greenhouse of volunteer sumpweeds from our experimental field. Later 12 plants were transplanted to the field. In the middle of the summer I noticed that 10 of the plants had two to four branches with abnormally thick stems along with normal ones. The abnormal branches later produced thick inflorescences with unusually large heads and I suspected they might be polyploid. However, examination of buds from two plants proved them to be diploid. Later when achenes were harvested from the normal and abnormal branches, it was found that those from the latter were much larger. One hundred achenes were measured from one plant and the length and width of those from the normal branch averaged 2.6 × 2.1 mm whereas those from the abnormal branch averaged 3.8 × 3.3 mm. The cause of the abnormality is not known nor is it yet known if the larger size is an inherited trait.

Why did sumpweed become extinct as a domesticated plant? Perhaps it was the introduction of corn and beans that led to the abandonment of the indigenous plants. The pollen of sumpweed is produced in great abundance and, like that of its relative ragweed, causes allergies in humans. Did people willingly give it up for that reason after they had other food crops? The sunflower, however, was kept, but perhaps more for its role as a dye and oil plant, rather than as a primary food source.

SQUASH, PUMPKIN, AND GOURD (*Cucurbita pepo*)

The presence of *Cucurbita pepo* in eastern North America before 2000 B.C., more than 1000 years before any of the native domesticates appear in the archaeological record, is regarded as evidence that agriculture in eastern North America did not have an independent origin (Chomko and Crawford 1978). It is well known that *C. pepo* was domesticated in Mexico by 5000 B.C. or earlier (Flannery 1973). But could it have been independently domesticated in the East as well? Such an independent domestication was suggested more than 30 years ago by Whitaker and Carter (1946; Carter 1945) and the wild Texas gourd, *C. texana*, was given as the possible progenitor. It is doubtful that these authors maintained that view, however. Whitaker (Whitaker and Bemis 1975) in a recent paper presents a figure showing *C. pepo* coming to the East directly from Mexico. Moreover, he has several times (for example, Whitaker and Bemis 1975) pointed out that there is no critical evidence to determine whether *C. texana* represents an escape from cultivation or is a truly wild plant.

The Texas wild gourd deserves more detailed consideration. Originally described as *Tristemon texana* by Scheele in 1848, it was transferred two years later to *Cucurbita* by Asa Gray (1850), who remarked that the "fruit is just that of *C. ovifera* [now *C. pepo* var. *ovifera*], of which our plant may possibly be only a naturalized variety." The influence of this statement is still being felt today, but Gray (1857) himself in a later paper wrote that the plant had the appearance of being native: "At least, this is the opinion of Mr. Lindheimer and Mr. Charles Wright [both well known botanical collectors], two good judges. The latter informs us that, from the stations and localities in which alone it is met with, he could not so feel it to be other than an indigenous plant." Unfortunately, sometimes there is no way by which a naturalized (i.e., an escape from cultivation that has reverted to the wild state and become firmly established) plant can be distinguished from an indigenous (i.e., a wild native) plant. All that we can do is rely upon the opinion of botanists who have given the plant careful study.

Coulter (1891–94) in his flora of western Texas considered it naturalized, but it is not known whether this resulted from personal observations or was simply on the basis of Gray's (1850) description.

One of the botanical authorities on cucurbits, L.H. Bailey (1930) visited Texas and along with his host, the Texas botanist B.C. Tharp, concluded that *C. texana* was probably an indigenous plant. Later Bailey (1943) stated that the fruits of *C. texana* vary greatly in nature and he thought it was possible "for the big oleraceous things we know as *Cucurbita pepo* to have developed from a plant much like *C. texana*."

A.T. Erwin (1938), another student of *Cucurbita*, also visited the locality where *C. texana* grows and decided that it was an indigenous plant and not an escape. He stated that, except in minor characteristics, it agrees with the ovifera gourds and clearly belongs to the same variety. He concluded that the preponderance of evidence indicated that it was the prototype of the cultivated forms of *C. pepo*.

The most recent treatment of *C. texana* is in the *Manual of the Vascular Plants of Texas* (Correll and Johnston 1970) where it is listed as an endemic, rare but abundant where found, occurring "in debris and piles of drift wood, often climbing into trees, along several rivers, especially the Guadalupe, that drains the Edwards Plateau" in central Texas.

More critical evidence to assess whether *C. texana* is indigenous or naturalized is to be desired, of course, but may never be forthcoming. The botanists who are most familiar with it, however, are inclined to regard it as indigenous, an endemic of central Texas. Perhaps it has been modified by hybridization with domesticated forms of *C. pepo*, which might explain the diversity in the fruits noted by Bailey. *Cucurbita pepo* var. *ovifera* is known to escape from cultivation at times. Steyermark (1963) and Mohlenbrock (1978) list several records for it from Missouri and Illinois, respectively. It is not known, however, how long it persists at these localities. Deam (1940) excludes it from *Flora of Indiana* as not becoming established.

That *C. texana* is nothing more than a form or variety of *C. pepo* seems clear, and it was included within *C. pepo* by Cogniaux, Naudin, and Coulter in the last century. More recent authors, however, continue to treat it as a distinct species. Bailey (1943) wrote: "In view of the fact that the connection between *C. ovifera* [= *C. pepo* var. *ovifera*, Bailey 1944] and *C. texana* has not been demonstrated in practice, I prefer in my time to keep the two things separate in nomenclature, that we may easier analyze our discussions." The connection between the two has now been demonstrated. In a recent numerical taxonomic study *C. texana* was found to link closely to the two accessions of *C. pepo* included in the study (Rhodes et al. 1968). Moreover, Whitaker and Bemis (1965) reported that hybrids between the two are fertile.

Thus we have a candidate for the progenitor of *C. pepo* north of Mexico. That the gourd can be grown north of Texas is evident. Gray grew it at Cambridge, Massachusetts, but it is not clear whether it came to fruit. However, it did fruit for Bailey at Ithaca, New York, for Erwin at Ames, Iowa and for me at Bloomington, Indiana.

It would be rather difficult to explain why only *C. pepo* would have come up from Mexico so much earlier than maize and beans. The problem does not exist, however, if an origin of *C. pepo* occurred in eastern North America. To what extent the material from this area was wild, cultivated or domesticated remains to be answered. The development of a domesticated form of *C. pepo* in eastern North America, of course, does not preclude a later introduction of other domesticated forms from Mexico.

Why did humans ever domesticate this plant in the first place? Certainly its rather fragile rind makes it very inferior to the bottle gourd for the ordinary uses of a gourd. There is little in the literature to suggest that *C. pepo* had very extensive use as a gourd; Speck (1941), however, does record its use as a utensil in the Southeast. It could perhaps also have served for a rattle at times. Its original use as a gourd, if it ever had any, could have largely been supplanted by the bottle gourd.

What little flesh the Texas gourd has is extremely bitter. So as a food plant we would have to assume that the seeds were eaten, as may well be true of the wild gourds that gave rise to the other domesticated species of *Cucurbita*. The plants could have originally been cultivated for the seeds, and mutants that gave rise to a greater amount of flesh and nonbitter types appeared after it was taken into cultivation (see Carter 1945).

If we accept an independent domestication of *C. pepo* north of Mexico from *C. texana*, how is the much earlier domestication of *C. pepo* in Mexico to be explained? Whitaker and Carter (1946) also suggest an origin of *C. pepo* in the Southwest or northern Mexico and give three species as possible progenitors. From the knowledge of the genus that has accumulated since that time, largely from Whitaker's work, it now seems most unlikely that any of these three species could be involved. *Cucurbita texana* remains the only possible progenitor. Did early Mexicans carry the seeds of it southward where it also underwent domestication? This seems rather unlikely, and it is more probable that *C. texana* or a plant very similar to it had a far more extensive distribution in earlier times than it does today (Heiser 1979b). How then are we to account for its extinction everywhere but in Texas? This is a difficult question to answer, and there is no good answer except to suggest, as has been done for the bottle gourd (Heiser 1979a), that the wild plant might have grown in the very sort of habitats that humans chose for their early settlements, and that humans eliminated it as a wild plant throughout most of its range by excessive harvesting or destruction of its habitat or that it was hybridized out of existence by the cultivated form. But, of course, this apparently didn't happen in central Texas.

BOTTLE GOURD (*Lagenaria siceraria*)

If the bottle gourd can be shown to be as old as *Cucurbita pepo* in central and eastern North America, it raises questions as to whether there was an independent domestication of the latter plant in that area, for the bottle gourd almost certainly came to North America from Mexico. The history of the bottle gourd has recently been treated in some detail (Heiser 1979a), so only a few points will be reviewed here. It is now thought that the bottle gourd is native to Africa, although that is scarcely proved. Thus it probably had to reach America across the Atlantic. Whether this journey was natural by floating of the fruits or whether it was carried by people is still an open question, although I support the former view. The most likely place for a bottle gourd to arrive in America is Brazil, but it is not impossible that it reached Middle America directly from Africa. One might even, I suppose, conceive of an arrival in southeastern North America by ocean currents, if not from Africa then from tropical America.[4] More than one arrival of the bottle gourd in America from Africa is perhaps unlikely, but hardly impossible. The bottle gourd could have arrived before humans appeared on the scene in the Americas, and it could have spread to some extent by natural means. One might immediately then ask why it isn't found as a wild plant in the Americas today. The answer could be for the same reason, whatever that reason might be, that it isn't found as a wild plant in Africa today.

The bottle gourd is known from Mexico at 7000 B.C. We cannot assume that it was necessarily cultivated or domesticated at this early date, for we do not yet know what differences, if any, existed between a wild and domesticated bottle gourd. It is perhaps reasonable to assume that it originally spread in the Americas as a weed following humans in their migrations. Thus one might suppose that it originally reached eastern North America as a weed. On the other hand, we certainly do not know that it didn't arrive as a fully domesticated plant. All that can be suggested here is that the presence of the bottle gourd in eastern North America does not necessarily indicate that it came with a knowledge of agriculture or with other plants from Mexico.[5]

CHENOPODS (*Chenopodium* Species)

Chenopodium is a difficult genus taxonomically, and identification of archaeological material has had to await adequate taxonomic treatment of the extant species which is only now beginning to appear. Asch and Asch (1977) have provided the most comprehensive treatment of the eastern archaeological chenopods. They showed that certain large seeds previously referred to as *Chenopodium* belonged to pokeweed. The remaining material they found most closely resembled *C. bushianum*. From measurements of archaeological fruits and those of modern *C. bushianum* they concluded that the archaeological material was within the size range of present day *C. bushianum*. Hugh Wilson (unpublished) who has also measured archaeological and modern fruits concludes that some of the archaeological samples are larger than would be expected for *C. bushianum*. Moreover, he points out that the pale fruits from Arkansas likely represent a domesticated form.

There are two historical accounts of a plant cultivated in the East that some have thought might refer to a chenopod. These accounts have been discussed in detail by Asch and Asch (1977) and Yarnell (1978). The original descriptions are so vague that certain identification is impossible. Possibly one or the other was a chenopod, but there is little in the descriptions that would rule out sumpweed.

In addition to *C. bushianum*, two other species require discussion, *C. nuttalliae* and *C. berlandieri*. For the present account heavy dependence has been made on H. Wilson (1976). *Chenopodium nuttalliae*, the domesticated chenopod of Mexico, exists as three main cultivars: *huauzontle*, used like broccoli, *quelite*, used like spinach, and chia used as a grain. As might be expected, chia has the largest fruits; fruits of the other two are often little or no larger than those of *C. bushianum*. The uses are mentioned to emphasize the possibility that the ancient chenopod of the East could have been used as a vegetable as well as for its fruits. *Chenopodium nuttalliae* may be an old domesticated plant, but as yet there is no archaeological evidence as to its age. From morphological, genetic and biochemical studies *C. nuttalliae* has been shown to be closely related to *C. berlandieri*, and it is now recognized as *C. berlandieri* ssp. *nuttalliae* (Wilson and Heiser, 1979). It is probably derived from *C. berlandieri* var. *sinuatum*. Gilmore (1931) called attention to the similarity of the plants from the Ozark bluff dwellings to *C. nuttalliae*. The possibility exists that this species was introduced north of Mexico and became cultivated there.

Chenopodium berlandieri is a widespread, variable species. Several varieties are recognized by Wahl (1952–53): var. *berlandieri* in Texas and Mexico; var. *sinuatum* in the southwestern United States and Mexico; var. *boscianum* from east Texas to Florida; and var. *zchackei* of the central and western United States and Canada, east to Ontario, Illinois, Arkansas and Texas with two collections known from Pennsylvania and Virginia. The last named is the most common chenopod west of the Mississippi River and most likely was the source of the wild chenopod fruits used by the Indians of the western United States (Wilson 1976).

Chenopodium bushianum, whose range Wahl (1952–53) gives as Massachusetts, Quebec, Ontario and North Dakota, south to Virginia and western Missouri, differs from *C. berlandieri* primarily, if not solely, by its larger size. Wilson (1976) has shown that it gives fertile hybrids with

C. berlandieri and it clusters with that species in a numerical taxonomic study. It links more closely to var. *sinuatum* than to the geographical adjacent var. *zchackei* (the other two varieties were not included in the study). Thus it is apparent that *C. bushianum* is nothing more than a subspecies or variety of *C. berlandieri* although the formal taxonomic change has not yet been made.

The new understanding of *C. bushianum*, although not as complete as one might desire, raises several possibilities, among them: (1) It was in the East by natural means before humans appeared on the scene. It may or may not have been intentionally cultivated. (2) It developed as a weed from *C. berlandieri* under human influence and was carried eastward, either intentionally or unintentionally. Attention should be called to the possible parallel to the sunflower. Again the weed may or may not have been cultivated. (3) It represents escapes from cultivation that have become naturalized, still retaining a somewhat larger size than the wild varieties. The last possibility perhaps is the least likely. The second one is perhaps the most reasonable and might also explain the larger size of *C. bushianum*, as would the third.

One final point needs to be made. Today *C. bushianum* is not one of the most abundant chenopods in the eastern United States. If distributions of the species several thousand years ago were similar to those today, why didn't the people use the more abundant species, such as *C. missouriense*? Perhaps it was simply the relative palatability of the species. On the other hand, if *C. bushianum* were actually cultivated we would have a ready explanation as to why other species were not collected.

From the evidence presently available it appears likely that a chenopod was cultivated prehistorically in eastern North America.

DEVIL'S CLAW (*Proboscidea parviflora*)

Although most of the comments in this paper are directed to agriculture in eastern North America, one plant from the Southwest deserves mention. As Yarnell (1977) has pointed out *Proboscidea parviflora* became a domesticated plant in the latter region. The domesticated variety is not known from the archaeological record, and it seems likely that it is a recent domesticate, ennobled for the fibers of its fruit which were used in basketry, and not as a food plant. The domesticate has white rather than the dark seeds of the wild variety and these give more rapid and even germination than do those of the wild type (Peter Bretting, unpublished). Perhaps the differences of the seeds developed through unconscious selection while deliberate selection was being carried out for increased pod size.

CONCLUSIONS AND SUMMARY

It is a fundamental difficulty of an historical science like evolution that one can never establish the cause of a past event. It is only possible to show that certain causes are plausible or at most likely, but because each species is a unique historical event we cannot say for certain what its genetic history was.

[Lewontin and Birch 1966]

With the words of Lewontin and Birch in mind—which I feel may be appropriate here—we should examine the plants bearing on early agriculture in central and eastern North America.

Sumpweed grows in this area today and the evidence strongly suggests that it became a domesticated plant here. The same statement applies to the Jerusalem artichoke, although there is no evidence to indicate that it was an early domesticate. The sunflower probably came to the eastern area from the West, but there is reason to believe that it first became a domesticated plant in the former area. *Cucurbita pepo* is an old domesticated plant in Mexico, but a plausible argument can be made for its domestication in the eastern half of North America, for it has a candidate for its progenitor in central Texas. The probability of the arrival of an entirely wild bottle gourd to the eastern area appears remote, but it did not necessarily come as a domesticate. The situation with the chenopods is most complex. In all probability there was a cultivated, or perhaps domesticated, chenopod in the eastern area, although with the present evidence an introduction from Mexico cannot be ruled out. For that matter there could have been an indigenous cultivated chenopod in the East, and a later introduction of the domesticated chenopod of Mexico.

From the botanical and archaeological evidence now available an independent origin of agriculture in central-eastern North America cannot be ruled out. The most critical plant is obviously the oldest domesticated plant in the region which appears to be *C. pepo*. If multiple origins of this domesticate did indeed occur, then it is likely that agriculture had an independent origin in central-eastern North America. Elsewhere I have expressed my opinion that the bottle gourd could have become a cultivated plant with very little effort on the part of humans (Heiser 1979a). Thus as a domesticated plant it could have several origins.

Certainly one has to agree with King's concluding statement as to the need for more well preserved plant remains from many sites at this early time before trying to reach any firm conclusions. One awaits with interest the exact dating of the pepos from Koster (Asch and Asch, this volume) and Cloudsplitter (Cowan, this volume).

NOTES

1. Except for the additions of comments on sumpweed and Note 5, the text is the same as that presented at the Symposium. Certain papers published since that time should be listed: Bretting (1982) on the domestication of *Proboscidea parviflora*, Conard et al. (1983) on the dating of archaeological materials from Illinois; H. Wilson (1981) on *Chenopodium*; and Whitaker (1981) on archaeological cucurbits. Conard et al. (1983) report the squash, "presumably *Cucurbita pepo*," from the Koster site as being 7000 years old. They, citing Cutler and Whitaker (1961), state that it was probably introduced from Mesoamerica or southeast Texas. They also state that the size of the rind of this squash is within the range of that of *C. pepo* var. *ovifera*, and for this reason I feel that it is better referred to as a gourd rather than a squash. I would suggest that this wild gourd, probably similar to *C. texana*, at one time could have grown wild as far north as Illinois so that calling for an introduction from the outside may be unnecessary.

2. The possibility that another annual species of *Helianthus* was also domesticated and has since become extinct also deserves mention. Very long, narrow achenes have been recovered in North Dakota. While these are probably nothing more than an extreme development of domesticated *H. annuus*, one might ask if they represent another species, for several of the annual species have much narrower achenes than does *H. annuus* (Heiser 1978).

3. Head size, or diameter of the disk, is clearly influenced by growing conditions. In order to show that and also to determine how achene number and size might be influenced, ten plants of a highly inbred cultivar "Commander" were grown in eight-inch pots and ten in four-inch pots in the greenhouse. The plants grown in the large pots were all taller and had larger leaves, larger heads (averaging 15.5 cm vs. 5.9 cm) and more achenes per head (803 vs. 174) than those grown in the smaller pots, as was expected. However, they also produced longer and wider achenes (12.42 × 8.13 vs. 9.56 × 6.45; ten achenes were measured from each plant); and the difference proved to be highly significant.

A similar experiment was carried out with weed sunflowers, using seed secured from sib crossings after four generations of plants from St. Louis, Missouri. Ten plants were grown in eight-inch and ten in five-inch pots. Again the plants in the larger pots were all taller, had larger leaves, larger teminal heads (4.5 cm vs. 3.7 cm), more achenes per head (330 vs. 180) as well as producing many more heads per plant. However, the mean length and width of the achenes was nearly identical in the two sets (5.55 × 3.16 vs. 5.55 × 3.20). For the archaeologist who may work with sunflower remains, the great variation that occurred in head size (from 2.0 to 5.5 cm) and achene size (from 4.6 to 5.8 mm in length) on the same plant should be pointed out. Moreover there is some variation in the size of the achene in the same head; usually this is not pronounced, but in one head the longest achene exceeded the smallest by 1.9 mm.

Another experiment was carried out with *Chenopodium bushianum*. Fruits from a single plant were supplied by H. Wilson. Plants were grown in the greenhouse under the following conditions: *A* in five-inch pots on a bench; *B* in two and one half-inch pots on a bench; *C* in five-inch pots under the bench; *D* in two and one half-inch pots under the bench. Thus plants in *A* and *B* received full light while those in *C* and *D* were shaded. Ten plants were grown in each set. Plants grown in *A* were the largest and produced by far the largest number of fruits, although exact counts were not made, whereas plants in *D* were the most depauperate. Fruits were sent to Wilson and 20 fruits per plant, a total of 200, were measured for each set. The mean diameters in mm were as follows: $A = 1.704$; $B = 1.643$; $C = 1.713$; $D = 1.709$. Further discussion of the results will be provided by Wilson, but it is apparent that environmental conditions produced little or no change in seed size. These results were predictable, for as Harper (1977) has pointed out, the seed is one of the least plastic organs on a plant. This statement would also apply to many kinds of fruit. See Harper (1977) for discussion of ecological significance of variation in seed size.

4. Dee Ann Story has called my attention to an interesting account of gourds from the travels of Cabeza de Vaca (Bandelier 1904:129; see also Smith 1871).

> In the afternoon we crossed a big river, the water being more than waist-deep. It may have been as wide as the one of Sevilla, and had a swift current. At sunset we reached a hundred Indian huts and, as we approached, the people came out to receive us, shouting frightfully, and slapping their thighs. They carried perforated gourds filled with pebbles, which are ceremonial objects of great importance. They only use them at dances, or as medicine, to cure, and nobody dares touch them but themselves. They claim that those gourds have healing virtues, and that they come from Heaven, not being found in that country; nor do they know where they come from, except that the rivers carry them down when they rise and overflow the land.

If we accept this as a reliable account, we are faced with the identification of the river and the gourd. Using Krieger's (1961) retracing of the explorer's route, I find that the "big river" must have been the Rio Grande near what is now Roma, Texas. The gourd most likely was a species of *Cucurbita* or *Lagenaria siceraria*. If it were the former, it could have been the buffalo gourd, *C. foetidissima*, which grows in the Rio Grande drainage. If it were the latter, it most likely would have come from cultivated fields unless we assume that in 1535 this species did grow as a wild plant or weed in the Southwest.

It has been postulated that rivers in Africa carried bottle gourds to the Atlantic which then may have washed upon the coast of South America (Heiser 1979a). One might also postulate that bottle gourds floating down rivers in Mexico or the West Indies reached the United States by ocean currents. The beaches of Florida as well as those of other parts of the eastern United States and the Gulf Coast receive tropical fruits and seeds carried by ocean currents (Gunn and Dennis 1976).

5. It should be pointed out that the size of the seed and the thickness of the rind of the bottle gourd from Phillips Spring (King, this volume) fall within the range of the smallest known for this species. This might indicate that they come either from a wild gourd or a primitive domesticated sort.

Early Cultivated Cucurbits in Eastern North America

Frances B. King
Illinois State Museum, Springfield

Cucurbits are among the oldest cultivated plants in the New World. Although never having achieved the status of maize or beans, they are an extremely popular and widespread group, including both the bottle gourd (*Lagenaria siceraria*) and five separate species of cultivated *Cucurbita*, attesting to their long association with humans. There is also evidence for the use, although not for the cultivation or domestication, of several wild species.

Three of the five cultivated species of *Cucurbita* occurred in North America in pre-Columbian times. These include *C. pepo* L. (scallops or pattypan, yellow crookneck, zucchini, and acorn squash; "pumpkins"; and yellow-flowered ornamental gourds, *C. p.* var. *ovifera*), *C. moschata* Poir. (Kentucky field pumpkin, butternut squash) and *C. mixta* Pang. (cushaw). The other species, *C. maxima* Duch. (hubbard, turban and banana squash) and *C. ficifolia* Bouche (fig-leaved gourd) were restricted to South and Central America.

Archaeological evidence suggests that both *Cucurbita pepo* and *C. mixta* originated from wild species of southern Mexico or Guatemala prior to spreading northward (Pickersgill and Heiser 1977). The oldest archaeological specimens of pepo come from Guila Naquitz Cave in the Oaxaca Valley of southwest Mexico (Fig. 4.1) and date 10,750–9200 B.P. (Whitaker and Cutler 1971). While pepo is present

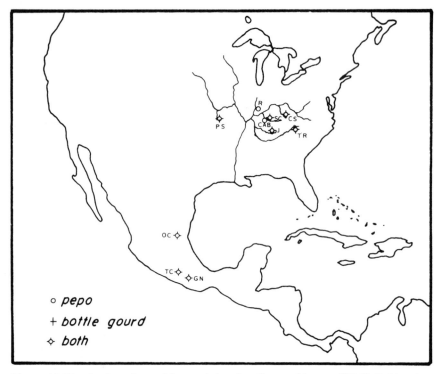

Figure 4.l. Distribution of cucurbit containing sites discussed in text. GN (Guila Naquitz, Oaxaca), TC (Tehuacán Caves), OC (Ocampo Caves), R (Riverton), CAB (Carlston Annis and Bowles), SC (Salts Cave), CS (Cloudsplitter), J (Jernigan II), TR (Tellico Reservoir), KNH (Koster and Napoleon Hollow).

in archaeological sites in eastern North America by 4300 B.P. for certain, and possibly by 7000 B.P., it apparently was not introduced into the southwestern United States until sometime after 3750 B.P. (Yarnell 1976). *Cucurbita pepo* var. *ovifera* is extremely similar to *C. texana*, a wild species of central Texas and several suggestions have been made regarding the relationship and evolution of the two species (Rhodes et al. 1968; Pickersgill and Heiser 1977; Heiser, this volume).

Like pepo, *C. mixta* was present in the Tehuacán Valley by 7000–5000 B.P. (Pickersgill and Heiser 1977) and can be linked with an unidentified wild species of southern Mexico that Whitaker and Bemis (1975) believe to also be feral derivative. *Cucurbita mixta* was not recognized as a species until 1930 and an English description did not appear until 1950 (Whitaker and Bohn). Prior to that time, archaeological material as well as modern specimens and cultivars were placed in *C. moschata*. The oldest material from the Southwest dates about 1050 B.P., and around 750 B.P. there was an increase in the use of hard shelled pepo and mixta as containers and a decrease in the use of bottle gourd. Cutler and Whitaker (1961) suggest that this may reflect either climatic change, increasing emphasis on the dual use of food plants, or demonstrates simply that pepo and mixta are easier to grow farther north. They note that pepo and mixta are common in modern Pueblos but that *Cucurbita moschata* and *Lagenaria siceraria* are not.

Cucurbita moschata lacks a clear wild ancestor, although it probably originated from the same southern Mexico–Guatemala complex of wild species that gave rise to *C. pepo* (Pickersgill and Heiser 1977). It is the only species with disjunct distributions, apparently having spread to South America before 5000 B.P. and the American Southwest by 1250 B.P. (Whitaker and Cutler 1965). Based on compatibility tests, *C. moschata* has been shown to be more closely related to the wild zerophytic and mesophytic species than are the other cultivated cucurbits. This, in combination with its broad interspecific compatibility among the cultivated cucurbits suggests that it may come the nearest to being a common ancestor to the other species (Whitaker and Bemis 1964, 1975).

Cucurbita maxima occurs late in the archaeological record (1350 B.P.) and was restricted to South America both in origin and evolution, probably evolving from the wild *C. andreana* which itself is common in archaeological sites dating about 5000 B.P. (Pickersgill and Heiser 1977). *Cucurbita ficifolia*, the only perennial species, occurs in the archaeological record in South America from 5000 B.P. and later in Mesoamerica.

Another species of the semi-arid regions of western North America, *Cucurbita foetidissima*, has as long an association with man as nearly any other *Cucurbita*. It was recovered with pepo and bottle gourd from the Ocampo Caves in strata dated 9000 B.P. (Bemis et al. 1978; Cutler and Whitaker 1961). However, because all parts of the plant excepting the seeds are extremely bitter and there is evidence of neither phenotypic modification indicating domestication nor cultivation by historic Indians, the species is not considered "cultivated." Whitaker and Bemis (1975) comment that modern civilization has probably extended the range of *C. foetidissima* and that it is an ideal fellow traveler, since the fruits are colorful and useful as trinkets and the seeds store well in the fruit. These characteristics are undoubtedly true of the other cucurbits as well.

Cucurbita foetidissima shows considerable potential for cultivation and domestication however, and Whitaker and Bemis (1975) suggest that its successful domestication would raise questions about how much influence humans may have had on the cultivated species. If cucurbits were essentially campfollowers growing on trash heaps, they would be only secondarily dependent on man and would be fully susceptible to the natural pressures of evolution. Alternatively, they may have been deliberately selected for, becoming increasingly dependent on humans for survival as they continuously lost more of the genetic variability which would allow them to evolve and adapt to new situations. Whitaker and Bemis also suggest that the campfollower hypothesis is supported by the independent evolution of the five cultivated species into cenospecies, separated by genetic barriers, as well as by the fact that each of the cultivated species, with the possible exception of *C. moschata* and *C. ficifolia*, shows much more compatibility with certain wild species than with other cultivated species.

Bottle gourds (*Lagenaria siceraria*) were perhaps the most widely distributed cultivated plant in the world in prehistoric times. They occur in the earliest levels of many archaeological sites: in Tamaulipas by 9000 B.P., Tehuacán by 7500 B.P., Oaxaca by 9400–9200 B.P., Peru by 8000–7500 B.P. (Cutler and Whitaker 1961; Pickersgill and Heiser 1983a; Cohen 1977) and in the midwestern United States by 4300 B.P. (Kay et al. 1980; Chapman and Shea 1977, Marquardt and Watson 1983a).

Although bottle gourd is found in archaeological sites in the New World, its occurrence in the wild has never been verified. It is also reported from a number of early archaeological sites in the Old World (Heiser 1979a). The presence of five species of *Lagenaria* in Africa, which are at least partially fertile with those of the New World, suggest that bottle gourd may originally have come from Africa. The question then becomes whether it arrived naturally or by human intervention. Since it has been shown that bottle gourds still contain viable seeds after floating in sea water for nearly a year and then being stored for an additional six years (Whitaker and Carter 1954, 1961; Richardson 1972), they *could* have drifted to the New World and humans were not necessarily involved in their transmittal. At the same time, the fact that bottle gourd might have floated to the New World and then grown does not prove that they actually did so. The answer to this riddle is tied up in the history of the New World: whether people arrived 11,500 years ago or much earlier; whether South America was populated by way of North America and the Bering Land Bridge or independently reached by seafaring people from Africa; and is too hot a controversy to be easily solved. Whatever the case, the antiquity of the New World material as well as the great variability between African and American gourds suggests that they probably spread prior to (or early in) their domestication.

While bottle gourd seeds are edible, the value of the plant is that they produce relatively heavy walled gourds of a wide variety of sizes and shapes and as noted by Heiser (1979a), and "for that reason alone it must have been one of man's most important plants before the invention of pottery."

CUCURBITS AS FOOD

Though widely cultivated at the present, nowhere are cucurbits of more than minor importance as food items (Whitaker and Bemis 1975). The same appears to have been generally true in the past. For example, cucurbits were not nearly so important to the pre-Hispanic Aztecs as maize or beans (Kaplan 1971) nor did they displace hickory nuts as the key plant food resource among the Indians of the United States Midwest as maize later did.

While it is easy to accept that cucurbits have never been primary food plants, it is unclear why they never achieved more importance. Cucurbit seeds contain high amounts of oil (an average of 47–48%) when crushed (Vaughn 1970), more protein and essential amino acids than sunflower seed (Whitaker and Davis 1962) and at 553 Calories/100 g are comparable in caloric value to corn (348 Cal./100 g), beans (349 Cal./100 g), sunflower (560 Cal./100 g), sumpweed (535 Cal./100 g) or hickory nuts (696 Cal./100 g) (Asch and Asch 1979; Watt and Merrill 1963). While the raw flesh of summer squash (20 Cal./100 g) and winter squash (44 Cal./100 g) have relatively low caloric values because they are approximately 90% water, dried squash, as was commonly prepared by the Indians has a respectable 325 Cal./100 g.

The small-fruited pepo are the best producers for oil since they produce large numbers of fruit per plant and relatively great numbers of seeds per fruit (Whitaker and Bohn 1950). In *Cucurbita foetidissima,* a potential oil producing crop, the greatest variability, and therefore potential for selection and increased yield, occurs in the number of seeds per fruit and fruits per plant (Bemis et al. 1978). Interestingly, the characteristics favoring maximum oil (numerous small fruits and many seeds) are opposite to the evolutionary trends evidenced by cultivated cucurbits, i.e., fewer larger fruits and fewer seeds (Whitaker and Bemis 1964). It appears therefore that, while pepo with thin inedible flesh may have been grown initially in eastern North America for the seeds, much of the later selectivity was for fruit with a relatively larger proportion of a better quality flesh. Presently in Mexico, seeds are more important as a food than they are in the United States, which may be an outgrowth of the relative abundance of other plant foods with high food value (such as hickory nuts) during prehistoric times in eastern North America.

Unless dried, pepo flesh keeps more poorly than other foods with lower initial moisture content (including all of the staples such as corn, beans, sunflower, sumpweed, hickory nuts, etc.). Because of the relatively large energy expenditure required for preparation of food items with low energy yield, pepo may have remained throughout much of their history a minor food plant grown only to add variety to the diet.

BITTERNESS

The characteristic of bitterness is common for nearly all wild species of *Cucurbita*. Whitaker and Bemis (1975) suggest that primitive peoples, while harvesting fruits of cucurbits for seeds, found and selected for nonbitter edible fruits which ultimately led to the cultivated species. Bitterness is due to a group of genetically controlled chemical compounds called *cucurbitacins*. This appears to be due to a three gene complex including a dominant gene for bitterness, a gene for suppressing it, and possibly a third gene controlling the enzyme system producing cucurbitacins (Whitaker and Davis 1962; Whitaker and Bemis 1975). If the situation involved straight dominance, preferably for bitterness over nonbitterness, it would be both a relatively simple and short-term project to select for edible fruit. However, because of the genetic complexity, it probably required selection over many generations to be relatively certain of having nonbitter fruit. The existence of bitter-fruited *C. pepo* var. *ovifera* and the presence of a bitter-fruited possible derivative (*C. texana*) on the pathway to eastern North America suggests that the earliest pepo in North America may have been bitter or frequently reverted to bitterness. This may have been an additional factor preventing pepo from becoming a major food plant in eastern North America.

ENVIRONMENTAL REQUIREMENTS

While cucurbits are vigorous growers and most are competitive enough for growth on the "trash heap" without much human aid, they also have tropical and semitropical origins. As a result, they are susceptible to frost damage and require a warm, long, frost-free period. For pumpkins and winter squash this period needs to be 120–140 days; it is less for summer squash and somewhat longer for bottle gourds which often rot if picked while immature. For this reason, bottle gourd remains are primarily recovered from more southern archaeological sites. It is naturalized (growing wild) from Florida to Texas and north to Missouri and Illinois (Steyermark 1963) which may correspond to the area in which it is most easily grown.

Because cultivated cucurbits originated in dry–mesophytic environments they are also subject to disease if there is excessive rainfall or long periods of very high humidity. While tolerant of soil and nutrient availability and capable of producing a crop on any good soil if the growing season and climate are adequate, they will not tolerate wet or poorly drained soils. They grow best on light, sandy soils with good drainage; such soils also warm up fastest in the spring and produce the earliest maturing crops (Whitaker and Davis 1962:145).

In much of eastern North America, sandy, well drained soils are common on alluvial terraces. Human subsistence activities have often revolved around the greater density of plant and animal resources found on floodplains and the light, easily worked, floodplain soils were probably the logical place to initiate early attempts at cultivation. It appears that cucurbits were, in some ways, preadapted to early cultivation in eastern North America.

CUCURBITS FROM LATE ARCHAIC SITES IN EASTERN NORTH AMERICA

The number of archaeological sites from which cucurbit remains have been recovered is growing rapidly in response to improved excavation and recovery techniques. The majority of cucurbit remains are fragmentary however, and frequently offer more questions than answers about the evolution of cultivated cucurbits in eastern North America.

For example, a number of *Cucurbita* rind fragments have been recovered from the Koster and Napoleon Hollow sites in the lower Illinois Valley. Accelerator radiocarbon dates on rind specimens themselves are as old as 7000 B.P. (Asch and Asch 1982; Conard et al. 1984). Unfortunately, it appears impossible to distinguish thin *C. pepo* rind fragments from those of *C. foetidissima,* a wild species that ranges over much of the Midwest and West. The problem of rind identification is discussed further in the section on rind characteristics.

For sites in the Tellico Reservoir on the Little Tennessee River (Iddins, Icehouse Bottoms, Bacon Bend, Patrick) only small pieces of pepo and bottle gourd seeds or rind appear about 4400 B.P. and 3300 B.P.

respectively (Chapman and Shea 1977; Chapman et al. 1982; Schroedl 1978). Likewise, only squash rind fragments occur at the Carlston Annis (younger than 4500 B.P.) and Bowles (older than 3440 B.P.) sites on the Green River in western Kentucky; two seeds identified as pepo by Chomko and Crawford (1978) were not (Crawford 1982). A single pepo rind fragment from the Riverton site on the Wabash River in eastern Illinois dates approximately 3200 B.P. (Yarnell 1976). Pepo and bottle gourd fragments have also been identified from the Jernigan II site (Crites 1978a, Bowen 1979) on the Duck River in southern Tennessee.

More abundant pepo and gourd material dating from approximately 2550 B.P. occurs in Salts Cave, also on the Green River in western Kentucky (Fig. 4.1). This material includes primarily pepo and gourd shells, many worked into vessels (Yarnell 1969:51). Pepo shell thickness ranges from 1.9–4.2 mm, while vessel diameter varies from approximately 12–25 cm. The majority of the material comes from "warty" squash (Yarnell 1969:51). Pepo seeds from human feces from Salts Cave range from 10–13 mm ($\bar{x}$ = 11.3 mm) in length and 6.9–8.1 mm ($\bar{x}$ = 7.3 mm) in width; $\bar{x}$ width/length = 0.65 mm. The pepo seeds

> suggest an intermediate form about midway between the edible squashes and the ornamental yellow flowered gourds. . . . There is a slight scalloping or lobing of the fruit. The thick-walled fruits probably had thin flesh and were similar to some forms of *C. pepo* var. *ovifera* still grown as decorative gourds. The seeds are small but differ from usual seeds of *ovifera*. [Letter from Hugh Cutler to P. J. Watson, cited in Yarnell 1969:51]

Cutler also noted that the seeds were like those of a cultivar grown by the Mandan and Omaha Indians and resemble some from the Ocampo Caves of Tamaulipas and the caves of the Tehuacán Valley in Mexico (Yarnell 1969:52).

Bottle gourd shells from Salts Cave, range in color from red to reddish brown, brown, tan and gray. Fruit diameter varies from 14.5–25.0 cm (similar to that of the pepo) and shell thickness varies from 3.2–6.2 mm ($\bar{x}$ = 4.9 mm) and includes many that are thicker and woodier than usual for species north of Mexico (Yarnell 1969:51).

Cucurbit remains are also abundant at the Cloudsplitter site on the Red River in eastern Kentucky. The following discussion of the Cloudsplitter material is based on information from Wesley Cowan.

Pepo remains appear at the Cloudsplitter Site at approximately 4700 B.P. (Cowan, this volume) and prior to bottle gourd. There are 43 measurable pepo rind fragments suggesting three rind types: a smooth rind ranging in thickness from 1.0–2.7 mm, a warty rind ranging in thickness from 1.8–3.0 mm, and a ribbed or lobed rind, 1.6–5.4

mm in thickness. Cowan feels that although the remains are fragmentary and that more than one type of rind surface might have occurred on a single fruit, the presence of three similar varieties in Late Woodland contexts in the Red River area substantiates their presence at Cloudsplitter.

There are 7 pepo seeds from the Cloudsplitter site, representing at least two types, a large seeded form (x̄ length = 12.7, x̄ width = 7.3 mm, N = 5, width/length ≃ 0.58) and a smaller seeded type (x̄ length = 8.7 mm, x̄ width = 5.4 mm, N = 2, width/length = 0.62). The smaller seeds have prominent raised margins covered with short hairs. Cowan notes that the pepo rinds from the Cloudsplitter site conform most closely to those of the modern cultivar "Mandan" he has examined, which has a thick, almost gourd-like shell and is the most primitive of the modern cultivated cucurbits.

Bottle gourd appeared at the Cloudsplitter site sometime after 3000 B.P. The five measurable rind fragments average 5.2 mm (2.8–6.5 mm) in thickness and represent a purplish-black and a reddish-brown fruit color. The single seed measures 10.3 × 6.45 mm and is smaller than Late Woodland seeds of the Red River area which average 14.7 × 7.5 mm.

Phillips Spring, on the Pomme de Terre River in western Missouri, contained abundant, well preserved, uncarbonized cucurbit (pepo and bottle gourd) remains in water-saturated spring sediments. The bulk of the material came from a widespread zone dating 4240 ± 80 B.P., 4310 ± 70 B.P. and 4222 ± 57 B.P. (Kay et al. 1980; King 1980) which contained 65 measurable pepo seeds and many seed fragments, rind fragments, as well as bottle gourd seeds and rind fragments. The seeds range in size from 8.3–12.2 mm in length (x̄ = 10.5 mm) and 5.4–8.5 mm in width (x̄ = 7.03 mm) (Fig. 4.2). Shape, represented by width/length, varies from a narrow W/L = 0.54 to a relatively broad W/L = 0.82. While not displaying a clear bimodal distribution, at least two rather different seed types appear to be present, and possibly several fruits are represented. There is both a relatively short broad type, some with marginal hairs similar to those found at the Cloudsplitter site, and a larger, relatively narrow type. The seeds from Phillips are discussed at more length later.

There are ten fragments of smooth, hard, relatively thin pepo rind, measuring between 0.6–1.8 mm in thickness, and blackish in color. Black is not a normal color for pepo and this is probably due to fire blackening or mold.

Bottle gourd remains from this zone include five measurable seeds (range 9.3–10.4 mm in length by 4.5–5.6 mm in width, x̄ = 9.8 by 5.0 mm). Other remains include two blossom scar buttons and two frag-

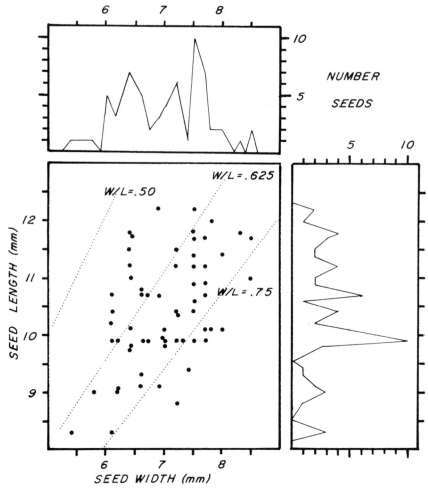

Figure 4.2. Relative length and width measurements for *Cucurbita pepo* from Phillips Spring.

ments of rind measuring 1.8 and 2.0 mm in thickness. All are reddish-brown in color.

Above this zone is an extensive rocklined pit containing mussel shell as well as plant remains including cucurbits. The pit dates 3938 ± 66 B.P. and 3995 ± 96 B.P. (King 1980) and includes approximately 50 small pepo seed fragments, 1 whole gourd seed (9.5 by 5.2 mm) and 1 gourd seed fragment. The seeds are all uncarbonized but have char-coal flecks adhering to them as if they might have been thrown into a cold fire pit.

Pepo seeds from this zone were originally reported by Chomko

(1978) and Chomko and Crawford (1978) who erroneously correlated them with earlier radiocarbon dates of 4310 B.P. and 4200 B.P. (Kay et al. 1980). These seeds were sent to Hugh Cutler who, in a letter to the author (19 March 1975) described them as "similar to early forms of a cultivar named 'Mandan.'" Based on size estimates made by Cutler, the four measurable seeds range from 8.9–10.6 mm in length by 6.7–7.6 mm in width, $\bar{x}$ = 9.9 by 7.2, width/length = 0.73.

Cucurbit seeds occur in an additional Late Archaic feature at Phillips Spring (one fragmentary pepo seed) and a Middle Woodland feature (two pepo seed fragments, one fragment gourd) dating 1999 B.P. Pepo seeds from a storage pit at nearby Boney Spring dating 1920 B.P. were likewise identified by Cutler as similar to the cultivar "Mandan" (personal communication, 18 October 1974; King and McMillan 1975).

COMPARISON OF CUCURBIT MATERIAL FROM LATE ARCHAIC SITES

All three of the sites discussed above with abundant cucurbit remains have small, relatively broad seeds (Fig. 4.3) similar to those of Mandan. Both Cloudsplitter and Phillips Spring material includes seeds with marginal hairs, as does a seed from Coxcatlán Cave, Tehuacán, dating about 7000 B.P. Marginal hairs are a rare characteristic in pepo seeds (Whitaker and Bohn 1950) but probably not of interpretative value. Although the range in seed size and shape is great at Phillips Spring, it encompasses only the smaller seed type from Cloudsplitter. Pepo rind from Phillips Spring is smooth and relatively thin compared to the thicker, smooth, warty and ribbed or lobed rinds from Cloudsplitter or the predominately warty shells from Salts Cave. Size measurements for fruit are available only for Salts Cave material. Assuming these sites to be in some way representative of their respective time periods, the tendency appears to be towards increasing rind thickness and seed size. Likewise, bottle gourd at Phillips Spring is represented by relatively small seeds and thin rind compared to Cloudsplitter or to Salts Cave.

Pepo cultivar Mandan is so named because it was grown by the historic Indians of the northern Great Plains, including the Mandan from whom it was originally acquired. It is illustrated by both Gilmore (1919:Pl. 128) and by Will and Hyde (1917:67, 150). Mandan squash has a medium thick, woody and brittle shell (3 mm) and is pale greenish underlain by a bright green layer. The surface is furrowed, unevenly and moderately warted. The moderately small broad seeds measure approximately 14.7 by 9.4 mm (width/length = 0.64), the seed surface is smooth and dull buff yellow with a rounded margin. The fruit measure 10–11 mm in diameter, 5–6 mm thick and weighs 3–4 pounds (Tapley et al. 1937:43–44).

The seeds of archaeological pepo have width/length ratios of more than 0.625, similar to cultivar Mandan (Fig. 4.3). A comparison of lengths and widths for seeds of cultivars listed in the *Vegetables of New York* (Tapley et al. 1937) shows that many seeds are, in fact, larger and narrower than Mandan, although Mandan is among the largest of the broader seeds (Fig. 4.4). This coupled with the historic Indian cultivation of Mandan indicates why it is so frequently used as an analog for prehistoric pepo.

SEED CHARACTERS

In order to address the problems of (1) determining the number of fruit or pepo types that might be represented by the Phillips Spring material and (2) apparent similarity between archaeological material as much as 4300 years old and modern Mandan, seed characteristics from various modern specimens were examined.

Length and width measurements were taken for 25 seeds from each of 50 fruits including 12 *Cucurbita pepo* (cv. Burpee bush acorn); 11 *C. foetidissima* collected in Arizona, Kansas, Missouri and Illinois; 20 *C. palmata* representing five vines of an isolated population on Lake Mead, Arizona; five different forms of *C. pepo* var. *ovifera* and two *C. texana*. The variability in length, width, and shape (width/length) of these seeds were compared by use of coefficient of variation and correlation coefficients.

Coefficient of variation, $V = 100s/\bar{x}$, where s = standard deviation and $\bar{x}$ = mean, is a useful statistic in this kind of comparison. It measures the variability relative to the sample mean, and is more valuable than standard deviation for comparing samples composed of different sized specimens or for comparing variability of two or more dimensions for the same specimen (Simpson et al. 1960:90). Correlation coefficients, $r = (X - \bar{X})(Y - \bar{Y})/(N - 1)s_x s_r$, where N = number of pairs of observations and s_x and s_r are the standard deviations of X and Y respectively, is a measure relating change in one variable to change in a second variable, in this case length and width (Simpson et al. 1960).

Coefficients of variation for individual fruit range from 2.6–7.2 ($\bar{x} = 4.2$) for length (Fig. 4.5), 2.7–8.8 ($\bar{x} = 4.7$) for width and 3.9–7.3 ($\bar{x} = 4.9$) for width/length. Coefficients of variation between fruit are

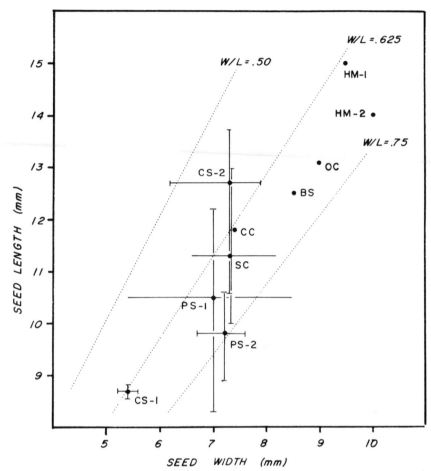

Figure 4.3. Relative length and width measurements for *Cucurbita pepo* seeds discussed in text. CS-1 (Cloudsplitter small seeds), CS-2 (Cloudsplitter large seeds), PS-1 (Phillips Spring 4300 B.P.), PS-2 (Phillips Spring 3900 B.P.), SC (Salts Cave), CC (Coxcatlán Cave, Tehuacán), BS (Boney Spring), OC (Ocampo Cave, Tamaulipas), HM-1 (historic Mandan seed, Tapley et al. 1937), HM-2 (historic Mandan seed, Cutler and Whitaker 1961).

greater. Based on average measurements calculated for individual species, coefficients of variation for length range between 6.4 for *C. palmata*, 7.7 for *C. pepo* cv. acorn, 9.4 for *C. foetidissima*, and 21.3 for *C. pepo* var. *ovifera*.

In comparison, Bemis et al. (1978) found coefficients of variation for seed wt./fruit, seed wt./100 seeds, and seed no./fruit of 36.9, 20.0 and 28.3, respectively for a much larger sample of *C. foetidissima*. For the same group they found a coefficient of variation for fruit diameter of

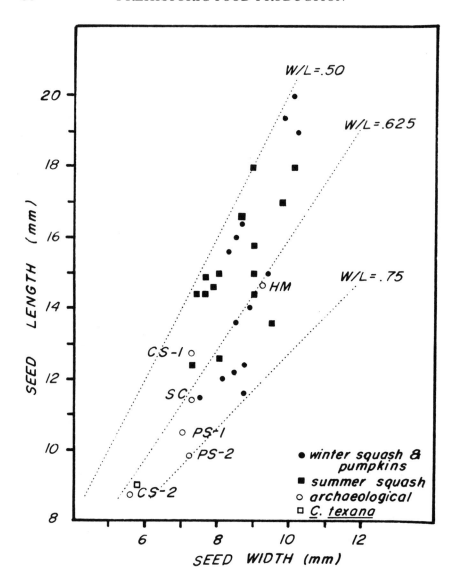

Figure 4.4. Relative length and width measurements for seeds of *C. pepo* cultivars listed by Tapley et al. 1937, also showing archaeological seeds. PS-1 (Phillips Spring 4300 B.P.), PS-2 (Phillips Spring 3900 B.P.), SC (Salts Cave), CS-1 (Cloudsplitter large seeds), CS-2 (Cloudsplitter small seeds), HM (historic Mandan).

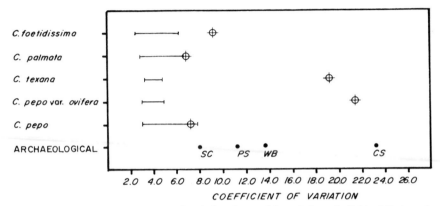

Figure 4.5. Range of coefficients of variation for seed length from individual fruit and calculated for species from average for individual fruit, as well as seeds from archaeological sites: CS (Cloudsplitter), SC (Salts Cave), PS (Phillips Spring), WB (Walth Bay).

9.1. It appears therefore, that seed size, like fruit size, is a relatively stable characteristic within a single specimen, population and even within a species of *Cucurbita*.

Not only are coefficients of variation for seed length and width similar but variation in length is also highly correlated with variation in width, i.e., as variability in one dimension increases variability increases proportionately in the other. A correlation coefficient for average length variation and width variation for the 50 specimens is 0.48 and is significant at the $P<0.001$ level.

Changes in length, however, correlate over a wide range with changes in width. This is due to the fact that in some fruit there is an almost linear relationship between increases in seed length and width while in others the two seem to vary independently, forming a cluster. Correlation coefficients for the 50 specimens, shown in Figure 4.6, vary from a low of 0.30, indicating little relationship between increases in length and width, to a high of 0.63, showing a statistically significant correlation between the two. Correlation coefficients calculated from average seed lengths and widths of a group of related specimens or for the combined seeds from two specimens of the same species are higher still, reflecting the stronger trends created by the combination of data from related specimens.

Plotting the coefficient of variation for length against correlation coefficient (Fig. 4.7) enables us to recognize some characteristics of modern seed populations that are probably applicable to archaeological collections. The modern data suggests that groups of seeds with coefficients of variation less than 6.5 probably represent a single fruit, fruit from the same vine, or possibly fruit from an isolated popu-

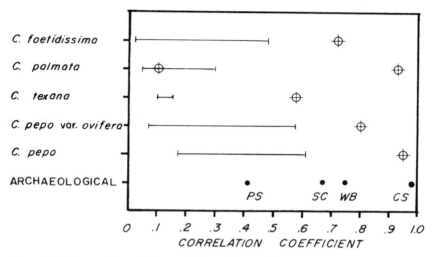

Figure 4.6. Range of correlation coefficients for seed length × width from individual fruit and calculated for species from averages for individual fruit, as well as for archaeological sites (see key, Fig. 4.5).

lation; coefficient of variation values between approximately 6.5 and 14.0 probably represent multiple, closely related fruit. Coefficients of variation above 14.0 may indicate the presence of seeds from unrelated specimens. Collections of seeds with high coefficients of variation and high correlation coefficients probably represent extremes within a single population. High coefficients of variation coupled with low correlation coefficients indicate the presence of seeds from unrelated specimens.

To return to the archaeological materials, also shown in Figure 4.7, the Phillips Spring seeds have a coefficient of variation greater than that of a single fruit or of most related fruit as well as a correlation coefficient lower than would be expected from related fruit. We can say, with more confidence than before, that the Phillips Spring seeds probably represent several fruits with at least two types of seeds. The seeds from Salts Cave, on the other hand, fall within the range of values for fruit from a single population. The Cloudsplitter seeds show more variability than would be expected from a single population; although the high correlation coefficient which suggests some relationship between the large and small seeds may be an artifact of the small sample size ($N = 5$).

For additional comparison, values are also shown for a late Prehistoric site, Walth Bay, in north-central South Dakota. Nickel (1974:36) notes that although these seeds show sufficient variation to

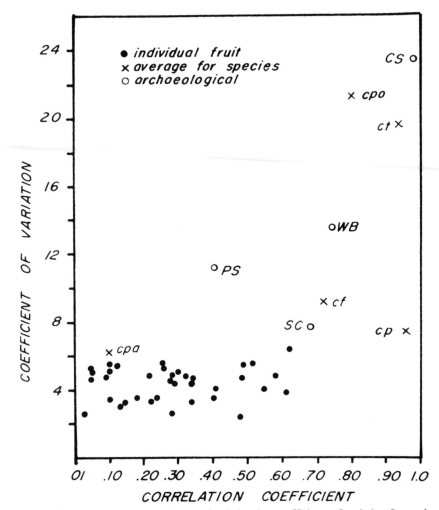

Figure 4.7. Summation of Figures 4.5 and 4.6 showing coefficients of variation for seed length plotted against correlation coefficients for length × width for individual fruit, species averages, and archaeological sites. CS (Cloudsplitter), PS (Phillips Spring), SC (Salts Cave), WB (Walth Bay), cf (*Cucurbita foetidissima*), ct (*C. texana*), cp (*C. pepo*), cpo (*C. pepo* var. *ovifera*), and cpa (*C. palmata*).

indicate more than one variety, many of them resemble the variety Red Lodge in shape and size. The Walth Bay seeds show more variability than the Salts Cave or Phillips Spring seeds and do definitely appear to represent two different types of seeds.

Based on a comparison between minimum fruit weight and seed length for the cultivars of *C. pepo* described by Tapley et al. (1937), there is a significant correlation between increasing seed length and heavier fruit weight. Based on Figure 4.8, the Phillips Spring pepo seeds, with an average length of 10.7 mm, indicate a fruit weighing approximately one pound. In comparison, the seeds of the cultivar Mandan (Tapley et al. 1937) measured approximately 15 mm in length and came from a squash approximately 10–18 cm in diameter and weighing three to four pounds. The measured fruit diameters from the Salts Cave pepo varied from 14.5 to 25 cm (Yarnell 1969:51).

Larger cucurbit seeds with their bigger embryos and correspondingly more endosperm grow with greater initial vigor than small seeds (Passmore 1930; Whitaker and Davis 1962:119). For this reason, increases in seed size through time might reflect not only human selection but natural selection as well, since seedlings from large seeds with rapid initial growth might have an advantage in outcompeting weeds or becoming established before summer dry spells. If cucurbits were campfollowers, natural selection may have been more important than human selection in cucurbit evolution.

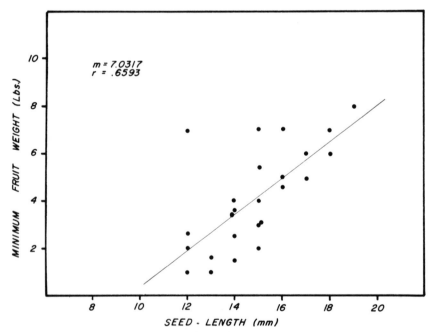

Figure 4.8. Relationship between seed length and minimum size based on measurements given for *C. pepo* cultivars listed by Tapley et al. 1937.

RIND CHARACTERISTICS

Although it is relatively easy to differentiate bottle gourd and *Cucurbita* on the basis of the cell structure present in the rind, the various species of *Cucurbita* are difficult or impossible to distinguish (Cutler and Whitaker 1961). This has not been considered a problem in eastern North America because only pepo was cultivated prehistorically. However, a wild species, buffalo gourd (*C. foetidissima*), has a modern distribution ranging from Missouri and Nebraska to Texas, Mexico, and California, as well as being introduced in Illinois and Indiana (Steyermark 1963:1426). Although there is apparently no evidence for aboriginal cultivation or domestication, buffalo gourd was utilized prehistorically; the seeds and rather foul smelling root were sometimes eaten, and the fruit served as a possible container. Remains of buffalo gourd have been recovered from archaeological sites at least as far east as Roaring River State Park in southwestern Missouri (Cutler and Whitaker 1961) and it seems likely that buffalo gourd might occur at other sites in the Midwest as well.

Measurements on a total of 24 buffalo gourds collected from six roadside sites in Kansas, Colorado, and Arizona found an average rind thickness of 0.7mm (range 0.2 to 1.5 mm, Table 4.1). An additional 20 archaeological specimens from Pre-pottery and Pine Lawn phases at Tularosa Cave, New Mexico, (Martin et al. 1952) averaged 1.0 mm (range 0.7 to 2.0 mm) with the thickest sections being adjacent to the peduncle or blossom scars.

Relatively thin cucurbit rind has been recovered from several archaeological sites in eastern North America in association with pepo seeds and feral *C. pepo* var. *ovifera* collected in the Illinois River valley also averaged 1.0 mm in thickness (Table 4.1). It is apparent that the rind thicknesses of buffalo gourd and pepo do overlap. As a result, unfortunately, rind fragments thinner than perhaps 2.0 mm (the maximum buffalo gourd rind thickness encountered in this study) cannot be conclusively identified unless they are accompanied by seeds or other readily identifiable material such as peduncles or, in the case of buffalo gourd, pulp fibers.

This problem needs to be considered in the identification and interpretation of archaeological cucurbit rind fragments, especially in areas within or bordering the range of buffalo gourd. Of all the sites which have thus far yielded *Cucurbita* rind, the problem currently appears most serious for some in the lower Illinois Valley. At other sites containing *Cucurbita* rind falling within the range of buffalo gourd (e.g. Phillips Spring, Cloudsplitter, Salts Cave), the presence of pepo seeds makes a positive identification possible. However, cucurbit rind frag-

TABLE 4.1
Cucurbita RIND THICKNESSES

Material	Max.	Min.	Average	σ^2	C.V.	N
C. foetidissima (modern)[1]	1.5mm	0.2	0.7	0.3	0.4	24
C. foetidissima (Tularosa Cave)	2.0	0.7	1.0	0.3	0.3	20
C. texana	0.9	—	—	—	—	1
C. pepo var. *ovifera* (modern)[2]	2.8	1.2	1.8	0.5	0.3	9
C. pepo var. *ovifera* (feral)[3]	1.0	0.9	1.0	—	—	3
Cloudsplitter Rockshelter, Ky[4]	5.4	1.0	—	—	—	43
Phillips Spring, Mo	1.8	0.6	—	—	—	10
Salts Cave, Ky[5]	4.2	1.9	—	—	—	25
Peter Cave, Tn[6]	1.1	0.7	—	—	—	2
Koster and Napoleon Hollow, Il[7]	1.7	0.5	0.9	—	—	8

[1]Based on four specimens each of six collections from Kansas, Colorado, and Arizona.
[2]Modern "ornamental" gourds
[3]Collected in the Illinois River valley near Starved Rock
[4]Cowan, 1979
[5]Yarnell, 1969
[6]Crawford, 1982
[7]Asch and Asch 1982

ments dated at approximately 7000 B.P. have been recovered from the Koster and Napoleon Hollow sites in the lower Illinois Valley (Asch and Asch 1982, this volume; Conard et al. 1984). These rind fragments average 0.9 mm (range 0.5 to 1.7 mm) and are unaccompanied by seeds or other material. The definite indentification of this material as *C. pepo* would provide important additional evidence that pepo may have originated in eastern North America, possibly derived from *C. texana* (Heiser, this volume). Without positive evidence of extremely early cucurbits from these, or some other eastern North American archaeological sites, however, the possibilities of *C. pepo* originating in Mexico or even of there having been independent domestications remain viable.

VALUE OF SEED AND RIND CHARACTERS IN DESCRIBING ARCHAEOLOGICAL CUCURBITS

Modern studies of the genetics and evolution of cucurbits are based on breeding experiments and involve the morphology of the seeds, rind, flowers, vine and roots. The majority of such criteria are not applicable to material recovered from archaeological sites. For example, of the 93 characters used by Bemis et al. (1970) and Rhodes et al. (1968) in their studies of the numerical taxonomy of the cucurbits, only 17 apply to seeds, fruit or peduncles, the most commonly pre-

served parts. The questions that are of most concern to the eth-
nobotanist in eastern North America involve subspecific variation and
the evolution of a single species, and the implications these in turn
have for culture or subsistence. The finer the separations desired,
however, the greater the number of characters that must be used in the
comparison. Thus, in attempting to discuss the development of cultivated cucurbits in eastern North America on the basis of the archaeological evidence, we are in the frustrating position of relying on
incomplete and inadequate data.

Although I have discussed seed and rind characters at length, they
are not necessarily the most representative of changes that have occurred in the species. Cutler and Whitaker (1956:256) in their description of *C. mixta* state "seed characters are inherited independently and
appear to be almost valueless for delimiting botanical varieties as are
colors or endosperm characters in maize." As noted earlier in this
paper, seed characters are also relatively conservative. For example, the
cultivated varieties listed by Tapley et al. (1937) shows the coefficient of
variation for seed length to be 19.5 while that for fruit weight is 112.13.
There is nearly six times more variation in fruit weight than there is in
seed size. Referring back to Figure 4.4, it can also be seen that there is
considerable overlap in length and width measurements for various
modern cultivars; therefore, very few can distinctly be separated on the
basis of seed characters. In a letter to the author (23 January 1980)
Bemis says that he does "not think that one can separate certain
cultivars of *C. pepo*, *C. pepo* var. *ovifera*, *C. texana* or species of the
sororia group based entirely on seed characteristics."

Likewise, in a summation of the inheritance of some fruit and vine
characters in *C. pepo*, Whitaker and Davis (1962:124) include some
fruit characters that are commonly seen in archaeological materials.
They show that warty surface is dominant over smooth and that hard
rind is dominant over soft. While a majority of smooth or soft thin rind
(seldom preserved in archaeological sites) might indicate that selection
and segregation for these characters was occurring, predominance by
warty and/or hard rind, typical of the remains from most Late Archaic
sites, is less informative. Even if selection was taking place, it might
have been for other, nonassociated, characters that are not equally well
preserved in the archaeological record. Nonbitterness is an example of
such a character.

Because of the restrictions imposed by having only seed and rind
data, it appears that in recognizing different varieties of *C. pepo* in
archaeological materials we are using the term "variety" rather loosely
for what might be considered by many taxonomists to possibly be no

more than a different form, a "commonly occurring type set off by a single usually conspicuous character" (Benson 1962:351).

The common names "pumpkin" and "squash" have been applied rather indiscriminately in the past, although it has been suggested more recently that the term pumpkin be used for the coarse and strongly flavored fruit of any species while "squash" is used for finer-textured, milder cultivars (Whitaker and Davis 1962; Whitaker and Bohn 1950). These terms are thus culinary rather than botanical and are almost entirely inapplicable to describing the types of cucurbit remains fround in archaeological contexts. Within *C. pepo* also occurs the ornamental, yellow-flowered "gourd" var. *ovifera*.

In examining and describing modern varieties, we are seeing the end-product of 7000–10,000 years of association with humans, domestication, and evolution. All of the tremendous variety of pepo seen today probably came from a single progenitor, so that as we go back in time, the distinguishing characteristics become less pronounced. While it may sometimes be possible to identify "pumpkin" or "squash" or "gourd" from seed or rind remains, this is based on comparisons with modern specimens, and becomes increasingly inappropriate for older material. It is also inappropriate to apply the nomenclature of modern cultivars to such material. Such identifications as "*C. pepo* var. *ovifera* (pumpkin/squash)" (Cowan 1979) and "*C. pepo* (squash)" (Kay et al. 1980; Yarnell 1969) for what are all basically intermediate forms between yellow-flowered gourds and edible squash point up the nomenclatural problems. Such differences in terminology can imply greater differences than may actually exist between specimens while neither style is particularly appropriate to the material being discussed.

A partial answer may be in doing for *Cucurbita pepo* what has already been done for *Chenopodium*, namely to make a common name from the botanical. Applying the term "pepo" as a common name for the botanical species has already been suggested by Tapley et al. (1937), Whitaker and Bohn (1950) and Cutler and Whitaker (1961). It has the advantage of conveying no connotation of size, shape or quality as do the terms "pumpkin", "squash", and "gourd" and is therefore ideal for discussing poorly known archaeological material. At the same time, it is important to continue to emphasize similarity rather than equality. Seeds or rind can be similar to those of cultivar Mandan or to var. *ovifera*; however, the total combination of characters possessed by the vine that produced those rinds or seeds may have been entirely different than those characterizing the modern specimens with which we are comparing them.

MECHANISMS OF INTRODUCTION

As evidence now stands, cucurbits were present in eastern North America by about 7000 B.P. and were widely distributed in the central Mississippi drainage by at least 3000 B.P., preceding both the appearance of cultivated cucurbits in the Southwest and the domestication of native plants in eastern North America. By 3000–2500 B.P. both tropical cultigens and native plant domesticates had become important subsistence items at sites such as Cloudsplitter and Salts Cave.

By about 4000 B.P., cultural exchange is shown in eastern North America by the distribution of exotic items such as marine shell and copper. Two regional exchange networks existed, one centered around the Great Lakes copper sources and the other representing the Atlantic and Gulf Coastal shell resources (Goad 1978). Indian Knoll, a series of shell mounds on the Green River in Kentucky (Carlston Annis and Bowles for example) is regarded as a prime center of exchange between these two networks (Winters 1968; Goad 1978).

Trade may either have been carried on by individuals or trading expeditions between exchange centers or in some combination with repeated, reciprocal (down-the-line) exhanges between neighboring groups. Directional exchange between distribution centers of regional networks may have operated along established trade routes such as those known for later periods. The occurrence of cucurbits at Indian Knoll sites show that cucurbits were present in the trading network, although they have not been found at Poverty Point, an exchange center with hypothesized Mesoamerican connections (Byrd and Neuman 1978; Webb 1977). The lack of cucurbit remains in sites along trade corridors in Texas and the Gulf Coast region (Story, this volume) supports the possibility that pepo might have originated in eastern North America or that it entered North America by a different route.

Alternatively, cucurbits are annually renewable resources which would not display the falloff in abundance with greater source distance which characterizes the distributions of other types of exotic goods in down-the-line exchange. Down-the-line exchange of cultigens as the result of reciprocal exchanges would allow for a more gradual entry of cucurbits into eastern North America, giving time for adaptation to a new environment and the addition of gardening to a hunting and gathering subsistence base (Kay et al. 1980).

The presence of cucurbits at Phillips Spring as well as the Indian Knoll sites, the similarity of Late Archaic burials between the two regions, and the lack of evidence indicating a direct relationship between Phillips Spring, Indian Knoll, Poverty Point or other sites in or near the lower Mississippi River valley suggests that the sites in the lower Pomme de Terre were not the focus of directional exchange but rather the beneficiaries of down-the-line exchange resulting in adoption of gardening practices (Kay et al. 1980).

At the same time however, the contemporaneous occurrence of bottle gourd and perhaps two types of pepo at Phillips Spring suggests that the mode of entry was not entirely down-the-line. Each time cucurbits were planted (by obviously inexperienced gardeners) there was a recurring risk of losing one or more of the types, and a falloff in types, if not in abundance, might be expected to occur with greater distance from the source. It seems likely, therefore, that cucurbits made their initial entry into eastern North America through a regional exchange system prior to being more widely distributed through down-the-line exchange.

There are two possible situations for the origination of cultivation: either it first occurred under population or environmental stress as food resources became short (e.g. Binford 1968) or alternatively, people already practicing limited agriculture might have turned more to planting as wild foods became increasingly inadequate (Bronson 1977; Caldwell 1977). Caldwell very plausibly argues that starving people unfamiliar with plant husbandry would eat seeds rather than put them in the ground, just as all too tragically happens in similar situations today with treated seeds. Cohen (1977:161) notes that the cultivation of bottle gourd and squash (*C. ficifolia*) in the Ancon-Chillon region of Peru occurred between 5600–4500 B.P., at least 700 and possibly as much as 2000 years after its appearance in the nearby Ayacucho highland region, yet there is evidence of repeated culture contact between the two regions well before this date. He suggests that, in this region the imbalance between growing population and food resources resulted in the beginning of agriculture.

Archaeological evidence, at least from the western Missouri Ozarks, suggests that Late Archaic peoples were under population stress (McMillan 1976; Klippel et al. 1979; King 1980). Following the models in which familiarity with cultivation is a necessary prerequisite for the adoption of intensive cultivation in the face of population or environmental stress (Caldwell 1977; Cohen 1977), it appears that cucurbits may have been being grown considerably earlier than 4700 B.P.— perhaps as early as 7000 B.P. based on the possible *C. pepo* remains from the Koster and Napoleon Hollow Sites in the lower Illinois Valley.

For many situations, the older an archaeological site, the poorer the preservation of plant remains. This probably relates to the recovery of primarily durable nutshells from most older sites or the apparent complete reliance by Paleo-Indians on meat. Among the cultigens, it has been shown that corn, beans, and sunflower seeds are more likely to survive burning and washing than squash or gourd seeds (Yarnell 1964:109). Because of such preservation problems, the farther back in the archaeological record we look for the history of cucurbits and their relationship with other types of wild or cultivated plants, the more fragmentary that record becomes.

Until recently, the ethnobotanical evidence suggested that native plants were being cultivated prior to the introduction of tropical cultigens. This was abruptly changed by the recovery of cucurbits from a number of sites in eastern North America considerably predating any evidence for native cultigens. The problem is, as Bronson (1977) points out, plants occur along a gradient going from selective exploitation, to intervention, near cultivation, quasi domestication and finally domestication. Generally it is not until a plant has reached the "domesticated" category that there have been sufficient artificially induced changes in that plant to set it apart from the normal phenotype. A considerable length of time might elapse between the initiation of selective exploitation (and the selection for specific characters) and the time when the population is recognizably changed. The exotics pepo and bottle gourd were introduced into eastern North America where there were no local endemic populations (excluding *C. foetidissima*) with which to confuse them. As a result, they have become, perhaps by default, the "earliest" cultigens.

While early cucurbits in eastern North America are relatively advanced along Bronson's gradient, their usage may actually have been less intensive than was that of ostensibly less "domesticated" native species such as marsh elder. We need well preserved plant remains from many more sites in this early time range before writing the last line on the origins of cultivation and domestication in eastern North America.

ACKNOWLEDGMENTS

I wish to thank the following for help in examining specimens or for their comments: the University of Illinois Herbarium, the Gray Herbarium, the Missouri Botanical Garden, W. P. Bemis, C. W. Cowan, B. K. Dawson-Saunders, J. E. King, R. A. Yarnell, and T. W. Whitaker.

The Impact of Early Horticulture in the Upland Drainages of the Midwest and Midsouth

Patty Jo Watson
Washington University, St. Louis

INTRODUCTION

As a result of what could be called "the flotation revolution" (Struever 1968; Watson 1976), a flood of new primary evidence for plant use in the Eastern Woodlands has become available and continues to appear almost weekly. Because the data base is changing so swiftly, a summary paper like this one is a highly ephemeral affair. It will certainly be out of date before it is published. Nevertheless, attempts at synthesis are essential if we are to discern significant patterns in the information about prehistoric subsistence that will enable us to trace the antecedents of horticulture in the eastern United States and also to understand subsequent economic developments. This task is complicated by the fact that there is clearly a considerable amount of local variation in plant use of both wild and cultivated species throughout the prehistoric and protohistoric time periods.

In this paper I present cultural-historical summaries for the upland regions now known to include some of the earliest evidence in North America for the use of cultivated plants (Fig. 5.1): the Pomme de Terre River valley in western Missouri; the Green River and Red River valleys of western Kentucky and eastern Kentucky, respectively; the Little

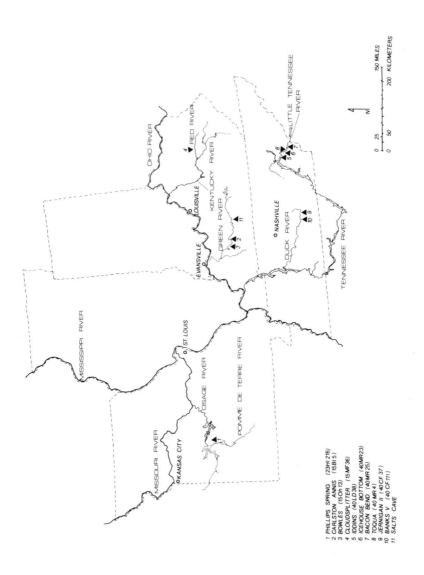

Figure 5.1. Location of archaeological sites.

Tennessee and the Duck River valleys in eastern Tennessee and central Tennessee, respectively. For ease of comparison among these five areas, I follow approximately the same format in describing the sites and specific proveniences for the cultigens, the regional environments, and the regional cultural-historical sequences. Information for the five areas varies somewhat, but there is sufficient evidence to enable at least an outline of cultural development for each. In three of the five, intensive and extensive surveys have been carried out as a result of federally financed dam construction (Truman Reservoir on the Pomme de Terre River; Tellico Reservoir on the Little Tennessee River; Normandy Reservoir on the Duck River), or the threat of it (Red River Gorge). The Green River in western Kentucky was surveyed by William S. Webb and his associates in the 1920s and 1930s, and several of the tributaries to the Green River (Barren, Nolin, and Rough rivers) were also surveyed more recently in advance of dam construction.

For each region my aim is to provide an account of the first appearance of cultivated plants, and then to summarize subsequent cultural-historical developments emphasizing the role played by the early cultigens. The earliest domesticated plant species in America north of Mexico now appear to be a gourd-like form of squash (probably *Cucurbita pepo*, var. *ovifera*) and bottle gourd (*Lagenaria siceraria*), both presumably imported originally from Mexico and both doubtless used primarily as containers rather than food. Native North American food species such as sunflower, sumpweed, chenopod, and maygrass were cultivated somewhat later (beginning between 2000 and 1500 B.C.), and maize is apparently still later (A.D. 400 or after; Yarnell 1983).

In trying to understand horticultural origins and effects, we need to muster as much of such specific comparative information as is available, but we should also be concerned with the more general implications of these data. On the present evidence, each of the five regions described is somewhat precocious with respect to the appearance of cultivated plants: If this precocity is not just a sampling error, did it have a significant effect on later developments in any of these regions? Predictably, the answer to this question appears to be somewhat complex. After the time of introduction of cultigens (pre–2000 B.C.), three of the five areas seem to have become quite provincial or parochial and to have remained so throughout the rest of the prehistoric time span. The other two—the Duck River and the Little Tennessee River drainage in Tennessee—appear to have supported much denser populations and to have been characterized by relatively complex cultural-historical developments. However, the details of the Tennessee sequences are only now being revealed by analyses currently underway, so conclusions about them must be rather tentative. Nevertheless, there is sufficient evidence from all five regions to support the suggestion just made, and further explored in the concluding section of this paper, that cultivated plants in the Kentucky and Missouri areas did not play as significant a role in cultural-historical development as in the Tennessee areas.

THE POMME DE TERRE RIVER VALLEY

Early cultigens have been reported from the Phillips Spring site (23Hi16) in western Missouri on the Pomme de Terre River in the extreme northern part of Hickory County, about 60 air miles north of Springfield, Missouri, and 95 miles southeast of Kansas City, Missouri. The Pomme de Terre River is a tributary of the Osage, which is a major tributary of the Missouri River. The Phillips Spring site lies on terrace 1b* of the Pomme de Terre. The site is centered on and in a small artesian spring—one of several on the alluvial terraces that line the river—which heads 80 m east of the river. The general region is an ecotonal one between the border of the Prairie Peninsula to the north and west and the oak-hickory forests of the Ozark Plateau to the south and east.

Site Description and Stratigraphy

Phillips Spring discharges between 25 and 30 gallons per minute and flows the year around (Chomko 1976:10). The archæological site extends over some four hectares of the 1b terrace north and south of the spring. Most of this terrace is presently under cultivation, but oak-hickory forest covers the hillside east of the terrace and there is bottomland forest along the river edge.

Detailed results are not yet available from all of the most recent (1977 and 1978) work at Phillips Spring, but at the end of the first season in 1974 Chomko had found evidence for four components: a Middle Archaic summer camp (to which he attributed Feature 2 containing squash seeds), two Late Archaic seasonal camps, and a more permanent Woodland occupation (Chomko 1976:108–9). The latter includes at least some Late Woodland material (Chomko 1976:104) as well as Middle Woodland remains.

The basal sediments (Unit A) at Phillips Spring are apparently late

---

*The terrace system was worked out by Vance Haynes (1976). T–1a dates between 13,000 and 11,000 B.P., whereas T-1b formed between 11,000 B.P. and 6000 B.P.

Pleistocene. They contain pine pollen, found so far only in late Wisconsin spectra for this region.

Above the Pleistocene sediments is a Holocene deposit (Unit C) equated by Kay, King, and Robinson (1980) with the Rodgers alluvium Haynes distinguished in his study of Rodgers Shelter and its physical setting (Haynes 1976). Unit C is cut by a series of channels; the channel fills (Unit C^2) contain uncarbonized plant remains and a possible hearth. The age of C^2 is indicated by radiocarbon determinations to be about 8000–6500 B.P.

The upper surface of C is truncated by another channel scar, Unit K^1, that "interfaces" with Unit K^2, the "Squash and Gourd Zone." There are three dates on the Squash and Gourd Zone (SMU–98, 4310 ± 70 B.P.; SMU–102, 4240 ± 80 B.P.; and SMU–483, 4222 ± 57 B.P.) which average 4257 ± 39 B.P. "This is the earliest acceptable age for cucurbits from Phillips Spring" (Kay, King, and Robinson 1980:812). These cucurbits comprise some 125 uncarbonized whole seeds and fragments of *Cucurbita pepo* plus 14 bottle gourd seeds and several pieces of bottle gourd rind (King 1980).

Overlying the Squash and Gourd Zone is a layer of sediment from the spring combined with riverine alluvium (King 1980). This matrix includes several Late Archaic features (4000 to 3000 B.P.), the oldest being a rock-lined pit that contained 24 fragments of squash seeds and a bottle gourd seed. One other somewhat younger, but still Late Archaic, pit also contained a squash seed.

Cucurbit seeds have also been found in flotation samples from a Middle Woodland storage pit at Phillips Spring dated 1999 ± 60 B.P. (King 1980).

Context of Early Cultigens

These come from deposits within the cone of saturation that surrounds the eye of the spring. They are uncharred, having been preserved by their saturated context, and were recovered both during excavation and by flotation (King 1980).

Together with the tropical cultigens in both the Late Archaic and Middle Woodland contexts at Phillips Spring, there is a variety of other plant material, carbonized and uncarbonized, such as grape, smartweed, chenopod, blackberry/raspberry, elderberry, and pondweed. Fragments of nutshell are also abundant (hickory, black walnut, oak, hazelnut).

So far, no native domesticates have been identified for Phillips Spring (Kay, King, and Robinson 1980). There is a sunflower present but it is a wild species (King 1980).

Context of the Site: Regional Culture History

Knowledge of Pomme de Terre Valley culture history dates back to 1946 when Carl Chapman initiated survey and test excavation in the area to be flooded by a proposed dam on the Pomme de Terre River (Chapman 1954; Wood 1961). The information accumulated by Chapman and Wood was supplemented by a larger University of Missouri salvage project carried out in the 1960s (McMillan 1971; Wood and McMillan 1976) in what was to become the Harry S. Truman Reservoir created by a dam constructed at Warsaw, Missouri, on the Osage River. The dam backs up water nearly to the Kansas-Missouri boundary and well up the Pomme de Terre Valley.

The modern vegetation pattern in the Pomme de Terre region was established about 12,000 B.P. when the late Pleistocene spruce forest disappeared (King and Lindsay 1976) to be replaced by dediduous species (walnut, hickory, elm, maple, a variety of oaks with prairie patches in some locations; Wood and McMillan 1976:25–35). Archaeological investigations in a number of the spring bogs on terraces along the Pomme de Terre were undertaken because of nineteenth century claims about an association between projectile points and mastodon bones. Cultural remains were found in three of the springs (Wood 1976): Trolinger, Boney, and Koch. Trolinger yielded only a single artifact, a projectile point interpreted as intrusive and probably less than 2000 years old. Deposits adjacent to Koch Spring, where a projectile point/mastodon association had been claimed in the nineteenth century, yielded a number of chipped and ground stone tools, a rock-lined hearth, and a burial with an associated artifact cache. Typologically the stone material indicates a long history of prehistoric use of the spring from Early Archaic to Woodland times.

A major prehistoric occupation was found around the margin of Boney Spring (Wood 1976; King and McMillan 1975) that included a basin-shaped pit containing a concentration of nuts and seeds as well as sherds of Woodland pottery. Among the plant remains are squash, dogwood, elderberry, cocklebur, giant ragweed, pokeberry, wild plum, and black haw. The context is referred to as Early Woodland, but the date is ca. A.D. 50 (one determination only; Wood and McMillan 1976:231; King and McMillan 1975:111; and Vehik 1978:18). Hence, the artifact/mastodon association claimed by Koch and others beginning about 1840 has so far not been substantiated.

The earliest attested human activity in the Pomme de Terre Valley as presently known is Dalton in age (ca. 10,500 to 9500 B.P.). Materials of this period have been excavated at Rodgers Shelter (and one Dalton point was found at site 23Hi23 in the Pomme de Terre reservoir according to Wood 1961:100). McMillan, who directed the Rodgers excavations, believes the Dalton settlement system was one of a series of transient occupations, with Rodgers Shelter being one such settlement (McMillan 1971:185–86). Deer and raccoon were apparently the focus of much of the hunting activity, although a variety of other game was also taken. Unfortunately there is very little direct evidence for plant use because only such charred remains as survived water-screening are available (no flotation was done, most of the excavation having been carried out just prior to the emphasis on this technique): hickory, walnut, hackberry, acorn, grape, persimmon, and black cherry were identified by Frances King (Parmalee, McMillan, and King 1976:141–43). Hickory nut fragments were present throughout the Archaic levels, and King calculated that the oak-hickory and bottomland forests within a 10 km radius of the shelter could have produced—at a minimum—several thousand bushels of hickory nuts per year (King 1976).

Middle Archaic use of Rodgers Shelter differed from the Dalton transient hunting-camp pattern. The shelter now functioned as a base camp (McMillan 1976:224). Less deer were taken but bison appear in Middle Archaic I (bison were not present in earlier or later occupations), although the focus of hunting was apparently on smaller game, especially squirrels and, later (Middle Archaic II), rabbits. Again, a few dozen fragments of hickory nuts, walnuts, and hackberries survived water-screening to be identified by Frances King. There were no identifiable storage pits found in the Archaic deposits, and McMillan notes that plant processing activities, as measured by functional analyses of the stone tools, were less important in Middle Archaic II than Middle Archaic I.

There is a long hiatus in the Rodgers sequence following Middle Archaic II, with reoccupation dating to about 3000 B.P. At this time deer hunting was again quite important, with emphasis also on some aquatic resources (mussels and turtles). No storage pits were located, but a few fragments of hickory nuts and walnuts were found as well as parts of 96 hackberry seeds.

Archaic materials elsewhere along the Pomme de Terre are rare, most traces comprising projectile points from open sites (Wood 1961:101). However, there are some pre–3000 B.C. Archaic strata (component A) at the bottom of another shelter, Blackwell Cave (Wood 1961:52–62, 87–90, 113–14; Falk 1969:88). Late Middle Archaic and Late Archaic occupations are suggested for the Miller site, an open site on the Osage River about five miles upstream from the Pomme de

Terre junction (Vehik 1974: 7–26). As noted below, Late Archaic components are present at open sites on the Osage and South Grand Rivers (Merideath, Thurman, and Fulton).

Woodland remains are more widely distributed. Above the Archaic component in Blackwell Cave are three Woodland components (B, C, and D), the first nonceramic (the Afton Complex), the other two with Hopewellian and Late Woodland/Mississippian parallels, respectively. The Rodgers Shelter Woodland component is Late Woodland in age (McMillan 1976:226; Wood 1961:114–15), and represents a transient occupation by deer and turkey hunters who also collected fish and mussels. The Afton Complex—a late preceramic manifestation which seems to occupy a more or less Early Woodland time slot—is found at two sites in the Pomme de Terre reservoir: Blackwell Cave (23Hi172, component B) and Holbert Bridge (23Hi135), the latter being a burial mound. Late or Terminal Archaic and Early Woodland material is reported from the Merideath open site (23Sr129) on the Osage River about 15 miles west-northwest of Blackwell Cave (Falk 1969:38–39, 110). Late Archaic and Woodland remains were recovered from two other open sites on the South Grand River (a tributary of the Osage from the north, it joins the main stream a few miles downstream of the Pomme de Terre/Osage junction), the Thurman site, which was occupied from the early first millennium B.C. to about A.D. 500–1000 (Falk and Lippencott 1974:7–53), and the Fulton site (1500 B.C. to A.D. 500 or somewhat later; Falk and Lippencott 1974:101–9). Apparently there is no earlier material than Late Archaic/Woodland anywhere on the lower South Grand River, and the several sites of this time period seem to be campsites. Lack of information on Dalton and Middle Archaic horizons may be because such materials are buried (Falk and Lippencott 1974:52, 118–19).

Next in time (the early centuries A.D.) are a few sites with Hopewellian-related pottery (Blackwell component C, and three sites west of the Pomme de Terre Valley; Wood 1961:102). The Hopewellian-influenced occupation of this part of western Missouri was not very intensive, and the majority of pottery-bearing sites in the Pomme de Terre basin are post-Hopewellian (Wood 1961:104). These include the Lindley Focus (village sites) and the Fristoe Burial Complex, both intermediate between Hopewellian and Mississippian complexes according to Wood (1961:108). A recent assessment of the Fristoe Burial Complex by means of factor analysis seems to indicate that both Late Woodland and Late Woodland-Mississippian traits are included (Vehik 1977). Wood (1967:125) notes that the creators of the burial tumuli are thought to have been semisedentary and partially dependent on horticulture, but there is no direct evidence bearing on either of these topics.

Late Woodland and Mississippian-related sites (Saba shelter, for instance; Vehik 1974:30–109) are also present, both occupation and burial sites being represented (Vehik 1974:100–101; Vehik 1978), but population is thought to have been rather sparse (Vehik 1978:38).

Finally, protohistoric and historic (Osage and Kickapoo) Indian occupations are attested in the general region (Wood 1961:110–12; Vehik 1978:42–43).

Role of the Early Cultigens in Pomme de Terre Cultural History

The archaeological remains from Phillips Spring indicate a multicomponent (at least Late Archaic, Middle Woodland, and Late Woodland) open site that probably usually functioned as a seasonal camp from which deer and lesser animals were hunted, mussels and fish were taken, and hickory as well as other nuts and wild plant foods (grape, plum, berries, etc.) were collected. The Archaic and Middle Woodland folk were growing two tropical cultigens—squash and gourd; the Woodland people who left the Boney Spring storage pit were also growing *pepo*. The uppermost stratum at Blackwell Cave (one radiocarbon determination of A.D. 1230±110) yielded gourd seeds and beans (Falk 1969:77, 85).

As indicated in the cultural historical sketch of the previous section, in spite of seeming precocity with respect to tropical cultigens, cultural evolution in the Pomme de Terre basin does not appear to have been particularly spectacular or outstanding. The area shares general similarities to developments in the rest of the southern Prairie Peninsula of central Illinois and Missouri, and the Ozark Highlands of eastern Kansas and Oklahoma (Kay, King, and Robinson 1980:820). There are not even any exotic materials in the Late Archaic assemblages now known from Phillips Spring, Rodgers Shelter, and Blackwell Cave. Kay et al. conclude that the tropical cultigens of Phillips Spring reached the area (by about the mid-third millennium B.C.) via a form of down-the-line exchange, and that gardening practices introduced at that time continued to the historic period.

On the present evidence from Phillips and Boney Springs, it appears that the gardening practices of the Late Archaic and Woodland peoples of the Pomme de Terre Valley were focused on squash and gourd. Such gardening may have been not primarily to intensify the production of plant foods, but rather to produce vessels or containers (which also had edible seeds).

Three sites in northwest Missouri and one in northeast Missouri outside the immediate Pomme de Terre region have recently yielded plant remains relevant to the question of plant use in Late Archaic and later periods for this general area: the Nebo Hill site (Root 1979), the Collins site (Klippel 1972; Yarnell 1978; Asch, Farnsworth, and Asch 1979), and the Yeo site (O'Brien 1982; King 1982). Macrofloral material from the Coffey site in northeastern Kansas (Schmits 1978) is also relevant here. At the Coffey site, over 4000 chenopod seeds were found (cf. *C. album* or *C. berlandieri*, with smaller amounts of *C. gigantosper-mum*; Schmits 1978:147–48) in a single hearth dated to approximately 3000 B.C. (the hearth dates are: N–1549, 4840 B.P. ± 95; WIS–618, 5155 B.P. ± 70; WIS–623, 5170 B.P. ± 70; Schmits 1978:85). Other seeds found in early Late Archaic context at the site include *Polygonum, Polygonatum* (Solomon's seal), bulrush, grape, and one hackberry seed. All these plants were presumably wild foods, but the abundance of chenopod may be significant.

Recent research on *Chenopodium* is revealing a complicated picture (Asch and Asch 1977; Fritz 1984; Smith 1984; H. Wilson 1981). It now appears that cultigen chenopod (*huauhtli; C. berlandieri* ssp. *nuttalliae*) together with cultigen amaranth (*huazontli; Amaranthus hypochondri-acus*) was introduced into the southeastern United States from Meso-america in prehistoric times, presumably late prehistoric times. Whether a species of *Chenopodium* native to the Eastern Woodlands was taken into cultivation prior to introduction of the Mesoamerican che-nopod is presently unknown, but *C. bushianum* was probably at least semidomesticated in some places by Late Archaic times.

At the Nebo Hill site, 119 chenopod seeds were found in a late Late Archaic pit (Feature 2). The pit has one radiocarbon determination of about 1605 B.C. (UGA–1332, 3555 B.P. ± 65). Also in the same pit were a few seeds (1 to 6) of the following species; amaranth, bedstraw, knotweed, dogwood, panic grass, plantain, hackberry, unidentified grass, and legume.

Domesticated *Iva* is reported from a Terminal Archaic–Early Wood-land context at the Collins site in the Salt River drainage of north-eastern Missouri (Yarnell 1978; Asch, Farnsworth, and Asch 1979:82); and radiocarbon determinations from the Napoleon Hollow site in Illinois indicate domestic *Iva* there by 4000 B.P. (Conard et al. 1984). This Napoleon Hollow sumpweed is at present the earliest evidence for domestication of a nontropical, native midwestern species.

Adair (1978; cited by Johnson 1979:88) found *Iva* as well as amaranth, chenopod, and sunflower at the Kansas City Hopewell Young site (near Parkville, Missouri) together with hickory, walnut, and hazelnut.

The Yeo site near Smithville, Missouri, is also a Kansas City Hopewell manifestation dating to the sixth or seventh century A.D. (O'Brien 1982). Plant remains were found in five pit features and identified by Frances King (1982). These remains include hickory nut (as usual, this species makes up the great bulk of the material: 82.8 g of approximately 105 g), black walnut (0.1 g), hazelnut (0.3 g), and seeds of four herbaceous species. The latter include 58 sumpweed seeds of cultigen size, 8 chenopod seeds, 6 grass seeds (cf. *Sporobolus*), and 3 knotweed seeds of the *Polygonum aviculare* type. O'Brien suggests the Yeo site is a limited activity plant-processing station, and may represent an example of the kind of cultivation described by Asch and Asch (1978:318–28) whereby sumpweed is transplanted from a floodplain to an upland area where it would not naturally be present. O'Brien (1982) and Johnson (1979) note the identification of sumpweed remains at the Trowbridge Hopewellian site near Kansas City, Kansas, which—like the Young site—is a village rather than a camp or special activity locus. Squash and corn are reported for Trowbridge as well, and corn has been found at several Hopewell sites in Illinois and Ohio (Ford 1979: Table 29.1), and at Meadowcroft (Adovasio and Johnson 1980). However, the Asches (1982; see also Conard et al. 1984) and Yarnell (1983) do not believe any Eastern Woodlands maize predates A.D. 400 on the present evidence. Finally, Robinson (1976) reports sumpweed seeds (some of which are large enough to have come from cultivated plants) at the Middle Woodland Fisher-Gabert site in central Missouri.

Back in the Pomme de Terre Valley, there are beans (another tropical cultigen) as well as bottle gourd reported from a Late Woodland context at Blackwell Cave (Falk 1969: 77; King 1980), but otherwise the present evidence, accumulated in the almost total absence of flotation, is not indicative of marked horticultural intensification (or horticulturally-based cultural intensification) in the prehistoric record of the Pomme de Terre basin. Hickory and other nuts seem to have been staples at least as far back as the Middle Archaic and to have remained central throughout the archaeological record of this region. The fanciest Pomme de Terre cultural development is probably the Fristoe Burial Complex and even it, Wood believes, reflects a "hill folk" kind of isolation to a certain degree, although there are elements included that demonstrate some kinds of trade relationships with more complex and sophisticated cultures outside the Ozarks.

> These contacts did not lead to an elaboration of the "hill folk" of this complex along the northwestern margin of the Ozarks because these complex and sophisticated alien groups embraced values or economic orientations or other cultural variables which were not valued by the hill folk, or which, at least, were not amenable to their way of life. [Wood 1967: 126]

THE MIDDLE GREEN RIVER REGION

Early cultigens have been reported from the Carlston Annis site (15Bt5), the Bowles site (15Oh13), and Peter Cave (15Oh94) (Crawford 1982; Marquardt and Watson 1983b). These sites are in Butler county and Ohio County, respectively, in western Kentucky. Bt5 is in the Big Bend of the Green River about 30 miles north of Bowling Green, 35 air miles south of Owensboro. The Green River is a major tributary of the Ohio. Besides Bt5, the Carlston Annis site, two other major shell middens lie inside the loop of Green River north of Morgantown known as the Big Bend. These are Bt6 and Bt11. All four sites are within 100 to 150 m of the river and thus are in a floodplain topographic and vegetational zone, partially drained by a series of heavily overgrown sloughs. The nearest uplands are the sandstone bluffs about one and a half miles east of the site, once covered with oak-hickory-tulip forest.

Oh13 is farther downstream, across the Green River from the little town of Rochester, which lies at the junction of the Mud River with the Green. There is a dam and lock system at this point on the Green River and the house of the lockkeeper's son-in-law stands on a portion of the site. Like Bt5, 6, and 11, Oh13 is on the floodplain a few dozen meters from the water's edge.

Peter Cave (actually a rockshelter) is in the uplands several kilometers northeast of Bt5 overlooking a prong of Indian Camp Creek, a small tributary of Green River.

Site Descriptions and Stratigraphy

Oh94, Peter Cave, is a large but shallow sandstone overhang, the deposits beneath which have been badly disturbed by vandals. Nevertheless, during the summer of 1975 a crew directed by William Marquardt was able to excavate a 1 × 1 m test pit through approximately 115 cm of intact deposit. Cucurbit remains (charred rind fragments of *C. pepo*) were found by Gary Crawford (1982) in flotation samples of the dark brown midden taken from the two bottom levels (7 and 8) in test pit A.

The present surface expression of Bt5 is a rounded oval approximately 100 m by 75 m east–west, and with a maximum height of some 2 m over the surrounding floodplain.

Oh13 was apparently a double-peaked mound, the eastern portion of which is still freestanding and is about 90 m in diameter. The maximum height of this eastern rise is close to 2 m above the flat. As noted above, the western rise is obscured by a modern house.

All four shell midden sites on the western limb of the Big Bend are under cultivation with corn or soy beans. There is an old barn on the south end of Bt5, and also a concrete wellbox. When we first visited Oh13 in 1972, it, too, supported a barn, but by the time of our fieldwork there in the summer of 1974 the barn had been removed and the entire field containing the mound was planted in corn.

During the summer of 1974 we spent two weeks excavating two 1 × 1 m pits at Oh13, only one of which, A3, reached sterile soil. We have also carried out systematic soil-coring programs at Bt6 and Bt11. Otherwise all our information comes from Bt5 where we have excavated several pits and trenches of varying dimensions and have completed a rather intensive coring project (Stein 1978, 1979). Hence, the bulk of the following discussion centers on Bt5.

The geological and geomorphological situation of the Big Bend sites has recently been worked out by Julie Stein (1979, 1980, 1983; Stein, Watson, and White 1981). The loop known as the Big Bend is created because the river is following a fault in the Mississippian and Pennsylvanian bedrock. The Green River in the vicinity of the Big Bend behaves in a rather unusual manner because, instead of flowing over a normal floodplain, it is incised into compact lake sediments deposited during the Terminal Wisconsin when the Ohio (and the Green River) were choked and partially dammed by fluvially transported gravel and sand carried by glacial meltwaters.

Stein notes that flood waters are not responsible for the buildup of the mound, a process which began after the river began to incise its way into the lake clays following draining of glacial Green Lake. Originally the mound was right at the edge of the river, but in the past 4000 years the river has migrated laterally (westward) some 150 m.

Bt5 and Oh13 were partially excavated by WPA crews some 40 years ago (Bt5: June, 1940, to September, 1941; Oh13: March, 1939). We turned to these shell mounds in our attempts to trace the antecedents of the Late Archaic/Woodland subsistence pattern documented in the large, dry caves of Mammoth Cave National Park 40 miles east of the Big Bend (Watson et al. 1969; Watson 1974).

In the spring of 1972 William Marquardt, then a graduate student at Washington University, and I formed the Shell Mound Archeological Project, and supervised 10 days of fieldwork at Bt5 with two major results: (1) we recovered sufficient charcoal for two radiocarbon determinations; (2) we recovered sufficient charred botanical material from throughout the 2 m depth of deposit in a 1 × 1 m stratigraphic test pit to demonstrate the feasibility of detailed analyses of prehistoric plant use at the site. These dates, plus eight more we obtained later (Table 5.1) and the five secured by Willard Libby and William S. Webb

TABLE 5.1*
RADIOCARBON DETERMINATIONS FOR SHELL MOUND
ARCHAEOLOGICAL PROJECT

Site	Cucurbit Proveniences	Proveniences for Radiocarbon Determination	
15Bt5 (Carlston Annis)		A1-8 105–120 cm	UCLA 1845B 4040 ± 180 B.P. 2090 B.C.
		A1-10 135–150 cm	UCLA 1845A 4250 ± 80 B.P. 2300 B.C.
	C1-3 (rind frags.) 40–50 cm		
	C1-6 (rind frags.) 80–90 cm		
	C1-20 (rind frags.) 220–225 cm	U. of Arizona Accelerator date on rind frags.	5730 ± 640 B.P. 3780 B.C.
		C3-5 75–85 cm	UCLA 2117B 3330 ± 80 B.P. 1380 B.C.
	C13-7 (rind frags.) 87–96 cm		
	C13-8 (rind frags.) 96–107 cm		
	C13-11 (rind frags.) 128–137 cm		
		C13-12 137–148 cm	UCLA 2117I 4500 ± 60 B.P. 2550 B.C.
		C13-15 167–177 cm	UCLA 2117D 2515 ± 80 B.P. 565 B.C.
		D14-2-9 84–94 cm	UGa 3393 5030 ± 85 B.P. 3080 B.C.
		D14-2-15 138–150 cm	UGa 3391 4670 ± 85 B.P. 2720 B.C.

TABLE 5.1
CONTINUED

Site	Cucurbit Proveniences	Proveniences for Radiocarbon Determination	
		D14-2-20 188–200 cm	UGa 3390 4350 ± 85 B.P. 2400 B.C.
		D14-3-7 60–70 cm	UGa 3395 4655 ± 540 B.P. 2705 B.C.
15Oh13 (Bowles)		A2-2 (burial just below plow- zone)	UCLA 2117E 1820 ± 300 B.P. A.D. 130
	A3-5 (rind frags.) 65–80 cm		
		A3-7 93–100 cm	UCLA 2117F 2420 ± 200 B.P. 470 B.C.
		A3-11 140–160 cm	UCLA 2117G 3440 ± 80 B.P. 1490 B.C.
	A3-12 (rind frags.) 160–175 cm	U. of Arizona Accelerator date on rind frags.	4060 ± 220 B.P. 2110 B.C.
	A3-15 (rind frags.) 200–210 cm		
15Oh94 (Peter Cave)		A-6 (sample from approx. 75 cm below surface)	UGa 3454 3415 ± 105 B.P. 1465 B.C.
	A-7 (rind frags.)		
	A-8 (rind frags.)		

*These radiocarbon determinations are uncalibrated, and were calculated with the Libby half-life and 1950 base-date.

in the very early days of development of the radiocarbon dating technique (Webb 1951; Libby 1952), indicate a Late Archaic age for the Bt5 deposits. The Libby/Webb dates are (Webb 1951):

C-116, 5149 ± 300 B.P. (shell from 6.5 ft. level)
C-251, 4900 ± 250 B.P. (antler from 6.5 ft. level)
C-739, 4333 ± 450 B.P. (antler from 5.5 to 7.0 ft. level)
C-180, 7374 ± 500 B.P. (shell from 3.0 ft. level)
C-738, 4289 ± 300 B.P. (antler from 1.5 to 2.5 level)

We also obtained four dates from Oh13 and one from Peter Cave (Table 5.1).

Finally, there are four Libby/Webb dates from Oh2, the Indian Knoll shell mound (Webb 1951):

C-741, 3963 ± 350 B.P. (antler from the 4.5 ft. level)
C-740, 4282 ± 250 B.P. (antler from the 1.0 ft. level)
C-254, 4894 ± 560 B.P.
        5709 ± 350 B.P. (antler from the 1.0 ft. level [the sample was run twice; Average: 5302 B.P.])

Context of Early Cultigens

From the outset of the excavation at Bt5, we were puzzled and frustrated by the lack of horizontal layering in the deposits. Our profiles did not at all resemble those at the Riverton shell mounds on the Wabash River (Winters 1969: Pl. 5) where a variety of banding and zonation was clearly discernible, as had also been the case in the Salts Cave Vestibule (Watson 1974: Fig. 11.4, for example). Hence, one of the first questions we asked geoarchaeologist Julie Stein when she began working with us was why Bt5 profiles were bereft of differentiation, except for greater or lesser quantities of shell and of sandstone fragments ("fire-cracked rock"). Her eventual answer was "faunalturbation." The churning activity of millions of earthworms over the millennia has homogenized the matrix but only minimally affected objects 2 cm or larger. Therefore, our clues to the vanished stratigraphy lie in microstratigraphic analysis of the depositional patterns of these objects (Stein 1980: Chapter VII, and 1983; Gorski 1979, 1980).

Meanwhile, however, analysis of flotation samples from both Bt5 and Oh13 revealed the presence of charred squash rind (*Cucurbita pepo*) in a context of wild plant foods, especially hickory nuts (Chomko and Crawford 1978; Crawford 1978, 1982; Marquardt and Watson 1976, 1983b; Wagner 1979; Watson 1976; Watson and Carstens 1979).

The present situation with respect to proveniences of the squash rind in the shell mounds and of our radiocarbon dates may be summarized as follows (see also Table 5.1): *C. pepo* fragments have been found in unit C1, levels 3, 6, and 20; and in unit C13, levels 7, 8, and 11. Both units are 1 × 1 m squares. Only one of the presently available radiocarbon determinations comes from a level or provenience that is so far known to contain squash remains: the accelerator date on the rind fragments from C1 level 20, which are at an absolute depth that is at or slightly below any of the other dates we have obtained. Our nine dates average 2418 B.C.; if the UCLA 2117D date is omitted (because it is so much younger than any of the others even though it is from one of the deepest levels so far dated), the arithmetic average is 2623 B.C. Hence, one could say the mean age of the Bt5 deposit we have tested between 75 and 200 cm below the surface is about 4500 years, and that most of the squash found so far is from that horizon (one occurrence above it and one slightly below). At Oh13 there are squash remains dated to 2110 ± 220 B.C. These come from 40–50 cm below a level dated 1490 B.C. ± 80; the arithmetic average of the three midden dates at Oh13 is 1357 B.C.

Cucurbita pepo rind as well as *Chenopodium* seeds from Peter Cave were identified by Crawford (1982). The Peter Cave squash apparently predates 1465 B.C. (Table 5.1); the *Chenopodium* seeds (not known to be from a cultigen form) are present in levels both above and below the radiocarbon determination.

Context of the Sites: Regional Culture History

The shell mound sites discussed here lie in Kentucky's Western Coalfield physiographic province, a basin approximately 4,680 square miles in area bounded by rugged hills capped with Pennsylvanian sandstones (McFarlan 1943: 201–3), and covered with oak-hickory forest. The basic topographic pattern is a dissected one of ridges and hollows, the hollows being valleys of various sizes with intermittent or permanent streams in them which are tributaries to larger streams and rivers like the Green River. The total relief may be as much as 400 feet. Where the sandstone outcrops along the ridge edges there are often springs, and also many overhangs forming an infinite variety of shelters.

The Green River heads far east in Lincoln County, Kentucky, but is the principal drainage channel for the Central Kentucky Karst in the Mammoth Cave area and for the Western Coalfield before joining the Ohio near Evansville.

Rainfall averages 41 to 46 inches per year, and the mean annual temperature is 56° (Commonwealth of Kentucky Department of Natural Resources 1965:7–10). Vegetation patterns are moisture dependent. Plant communities range from those characterizing the dry uplands (hickory, walnut, elm, maple, various oaks, tulip) to those at home on the wet and humid river floodplains (willow, birch, cottonwood, sycamore, vine, and cane stands; Wagner 1979).

Riverside locations like those of the shell mounds are subjected to annual flooding from late winter to early spring. Variety in trees increases as one moves away from the immediate vicinity of the river, but concentration of any one species decreases. A feature of the Green River floodplain in the Big Bend is the presence of many sloughs, some with permanently standing or sluggishly flowing water, others that flow only after a rainfall or in the spring thaw. Vegetation in the bottoms shifts continually in response to flooding, slip-ins, and, farther back from the river, gradual filling-in and drying of some areas.

The Green River fauna must also have been rich and varied. We do not yet have detailed reports on the vertebrate remains from Bt5, but deer and turkey bone are common as are remains of several kinds of smaller animals especially squirrel and rabbit. Webb reported about 90% deer bone in a total of 25,757 identifiable fragments from Indian Knoll. There is also a quantity of fish bone of various sizes (drum remains are conspicuous among them) and, of course, thousands of unionid (mussel) shells. The unionids were the subject of a detailed study by Diana Patch (1976), who concluded that the great majority were shallow water (riffle-run) species. Thus, her work provides empirical support for the suggestion that the river near the site differed somewhat at the time of occupation from its present appearance. There is no riffle or run near Bt5 now. Another possibility is that contemporary records available on natural habitats of the various mussels are skewed towards riffle-runs because they are so much easier to collect there than in deeper proveniences. Perhaps several or all of the species regarded as riffle-run indicators may and do also occur in deeper, slower water. In any case, the river has now been severely altered by dams (one at Woodbury at the base of the eastern limb of the Big Bend, and one at Rochester downstream of the Big Bend; the one at Woodbury collapsed several years ago), and by dredging to facilitate river boat traffic. The mussel population is greatly reduced in size and variety from the prehistoric situation because of this recent meddling with the riverine regime and because of high density in the modern human populations along the Green River.

Cultural History of the Middle Green River

Martha Rolingson's detailed analysis of the Green River Archaic (1967) led her to a series of conclusions about the culture history of this region, and about relationships of the shell mound phase to other areas. A summary of her results and of ours is presented below, followed by a comparative synthesis for the Mammoth Cave area centering on Salts Cave and Mammoth Cave.

Rolingson's temporal analyses, not all of which are published, even preliminarily, are based on an intensive study of projectile points and pottery from a series of 12 Green River Archaic sites in Butler, Ohio, Muhlenberg, and McLean counties:

Bt5	—	Carlston Annis, shell mound
Bt10	—	Read, shell mound
Oh1	—	Chiggerville, shell mound
Oh2	—	Indian Knoll, shell mound
Oh12	—	Jackson Bluff, shallow shell mound
Oh13	—	Bowles, shell mound
Oh19	—	Jimtown Hill, shallow shell mound
Mu12	—	Baker, shell mound
McL4	—	Barrett, midden with very little shell
McL7	—	Butterfield, midden with shell lenses
McL11	—	Ward, midden with very little shell
McL12	—	Kirkland, midden with very little shell

Paleo-Indian and Archaic

Like many other parts of the eastern United States, the Middle Green River was occupied to some degree by makers of fluted projectile points. Fluted points were found at Carlston Annis (two), Indian Knoll (one), and Jimtown Hill (one). Early Archaic lanceolate projectile points like Dalton, Kirk Serrated, and Lecroy are somewhat more common; they were found at eight of Rolingson's twelve sites (lacking at Carlston Annis, Bowles, Jackson Bluff, and Kirkland). Dates for these points from elsewhere in the Midsouth and Southeast place them between 8000 and 6000 B.C. There are also slightly later, early to middle Archaic point types, such as Eva Basal Notched, at several of the sites and a "Laurentian-like" early Late Archaic (Rolingson 1967:446). But the major occupation of the Middle Green River is the Late Archaic Indian Knoll phase characterized by a series of projectile points Rolingson has grouped and defined as "Cluster V": most are parallel or expanding stemmed points with sloping to barbed shoulders. These points are present at Carlston Annis, Read, Bowles, Chiggerville, Indian Knoll, Ward, Kirkland, and Barrett. Other traits of the Indian Knoll phase as defined by Rolingson include a complex of grave goods accompanying some of the burials: disc and tubular shell beads, conch shell gorgets and pendants, turtle shell cups and rattles, animal mandibles, dogs, atlatl parts, copper, red ocher, bone hairpins, shell earplugs (Rolingson 1967:409–410). Rolingson dates the Indian Knoll phase Late Archaic between 2500 and 1500 B.C. on the basis of typological comparisons with other Archaic assemblages. This time-span is in reasonable agreement with the majority of our radiocarbon determinations. As indicated by some of the exotic items in the grave goods complex, the Indian Knoll people were participating in long distance trade both to the north (copper, plus some projectile point forms) and to the south and/or east (conch and other marine shells; Goad 1978: Chapter VI). This Indian Knoll phase is limited to the Middle Green River basin, but there are other Archaic sites—small and thin compared to the Indian Knoll ones—on the tributaries of the Green River (Nolin River, Barren River) and on the upper Green (Rolingson 1967:416; Schwartz 1960).

We recently found a small and badly damaged shell mound of un-known age in the loop of the Big Bend north of Bt6, and Charles Hockensmith of the Kentucky Heritage Council is presently carrying out a shell mound survey of the entire middle Green River-Western Coalfield region. He has located a number of mounds not previously recorded. When the results of this work are available we should have a much clearer idea of the chronological and geographic patterning of these sites.

Rolingson believes—still on the basis of projectile points—there is a third Late Archaic phase, following the "Laurentian-like" and the In-dian Knoll phases, represented in the Middle Green River which is related to the Riverton culture of the Wabash River valley (Winters 1963, 1969; Rolingson 1967:447).

Woodland and Mississippian

A few Early Woodland sites are reported for the upper Rough River drainage (Schwartz, Sloan, and Walter 1958) and for the Nolin River (Schwartz 1960). Several minor Early Woodland components are pre-sent at the Indian Knoll phase sites on Green River as indicated by sherds of grit-tempered pottery types such as the Baumer and Alex-ander series at several of them (of Rolingson's 12-site sample, only Read, Bowles, Baker, and Jackson Bluff had no ceramics), the great majority of sherds being in the upper part of the deposit (no more than 2 to 2.5 feet below the surface). Rolingson believes three separate periods of Woodland occupation are represented by the pottery (Rolingson 1967:390–91): Early Woodland types (Fayette Thick and Baumer at Carlston Annis, Jimtown Hill, Butterfield, Kirkland, and Barrett); and later Early Woodland (sand-tempered types like O'Neal Plain, Alexander Incised, Columbus Punctated, and perhaps the

Rough River limestone-tempered series) at Butterfield, Jimtown Hill, Carlston Annis, Indian Knoll, Ward, and Barrett. Finally, there is a Middle or Late Woodland occupation at some of the sites as indicated by the presence of such types as Baytown Plain and Mulberry Creek Cord Marked at Carlston Annis, Chiggerville, Indian Knoll, Jimtown Hill, Butterfield, Ward, Kirkland, and Barrett; and by a single complicated stamped sherd at Indian Knoll. See also the discussion of Bt1 below.

Early Woodland or Adena point types are also present at ten of the twelve sites (all but Baker and Jackson Bluff), and Woodland remains have ben found elsewhere in the region as well. There are at least two Early to Middle Woodland burial mounds nearby, one (the Ashby site, Mu4; Hoffman 1965) in Muhlenberg County and the other (Jones Mound, Hk11) in Hopkins County (Purrington 1966; Rolingson 1967:318–23). There are Hopewellian Snyders Notched points at Read, Chiggerville, Butterfield, and Barrett. Mississippian Triangular points were found at seven of the twelve sites (Bowles, Baker, Jackson Bluff, Jimtown Hill, and Barrett lack these points).

Shell-tempered pottery is also present on eight of Rolingson's twelve sites (all the pottery-bearing sites had some shell-tempered pottery). These pottery types include: Neeley's Ferry Plain, Bell Plain, McKee Island Cord Marked, and Wolf Creek Check Stamped, plus a few decorated sherds (incised or red painted). All these pottery types are also present at a Mississippian village and mound site (Bn21, the Jewell site) on the Barren River in Barren County (Rolingson 1967:391). There are three radiocarbon dates for different construction phases of the Jewell site mound: I–1110, A.D. 1028 ± 125; I–1109, A.D. 1293 ± 100; I–1108, A.D. 1423 ± 120.

There is a small Mississippian village site between the Ward and Butterfield sites (McL19, the Kirtley site: Rolingson 1967:324) comprising six house patterns and exclusively shell-tempered pottery, mostly of the same types as found on the Green River shell mounds.

Excavated Mississippian sites in the Big Bend region itself include Bt2 and Bt20, a stockaded village and mound complex on the east limb of the Big Bend. This site was dug by the WPA but never published. It is the largest known Mississippian site in the Middle Green River area, and there are possibly associated burials in a nearby Woodland mound, Bt1 (the Martin mound). A small pit was found at Bt20 that contained charred corn cobs (Marquardt 1971:73, 80; Young 1962). Webb's surveys also located several other sites in and near the Big Bend designated "Mississippian": Bt1, 4, 14, 16, 23; McL6, 19, 20, 25. Schock and Langford (1979:76–77) note Mississippian stonebox cemeteries in Allen and Barren Counties, and Rolingson makes reference to the Corbin site, another stockaded village and mound site on the upper Green River (Rolingson 1967:418).

Bt1 and 29 (the Martin mound and camp), near Bt2 and 20, were excavated by the WPA but have not been published. According to the fieldnotes (Marquardt 1971:51–52, 71–72), Bt1 was an earth mound containing 28 burials, at least some of which were in sandstone slab graves. The pottery found at the site indicates that it was sporadically occupied by Woodland people, then served as a burial mound for the Mississippian folk of Bt2/20.

Rolingson concludes (1967:392) that the occupations of the pottery-making Woodland and Mississippian peoples on the Green River shell mound sites were not long or intensive, but that there is too much pottery to be a result of transient camping alone. Woodland and Mississippian people reoccupied the sites and probably added somewhat to the total deposit.

Schock reports a small, possibly Early Archaic site and a possibly Late Archaic/Early Woodland site in the Little Bend of Green River immediately west of the Big Bend (Schock 1984a and b).

Distribution of Projectile Point Types, Ceramics, and Other Cultural Materials at Bt5 and Oh13

Because there is still so little precision in the chronological framework for the Green River shell mound sites, it seems useful to include Rolingson's detailed data on point types and sherd distributions for the Carlston Annis and Bowles sites (Tables 5.2–4). These distributions indicate both Woodland and Mississippian activity at both sites.

Carlston Annis, Indian Knoll, Ward, Barrett, and Read form a cluster of sites distinguished from the other seven in Rolingson's sample by the large number of burials present and the number of burials with artifacts (Rolingson 1967:333). At most of the sites, Rolingson believes, the burials were clustered rather than scattered. For Bt5 she thinks the burials were more abundant to the south and west than to the north and east.

So little of Bowles was dug that burial distributional data are inadequate for any generalizations.

As for grave goods, "Carlston Annis, Barrett, Ward, and Indian Knoll have the greatest variability of artifact forms and the larger number of artifacts included in graves" (Rolingson 1967:339). Exotic shells at Carlston Annis and Indian Knoll include *Olivella*, *Marginella*, and conches (the latter found at a number of other Green River sites) (Rolingson 1967:342–43; Winters 1968:Table 3 and 215). These came from the Carolina or Florida coastal waters and had to be conveyed

TABLE 5.2*
TABULATION OF PROJECTILE POINT TYPES AT CARLSTON ANNIS (Bt5)

  2 fluted points.

  7 points belonging to an analytical unit defined by Rolingson which she calls "Cluster I." These are similar to Palmer Corner-Notched from the Hardaway site (Coe 1964), and hence probably Early Archaic in age.

  1 serrated-edged point with incurvate blade and convex base; a type similar to the Pine Tree Corner-Notched point of northern Alabama considered to be Early Archaic (Rolingson 1967: 131).

 60 points belonging to the Cluster II unit (lanceolate and fish-tail points) which may be Early Archaic (Rolingson 1967: 312).

  2 points of Cluster III, diagonally-notched specimens with heavy grinding of the base and haft element edges, probably Early Archaic in age (Rolingson 1967: 153).

 21 Cluster IV points, a side-notched type which is probably Late Archaic in time (Rolingson 1967: 313).

738 points of Cluster V with long, narrow blades and straight to subconvex stems; shoulders are sloping or contracting, or barbed. These points are thought by Rolingson not only to be Late Archaic but also to be especially characteristic of the Indian Knoll phase of the Green River Late Archaic (Rolingson 1967: 313). They are the predominant forms included with burials (Rolingson 1967: 281).

 83 contracting stemmed points, probably a Late Archaic type (Rolingson 1967: 222–223).

 86 broad bladed, shallowly side-notched points somewhat similar to Brewerton points (Late Archaic).

 39 Cluster VI points, another Brewerton-like form.

 27 Cluster VII points, stemmed and with thick, narrow blades somewhat like Lamoka stemmed and notched points (Rolingson 1967: 239); Late Archaic.

 20 Cluster VIII points; small, thin points with thin carefully finished haft elements, probably Late Archaic (Rolingson 1967: 313).

 15 points of 5 miscellaneous categories, possibly Late Archaic.

 64 contracting stemmed points, probably Early Woodland.

  7 Madison Triangular points (Mississippian).

1172 Total

*Data from Rolingson 1967: Table 1.

600 to 750 miles overland to reach the Middle Green River. Similarly, copper was imported from the Great Lakes area. A total of 13 to 16 artifacts and fragments were found in graves at Indian Knoll and Barrett, and in the midden at Carlston Annis (Rolingson 1967:344–45 and Winters 1968:Table 10; their respective tabulations differ somewhat from each other and from the figures in the University of Kentucky publications). Thus, it is clear that the shell mound people had

TABLE 5.3*
TABULATION OF PROJECTILE POINT TYPES AT BOWLES (OH13)

(For notes on time assignments of these types, see Table 5.2)
         2 points of Cluster II
         1 point of Cluster III
         4 points of Cluster IV
        67 points of Cluster V
         7 contracting-stemmed points
         2 points of Cluster VIII
         2 miscellaneous
         1 contracting-stemmed Early Woodland-like point

        ——

        86 Total

*Data from Rolingson 1967: Table 1.

TABLE 5.4
VERTICAL DISTRIBUTION OF SHERDS AT Bt5

| Pottery Type | Depth in Feet Below the Surface According to WPA Notes | | | | | | | | | | | Total |
	0.5	1.0	1.5	2.0	2.5	3.0	3.5	4.0	4.5	5.0	5.5	
Neeley's Ferry Plain	5	21	9			1						36
Bell Plain		1	4					1				6
Kimmswick Plain				1								1
McKee Island Cd. Mkd.		2										2
Subtotal	5	24	13	1		1		1				45
Rough River Plain		2	2									4
Rough R. Simple Stpd.		1								3		4
Baumer Cord Marked		1										1
Baytown Plain	3	4	2	2								11
Mulberry Creek Cd.Mkd.		3	3		1							7
Subtotal	3	11	7	2	1					3		27
Total	8	35	20	3	1	1		1		3		72

(Rolingson 1967:379)

rather far-flung trade connections (Goad 1978:90–105), and therefore provide a considerable contrast to the Late Archaic inhabitants of the Pomme de Terre Valley.

There are more than twice as many features recorded for Bt5 (a total of 118; Rolingson's count varies somewhat from Webb's in the Bt5 report, Webb 1950:271, where he presents a total of 129 features) in the WPA notes and publications than at any of the other Green River sites

(Rolingson 1967:Table 14, p. 348). Of these, 31 are "scattered burned rocks and refuse," and 34 are "compact concentrations of burned rocks and refuse." However, there is an unknown but perhaps very large error factor here with respect to WPA reportage because only 12 features were recorded for Indian Knoll, and that hardly seems credible.

Be that as it may, the recorded Carlston Annis features are nearly all of a sort most readily interpretable as resulting from or associated with food preparation (Rolingson 1967:347): prepared hearths, hearth areas, mussel-steaming locales, refuse pits. There were also 19 post molds, patterned in a rough parallelogram shape (but with post molds on only three sides) measuring about 12 × 15 feet. These were first noticed at a depth of about 4.4 feet below the surface and extended to 5.8 feet (Rolingson 1967:358), but it is unclear what they represent.

Chronology and Significance of the Early Cultigens

Our own excavation at Bt5 has been much more limited than that of the WPA, and we are still doing research on and about the mound. For purposes of this paper I can summarize our results as follows (see also the geological, botanical, and microstratigraphic analyses of Stein, Wagner, and Gorski in the references; a detailed comprehensive report is in preparation):

1) According to our ten radiocarbon determinations, the Bt5 deposits date between the late fourth millennium B.C. and the mid-first millennium B.C. If the UCLA 2117D date is ignored—one of the oldest samples according to absolute depth below the surface but by far the youngest determination—then the span is approximately from 3000 B.C. to 1500 B.C. Webb's five dates range from sixth millennium B.C. to latter third millennium B.C., but these are perhaps not reliable having been run so early in the history of the technique, and on solid carbon obtained from antler and shell.

As Table 5.1 indicates, only one occurrence of cucurbit remains comes from a directly dated level at Bt5: rind fragments from level 20 (over 2 m below the surface) in pit C1.

Given the present distribution of cucurbit proveniences and radiocarbon determinations, I think a conservative age assignment for the earliest squash rind at Bt5 is early third millennium B.C. At Bowles (Oh13), the rind fragments in A3, level 12, are dated 2110 B.C.±220, and there are more fragments in level 15 of A3, 30 cm or so below those in level 12. So both sites contain squash rind that certainly predates 1500 B.C. and almost certainly predates 2000 B.C.

2) Our investigation of shell mound formation processes is not com-

plete, but it is clear that Griffin's and Rolingson's suggestion (Rolingson 1967:32) is correct: Contrary to Webb's interpretation of the shell mound people as sedentary mussel gatherers, these sites represent relatively transitory, probably seasonal, occupations accumulated over hundreds of years. Thus, the deposit built up sporadically over a long time period (at least 1000 years for Bt5); and surely not in a straightforward vertical fashion but at least partially horizontally and probably often interleaving and mixing older with younger deposits. It follows that there are one or more components of the shell mound settlement system located elsewhere; these other components may include some of the so-called "dirt mounds" like the Barrett, Ward, and Kirkland sites, and probably also include rockshelters in the nearby uplands. We have begun looking for such upland shelters and have so far found only one, Peter Cave, that seems contemporaneous with the shell mound occupations.

In three important papers, Howard Winters has discussed the possible subsistence-settlement system that characterized the Green River Archaic (Winters 1968, 1969:131–37, 1974). He suggests that the Carlston Annis and Read sites functioned together in a single system, the "Read unit," (Winters 1968:176) as did Indian Knoll and Chiggerville, forming the "Chiggerville unit." There may well have been important relationships between Carlston Annis and the Read site.

The Read site is in the Little Bend of Green River about 2.5 miles straight line distance from Carlston Annis on the opposite side of the river; the river distance between the two sites is at least three times the straight line distance. Whether or not the two communities were contemporary is not known, however, because there are no radiocarbon determinations or other independent dates for Bt10, the Read site. But if Carlston Annis and Read were part of one system, then it is even more likely that Bt6 and/or Bt11 also participated in that system because they are much closer to Bt5 than is Bt10. Bt6 is about one mile north of Bt5, and Bt11 is about one mile south. However, once again, there are no radiocarbon determinations for either Bt6 or 11, so we cannot be certain how much either or both overlapped Bt5 and/or Bt10 in time.

The other difficulty one immediately faces in trying to evaluate Winters' proposition is the nature of recovery and reporting for the data he is using. Winters is aware of these problems, and his attempts to extract important information from the WPA excavations in spite of grave uncertainties are admirable. However, one must be extremely wary of coming to definite conclusions about subsistence activities that may have characterized the Green River sites solely on the basis of artifactual data obtained without the use of screens or flotation. More detailed study of each of these complex sites is necessary before we can test Winters' ideas and accept, modify, or reject them.

In any case, on the basis of the present evidence (not yet completely analyzed), I believe Bt5 to be a seasonal camp, probably occupied more or less yearly by a few dozen people for varying periods from early summer to late fall, an interpretation based on botanical and zoological data (Claassen 1983; Wagner 1979). These people were fishing and hunting, collecting mussels and hickory nuts, and they also buried their dead in the mound. The quantity of hickory nutshell is overwhelming. Its ubiquitous presence in the archaeological record at Bt5 and elsewhere may be partially because it was a superior fuel rather than being a direct reflection of food processing practices. Another likely explanation for the nature of the remains (rather well crushed shell fragments), however, is that the nuts were pounded up and thrown in water to make hickory nut butter or oil (Wagner 1979). Some of the shell fragments may have been carbonized during this process, but most of them probably wound up in the fire as fuel.

3) The squash was doubtless primarily used as a container, although we know from the Salts Cave fecal deposits that these Late Archaic/ Woodland cavers sometimes ate squash (and gourd) seeds.

Comparison of Plant Use at the Carlston Annis Shell Mound, Salts Cave, and Mammoth Cave

Radiocarbon determinations from the two caves indicate a use span beginning about 2000 B.C. and continuing for two millennia (Watson et al. 1969; Watson 1974:236–37). Five dated fecal specimens from Salts Cave contained the plant foods shown in Table 5.5.

These dates put the dietary complex represented in the feces into the Early Woodland horizon with some suggestion of Late Archaic overlap. Dates from Salts Cave Vestibule—where there is a sequence of charred plant remains including squash, gourd, sumpweed, sunflower, and chenopod derived from flotation—are difficult to interpret, but include three that are approximately mid-second millennium B.C. ± 100 to 200 years. The other two published dates are 710 B.C. ± 100 and 990 B.C. ± 120. In addition there are eight more as yet unpublished Salts Cave Vestibule dates obtained by Paul Gardner and Richard Yarnell from Beta Analytic. These range from 250 B.C. ± 60 to 570 B.C. ± 60. Hence, it appears that squash, gourd, sumpweed, sunflower, and chenopod were present in the Salts Cave region shortly after 1000 B.C. at the latest, and continued to be used in varying combinations at least to the beginning of the Christian era as indicated by the intestinal contents of the prehistoric Salts Cave and Mammoth

TABLE 5.5*
PLANT FOOD REMAINS IN SALTS CAVE FECAL SPECIMENS

Specimen No.	Remains of Plant Food	Date
SCM 1	sunflower sumpweed (marsh elder) chenopod hickory	M-1770 2660 ± 140 B.P. 710 B.C.
SCM 5	sunflower sumpweed (marsh elder) chenopod grape maygrass squash pollen	M-1577 2350 ± 140 B.P. 400 B.C.
SCU 38	squash sunflower sumpweed (marsh elder) chenopod grape hickory	M-1573 2240 ± 200 B.P. 290 B.C.
SCU 39	gourd sunflower sumpweed (marsh elder) chenopod sumac hickory maygrass	M-1574 2570 ± 140 B.P. 620 B.C.
SCU 105	sunflower sumpweed (marsh elder) chenopod hickory	M-1777 2270 ± 140 B.P. 320 B.C.

*Data from Yarnell 1969, Table 6.

Cave bodies. Little Al of Salts Cave (M–2259, A.D. 30 ± 160; M–2258, 10 B.C. ± 160; both dates on intestinal tissue) had eaten hickory nut, sumpweed, and chenopod (Yarnell 1974b:109), and Lost John of Mammoth Cave (SI 3007A, 445 ± 75 B.C.; SI 3007C, 15 B.C. ± 65; the older date on matting wrapped around the body, possibly contaminated by a hydrocarbon-based preservative, the younger one on intestinal tissue) contained sunflower, sumpweed, hickory, a few chenopod seeds, and one large *Polygonum* seed (Yarnell 1978:292; personal communication, 1976).

Prehistoric plant foods from Mammoth Cave (Bryant 1974; Marquardt 1974) are less well known than those in Salts Cave, but the pattern is certainly generally similar. However, Yarnell (1978:296) suggests that, on the basis of their size, the sunflower seeds N.C. Nelson recovered from Mammoth Cave Vestibule in his 1916 excavation are

Late Woodland in age (the Mammoth Cave Vestibule remains have usually been viewed as Late Archaic).

The diet abundantly represented in the human paleofeces from the caves is dominated by hickory nut and a series of seeds, some of which were from cultivated plants: sunflower, sumpweed, and chenopod. Squash and gourd seeds were occasionally eaten. Yarnell's percentages for the plant foods in 100 Salts Cave fecal samples are as follows (Yarnell 1974b:120, Table 16.5): squash and gourd seeds 3%; sunflower achenes 25%; sumpweed achenes 14% (making a total of 42% definite cultigens); chenopod seeds 25%; amaranth, knotweed, panic grass, pokeweed, purslane, and unidentified seeds 2%; maygrass 5%; blackberry, blueberry, viburnum, sumac, grape 1%; hazel nutshell 1%; acorn shell 2%; hickory nutshell 16%; rhizomes and tubers possibly 1%; and animal remains (insect parts, fish scales, mouse bones, etc.) possibly 5%. The Mammoth Cave fecal specimens analyzed by Stewart, reported in Marquardt (1974) present a similar picture, although the sample is smaller (27 specimens).

Evidence for use of squash and gourd by the Salts and Mammoth Cave aborigines also comes from fragments of these vessels left in the dry portions of the caves (Cutler in Yarnell 1969; Watson 1974; Wilson n.d.). Both species were obviously used as containers and were available in some quantity.

Role of the Early Cultigens in
Middle Green River Cultural History

Since the publication of the 1974 report (Watson, ed., 1974) we have conducted a number of surface surveys in various parts of Mammoth Cave National Park (Carstens 1974, 1980; Wagner 1978). Although there are many rockshelters containing prehistoric cultural debris, most of them postdate the Salts-Mammoth Cave use period on the basis of radiocarbon determinations plus diagnostic sherd and projectile point types (Carstens 1980), and so far, although there is no shortage of hickory nutshell fragments, have revealed no trace of cultigens, tropical or North American (Wagner 1978:67). It is possible that all of these shelters were special purpose sites, the best documented example being Blue Spring Hollow shelter which looks like a late fall nut gathering station. Perhaps the evidence for cultigens at such places might be less abundant than at base camps, but in spite of a very great deal of flotation, no seed remains of cultivated or possibly cultivated plants have been found there.

My own interpretation of this evidence so far is that some of the Middle-Late Woodland and Mississippian occupants of the Mammoth

Cave area rockshelters and cave entrances used some cultigens (Little Al and Lost John, both dating to the Middle Woodland range, between them contain sunflower, sumpweed, and chenopod as well as hickory), but these were not very important in their diets, or were important only seasonally or in special situations as when caving. They probably depended more on nuts and on the hunting of small mammals, amphibians, and fish for food than they did on sunflower, sumpweed, and chenopod. And they were using pottery instead of, or in addition to, squash and gourd vessels. These people did not spend much time in the caves, or if they did, they did not lose any pottery there, nor leave enough other debris to affect our dating framework on organic materials from the caves (Watson 1974: Fig. 31.1, p. 237).

On the other hand, their Early Woodland predecessors, who were probably the best cavers in the world, relied heavily on cultivated plants, at least while in the cave. Perhaps as indicated above, this heavy reliance on cultigens is simply the expression of the most appropriate food for carrying into the cave. However, regardless of how representative or nonrepresentative this diet is, the fact remains that the cultigens were available in the cave region (probably a backwoods area in so far as Late Archaic/Early Woodland communication lines were concerned) for such emphasis by at least 1000 B.C. There is, then, a crucial gap in our knowledge of plant use and cultigen development along the Green River: What happened between the Late Archaic hickory nut-and-squash of the shell mound area and the Early Woodland sunflower-sumpweed-chenopod and squash-gourd of the big caves? The crucial time period is the millennium after 2000 B.C. We may yet find material in or near Mammoth Cave National Park to help us understand where and how the native North American cultigens entered the picture, but at present we do not know.

As noted above, the Salts Cave–Mammoth Cave area, somewhat like the Phillips Spring region, was probably not in the mainstream of Late Archaic trade networks, but the shell mound sites—especially Indian Knoll and Carlston Annis—are usually thought to have occupied a pivotal position in those networks (Rolingson 1967:419ff; Winters 1968; Kay, King, and Robinson 1980; Goad 1978). Copper was coming into the Middle Green River sites[1] from the Great Lakes, and marine shells[2] were arriving from the south Atlantic coast. Interestingly enough, for both copper and shell nearly 50% of the items were apparently in the graves of infants and children (Winters 1968:202–04). It is possible that cave minerals from Salts and Mammoth were conveyed downstream to the Big Bend and were entered into this trade network, too, and that the spread of both tropical and native North American cultigens was tied to trade in other substances, but the whole picture is very unclear at the moment. Even if one uses the already documented trade in luxury goods as a mechanism to explain diffusion of cultigens through the Midwest and Midsouth, one is still left with the very early squash and gourd of Phillips Spring where there does not seem to be evidence of any luxury goods trade. On the other hand, squash at the Schultz site in Michigan by 500 B.C. (Ford 1974:401) seems perfectly acceptable; in fact, one might expect squash and gourd to be present in the Great Lakes area considerably earlier than that in the wake of the third millennium B.C. copper trade.

In summary, the impact of squash on the diet of the later Late Archaic/Early Woodland cavers farther upriver in the Mammoth Cave region was very slight. However, these latter folk, at least while in the cave, ate very different plant foods from those of the shell mound dwellers and were relying heavily on native North American cultigens at least by the first millennium B.C. (between 700 and 200 B.C.), and perhaps earlier. This dietary pattern apparently disappears with the cessation of intense use of the caves. Later inhabitants (Late Woodland and Mississippian) of the Mammoth Cave area rockshelters were probably eating much the same diet as the Late Archaic shell mound dwellers of the Middle Green River (Wagner 1978). Other than the reference to a pit full of charred corn cobs at Bt2, there are no available data on the plant foods of those Mississippian-related populations who built the Bt2/20 stockaded village and pyramidal mound complex, and who left the shell-tempered pottery on some of the Archaic shell mounds of the Middle Green River.

RED RIVER GORGE

Early cultigens have been reported from Cloudsplitter rockshelter (15Mf36) on the North Fork of the Red River, Menifee County, eastern Kentucky, in the Red River Gorge. The Red River joins the Kentucky River at Richmond, the Kentucky River in turn flows into the Ohio. Red River Gorge forms the northwestern corner of the Cumberland Plateau where it has created "a maze-like complex of valleys and ridges" (Wyss and Wyss 1977:6). The gorge, as the name indicates, is a narrow stream bed without expanses of bottomland. The change in elevation from ridgetop to river bottom averages 600 feet.

The plateau caprock is sandstone, and this outcrops as cliffs lining the valleys, isolating them from each other and from the uplands. Only where there are gaps in the cliff, or where the sandstone is tiered rather than sheer, is one able to climb from valley bottom to ridgetop. Thousands of rockshelters, formed by the sandstone cliff weathering into overhangs, are present in the gorge. Most of these are at least partially dry, and provide conditions of maximum preservation for ordinarily perishable remains: plants and plant parts, wooden and leather artifacts, etc.

Site Description and Context of the Early Cultigens

Cloudsplitter shelter was discovered during a survey of the North Fork of Red River for the Kentucky Heritage Commission (Cowan and Wilson 1977:13–18). It is a large sandstone overhang (about 40 m long by 4 to 5 m deep), facing west, and lying several hundred meters above the stream. The floor of the shelter is bounded on the front by a series of large breakdown blocks. As is so often the case in these rockshelters, the abundant breakdown, the action of the dripline, and the ubiquitous pits of looters make excavation very difficult. The stratification of the deposits is also quite complex. The basic situation is one of excavation in a series of discontinuous patches or pockets of deposit separated by breakdown or areas disturbed by vandals. Crossties between these patches or pockets are often impossible to make unless they contain diagnostic artifacts or can be radiocarbon dated.

On the present evidence it appears that the site contains deposits dating from 8000 B.C. to about A.D. 1200, but with numerous gaps in the sequence. The site appears to have been utilized most intensively during the Early Woodland period. A total of more than 80 features were recorded.

Analyses of the Cloudsplitter materials are presently underway and no final results are available. However, C. Wesley Cowan, the site supervisor, provides the following preliminary summary of the early cultigen situation there:

> On the basis of stratigraphy and currently available radiocarbon dates, presumably tropical cultigens make their first appearance in the Cloudsplitter deposits sometime prior to 1700 B.C. Squash rind has been recovered from a deposit immediately below a lens containing a Merom stemmed/Trimble side-notched point. A single radiocarbon date of 1178 ± 80 B.C. (UCLA 2313–K) is available for this deposit.
>
> Seeds from a small-fruited squash have also been recovered from a deposit superimposed over a thick layer of hemlock needles. The seeds were found adjacent to a small surface hearth lying directly on the hemlock needle layer. The hemlock needle layer has been radiocarbon dated to 7265 ± 290 B.C. (GX–5873); the hearth yielded a date of 7268 ± 100 B.C. (UCLA 2313–I). Obviously these dates are quite controversial, and additional samples from adjacent deposits are now being processed. It should be noted, however, that the seeds are similar in size and general appearance to the wild squash, *Cucurbita texana*, although Thomas Whitaker, who has examined them, has suggested they are probably from *C. pepo*.
>
> Remains of the Eastern North American cultigens (sumpweed, chenopod, sunflower, maygrass, and perhaps ragweed) are sparse to absent in the Cloudsplitter

deposits prior to 1000 B.C., but increase dramatically thereafter. A small pit feature dated to 841±60 B.C. (UCLA 2313–A) yielded squash, sumpweed, chenopod, sunflower, and maygrass, and by at least 400 B.C. Eastern Complex cultigens are present in abundance. [Personal communication from C. Wesley Cowan, 21 July 1980; radiocarbon determinations uncorrected]

Environment and Cultural History of the Red River Gorge

Dominant vegetation is distributed in three different ecozones in the gorge: ridgetops, slopes, and streambanks (Cowan 1975:2–6). An open oak-pine community grows on the ridge tops where one finds a variety of oaks including chestnut oak, with hickories also present.

The slope ecozone includes short slopes above the sandstone cliffs but below the ridgetops, and the longer, steeper slopes below the cliffs, the latter woodland being the more diverse. American beech, tulip poplar, basswood, sugar and red maple, eastern hemlock, and white pine are all found here. Before the chestnut blight of 1905, this tree was quite common below the cliffs. On the lower portions of the slopes are black walnut, butternut, and mockernut hickory, together with a variety of shrubs and many herbaceous plants.

The stream and riverbank communities share a number of species with the lower slope woodland, and add cottonwood, river birch, American hornbeam, hazel alder, black willow, American and slippery elm, and cane.

The fauna inhabiting these woodlands is basically similar to that of western Kentucky. Turkey and passenger pigeon were prominent among game birds, and a variety of fish and mussels, though not so diverse an array of the latter as in the Green River, were available in the river and its tributaries.

There is presently no clear evidence for Paleo-Indian occupation of Red River Gorge, but Kirk and LeCroy projectile points indicate the presence of Early Archaic people (Cowan 1976:121–24; Weinland and Sanders 1977:Fig. 3 and p. 28). The points were found by survey teams in bottomland or terrace sites and in one rockshelter. One LeCroy point has been found at Cloudsplitter as well as another early point similar to the Charleston Corner Notched type defined by Broyles at the St. Albans site; the point type is dated to about 7900 B.C.

Elsewhere in the gorge, Late Archaic projectile points are known from one bottomland, Po17; and two rockshelter sites, Mf132 and 139 (Cowan 1976:68–71, 126; Wyss and Wyss 1977:183–88, 194–95). Cowan believes there is probably Middle Archaic present, also, but the evidence is not very clear (Cowan 1976:124, 126; Weinland and Sanders 1977:85). Po17, the Seldon Skidmore site, may have been part of the settlement system of the Cloudsplitter folk.

Woodland use of the gorge is indicated by the presence of a series of ceramic types as well as suspected Woodland projectile point types in bottomland and rockshelter sites (Cowan 1976:124–26; Wyss and Wyss 1977:Table 6, 229–31; Weinland and Sanders 1977:85). At the Seldon Skidmore bottomland site, limestone-tempered plainware sherds were found above Late Archaic materials, and Early Woodland sherds were also discovered at another bottomland site Po42, the Martin site (Cowan 1976:76–82, 127). Newt Kash Hollow shelter (Webb and Funkhouser 1936) is apparently Early Woodland, at least in part, according to the radiocarbon dates (Crane 1956; Cowan 1979:10); and Cloudsplitter has an extensive Early Woodland component, to judge from the radiocarbon dates and the nature of many of the remains.

There is also some evidence for Middle Woodland occupation of rockshelter and bottomland sites in the Red River Gorge (Cowan 1976:128; Wyss and Wyss 1977:176, 178–80, 230). Cowan thinks bottomland site Po31 (the Anderson site) may have been a major Middle Woodland settlement; Po32, another but smaller bottomland site near Po31, yielded two Middle Woodland sherds; and the Wysses report at least three rockshelters with Middle Woodland pottery (Mf125, 127, and 129).

Late Woodland remains are known from several rockshelters, most notably Haystack rockshelter (Cowan 1976:82–113; 1979). Here a series of plant remains were found including several cultigens: squash, gourd, sunflower, sumpweed, chenopodium, and maygrass. Similar plant remains were recovered from another set of Late Woodland rockshelters—the Rogers shelters, Po26 and Po27—a few miles south of the Haystack shelter.

Cowan suspects, on the basis of ceramic evidence, that there is a transitional Late Woodland-Fort Ancient phase in the Red River valley. So far there is only one bottomland site where such a transitional phase is fairly clearly present: the Martin site, Po42. Probably transitional wares were found at several of the rockshelters excavated by Webb and Funkhouser in the 1920s and 1930s and located by the Wysses in the 1970s (Wyss and Wyss 1977), but the only such site with stratigraphic data is Hooton Hollow excavated by Haag and a number of other WPA supervisors in the summer of 1940 (Cowan 1976:129; Haag 1974:138–41).

The latest prehistoric period represented in the Red River valley is the Fort Ancient, characterized by shell-tempered pottery and small, stemless triangular projectile points. The diagnostic ceramics are found in both rockshelters and open sites (Wyss and Wyss 1977:35, and 229–31 with accompanying site descriptions; Weinland and Sanders 1977:Fig. 3 and p. 85). Cloudsplitter shelter contains Fort Ancient ceramics, and is said to exhibit at least a minor occupation as late as A.D. 1200.

Role of the Early Cultigens in Red River Gorge Cultural History

This region is the least well known of those discussed in the present paper. To a considerable degree this situation is a result of extensive vandalism rather than simply lack of survey and excavation. Hence, our ignorance is, to a certain extent, irremediable. However, there are more data on Late Woodland plant remains than in any of the other areas except the Tennessee sites. This information comes from four rockshelters: Haystack (Po47), Rogers (Po26 and 27), Cloudsplitter, and site Mf32 (Cowan 1979).

Although the Cloudsplitter data are still being analyzed, it is clear that squash is present in the Late Archaic, dated 4700 ± 250 B.P.; and there is certainly an Early Woodland cultigen complex dating to the early first millennium B.C. that includes squash, sunflower, and possibly sumpweed, chenopod, and giant ragweed. If the old radiocarbon dates (Crane 1956:2650 ± 300 B.P. and 2600 ± 300 B.P.) for Newt Kash Hollow (Mf1) are more or less correct, then at least some of the plant remains described by Jones (1936) are also Early Woodland in age. These include chenopod, sunflower, sumpweed, giant ragweed, maygrass, pawpaw, and honey locust as well as squash, gourd, and maize. Two squash seeds were found in Stratum II at the Sparks shelter in Johnson County, eastern Kentucky (Applegarth 1977). A radiocarbon date of 860 ± 70 B.C. was obtained from the top of Stratum II; if the context is secure, this is another instance of Early Woodland squash in eastern Kentucky. Hooton Hollow shelter, which may be in part Early Woodland, yielded sumpweed and maygrass (Cowan 1979), and, finally, in the Late Woodland Haystack and Rogers shelters, there are the remains of squash, gourd, sumpweed, sunflower, and maygrass. The latter is also present at a Fort Ancient rockshelter, Mf32 (Cowan 1979).

In other words, the present evidence from the Red River sites indicates continued dependence on both tropical and native cultigens in a manner quite different from the Mammoth Cave National Park region as we now know it. For the Big Bend of the Green River, paleoethnobotanical data are simply lacking from sites postdating the Late Archaic Indian Knoll phase. For the Pomme de Terre Valley, there is indication of Middle Woodland use of the tropical cultigens (at Phillips Spring and Boney Spring), although the use of the Eastern

Complex of cultigens is less well documented in the valley at the moment.

LITTLE TENNESSEE RIVER

Early cultigens have been reported from two sites in Monroe and Loudon Counties in eastern Tennessee, some 20 to 30 miles southwest of Knoxville on the Little Tennessee River within the Tellico Dam reservoir: Bacon Bend (40Mr25), and Iddins (40Ld38). The Bacon Bend site is several miles upstream from Iddins, above the junction of the Tellico River with the Little Tennessee; Iddins is only a short distance above the Tellico Dam site, which is where the Little Tennessee runs into the Tennessee. Both sites are deposits of midden and occupational debris stretching along the river terrace.

Cultigen Occurrence

Plant foods from these and related sites have been preliminarily reported in several places (Chapman 1973; Chapman and Shea 1977, 1981; Chapman 1978:96–97, 126–27) but analyses in progress may make this summary obsolete even as it is being written.

Both sites were found during a several-year long reconnaissance of the river terraces along the Little Tennessee. The Archaic period was a special focus of these surveys, which included backhoe testing to locate buried sites. In 1976 such backhoe testing at the Iddins site, previously located and assigned to the Early and Middle Woodland periods, revealed a buried Late Archaic midden referred to as Stratum III and some 350 by 75 feet in extent (Chapman 1978:96–97). There are three radiocarbon dates for Stratum III: GX–4705, 3655 ± 135 B.P.; GX–4706, 3205 ± 145 B.P.; UGa 1883, 3470 ± 75 B.P. Chapman and Shea (1981) report 129 fragments of squash from 24 features and 10 midden samples, plus two fragments of gourd rind, the latter from a feature dated to 1255 B.C. Other plant foods represented in the flotation samples from Iddins include hickory nut, acorn, walnut, chestnut, one wild rice seed, and one sunflower seed (wild size).

A series of flotation samples was analyzed for the Bacon Bend site from a buried Savannah River component (Late Archaic) ca. 2500–1800 B.C., 25 by 30 feet of which were excavated. The site also includes an Early Woodland occupation (Chapman 1978:126–27). Eighteen fragments of carbonized squash rind were found in the Late Archaic samples; three of these fragments came from a firepit dated 2440 ± 155 B.C. (Chapman and Shea 1981). Also present in the Late

Archaic archaeobotanical remains at Bacon Bend are charred fragments of hickory, acorn, walnut, canary grass, grape, chenopod, sumac, poke, and grass seeds, three of which are wild rice (Chapman and Shea 1981).

Other early cultigens, or possible cultigens, comprise: sumpweed in the Early Woodland levels (ca. 300 B.C. to A.D. 200) of three sites (Rose Island (40Mr44), Calloway Island (40Mr41), and Patrick (40Mr40); sunflower in the Early Woodland levels of the Patrick and Rose Island sites; *Chenopodium* in the Late Archaic horizon at Iddins (second millennium B.C.); and maygrass in the Savannah River Late Archaic (2500–1800 B.C.) at Bacon Bend. Following these initial appearances, these species are found throughout the Woodland periods and into the Mississippian horizons of the Little Tennessee River sites. The earliest evidence for domestic sunflower comes from Terminal Archaic (ca. 900 B.C.) strata at the Higgs site (40Lo45) in Loudon County, Tennessee. This site lay in the I–75 right-of-way on the north bank of the Tennessee River some 10 to 12 miles southwest of Lenoir City (McCollough and Faulkner 1973; Brewer 1973). One hundred ten carbonized sunflower seeds as well as 360 chenopod seeds and 60 fragments of acorn were recovered by flotation of a roasting pit or earth oven (Feature 11 in Structure I of Stratum IV; Brewer 1973:141–42)[3]. Early Woodland deposits (Stratum II) at the Higgs site yielded only hickory and walnut remains with two seeds of chenopod.

Environmental Setting

The Little Tennessee River drains parts of Tennessee, North Carolina, and a small portion of Georgia before it joins the Tennessee River at Lenoir City, Tennessee. The Bacon Bend and Iddins sites lie in the lower course of the Little Tennessee, after it emerges from the mountainous country to the east and flows through a fertile but narrow floodplain consisting of alluvial terraces. This general region is a part of the Ridge and Valley physiographic province, and is characterized by temperate, deciduous forest vegetation featuring an abundance of nut-bearing trees such as hickory, oak, and chestnut. The climate is humid mesothermal with precipitation averaging a little over 51 inches per year and temperatures ranging from 10° to 80°F.

Fauna was originally varied and abundant. Chapman (1975:218) mentions 37 species of game animals, 78 fish species, 58 species of amphibians and reptiles, 25 species of ducks and other waterbirds, 26 species of shore and wading birds, 102 resident and migrant predatory and song birds.

The Little Tennessee River valley was occupied from Paleo-Indian times to the historic period. The carrying capacity was high, and many human groups were using the local resources fairly intensively from the Early Archaic period on (Chapman 1975, 1977; Chapman and Shea 1977, 1981).

Site Contexts of the Early Cultigens, and Regional Cultural History

Neither Bacon Bend nor Iddins is yet published in sufficient detail to enable much discussion of site context. Apparently the remains all derive from flotation samples taken of features and general midden deposit.

Since 1970 Chapman has been carrying out research in the Little Tennessee valley on Archaic and later prehistoric occupations, beginning with excavation at the Icehouse Bottom site (Chapman 1973, 1977) for which only the Early and Middle Archaic materials have so far been published in detail (Chapman 1973, 1975, 1977, 1978). There are five other major Early Archaic sites in the Little Tennessee River valley: Bussell Island, Bacon Farm, Rose Island, Thirty Acre Island, and Calloway (Chapman 1978). These large sites were places of long-term occupation and are all in areas of maximum microenvironment and resource diversity (Chapman 1978:142). There are also smaller camps along the first terrace from Bacon Bend to the mouth of the Little Tennessee. These were perhaps hunting or other special purpose camps.

Early and Middle Archaic plant foods from the Little Tennessee River sites consist primarily of hickory nuts, acorns, and walnuts in varying proportions. There are also a few seeds of grape, sumac, amaranth, chenopod, poke, knotweed, honey locust (Chapman and Shea 1981: Tables 2 and 4).

Woodland and Mississippian plant remains from the Little Tennessee River sites are also dominated by nut remains, especially acorn and hickory but, as already noted, the cultigen and potential cultigen species (squash, gourd, sunflower, chenopod, and maygrass) are found throughout as are various wild seeds and fruits (Chapman and Shea 1981: Table 4). Maize is definitely present in the Middle Woodland component at Icehouse Bottom (Chapman and Shea 1981). Both eight- and twelve-rowed cobs were found in contexts dated to A.D. 439 ± 75 (weighted average of eight dates), this being one of the earliest well documented occurrences of maize in the Eastern Woodlands. Maize becomes much more abundant in Early Mississippian and later periods, but beans do not appear until Late Mississippian times. Only with increasing abundance of maize in the Early Mississippian do nuts decline in frequency.

Comparative data on the later time periods from the Duck River/ Normandy Reservoir area, about 150 miles west of the Little Tennessee's confluence with the Tennessee, are presented in the next section. Summary interpretive discussion is deferred until then.

DUCK RIVER/NORMANDY RESERVOIR AREA

The earliest cultigens presently reported are from the Jernigan II (40Cf37) site in Coffee County, about 50 miles south of Murfreesboro, on the upper Duck River in central Tennessee. Jernigan II is one of several hundred sites located and recorded by the University of Tennessee in a long-term attempt to mitigate effects of a dam across the upper Duck River at Normandy, Tennessee (Faulkner and McCollough 1973, 1974, 1977, 1978; McCollough and Faulkner 1976, 1978; Crites 1978a).

Cultigen Occurrence

Squash and gourd rind fragments were found at Jernigan II in flotation samples from Feature 54, a circular pit 2.95 × 3.00 × 3.27 feet deep, which was either a deep earth oven or a storage pit. The context is Late Archaic (Ledbetter phase; see p. 141 for the regional chronological sequence) with an estimated date of 1500–1200 B.C. The site is an accumulation of occupation debris, some two acres in extent, on the first terrace of the Duck River.

Environment

The Duck River is a tributary of the Tennessee River. The Normandy Reservoir portion of the upper Duck River lies in the Interior Low Plateaus physiographic province between the Cumberland Plateau and the Nashville Basin on what is known as the Eastern Highland Rim. The Duck River's headwaters are in the hilly eastern part of the Rim, the major tributary being the Little Duck River. Also tributary to the Duck from the south is Carroll Creek. Below its confluence with the Duck in the lower reservoir of the Normandy Dam area, there is a broad floodplain with bordering terraces where the Duck River flows into the Nashville Basin. Above the Carroll Creek/Duck River confluence is the upper reservoir where the river is held between steep walls lined by narrow floodplains and alluvial terraces.

There are four major topographic zones in the upper Duck River:

floodplain (T–0), older alluvial terraces (T–1 and T–2), valley slopes and bluffs, and uplands.

Mean annual temperature here ranges from 60°F for the Nashville Basin to 55°F for the Highland Rim. Average annual rainfall is a little over 54 inches with the greatest amounts falling in winter and spring.

The upper Duck lies in a transition zone between the western mesophytic (Nashville Basin) and the mixed mesophytic (Highland Rim) forest. Nut trees are present in each of these forest regions (oaks, hickory, chestnut, walnut, beech). The older alluvial terraces supported a dense deciduous forest that included nut trees (walnut, hickory, buckeye, beech, oak) and fruit trees (persimmon, pawpaw, mulberry), and other food-producing plants such as grape, jack-in-the-pulpit, raspberry/blackberry, greenbriar (edible tubers and green shoots). Valley slopes and bluffs again included a variety of nut trees (hickory, walnut, oak, butternut), fruit trees (persimmon, black cherry, serviceberry), and annuals (raspberry/blackberry, jack-in-the-pulpit) and vines (grape, greenbriar). Floodplain species such as sweetgum, maples, ash, willow, and sycamore grow in the bottomland near the river, as do herbaceous plants like giant ragweed, chenopod, and smartweed or knotweed.

The Normandy Reservoir is in the Carolinian biotic province, a region rich in fauna that includes at least 303 species of vertebrates excluding fish (25 amphibians, 45 reptiles, 166 birds, and 52 mammals)(Cleland 1966: Appendix G; McCollough and Faulkner 1973:34). Nearly all of these species are at least partially edible. There are numerous fish species in the river: bass, bluegill, crappie, suckers, catfish, buffalo, and gar, for instance. At least 54 molluscan species have been reported in the Duck River and there were possibly more in prehistoric times (Faulkner and McCollough 1973: Ch. I; Crites 1978a: Ch. II).

Site Descriptions and Cultural-Historical Context

Jernigan II "is the most intensively occupied open habitation site known to exist on the right bank of the Duck River in the extreme lower reservoir zone" (McCollough and Faulkner 1976:27). The two-acre site contains occupation material of the Early, Middle, and Terminal Archaic, as well as the Middle and Late Woodland periods (McCollough and Faulkner 1976:27). There are also two "shaft-and-chamber" graves belonging to the Mason phase (Late Woodland).

As Jernigan II illustrates in a microcosmic fashion, "cultural material from every major prehistoric period recognized in eastern North America has been found on sites in the Normandy Reservoir"

(Faulkner and McCollough 1973:412). An even better example is the site of Eoff I, one of the largest sites in the Normandy Reservoir (1500 × 1000 m). Eoff I is in a bend of the river opposite the mouth of Carroll Creek, a major tributary, and within the transitional zone between the upper and lower reservoir zones. Archaeobotanical remains were analyzed by Andrea Shea (Faulkner and McCollough 1977), and by Gary Crites (1978a). Although there are no cultivated species as early as the squash and gourd from Feature 54 at Jernigan II, there is a considerable variety and abundance of charred plant material spanning six occupational horizons (Ledbetter, Wade, McFarland, Owl Hollow, Mason, and Mississippian).

In the following discussion I summarize first the archaeological phases in the Normandy Reservoir, and then the archaeobotanical remains from seven sites for which detailed information is now available (Crites 1978a).

The earliest prehistoric period represented by occupational debris in Normandy Reservoir sites is Middle Archaic, although Faulkner and McCollough (1974:573–74; 1977:297) note the presence of Early Archaic projectile points (Kirk and bifurcated base types) at several sites. Middle Archaic (Morrow Mountain) activity is not nearly so well documented as Late Archaic (Ledbetter) and succeeding periods, however. Plant food remains from a Middle Archaic feature at the Eoff III site comprised primarily hickory nutshell with a little black walnut— no acorn, no herbaceous seeds. It appears that Early and Middle Archaic people occupied the T–0 seasonally, from late summer to early fall, but by Late Archaic times the local population was probably occupying the Eoff I site on T–1 through the winter: T–0 would be flooded in late winter/early spring. At any rate, there are deep cylindrical Late Archaic storage pits here which imply a longer term occupation than at Eoff III. There are also Ledbetter (Late Archaic) storage pits at the Banks I and Banks III sites, and Banks I revealed traces of a simple shelter (a semicrescentic array of post holes around a living floor) of a sort that was probably widespread in the Late Archaic of the Midsouth (Faulkner and McCollough 1974:201, 204–208).

In the next, or Wade phase, there is apparently an increase in population and the beginning of long distance trade resulting in importation of steatite and chert (Faulkner and McCollough 1974:576). The Early Woodland period is marked by the first appearance of pottery (quartz and limestone tempered, fabric marked), but is not well represented in the upper Duck valley (McCollough and Faulkner 1978:vi). The earlier of the two local Middle Woodland phases (McFarland) is better known. McFarland sites, although still fairly small, were more intensively occupied than those of the Wade phase (Faulkner and Mc-

Collough 1974:577), and are characterized by pole houses with interior cylindrical storage pits and outdoor earth ovens. Fabric-marked pottery is gradually replaced by check-stamped pottery during the McFarland phase.

During the Owl Hollow phase (late Middle Woodland) at least some sites (e.g., Banks III and Banks V) seem to have been permanently occupied by people living in large houses with interior earth ovens during the winter, and in smaller structures during the summer (Faulkner 1977). This change in settlement pattern to year-round occupation at some sites is thought to be correlated with increasing dependence on cultivated and domestic plants (Cobb 1978:199–200; Crites 1978b; Shea 1978). The pottery differs from that of the McFarland phase: fabric-marked pottery was not produced but stamped (particularly simple stamped) continues, although plain surfaced pottery predominates on some sites (Faulkner and McCollough 1974:578; Cobb 1978:199).

The Mason phase represents a Late Woodland component in the upper reservoir zone which is at least partly contemporaneous with the Banks Mississippian phase (Faulkner and McCollough 1978:51). The pottery is distinctive from Banks ware.

There is evidence at Banks V for intensive early Mississippian occupation characterized by shell-tempered pottery and at least one wall-trench structure. These Mississippian-related materials are referred to as the Banks phase, and appear primarily in the lower reservoir stretch of the river on the Banks V, Parks, and Eoff I sites (Chapman 1978). Shea (1978) analyzed plant remains from 29 Banks phase features at the Banks V site. Again, nuts predominate making up 93.7% of total plant foods (acorn, walnut, chestnut, hickory, with hickory comprising 89% of total plant food). Cob fragments, cupules, and kernels of maize were recovered from 14 features and make up 5.1% of total plant food remains. [14]C dates on these features range from A.D. 735 ± 145 to A.D. 1045 ± 90 (Shea 1978:628). Twenty cobs are represented (details by Hugh Cutler) with 35% 8-rowed, 30% 10- and 12-rowed, 5% 14-rowed. Median row number is 10.1, medial cupule width is 7.1 mm. The 8-rowed samples are Eastern Complex or Northern Flint; the 12–14-rowed is probably tropical flint or popcorn type. Also present in one feature was a squash peduncle fragment.

Other Banks phase plant remains include grape, pokeweed, chenopod, honey locust, persimmon, bedstraw, purslane, bulrush, burreed, asters, cowlily, bearsfoot (*Polymnia uvedalia*), *Polygonum*, clover, sumpweed (seed sizes = 4.0 × 3.0 mm, 3.5 × 2.0 mm, 3.0 × 2.0 mm), sumac, spikerush (*Eleocharis*), beggar's lice, legume, morning glory, panic grass, *Prunus*, false Solomon's seal, and hackberry.

Shea notes striking similarities in Middle Woodland and Banks phases (the latter is early Mississippian) plant food remains (Shea 1978:631). She characterizes Middle Woodland subsistence as based on wild foods supplemented by incipient agriculture, and the Mississippian as based on intensive agriculture with wild foods as a supplement. However, in spite of the intensification of agriculture, wild plant foods were heavily utilized in early Mississippian times. Even the relative percentages of nut remains found in the two time periods are similar. Probably as an accident of sampling chestnut is present in the Mississippian rather than the beechnut as found in Middle Woodland contexts. A greater variety of plant foods is found among the Mississippian remains: 25 seed genera, 1 inflorescence type, and 6 fruit genera in Mississippian contexts vis-à-vis 12 seed genera, 1 inflorescence type, and 3 fruit genera in Middle Woodland contexts. There is no clear evidence that chenopod, sumpweed, or knotweed were cultivated. Shea suggests the diversity in plants used by the Mississippian occupants of the Banks V site may be explained by reference to local population increase at that time.

Robison's analysis of the Banks phase faunal remains at the Parks, Eoff I, and Banks V sites (Robison 1978:583–95) resulted in similar conclusions about the similarity between hunting patterns at these Mississippian sites and hunting patterns of earlier Archaic and Woodland groups. That is, even the introduction and fairly intense use of maize agriculture did not cause major changes in the types of animal species hunted. Deer, raccoon, fish, migratory waterfowl, turkey, beaver, possum, rabbit, turtle, dogs, squirrels, black bear, and elk were preferred meat foods of most Archaic to Mississippian peoples for whom evidence is available. A more detailed outline of plant use at seven sites with remains ranging in age from Late Archaic to Mississippian is a useful supplement to the general cultural-historical summary just provided. The discussion below is based upon data presented by Gary Crites in his M.A. thesis and in a published paper (Crites 1978a, b).

The archaeological phases variously represented at the sites are:

LOCAL PHASE NAME	GENERAL CULTURAL HORIZON	DATE
Banks	Mississippian	ca. A.D. 800–1350
Mason	Late Woodland	A.D. 600–1000
Owl Hollow	Late Middle Woodland	A.D. 200–600
McFarland	Early Middle Woodland	100 B.C.–A.D. 200
Long Branch	Late Early Woodland	ca. 200 B.C.
Rounded Base	Early Woodland	800–200 B.C.
Wade	Terminal Archaic	1200–800 B.C.
Ledbetter	Late Archaic	2500–1200 B.C.

The sites in question are:

NAME AND NUMBER	PHASES
Wiser-Stephens I, 40Cf81	Ledbetter, Wade, McFarland, Mason
Ewell III, 40Cf118	Ledbetter, Wade, McFarland, Mason
Jernigan II, 40Cf37	Ledbetter/Wade, Long Branch, McFarland, Mason
Banks III, 40Cf108	Ledbetter, Wade, Long Branch, Owl Hollow, Banks
Parks, 40Cf5	McFarland, Mason, Banks
Eoff I, 40Cf32	Ledbetter, Wade, McFarland, Owl Hollow, Mason, Banks
Banks V, 40Cf111	Ledbetter, Wade, Long Branch, McFarland, Owl Hollow, Mason, Banks

Plant remains of the Ledbetter and Wade (Late and Terminal Archaic) phases present a continuation of narrow-spectrum plant food use focused on nuts that began in the Early Archaic of the Eastern Woodlands. Hickory nuts predominate, but walnuts and acorns were also important. At the Jernigan II site, squash and gourd are present as well, but only as minor components.

Sites of the Long Branch (late Early Woodland) phase yielded quantities of nut remains but also some chenopod, knotweed, *Galium*, grape, and honey locust. Introduced cultigens comprise squash, probably gourd, and perhaps maize (from a Long Branch phase pit at Jernigan II, but one that was intruded by a McFarland phase feature).

The McFarland (early Middle Woodland) phase provides the first evidence in the upper Duck valley for the presence of native cultigens together with imported ones. Maize, sunflower, squash, and perhaps gourd are present at Ewell III, and squash, sunflower, and chenopod at Eoff I (Crites 1978a:63, 124). There is also continuing dependence on nuts. Late fifth century A.D. maize is present in Owl Hollow phase components of several sites in the upper Duck and Elk river valleys (Crites 1978b).

Plant food remains from the Middle Woodland components at the Banks V site were identified by Andrea Brewer Shea (1978) with both McFarland and Owl Hollow phases considered together, and more recently by Gary Crites (1978a:149–74) with McFarland and Owl Hollow phases distinguished. Nut remains make up over 90% of the total. Other plant foods represented include honey locust, flowerheads of asters, grape, grass seeds, chenopod, bedstraw, persimmon, squash (from three different features with radiocarbon dates of A.D. 395 ± 70, A.D. 455 ± 65, and 90 B.C. ± 95, respectively), pokeweed, purslane, bulrush, burreed, evening primrose, cow lily. Maize kernel and cob fragments were also found in several features, although for some of these the possibility of intrusion from the Mississippian occupation of Banks V must be seriously considered (Shea 1978:617).

Use of squash and maize increases in the Owl Hollow phase, seemingly at the expense of the semicultivated or cultivated weed seeds, e.g., goosefoot (chenopod) and maygrass, and with continuing use of nuts. However, the weed seed picture is different for the Owl Hollow phase in nearby Elk River Valley and at Thompson Creek, a tributary of the Duck River:

> Hundreds of goosefoot and maygrass seeds were found in association with squash and maize remains in the Elk Valley and Thompson Creek samples, indicating that an increasing reliance upon cultigens, particularly maize, did not halt the exploitation of locally abundant herbaceous plants in those areas. [Crites 1978a:198; see also Crites 1978b]

Crites goes on to conclude that the lack of weed seeds in the Owl Hollow levels of his upper Duck River site sample is probably an accident of sampling: plant remains from this phase in the Duck River sites came almost exclusively from roasting pits or earth ovens rather than storage pits which were the sources of the Elk Valley/Thompson Creek samples. One of the Elk Valley sites, the type-site for the Owl Hollow phase (site 40Fr7), has also yielded several sunflower seeds and achenes (Crites 1978a:110 and 1978b; Cobb and Shea 1977).

The Mason phase also reveals few weed seeds, but there is squash present. At the Mason phase type site (40Fr8) in Franklin County in the upper Elk River valley, one sunflower seed has been found in the Mason levels, and it seems to have come from a cultivated plant (Crites 1978a:110).

The Banks phase sites show the most diverse plant food spectrum in the Normandy sequence. The tropical cultigens squash and maize were very important, especially maize, but nuts were still being used as well as weed seeds (chenopod, poke, sumpweed, knotweed, purslane)—although none is present in any quantity—and fruits (grape, plum or cherry, persimmon). An even clearer picture of Mississippian plant use is supplied by the Duck's Nest site (Kline and Crites 1979), some 25 to 30 miles northeast of Normandy, but this is a small site, not entirely comparable to the larger sites in the river valleys). Nuts made up somewhat more than 95% of the total plant food quantity from feature and midden flotation samples with hickory, walnut, and butternut predominating. Also present were several hundred seeds of goosefoot, knotweed, and maygrass, respectively, a few seeds of sumpweed, grape, and *Rubus*, as well as fragments of squash and maize. The authors think the sumpweed was probably domesticated.

Thus, there is beginning to be sufficient archaeobotanical data from the Normandy Reservoir to enable one to see major trends in plant use through time. This is also true of the Little Tennessee region where there is documentation of plant foods from the Early Archaic to the early historic periods.

Two tropical cultigens, squash and gourd, are added in Late Archaic times to an old acorn and hickory nut-centered subsistence pattern (which goes back to at least the Early Archaic in both Normandy and Little Tennessee river valleys).

As in the Green River region, it is unlikely that the cucurbits played any very important dietary role at first. Although the seeds, expecially squash, are nutritious, the primary function of the fruits was probably as containers, and perhaps also as rattles. However, by Early Woodland times in the Little Tennessee River valley (3000 to 2000 B.P.), some members of the Eastern Complex, notably sunflower and sumpweed, were apparently beginning to be grown. Chenopod and maygrass appear even earlier—4000 to 3000 B.P.—but their cultigen status is uncertain.

Early Woodland plant remains in the Duck River valley are less well known, but by Middle Woodland times Eastern Complex plants are definitely present (sunflower, maygrass, chenopod; there is apparently little evidence for domestic sumpweed prior to the Mississippian period) as well as maize and squash. Plant use in general in the Mississippian was apparently quite intense in the Duck River valley, including nut collecting and reliance on a variety of other wild species as well as cultivation of the plants noted above.

In the lower Little Tennessee River valley, *Cucurbita pepo* appears first in the mid-third millennium B.C. followed by gourd before 1000 B.C. Sunflower and sumpweed are added in the first millennium B.C., then maize about A.D. 400 with beans finally evident approximately 800 years ago. A record of increasing diversity and abundance of these cultigens is paralleled by increase in other plant species characteristic of disturbed ground.

CONCLUSIONS

A thumbnail summary of the role cultigens played in the five areas discussed in this paper might run as follows: We have virtually no post–Late Archaic data for the Middle Green River, but Woodland and Mississippian cultural developments seem quite skimpy. For the Mammoth Cave area there is no evidence so far, perhaps because of sampling error, that the cultigens so well documented in the big caves during the Late Archaic/Early Woodland period were much used in later Woodland to Mississippian times. The Red and Pomme de Terre regions seem to show a pattern of a rather provincial or "backwoods" kind of cultural development that includes cultigens but does not so far give the impression of either horticultural intensification or cultural intensification on a horticultural base.

In the Tennessee river valleys, on the other hand, the situation as presently known contrasts with the others. This contrast may be partly a result of the considerable difference in the nature of available evidence. In any case, the stream valleys of southern Tennessee appear to have been population centers from Archaic times on, and there may have been a population peak along the Duck River in the Early Woodland period (Dickson 1979) which more or less coincides with the beginnings of horticultural intensification there. Increased emphasis on horticulture is thought to have enabled the sedentariness seen as characterizing Owl Hollow phase (later Middle Woodland) settlements in contrast to earlier, seasonal settlements. Shea (1978) stresses the diversity of Banks phase (Mississippian) subsistence, which might have been necessitated by continued population pressure. At any rate, use of both wild plants and wild animals seems to have been fairly intense, even though maize and squash were being cultivated in some abundance.

In the lower Little Tennessee River valley, a shift from temporary to semipermanent settlement in Late Archaic to Early Woodland times was followed by the appearance of permanent villages by 2000 B.P. Land clearance and cultivation, especially on the lower terraces, were apparently sufficient to cause major alterations in the local vegetation patterns reflecting rather intense use of these terraces which, in turn, must mean local increase in population density (Chapman et al. 1982).

In sum, although the role played by early horticulture in the Tennessee river valleys is not yet completely defined, it is clear that that role was a much more important one than in the other areas.

In all five of the regions discussed in this paper—and also in the lower Illinois Valley (Conard et al. 1984; Asch and Asch, this volume) the first cultivated plants are non-native species probably valued more as containers (and as rattles?) than as food: gourd-like squash (a variety of *Cucurbita pepo*) and true gourd (*Lagenaria siceraria*). Later, probably between 2000 and 1500 B.C., the exotic cultigens are combined with local, north-of-the-Border cultigens in regionally distinct horticultural complexes whose origins are as yet obscure, but which do not appear to be indigenous to any of the five river drainages discussed in this paper. Nor in any of the five does the initial impact of the earliest squash-gourd horticulture seem to be very great. In three of the five regions, introduction of the post–2000 B.C. horticultural complex does not seem to have resulted from nor to have stimulated developments toward significant cultural complexity, but in the Duck and

Little Tennessee river drainages permanently nucleated settlement beginning in Middle Woodland times was seemingly enabled by the combined exotic and native cultigen complex added to the use of wild plant and animal species.

Why was there this difference in horticultural impact among the five study areas? Perhaps because the carrying capacity for human hunter-gatherers and the horticultural potential of the alluvial terraces along the Duck and Little Tennessee were significantly greater than those of the Pomme de Terre, the Middle Green River, or Red River Gorge. Dickson notes that the Duck River drainage and middle Tennessee in general are optimal areas even now (Dickson 1979:114). Certainly human population seems to have been denser in the Tennessee areas than in any of the other three at all prehistoric time periods.

There is now clear evidence that gourd-like squash was being grown in the lower Illinois River valley by 7000 B.P. (Conard et al. 1984; Asch and Asch, this volume). This is far earlier than the evidence for cultigens at any of the sites or regions discussed in this paper. However, the combined horticultural complex (squash and gourd, plus varying combinations of the eastern United States species: sumpweed, sunflower, maygrass, chenopod, knotweed) is not well evidenced in the lower Illinois River areas until Middle Woodland times, approximately 2000 B.P. Yet the combined complex is documented in Early Woodland contexts by approximately 3000 B.P. in the Green River, Red River, and Little Tennessee River regions. It is apparently this combined horticultural complex, together with significant dependence on wild plants and animals that formed the economic basis for Woodland societies throughout much of the eastern United States (including the impressive Adena and Hopewell developments). Maize does not seem to have been important until Mississippian/Fort Ancient times anywhere for which there is good evidence, and even nuts, other wild plant foods, and hunting were still highly significant subsistence activities (Bender et al. 1981; Broida 1983; Chapman and Shea 1981; Johannessen 1982, 1984; Shea 1978; Wagner 1983; Wymer 1983).

On the basis of the data from the lower Illinois River valley one might suggest that squashes and gourds were grown in the principal river valleys of the Midwest and Midsouth (the Mississippi, the Ohio, the Illinois, the Tennessee, etc.) and their major tributaries long before these plants were cultivated in the upland regions described here. But it is not clear from the present evidence whether the combined horticultural complex just referred to (which was much more important dietarily) was developed first in those principal river valleys or in the hilly lands above them. It is quite possible that the process occurred in both places at various times in various ways. In any case, it is abundantly obvious that the issue of horticultural origins in the East is a highly complex one, and that local patterns of plant use must have produced a rich and intricately varied mosaic across the whole expanse of the Eastern Woodlands from Early Archaic to Contact times.

ACKNOWLEDGMENTS

Several people aided me very generously in assembling the bibliography for this chapter, and in obtaining—and permitting me to refer to—unpublished material: Leonard Blake, Kenneth Carstens, Jefferson Chapman, Wesley Cowan, Gary Crites, David Dye, Charles Faulkner, Marvin Kay, Frances King, Major McCollough, William Marquardt, Alan May, Patricia O'Brien, Jack Schock, Ann Tippitt, Gail Wagner, and Richard Yarnell. I am deeply grateful to all of them. In addition, I am indebted to David Browman, Gary Crites, Charles Faulkner, William Marquardt, and Gail Wagner for thoughtful comments and suggestions about revision of the preliminary manuscript, and to Mary Kennedy for typing, cutting-and-pasting, and photocopying the revised draft for submission to the Press.

Finally, I wish to acknowledge the deep debt of gratitude I owe, as do all members of the Shell Mound Archeological Project, to the wonderfully kind and hospitable inhabitants of the Big Bend in and around Logansport, Kentucky. Without their interest and help we could not have carried out our work at the shell mounds and in the surrounding area. We are especially thankful to the owners of Bt5, Bt11, and Oh13 for permitting and aiding our investigations at those sites: Mr. and Mrs. Waldemar Annis, who have also greatly facilitated our study of their shell mound, Bt5, by providing us with a fine fieldhouse; Dr. Marvin W. Russell; and Mr. Shelton Brown. We are particularly grateful to Mr. John L. Thomas of Logansport for enthusiastic and invaluable assistance in every aspect of our work.

NOTES

1. Only 13 copper items have been found according to Winters' summary of the published data (Winters 1968:Table 10): 6 copper items from Indian Knoll, 5 from Barrett, 2 from Carlston Annis. But, as already noted, Rolingson's count (1967:344–45) is slightly different: 8 copper items from Indian Knoll graves, 4 from Barrett graves, and 4 items found in "village midden" (site not specified).

2. Present at several dozen graves at the sites of Barrett, Carlston Annis, Read, Chiggerville, Indian Knoll, Ward, and Kirkland (Winters 1968:Table 4).

3. Yarnell (1976:269–70) notes a single sunflower seed possibly from a domesticated plant in a late second millennium B.C. context at the Riverton site (on the Wabash River in Illinois); and also a single carbonized sunflower seed from a Terminal Archaic feature at the Westmoreland-Barber site in eastern Tennessee. Finally, Crawford (1978) reports a possible sunflower achene from level 7, trench C13, at the Carlston Annis site.

Prehistoric Plant Cultivation in West-Central Illinois[*]

David L. Asch and Nancy B. Asch
Center for American Archeology, Kampsville, Illinois

The aim of this paper is to provide an outline of prehistoric horticultural development in west-central Illinois. Specifically, the paper will detail evidence from which the cultivation of 11 plants has been recognized in this region and it will set the course of cultivation and domestication into a chronological framework.

As we use the term, *cultivation* will refer to deliberate human encouragement of the reproduction of a plant species. This could include the sowing of seed or tilling to extend the area of a perennial root crop. It will exclude activities such as tending nut trees to increase canopy development and the size of the mast. Also excluded are relationships with weedy species which thrive in areas of human disturbance and which are utilized but not intentionally propagated.

A dichotomization of *gathering* and *food production*, as Ford points out (this volume), tends to disguise the existence of a continuum in human-plant relationships that ranges from a parasitic gathering to toleration, to encouragement, and to progressively greater control of a plant's life cycle and biology. Nevertheless, cultivation, as we define it, can be a critical juncture in the management of a plant resource—the point at which local productivity of the plant can be greatly extended,

---

[*]Archeobotanical Laboratory, Center for American Archaeology, Report No. 67.

at which the plant can be propagated beyond its natural range, and at which genetic modifications are more likely to accumulate that further increase the plant's usefulness. It is such changes which tend to make cultivation more readily recognizable in an archaeological record than other forms of management.

One other terminological distinction is that *domestication* here refers to genetic changes that occur in plants under cultivation, either through deliberate human selection or through unintended adaptations of the plant to the human-manipulated environment. If effects of domestication are not perceptible, then we may speak of the cultivation of a wild-type plant.

How can cultivation be recognized prehistorically? Three strong kinds of evidence include:

1) Recognition of morphological changes in the prehistoric material that are a consequence of domestication.

2) Recognition of a change in the plant's geographic range as a consequence of its introduction beyond the region in which it occurs naturally.

3) Recognition of a level of utilization that could not have been sustained by gathering from natural stands alone.

Such kinds of evidence are not infallible indicators of cultivation, as there are usually alternative possibilities which might account for the observed record. As one example, Heiser (1954) has suggested that when people entered the New World, the wild common sunflower, *Helianthus annuus*, became a weedy campfollower that moved with man from its western range into the East. Part of that journey, at least, could have occurred without saving and sowing of seed. Also, Heiser suggests that new forms of common sunflower evolved as the plant became adapted to new niches created by human disturbance and as the eastern sunflower became genetically isolated from western populations. Many of these changes, undoubtedly, were not dependent on cultivation.

Besides the stronger types of evidence, archaeologists have employed a number of weaker arguments to support the plausibility of cultivation:

1) A plant has economic potential—that is, it is worthy of cultivation.

2) A plant has attributes that make it relatively simple to bring under human propagation.

3) In other regions the same species, a biologically related species, or an economically comparable species has been cultivated, thus demonstrating the feasibility of the undertaking.

4) The plant occurs in prehistoric association with other cultivated species, so that its cultivation need not be established as a special case.

5) There is ethnohistoric evidence from the region of investigation for the plant's cultivation.

6) An increase in abundance in the archaeological record suggests a change in the plant's prehistoric economic status, perhaps because of its cultivation.

7) Increases in sociocultural complexity and growth of population either required or reflect an agricultural basis of support.

The present paper deals primarily with the stronger forms of evidence for prehistoric cultivation. The aim of such a conservative approach is to provide inferences that may be used with a degree of confidence in developing cultural historical arguments. We do not intend, however, to denigrate informed but speculative approaches, for they serve different functions. Since early horticulture is likely to be scarcely differentiable archaeologically from wild gathering, a more venturesome evaluation can direct attention toward occasionally rewarding, if often unprofitable, new lines of research.

The Region

The west-central Illinois region, as defined here, is the research universe within which the Center for American Archeology and its predecessor has concentrated most of its research efforts during the past 25 years. Basically, this region consists of the lowermost 70 miles of the Illinois Valley, the adjacent Mississippi Valley, and the local tributaries to the Illinois and Mississippi rivers.

The beginning of archaeobotanical research in this region dated, effectively, to the development by Struever (1968a) of a practical system for large-scale, systematic recovery of carbonized plant remains: the water and chemical flotation system. Over the past 25 years a very large archaeobotanical data base has accumulated for this region with information spanning virtually the entire period between 6700 B.C. and A.D. 1300.*

Data contributing to the present paper have been gleaned from excavations, large and small, conducted at dozens of sites. Sites mentioned specifically in the text are shown on the locator map (Fig. 6.1). The excavation/research directors for sites that have contributed critical and/or large archaeobotanical data sets are listed in the acknowledgments at the end of this chapter, but space limitations unfortunately do not permit citation of all whose collaboration has made this summary paper possible.

---

*B.C./A.D. dates and B.P. ages cited in this paper are based on the Libby half-life for radiocarbon and are not calibrated for fluctuation in atmospheric ^{14}C.

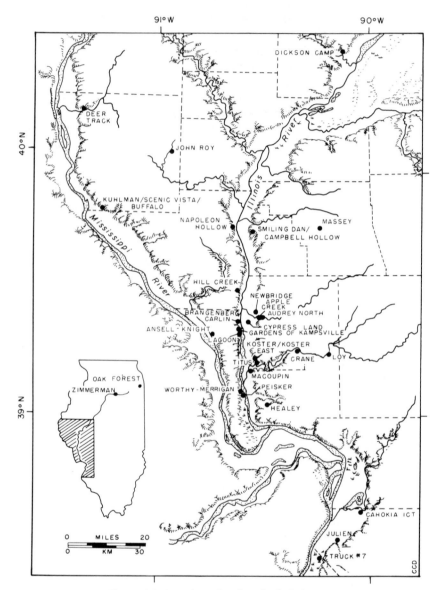

Figure 6.1. Location of archaeological sites.

TABLE 6.1
SQUASH FROM ARCHAIC CULTURAL CONTEXTS

Site/Component	No. Samples with Rind	Associated Radiocarbon Dates
Koster		
Horizon 8B	3	7100 ± 300 B.P.: 5150 B.C. (NSRL-298)[a]
		7000 ± 80 B.P.: 5050 B.C. (ISGS-809)
		6960 ± 80 B.P.: 5010 B.C. (ISGS-848)
		6910 ± 100 B.P.: 4960 B.C. (ISGS-1082)
Horizon 8A	1	6860 ± 80 B.P.: 4910 B.C. (ISGS-835)
Napoleon Hollow		
Lower Middle Archaic component	3	7000 ± 250 B.P.: 5050 B.C. (NSRL-299)[a]
		6800 ± 80 B.P.: 4850 B.C. (ISGS-817)
		6730 ± 70 B.P.: 4780 B.C. (ISGS-937)
		6630 ± 100 B.P.: 4680 B.C. (ISGS-786)[b]
Upper Middle Archaic component	2[c]	6130 ± 110 B.P.: 4180 B.C. (ISGS-909)
		6080 ± 90 B.P.: 4130 B.C. (ISGS-972)
		5670 ± 90 B.P.: 3720 B.C. (ISGS-806)
		5350 ± 70 B.P.: 3400 B.C. (ISGS-938)[b]
		5280 ± 70 B.P.: 3350 B.C. (ISGS-1038)
		5140 ± 70 B.P.: 3190 B.C. (ISGS-1036)
Titterington component	1	4060 ± 75 B.P.: 2110 B.C. (ISGS-823)[b]
		3920 ± 90 B.P.: 1970 B.C. (ISGS-933)
Lagoon		
Titterington component	1	4300 ± 600 B.P.: 2350 B.C. (NSRL-303)[a]
		4030 ± 75 B.P.: 2080 B.C. (ISGS-804)
		4010 ± 150 B.P.: 2060 B.C. (ISGS-798)
Kuhlman		
Titterington component	1	4010 ± 130 B.P.: 2060 B.C. (ISGS-982)[b]

[a]Accelerator date obtained directly on squash rind.
[b]Date is on dispersed charcoal from same cultural feature in which rind was identified.
[c]One sample is a midden context which could possibly include admixture with the lower Middle Archaic component.

Cucurbita pepo, Squash

The first plant to have been cultivated in eastern North America was a cucurbit, probably a variety of pepo squash, *Cucurbita pepo*. We shall refer to the early archaeological material as a squash, although if one makes the distinction of common usage between *squash* for cucurbits having an edible fleshy rind and *gourd* for cucurbits with inedible, hard-shelled fruits, then probably the early material was more gourd-like than squash-like.

The oldest squash remains found in eastern North America are from west-central Illinois (Conard et al. 1984). Squash rind dating to between 7000 and 4000 years ago has now been recorded for seven archaeological components at four sites in the region (Table 6.1). The oldest material from Koster and Napoleon Hollow sites dates to about 5000 B.P. Koster (Brown and Vierra 1983) and Napoleon Hollow (Wiant, Hajic, and Styles 1983) are habitation sites that were occupied repeatedly during the Holocene. Situated on colluvial fans of redeposited loess, these sites have well marked stratigraphies that are substantiated by numerous radiocarbon dates.

At Koster, rind fragments have been identified from cultural Horizons 8B and 8A from four midden excavation units. These occupations, which are sealed from more recent occupation by overlying zones of sterile colluvium, lie 3½–4 m below the surface. The quantities of squash recovered are very small. From 516 g of Horizon 8B charcoal, seven squash rind fragments weighing 27 mg were identified in just 3 of 239 flotation samples. The date of 5150 B.C. listed in Table 6.1 is an accelerator radiocarbon date on a Horizon 8B rind fragment (Conard et al. 1984). The other dates listed for Koster were determined by conventional β–decay methods and are from cultural Horizons 8B and 8A but not from the particular excavation units that yielded the squash.

At Napoleon Hollow, squash rind has been identified in each of three stratigraphically distinct Archaic occupation units on a colluvial slope. The oldest squash came from three levels in a 2-meter-square excavation unit from the older of two Middle Archaic components. Accelerator radiocarbon dating of one of these fragments, recovered 2.6 m beneath the surface, gave a date of 5050 B.C., which is a little earlier than the range of 4850–4680 B.C. obtained from β–decay dates for charcoal from this component (Conard et al. 1984).

Rind fragments were identified from two contexts associated with the younger Middle Archaic component at Napoleon Hollow. One was from a midden context in a location where there was possible admixture with the older Middle Archaic component. The other rind fragment was recovered from a pit feature containing charcoal dated at 3400 B.C. Six β–decay radiocarbon dates on charcoal from the younger Middle Archaic component range from 4180 B.C. to 3190 B.C. A single rind fragment was present in a Late Archaic Titterington phase pit at Napoleon Hollow, from which a radiocarbon date of 2110 B.C. has been obtained.

Two other sites in west-central Illinois have yielded squash from Titterington Archaic contexts: Lagoon (Cook n.d.) and Kuhlman (Farnsworth and Walthall 1983). Lagoon has six rind fragments from two levels in a shallow pit truncated by plowing. Occurrence of a Sedalia point within the pit supported attribution of the squash to the site's dominant Titterington occupation. This was confirmed by an accelerator date on the squash of 2350 B.C. ± 600 (Conard et al. 1984). β–decay dates, which were obtained from dispersed charcoal in other pits, suggest that the occupation actually occurred at about 4000 B.P. They have smaller standard deviations than the accelerator date.

The Kuhlman site, located on a blufftop overlooking the Mississippi Valley, had surface occupations by a Titterington Archaic group and by Late Woodland groups. Squash rind was identified in a flotation sample from a shallow Archaic pit feature truncated by plowing. The pit, which was a repository for 8 kg of chert manufacturing debris, contained three Wadlow/Sedalia blades. Nutshell from the flotation sample gave a date of 2060 B.C. Complicating the interpretation of cultural context was the presence of a single carbonized maize glume in the flotation sample from the pit—probably as a contaminant from the site's occupation by Late Woodland maize growers. Because of soil leaching, there was uncertainty in defining the limits of the pit. Squash rind was not common in flotation samples from Late Woodland contexts at Kuhlman; it was present in just 17 of 338 samples. While it remains plausible that Archaic squash was indeed present in the Archaic pit feature, accelerator dating of the rind fragments will be required for a certain determination of their age.

The squash rind fragments from Koster, Napoleon Hollow, Lagoon, and Kuhlman are all very small. Nevertheless, they are readily identified from their distinctive structure (Cutler and Whitaker 1961). Figure 6.2 illustrates one of the Koster site fragments. An important characteristic pointing toward placement of this material within the family Cucurbitaceae is the occurrence in the epidermis of tiny calcium carbonate-containing cells called cystoliths (Esau 1967). In carbonized archaeological specimens, these show up as white dots, or as small craters (lithocysts) if the cystoliths have dissolved or fallen out. To our knowledge, the only eastern North American plant materials which could conceivably be confused with cucurbit rind are carbonized fragments of *Nelumbo* (American lotus) tubers. However, *Nelumbo* tubers lack stone cells and lithocysts, and they have numerous vascular bundles; parenchyma cells of the tubers often are oriented radially with respect to the vascular bundles.

As Cutler and Whitaker (1961:479) have observed, cells of the inner rind of the squash genus *Cucurbita*, viewed in cross-section, are isodiametric; those of the bottle gourd genus *Lagenaria* are elongated. In *Cucurbita* these cells are somewhat regularly arranged; in *Lagenaria* they are loosely organized. The cross-sectional characteristics of the Archaic rind fragments indicate that the rinds can be ascribed to *Cucurbita*.

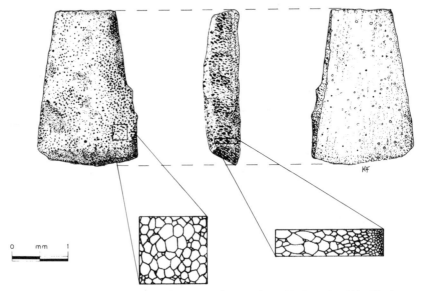

Figure 6.2. Rind fragment of squash, Koster site, Horizon 8B, Sq. 164–027. The inner surface, cross-section, and outer surface of the rind are illustrated from left to right.

On archaeological and biogeographical grounds, two species of *Cucurbita* are plausible candidates for attribution of this material: *C. foetidissima* (buffalo gourd) and *C. pepo* (pepo squash). Buffalo gourd is a wild plant which ranges into Missouri from Mexico and the Southwest (Bemis et al. 1978). Mohlenbrock (1978:278) maps a few modern records for this species in Illinois and describes its habitat in the state as being "along railroads." Following the common botanical opinion, Mohlenbrock regards the buffalo gourd as adventive east of the Mississippi River. Speculatively, the Hypsithermal climatic conditions of 7000 years ago might have favored a temporary eastward extension of this species' natural range.

The squash species that was cultivated prehistorically by Indians of the Midwest was *C. pepo*. Of special interest for comparison is the thin-shelled variety *C. pepo* var. *ovifera*, sometimes called yellow-flowered gourd, which is grown today as an ornamental.

One character which separates the archaeological rinds from *C. foetidissima* is thickness of the rind. *C. foetidissima* has a very thin shell. We measured 11 modern buffalo gourd fruits from seven localities in Kansas, Texas, New Mexico, and Arizona. The rinds were generally 0.4–0.7 mm thick, with a range of 0.15–0.9 mm. The stated range takes into account the variability over all part of the fruit except where the peduncle and corolla attach.

For *C. pepo* var. *ovifera*, we determined rind thickness for 24 fruits from two self-propagating stands of the plant in the lower Illinois Valley and from fruits present in the river's flood drift. They were most often 1.0–1.2 mm thick with a range of 0.5–1.8mm, the range being determined in the same manner as for buffalo gourd. For uncarbonized *C. pepo* rind from Phillips Spring, southwest Missouri, F. King (this volume) determined a range in thickness of 0.6–1.8 mm. These rinds, which date to about 2300 B.C., could be ascribed to *C. pepo* at Phillips Spring because they were associated with small seeds of *C. pepo*.

Rind thickness of the Koster *Cucurbita* and the oldest Napoleon Hollow *Cucurbita* ranged between 0.5 mm and 1.7 mm, with a median of 0.9 mm. If one makes an allowance for shrinkage due to carbonization, the difference with respect to *C. foetidissima* is even greater. Thus, it is concluded that the Archaic squash rind from west-central Illinois is *C. pepo*.

Pepo squash probably was introduced from Mexico or southeast Texas in a form much resembling var. *ovifera* (Cutler and Whitaker 1961:477–78; F. King, this volume; Heiser, this volume). The thin flesh of the early squash would have had little value as food, and perhaps selection had not yet eliminated the bitterness of the wild fruits (Whitaker and Bemis 1975). The seeds would have been edible, but the plant's technological value (as containers, net floats, etc.) may have exceeded its importance as food, as Munson's (1973) etymological study of Indian names for squash would suggest.

C. pepo, especially var. *ovifera*, has a pronounced capacity for self-propagation. Today var. *ovifera* is sometimes found on disturbed soils along streams in Illinois (Mohlenbrock 1978:281). We have noted that the fruits are common in flood drift along the Illinois River, and it is a very abundant weed of some floodplain fields of the Illinois Valley. It is necessary, therefore, to consider possibilities that (1) var. *ovifera* actually is indigenous to the region or that, (2) if introduced, it persisted without cultivation.

Establishment of *C. pepo* var. *ovifera* as a floodplain weed in Illinois apparently is a very recent phenomenon. The plant is not mentioned in any treatments of Illinois' natural flora from the nineteenth century; nor is it mentioned among the species introduced to Illinois before the twentieth century (Brendel 1870, Darlington 1922). As recently as 1955, it was omitted from a catalog of "every species of vascular plant that is known to grow spontaneously in Illinois" (Jones and Fuller 1955:vii, 339). Of course, the conspicuous capacity for self-propagation of *C. pepo* and other escaping cucurbits was well known, but the following comment from *The New Britton and Brown Illustrated*

Flora of Northeastern United States and Adjacent Canada (Gleason 1952:311) was representative of botanical opinion: They "are frequently spontaneous in waste ground, especially on dump-heaps where their seeds have been discarded, but none is naturalized in our range." In contrast, Gleason considered the common sunflower and tobacco—two other Indian crop plants—as being more persistent escapes into the regional flora. In sum, the present frequency of *C. pepo* var. *ovifera* apparently represents a recent naturalization of the plant in extensive, highly disturbed floodplain fields; and the prehistoric presence and persistence of squash in west-central Illinois implies at least occasional replanting by Indians.

Not until about 2000 years ago during the Middle Woodland period did squash begin to occur frequently in the archaeobotanical record for west-central Illinois. In bulk, carbonized rinds always were insignificant among archaeobotanical remains but they have commonly been recorded in 20% or more of flotation samples at sites younger than 2000 years (D. Asch and Asch 1978:331–32).

Lagenaria siceraria, Bottle Gourd

Besides pepo squash, the other cucurbit species cultivated prehistorically in eastern North America was *Lagenaria siceraria* (bottle gourd). Bottle gourd is unknown for the Archaic in west-central Illinois, although it was found at Phillips Spring, Missouri in an occupational zone dating to 2300 B.C. (Kay, King, and Robinson 1980; King, this volume). During the first millennium B.C., bottle gourd was in common use as a container in the Mammoth Cave area, where it also has been found as a minor constituent in human paleofeces (Yarnell 1969; Watson 1974).

In other papers, we have stated that cucurbit rind—including that of *Lagenaria*—is ubiquitous in west-central Illinois contexts beginning with the Middle Woodland period (D. Asch and Asch 1982). With more adequate comparative material at hand, we have reexamined the prehistoric cucurbit rinds and conclude that very few are actually *Lagenaria*. Rather, almost all can be assigned to *Cucurbita*. Bottle gourd was positively identified from only two Middle Woodland component (Loy and Macoupin), and it was uncommon at later sites as well: The reported occurrence of bottle gourd rind from Dickson Camp in the central Illinois Valley (N. Asch and Asch 1980) is in error; it is actually *Cucurbita* rind. From a Middle Woodland context at the Smiling Dan site, one seed coat fragment that is probably *Lagenaria* was discovered (D. Asch and Asch 1983); seeds have also been found at a few later sites. James Schoenwetter identified a pollen grain that was possibly

Lagenaria from a near-surface Middle Woodland pit at the Macoupin site (Struever and Vickery 1973:1205). Finally, a ceramic vessel in the shape of a bottle gourd was excavated from a Middle Woodland cemetery—Brangenberg Mound 2 (Griffin and Morgan 1941:42).

Iva annua, Marsh Elder or Sumpweed

Iva annua, an oily-seeded annual, is native to west-central Illinois where it occurs in open, disturbed, wet floodplain habitats (D. Asch and Asch 1978). The oldest Illinois Valley record is an achene identified in a noncultural context radiocarbon dated to 12,000 ± 1000 B.P. (ISGS–911). The achene was present in a core sample of upper Keach School terrace sediments about 4 m below the present surface (Hajic 1982). The earliest appearance of *Iva* in an archaeological context is from Koster Horizons 8D and 8C. Five small achenes have been identified in samples from these components. The older occupational unit, Horizon 8D, has a radiocarbon date of 7320 ± 70 B.P.: 5370 B.C. (ISGS–859); the younger unit, Horizon 8B, has several dates of about 5000 B.C. (Table 6.1).

From Horizon 6 at Koster, *Iva* comprised 40% of a large sample of identifiable seeds, and the concentration of *Iva* achenes per kilogram of charcoal surpassed that found at most Woodland period sites in the region. Radiocarbon dates for the Horizon 6 occupation range from 3800 B.C. to 2900 B.C. (Brown and Vierra 1983). We have speculated (D. Asch and Asch 1982) that *Iva* may have been cultivated during this occupation. If such was the case, selection for domesticated forms was not yet evident in the archaeological specimens, which fall within the wild size range (D. Asch and Asch 1978:324). Alternatively, *Iva* from Horizon 6 plausibly could have been the product of a wild harvest, since today the plant is common enough to harvest effectively in some floodplain habitats (D. Asch and Asch 1978:311–15).

Archaeobotanical documentation of a gradual increase in *Iva* achene dimensions provides persuasive evidence for a domestication of the plant in eastern North America (Yarnell 1978, 1981; D. Asch and Asch 1978). Figure 6.3 shows histograms of achene lengths for *Iva annua* from some west-central Illinois archaeobotanical collections. The process of *Iva*'s domestication evidently was underway in the lower Illinois Valley at least by 2000 B.C.

From the Napoleon Hollow site, 79 achenes of *Iva annua* were recovered from a shallow pit associated with the Titterington occupation (Conard et al. 1984). Their dimensions are larger than mean achene sizes from modern wild stands (ca. 2.8 mm × 2.2 mm) or from older archaeological contexts, and they are smaller than achenes from Mid-

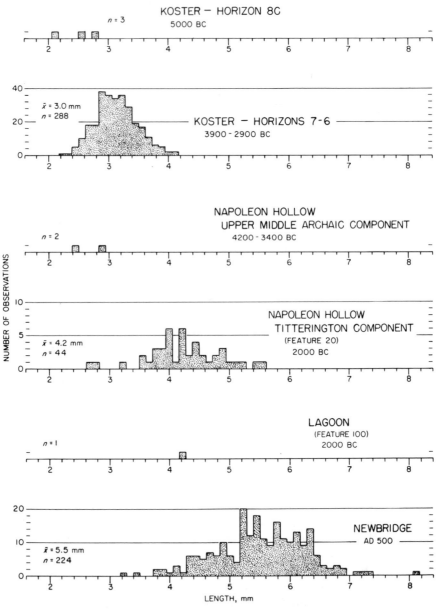

Figure 6.3. *Iva annua* achene lengths from selected prehistoric occupations. Measurements are corrected by Yarnell's (1972) method.

dle and Late Woodland sites (D. Asch and Asch 1978:322). Their sizes are comparable with those reported by Yarnell (1978) from about 1000 B.C. at Salts Cave, Kentucky. The pit in which these *Iva* achenes were contained, Feature 20, was 0.9 m below ground surface at the base of a buried A-horizon within which Titterington Archaic cultural remains were plentiful (Wiant, Hajic, and Styles 1983). A date of 3920 ± 90 B.P.: 1970 B.C. (ISGS–933) obtained on dispersed charcoal within the pit is consistent with the age of the Titterington cultural phase as documented elsewhere in Illinois (Cook 1976, n.d.). Woodland period cultural remains overlie the Titterington horizon. The slight probability of a downward contamination by post-Titterington achenes was discounted through a date that was obtained directly upon one of the large achenes by the method of direct detection accelerator radiocarbon dating (Conard et al. 1984). The date is 4500 ± 500 B.P.: 2550 B.C. (NRSL–297). Though the standard error is large, a 5σ error in the date would be necessary to account for this specimen as a product of Napoleon Hollow's Middle Woodland occupation.

Also present with *Iva* in Feature 20 were seeds of *Chenopodium berlandieri* (goosefoot), *Ambrosia trifida* (giant ragweed), and *Helianthus* sp. (sunflower). We have speculated that together with *Iva* and *Cucurbita* these plants may have belonged to a Titterington Archaic horticultural complex (D. Asch and Asch 1982).

Feature 20 had 44 specimens of *Iva* that are measurable for length (33 missing the pericarp). To estimate original *Iva* achene dimensions from a carbonized sample, a common procedure is first to add 0.7 mm and 0.4 mm, respectively, to the observed length and width if the specimen is a naked kernel, and then to make a correction for 10% shrinkage due to carbonization (Yarnell 1972:336–37). Applying Yarnell's corrections to the Napoleon Hollow specimens results in an estimate of 4.2 × 2.8 mm for mean length and width, with standard deviation of 0.6 × 0.4 mm. The index of length × width in mm is 11.9. The range of corrected specimen lengths is 2.7–5.5 mm, and the range of widths is 2.0–3.8 mm. Specimens for which the pericarp is questionably present were counted as entire achenes for the computations, thus protecting against an overestimation of the difference with respect to wild populations.

Figure 6.4 compares the size distribution of the Napoleon Hollow achenes with the size distributions for harvests from the largest-seeded and smallest-seeded of 11 modern wild stands (D. Asch and Asch 1978:322). The Napoleon Hollow achenes from Feature 20 average one-third longer and 10% wider than the mean dimensions for the wild population with the largest achenes. In any wild population of *Iva* there are occasional achenes longer than 4.0 mm, but these are a very

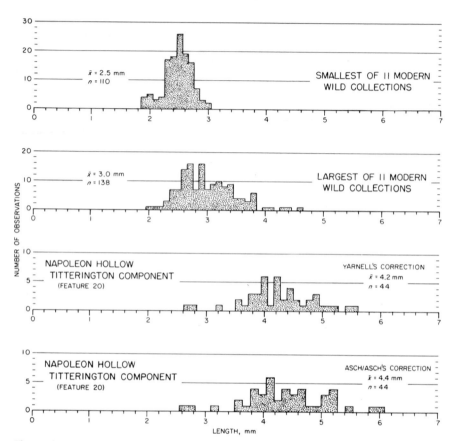

Figure 6.4. *Iva annua* achene lengths: Titterington Archaic occupation of Napoleon Hollow and modern wild stands.

small percentage of the total. We have found no technique of selective collecting from different regions or different habitats, from large or small plants, or from different parts of a plant that could raise the mean size of achenes in a wild harvest sample significantly above the natural mean (D. Asch and Asch 1978:322).

The Titterington achenes from Napoleon Hollow probably were somewhat larger than indicated by the estimate based on Yarnell's method. Yarnell's correction method assumes a constant difference between dimensions of the entire achene and the enclosed kernel, whereas the difference is actually an increasing function of achene size (D. Asch and Asch 1978:326–27). Yarnell's method apparently over-compensates for pericarp loss in specimens of average wild size and undercompensates for larger specimens. We derived correction equations based on modern data that were used to plot Figure 3 in D. Asch and Asch (1978:327) from the Crawford Creek (CAA–270) and Michael (CAA-274) *Iva* collections in Calhoun County, Illinois. Mean dimensions were recorded at three size levels for groups of 20 specimens from each of the modern collections, and linear regression equations were fitted separately to the data on mean lengths and widths of achenes and kernels. The following equations were obtained to estimate entire uncarbonized achene dimensions from the observed dimensions of carbonized kernels:

Uncarbonized achene length = 1.36 × (carbonized kernel length) + 0.17 mm

Uncarbonized achene width = 1.45 × (carbonized kernel width) − 0.06 mm

The equations include the 10% correction for shrinkage due to carbonization.

Applying this technique to the Napoleon Hollow kernels, the mean size of entire uncarbonized Titterington achenes is re-estimated as 4.4 × 3.0 mm, standard deviation as 0.6 × 0.5 mm, size index as 13.0, and size range as 2.7–6.0 × 2.1–4.3 mm.

A single kernel of *Iva annua* has been recorded from one other Titterington component—in a shallow pit at the Lagoon site. The estimated dimensions of the entire achene before it was carbonized and divested of its pericarp are 4.2 × 3.2 mm (by Yarnell's correction method) or 4.6 × 3.6 mm (by our correction method), about the same size as Titterington achenes from Napoleon Hollow. Charcoal from the same pit gave a radiocarbon date of 4030 ± 75 B.P.: 2080 B.C. (ISGS–804).

Use of wild-size *Iva* continued in Illinois after 2000 B.C. A Terminal Archaic midden at the Titus site, with radiocarbon dates of 3240 ± 75 B.P.: 1290 B.C. (ISGS–826) and 2860 ± 80 B.P.: 910 B.C. (ISGS –990), produced small *Iva* (D. Asch and Asch 1978:324). A large sample of achenes dating to about 1200 B.C. has been reported from the Cahokia Interpretive Center Tract in the American Bottom by Lopinot (1983). They were also from a wild-size population. Another collection from a site near west-central Illinois—the Collins site in Monroe County, northeastern Missouri—has been attributed to a Terminal Archaic component radiocarbon dated to about 600 B.C. (Klippel 1972). Collins site *Iva* is comparable in size to the Titterington *Iva* from Napoleon Hollow, or slightly larger (Yarnell 1978). Archaeobotanical investigations for Early Woodland components in Illinois, including the American Bottom area (Johannessen 1984), have re-corded no *Iva* nor evidence of any kind of seed horticulture. Begin-ning with the Middle Woodland period, achenes of domesticated size once again were present in low frequency as part of the region's hor-ticultural complex (D. Asch, Farnsworth, and Asch 1979; D. Asch and Asch 1983).

To conclude: archaeobotanical studies conducted in west-central Illinois have provided the oldest record for substantial exploitation of *Iva annua* and, at 2000 B.C., the oldest record for its domestication. Yet subsequently, its cultivation in the region may have been inter-rupted, not continuing on a consistent low-scale basis until about 2000 years ago. In contrast, domesticated *Iva* (with achenes about the same size as the Titterington *Iva*) was an important component of the hor-ticultural complex that flourished in Kentucky during the first millen-nium B.C. (Watson 1974; Yarnell 1978; Cowan et al. 1981).

Helianthus annuus, Common Sunflower

Among the cultivated plants of New World origin, the only one from north of Mexico that has become an important crop in modern times is the common sunflower (*Helianthus annuus*). In papers published dur-ing the last 30 years, Heiser has sketched hypotheses concerning its evolution (Heiser 1951, 1954, 1965, 1978, this volume; Heiser et al. 1969). To simplify, he has proposed a two stage sequence for the course of its prehistoric cultivation and domestication. First, common sunflower moved eastward with man as a weedy campfollower from its original home in the West. Second, domesticated forms developed in eastern North America.

Archaeological documentation of eastward range extension from the West is lacking, and the degree to which such range extension was aided by cultivation of the plant, rather than occurring solely by self-propagation in disturbed habitats, is uncertain. On the central Plains, intentional human propagation probably was not essential for the plant to persist prehistorically, and weed forms somewhat different than western populations have evolved there (Heiser 1954; Heiser et al. 1969). In Illinois, uncultivated common sunflower has generally been regarded by botanists as adventive after major Euroamerican settlement (Mohlenbrock 1975:417), although the plant had long been cultivated in the state by the Indians. Darlington's (1922) review of nineteenth century publications on Illinois flora and weed introduc-tions supports this position (see also Jones and Fuller 1955:494). As late as 1859, wild *Helianthus annuus* had not been cited as an immigrant to the state. The variety and massiveness of modern disturbance have enabled establishment in west-central Illinois of a rural form and an urban weed form (authors' observations and Heiser et al. 1969). The urban form, in fact, now occurs sporadically to the Atlantic Coast (Heiser et al. 1969).

It is reasonably certain that the prehistoric occurrence and persistence of common sunflower in Illinois—even were there no selection for domesticated forms—would have required some degree of cultivation. Farther to the east in regions formerly covered by a continuous deciduous forest, one could even more securely infer a cultivation of common sunflower merely from evidence that it was present prehistorically.

Achene dimensions are the commonest source of archaeological information about the progress of sunflower domestication. Measurements assembled by Yarnell (1978, 1981) from across eastern North American show that Mississippian sunflower achenes were larger than Middle/Late Woodland achenes and that achenes as old as 3000 years were slightly larger, on the average, than those of wild and weedy sunflowers. Excluding outliers, Yarnell (1981) obtained the following trends in achene size indexes (length × width, in mm):

20 to 24	Terminal Archaic
22 to 26	Early Woodland
25 to 35	Middle Woodland
35 to 60	Early Late Woodland
50 to 100	Mississippian

Yarnell cautions that sunflower achenes display more size diversity at sites of comparable age than do achenes of *Iva annua*.

With one exception, no excavated site in west-central Illinois has yielded many sunflower achenes. They have been found with three Archaic components, with ten Middle or Late Woodland components, and with two Mississippian components. Measurements are given in Table 6.2 and are graphed in Figure 6.5. Data are also presented from two late prehistoric/contact sites in northeastern Illinois whose plant remains have been studied by the Archaeobotanical Laboratory. Measurements are corrected to compensate for shrinkage due to carbonization and, if applicable, for loss of pericarp, following the recommendations of Yarnell (1978:296): Increase achene lengths and widths by 11% and 27%, respectively; increase kernel lengths and widths by 30% and 45%, respectively.

Eleven Archaic sunflower achenes recovered from the Koster and Napoleon Hollow sites are, to our knowledge, the oldest that have been recorded from prehistoric sites in eastern North America. Nota-

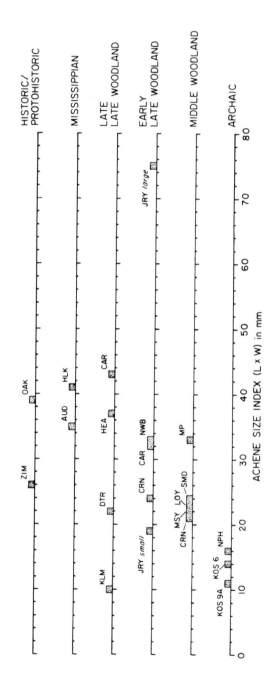

ARCHAEOLOGICAL *HELIANTHUS*

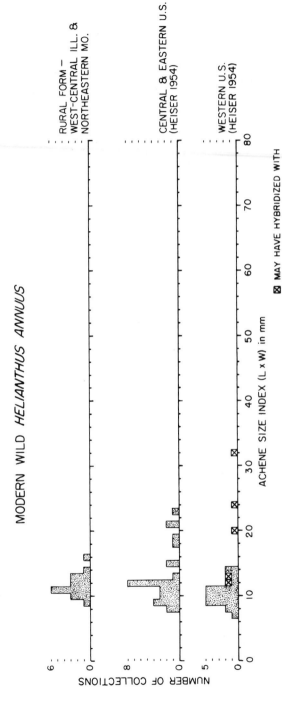

Figure 6.5. Prehistoric and modern achene sizes of *Helianthus annuus*. Measurements are corrected by Yarnell's (1978) method. Site abbreviation key: AUD, Audrey North; CAR, Carlin; CRN, Crane; DTR, Deer Track; HEA, Healey; HLK, Hill Creek; JRY, John Roy; KLM, Kulhman; KOS 6, Koster Hor. 6; KOS 9A, Koster Hor. 9A; LOY, Loy; MP, Macoupin; MSY, Massey; NPH, Napoleon Hollow (Titterington component); NWB, Newbridge; OAK, Oak Forest; SMD, Smiling Dan; ZIM, Zimmerman.

TABLE 6.2
DIMENSIONS OF *Helianthus annuus* ACHENES

	No. of Measure-ments	CORRECTED ACHENE DIMENSIONS (L×W)			Index (L×W), mm
		Mean, mm	Std. dev., mm	Range, mm	
Middle Archaic					
Koster, Horizon 9A	1	4.4×2.5	—	—	11
Koster, Horizon 6	1L,2W	6.0×2.4	− ×0.1	− ×2.3–2.4	14
Late Archaic					
Napoleon Hollow, Titterington	4	6.1×2.7	0.2×0.3	6.0–6.4×2.5–3.0	16
Middle Woodland					
Crane	5L,8W	6.6×3.3	2.2×0.9	4.2–9.4×1.9–4.6	21
Loy	2L,4W	6.5×3.6	2.4×0.7	4.8–8.2×2.7–4.2	23
Massey	8L,11W	6.8×3.2	0.9×0.7	5.5–8.7×2.2–4.8	22
Smiling Dan	3L,15W	7.2×3.4	0.8×0.4	6.2–7.8×2.8–4.1	24
Macoupin	1	8.5×3.8	—	—	33
Early Late Woodland					
John Roy (large)	2	11.3×6.7	1.3×0.6	10.4–12.2×6.2–7.1	75
(small)	1	5.9×3.3	—	—	19
Newbridge	3	8.3×4.0	1.3×0.5	6.7–9.1×3.4–4.4	33
Carlin	1	7.9×4.1	—	—	32
Crane	64L,114W	7.1×3.3	1.2×0.6	5.2–11.1×2.2–5.6	24
Late Late Woodland					
Koster East	3W	− ×3.9	− ×0.6	− ×3.4–4.5	—
Deer Track	1	6.1×3.6	—	—	22
Carlin	3L,4W	9.7×4.5	0.6×0.4	8.8–10.1×4.1–4.9	43
Kuhlman	1	3.9×2.7	—	—	10
Loy	1W	− ×3.6	—	—	—
Healey	2	8.7×4.1	1.7×0.4	7.5–9.9×3.9–4.5	37
Mississippian					
Audrey North	2	10.3×3.4	0.6×0.5	9.9–10.8×3.0–3.8	35
Hill Creek	3L,9W	9.0×4.5	1.8×0.9	7.4–10.9×3.2–5.7	41
Historic/Protohistoric					
Oak Forest*	1	9.4×4.2	—	—	39
Zimmerman*	7L,10W	7.0×3.3	0.5×0.3	6.5–7.7×2.9–3.8	23

*Located in northeastern Illinois.

bly, the older Archaic achenes are smaller, the younger ones larger; and the apparent trend toward larger size dovetails nicely into the size trend proposed by Yarnell for the last 3000 years. The oldest achene was collected from Horizon 9A at the Koster site. Radiocarbon dates associated with that cultural stratum are 7800 ± 160 B.P.: 5850 B.C. (ISGS–316) and 7910 ± 100 B.P.: 5960 B.C. (ISGS–229). Reconstructed dimensions yield a size index of 8. At Napoleon Hollow, six long narrow kernels were identified from the Titterington occupational stratum, four of them from the 3920-year-old radiocarbon-dated Feature 20 which also contained domesticated *Iva annua*. The four measurable specimens have a reconstructed size index of 16.

For comparison with the archaeological measurements, Figure 6.5 provides data on the size range of modern uncultivated *H. annuus*. Two sources of information on modern size are used. (1) Heiser (1954:Fig. 3) recorded the mean length and width of achenes from 28 populations throughout eastern and central United States and from 27 western populations. (2) We measured 25 achenes per plant for three plants from each of six collecting sites in west-central Illinois and northeast Missouri. The model size index from modern measurements is between 8 and 13. Histograms from Heiser's measurements have long tails of occasional populations from which achenes were recorded that were much larger than the model size. For the western collections, Heiser suggested that this tail probably was a consequence of recent hybridization between wild and domesticated sunflowers. In the 1954 paper, Heiser did not discuss the probability that the same explanation could account for the large achenes in central and eastern populations. However, it would seem that such hybridization is more likely to occur in the east than in the west. In another paper, Heiser (1965:395) does propose that some of the traits observed in the eastern, urban sunflower form are a result of hybridization between weed sunflowers and cultivated sunflowers.

In conclusion, it is plausible that the 4000-year-old achenes from Napoleon Hollow represent an early stage in the domestication of common sunflower. Their size index of 16 is slightly larger than expected for modern populations of uncultivated sunflowers that have not hybridized with domesticated plants, although individual achenes from modern uncultivated plants are often as large. However, we cannot even be certain that any of the Archaic achenes are *H. annuus* rather than an indigenous perennial species. For instance, the indigenous *H. tuberosus* (Jerusalem artichoke) produces achenes as large as those found at Napoleon Hollow. Neither is it certain that our interpretation of size variation in modern uncultivated *H. annuus* is correct. Nevertheless, should future measurements on Archaic sunflowers conform to the temporal trend of the present small data set, the inference of domestication in *H. annuus* would provide the simplest means of accounting for the trend.

No sunflowers have been identified at Terminal Archaic or Early Woodland sites in west-central Illinois. Illinois sunflower achenes dating from Middle Woodland into contact times have sizes indicative of domestication (Fig. 6.5), except for a single tiny Late Woodland achene from the Kuhlman site. Size indexes for sunflowers from the various components fall within the range of 22 to 42, with an outlier of 75 from the John Roy site.

By a judicious exclusion of outliers, one may be able to discern a weak temporal trend in the Woodland and post-Woodland scatter of data. Unlike most other plants, *Helianthus annuus* does not have strictly canalized seed size; achene size is not uniform even within a single disk (Harper 1965; Heiser, this volume). Consequently, the effects of selection under domestication may be partially obscured by diverse environmental conditions, the more so because of the very small prehistoric samples available for study.

The only large sample of achenes from west-central Illinois comes from an early Late Woodland pit at Crane, which has an associated radiocarbon date of 1330 ± 70 B.P.: A.D. 620 (ISGS–1079). The mean index of 24 is smaller than predicted for an early Late Woodland sample from Yarnell's trend chart. In contrast, John Roy has two specimens which are much larger than any found in the Crane collection of about the same age. The John Roy kernels were within a maygrass-knotweed-chenopod seed mass from which a radiocarbon date of 1400 ± 70 B.P.: A.D. 550 (ISGS–971) was obtained. Their size index of 75 is comparable with that of Mississippian sunflowers from other regions. In uncultivated sunflowers, we have noted that insect damage can result in inflated achenes. This factor can be discounted for the John Roy specimens since both are entire, well-preserved kernels. As Heiser (this volume) observes, large achene size is associated with disk enlargement and suppression of lateral disks in favor of a central head. It is probable, therefore, that the John Roy sunflower was monocephalic and had a large disk. The size contrast with the contemporaneous Crane site sunflower suggests that more than one cultivar was maintained in the region 1500 years ago.

Mississippian size indexes of 35 to 40 for west-central Illinois sunflower are considerably smaller than the range of 50 to 100 given by Yarnell (1981) for that period. The occurrence of small achenes in late contexts is further documented in northeastern Illinois, where size indexes of about 40 were recorded for two late prehistoric contact sites. Yarnell had excluded from his trend chart a collection of small Mississippian achenes from the state of Mississippi on the grounds that sunflower at the southern margin of its cultivation might be aberrant. The Illinois data suggest, rather, that a greater allowance should be made for variability in late prehistoric times. This would be in accord with the size variability documented by Heiser (1951) for traditional Indian varieties grown in the twentieth century.

Chenopodium berlandieri, Goosefoot

Initial archaeobotanical research in the lower Illinois Valley implicated small starchy seeds as an important part of Middle and Late Woodland subsistence (Struever 1962, 1964, 1968b, 1968c; Maina 1967; Kaplan and Maina 1977). The starchy-seed complex of this region is now known to consist of four plants: *Chenopodium* (goosefoot), *Polygonum erectum* (knotweed), *Phalaris caroliniana* (maygrass), and *Hordeum pusillum* (little barley) (D. Asch and Asch 1978, 1982, 1983; N. Asch and Asch 1980; Johannessen 1984). The most notable early discovery in the region pertaining to this complex was made at the early Late Woodland Newbridge site, where large masses of carbonized goosefoot and knotweed seeds were recovered from two pits. This was unmistakable evidence for starchy-seed harvesting and storage.

Struever (1964, 1968b, 1968c) elaborated an hypothesis that the Hopewellian cultural phenomenon of Middle Woodland times developed as an adaptive-functional response to subsistence upgrading in certain riverine locations. This included an amplified reliance on native seed-bearing plants such as goosefoot. He proposed that goosefoot became an important food plant by one of two means: (a) an intensive harvest collection of naturally propagating goosefoot stands which were thought to occur extensively on floodplain mudflats; (b) a technologically simple cultivation of goosefoot on mudflats.

Subsequent archaeobotanical studies in west-central Illinois have confirmed that the starchy-seed complex, including goosefoot, was important from Middle Woodland into Mississippian times. As Struever suspected, this complex and the other cultivated plants are virtually unrepresented in the region during the Early Woodland period (Morgan et al. 1982; N. Asch and Asch 1983; Farnsworth and Asch n.d.; Johannessen 1984). The archaeological record in west-central Illinois is thus dissimilar from that of Kentucky, where along with other eastern North American plants, goosefoot was a major food during the first millennium B.C. (Watson 1974; Cowan et al. 1981).

Goosefoot probably was a minor plant food in west-central Illinois during most of the Archaic period (N. Asch and Asch 1979a; D. Asch and Asch 1982). The earliest archaeobotanical remains that have been studied from the lower Illinois Valley—which date to about 6500 B.C. from the Koster site—have a few goosefoot seeds. A small scale of utilization is implied from the fact that goosefoot constitutes only a low percentage of seeds in most Archaic seed spectra, even though seeds in general are poorly represented at these sites.

The Titterington cultural phase at 2000 B.C. may constitute an exception to the Archaic goosefoot pattern (D. Asch and Asch 1982). As a percentage of seeds recovered, goosefoot is well represented in three Titterington components that have been studied—Napoleon Hollow, Lagoon, and Koster. Among the Titterington samples from Napoleon Hollow, more than 60% of identifiable seeds were goosefoot, and overall seed frequencies (2.9 seeds/g charcoal) were at a level considered typical of Middle and Late Woodland occupations in the region. In contrast, for earlier occupations at Napoleon Hollow, no more than 4% of identifiable seeds were goosefoot, even though overall seed frequencies were very low (0.2 seeds/g charcoal). No other member of the Woodland period complex of starchy seeds was common at Titterington Archaic sites.

As noted above, Struever was uncertain whether goosefoot was harvested prehistorically from self-propagating stands or whether it was a product of cultivation. Yarnell (1969:46), writing at about the same time as Struever, also was ambivalent about how goosefoot was procured in the Salts Cave area of Kentucky: "Evidence for intentional Early Woodland cultivation of chenopod is insufficient, though it is not immediately obvious where such a quantity of seeds could have been harvested if not from cultivated fields. . . . [I]t is quite possible that chenopod was an encouraged, self-propagating weed in the cultivated fields" where plants such as sunflower, *Iva* and cucurbits were grown.

As early as the 1930s, Gilmore (1931) had claimed, on the basis of studies of plant remains in Ozark bluff shelters, that a domesticated goosefoot was grown prehistorically in eastern North America. A conclusive demonstration that some *Chenopodium*, at least, was domesticated was not achieved until Wilson (1981) reexamined and described exsiccated material from Holman bluff shelter in northwestern Arkansas. This *Chenopodium* probably is of Mississippian age (Fritz 1984).

At present, two strong arguments can be advanced for a prehistoric cultivation of goosefoot in west-central Illinois. One is an ecological/economic argument that the species of *Chenopodium* which was exploited prehistorically would have had to be cultivated in order to achieve a significant harvest potential in the region (D. Asch, Farnsworth, and Asch 1979; N. Asch and Asch 1980, 1981). The second argument rests on evidence for the presence of domesticated forms (D. Asch and Asch 1982, 1983). Domestication is the stronger of the two. However, the ecological/economic argument is important because there may have existed a stage (Titterington Archaic) during which *Chenopodium* had been taken into cultivation but before the seeds had developed characters attributable to a process of domestication. Also, not all of the seeds from Woodland contexts are of domesticated form.

The new understandings of the economic status of goosefoot have depended on taxonomic clarification of prehistoric and modern *Chenopodium* and on field studies that give a more accurate picture of the availability of *Chenopodium* seeds in natural stands. Subgenus classification of prehistoric materials is necessary in order to be able to assess the wild resource potential of the species that actually were exploited prehistorically. Also, to be able to infer that morphological peculiarities of prehistoric material are a consequence of domestication, one should be familiar with natural variability within the species, including occurrence of seed polymorphism.

Whereas archaeobotanists once routinely assigned prehistoric *Chenopodium* to *C. album* (a taxonomic catchall) or, if the fruits were unusually large, to *C. hybridum* var. *gigantospermum*, it now is recognized that almost all prehistoric *Chenopodium* from eastern North America belongs to subsection *Cellulata* of section *Chenopodia* (D. Asch and Asch 1977; Wilson 1976a). A characteristic feature of the species belonging to *Cellulata* is the prominent reticulations of the pericarp (Aellen and Just 1943; Wahl 1954; Wilson 1980). The two wild species of *Cellulata* from interior North America are *Chenopodium bushianum* Aellen and *C. berlandieri* ssp. *berlandieri* sensu Wilson (1980). *C. bushianum* grows from the Atlantic coastal plain westward to Missouri and North Dakota (Wahl 1954:45). The Plains variety of *C. berlandieri*—var. *zschackei* (Murr.) Murr. in Wahl's (1954:41) treatment—presently ranges into Illinois, although we have not found it to be common in the west-central part of the state. Wilson (1980) has demonstrated that the two species are completely interfertile, and he notes that morphological intergrades occur within the area of sympatry. Consequently, he concludes (Wilson 1980:283) that "the two might better be treated as a single species."

In prehistoric collections of *Chenopodium*, the thin pericarp that encloses the seed rarely is preserved. Nondomesticated *Cellulata* seeds, if otherwise well preserved, are readily identifiable as belonging to this subsection because the seed coats have a distinctive, alveolate surface. When the pericarp is missing, the only criterion by which *C. bushianum* can sometimes be distinguished from *C. berlandieri* spp. *berlandieri* is seed diameter. The size range for *C. bushianum* seeds usually is given as 1.5–2.0 mm, and for Plains *C. berlandieri* spp. *berlandieri* a range of 1.2 to 1.6 mm is commonly cited (D. Asch and Asch 1977:18–19). Some modern collections of *C. bushianum* have seeds averaging slightly less than 1.5 mm in diameter (D. Asch and Asch 1977:Table 2). Examining herbarium sheets of *C. berlandieri* spp. *berlandieri* at the Missouri Botanical Garden, St. Louis, we have noted that the seeds of individual plants commonly average between 1.4 mm and 1.5 mm in diameter.

In previous studies we have identified prehistoric west-central Illinois seeds as *C. bushianum*. However, we now prefer to assign them to the inclusive taxon *C. berlandieri*, within which *C. bushianum* is relegated to a subspecies or varietal level. Wilson and Heiser (1979) also have shown that the domesticated *Chenopodium* grown today in Mexico belongs to the *berlandieri* complex, and they classify it as *C. berlandieri* spp. *nuttalliae*. Besides the biological justification for merging *C. bushianum* with *C. berlandieri*, which rests on the research of Wilson, the classification of the prehistoric material as *C. berlandieri* is attractive for pragmatic reasons. First, pigeonholing individual specimens or entire collections into one taxon or the other is less informative than providing data on the distribution of seed diameters in a prehistoric collection. Second, as discussed below, the domesticated *Chenopodium* of eastern North American clearly can be placed within the inclusive taxon *C. berlandieri*. At present, we prefer a conservative approach to classification of the prehistoric material that does not further assign it to a formally defined subspecific taxon. This avoids prejudging important questions concerning: (1) the relationships of domesticated eastern North American materials to wild spp. *berlandieri* or *bushianum*, (2) putatively definitive characters separating wild-type from domesticated seeds, or (3) the issue of indigenous evolution of a domesticate versus introduction from Mexico.

The identification of prehistoric *Chenopodium* as *C. berlandieri* is important for assessing the prehistoric wild harvest potential of goosefoot. Goosefoot is very abundant today in west-central Illinois on ground subject to human disturbance, but almost all of it is *C. missouriense*. *C. missouriense* is considered by botanists to be indigenous to the region, but it is very rare or absent in archaeological contexts. If habitat relations of the indigenous chenopod species are the same as in the past, then *C. berlandieri* must have been very uncommon on disturbed soils of prehistoric villages. In other regions where it is abundant, the Plains form of *berlandieri* thrives on dry disturbed ground. However, despite the fact that massive modern disturbances should have increased habitats favorable to its survival in west-central Illinois, after several years of searching we have found only a few plants belonging to this Plains-type *berlandieri*.

The *bushianum* type of *C. berlandieri* is a minor chenopod in the region. We first identified it in a small, linear stand on a semi-open, sandy bank of an island in the Illinois River (D. Asch and Asch 1977:19–20). Other stands have since been located in essentially the same type of habitat. Even within this restricted environmental setting, the *bushianum* type occurs sporadically. Small harvests of the seed are possible from a few stands of lower Illinois Valley *bushianum* (D. Asch and Asch (1978:313–14), but wild *bushianum* falls far short of suitability for "intensive harvest collection."

In a few instances, we have observed straggling plants of the *bushianum* type on mudflats at the river margin, but they are infrequent there by comparison with the better drained floodplain setting described above. In field studies we have found that *Chenopodium* belonging to any species is rare on mudflats. This observation is reinforced by results of a floodplain plant study conducted by Klein, Daley, and Wedum (1975) in the lower Illinois and adjacent Mississippi valleys. In the central Illinois Valley, Munson (n.d.) censused mudflat vegetation and found no *Chenopodium*.

It is improbable that mudflats would have made attractive settings to cultivate goosefoot (D. Asch, Farnsworth, and Asch 1979:84). Wild *bushianum*-type seeds are continually dispersed today by flooding into these wet microhabitats where they do not thrive because of competition with other pioneer annuals such as water hemp and giant ragweed. The existence of a preadapted complex of quickly germinating, fast growing weeds would pose serious problems for mudflat cultivators. Also, Illinois Valley mudflats were reservoirs not only for spring floodwaters but also for runoff from small side valleys. Historically, these small, nonpermanent streams did not cut channels across the Illinois Valley to reach the main river directly but dumped their discharge into backswamps behind the river's natural levee (Andreas, Lyter, and Co. 1873; Woermann 1905; Rubey 1952). Consequently, mudflats were subject to flooding throughout the summer and fall, and to attempt to cultivate them could have been foolishly risky.

Having provided background information on *Chenopodium* taxonomy and the wild resource potential of *C. berlandieri* in modern environments, we can now review more closely the question of prehistoric cultivation and domestication. If, as we have suggested, *C. berlandieri* was utilized to a significant extent at 2000 B.C. during the Titterington cultural phase and if this species was no more abundant than at the present time, then it is likely that this harvest was made possible through cultivation.

The plausibility of goosefoot cultivation 4000 years ago is increased by the fact that such a cultivation does not have to be established as a special case. Already at that time there was a horticulture that included

marsh elder, squash, perhaps sunflower, and possibly even giant ragweed. Goosefoot, however, would have been the first starchy seed taken
into cultivation.

A counter argument against Titterington cultivation of goosefoot
could be developed (1) if future archaeobotanical studies do not substantiate that goosefoot was extensively harvested (the present archaeobotanical data base is rather small) or (2) if one could establish a case
that *C. berlandieri* was more widely available in west-central Illinois
during prehistoric times than at present.

To the west, Plains-type *C. berlandieri* is common in disturbed habitats that should be comparable to those existing around a prehistoric
campsite. To the north and east, the *bushianum* type is not restricted to
the specialized floodplain habitat in which it is found in west-central
Illinois. P.J. Munson has pointed out to us that in the vicinity of Bloomington, Indiana, *bushianum* is frequently found in waste places and
cultivated fields, as well as in floodplains (N. Asch and Asch 1980:158).
Examining its distribution on a trip between Bloomington and
Kampsville, we observed that *bushianum* drops out of its wider weedy
niche in the vicinity of the Wabash Valley at the Illinois/Indiana state
line. In prehistoric times, could west-central Illinois have been within
the geographic area where *C. berlandieri* is common around human
disturbance? Actually, it is more likely that this range has extended
rather than retracted in modern times in response to the great increase
in disturbance. Such has been the response of most weedy species.

For the sake of argument, let us suppose that *C. berlandieri* was a
harvestable wild resource in prehistoric west-central Illinois. Then a
new problem is raised: explaining why an easily harvested and processed campsite weed was little used during most of the Archaic
period. At the stratified site of Napoleon Hollow, the problem is illustrated by the contrast of goosefoot abundance from the
Titterington stratum and its near absence from pre-Titterington
strata. Napoleon Hollow had intensive, long-term occupations at
5100–4650 B.C., later at 4200–3200 B.C., and again at about 2000
B.C. (Wiant, Hajic, and Styles 1983). If the 2000 B.C. Titterington
habitation area was overgrown with self-propagating goosefoot, so too
should have been the equally disturbed occupation areas from earlier
millennia. Giant ragweed and wild bean were present in the earlier
occupations, indicating that there was some interest in utilizing small
edible seeds (D. Asch and Asch 1982). Cowan (this volume) presents
experimental evidence that the return in harvesting giant ragweed is
very low. If pre-Titterington groups turned to giant ragweed as a
source of seeds, why then would they have virtually ignored the
putatively abundant wild goosefoot?

To evaluate evidence for prehistoric domestication, it is preferable to have uncarbonized *Chenopodium*. Still, some carbonized seed collections can provide a remarkable amount of reliable information concerning seed morphology. When *Chenopodium* fruits are carbonized, the starchy perisperm usually pops in the seed's vertical dimension, i.e., parallel to the vertical axis of the seed in the infructescence. The thin pericarp of the fruit is rarely preserved, and often the seed coat is lost or adheres in fragments. The embryo, which encircles the perisperm, commonly is missing as well. Even when a popped perisperm is all that remains of a seed, one can usually gain a rough impression of the original seed diameter. Important characters for subgenus classification and for detecting effects of selection under domestication include the seed coat cross-sectional shape, seed coat thickness and markings, and seed diameter.

Seeds from Titterington Archaic contexts have a thick, alveolate seed coat and a biconvex seed cross-section. These are characteristic features of wild-type *C. berlandieri*. (See discussion below for the Smiling Dan site.) Figure 6.6 is a scanning electron micrograph of a typical specimen from the Titterington occupation at Napoleon Hollow. If goosefoot was grown in the region at 2000 B.C., then cultivators were using seed that was not differentiated from the wild type.

By Middle Woodland times, however, domesticated *Chenopodium* was grown in west-central Illinois (D. Asch and Asch 1982, 1983). The case for goosefoot domestication in the region is stated most fully in a report on plant remains from the Middle Woodland occupation at the Smiling Dan site (D. Asch and Asch 1983).

Basically, the Middle Woodland *Chenopodium* seeds from Smiling Dan fall into two types that occur in roughly equal numbers. One type has a thick, alveolate seed coat, a biconvex seed cross-section, and a prominent beak due to the slight overlap of the annular embryo onto itself. The seeds have a modal diameter of 1.5 mm and a mean diameter of 1.4 mm.

The second seed type (Fig. 6.7) has a thin seed coat approximately one-third the thickness of the first type. Its surface is smooth or at best faintly marked. The seed has a truncate margin. Beak configuration is similar to the first type. Few of the thin-coated seeds are complete enough for an accurate determination of diameter, but 24 measurable specimens have diameters between 1.4 mm and 1.8 mm, with a mean of 1.6 mm. Adhering to two of the thin-coated seeds are remnants of a reticulate pericarp, which is a diagnostic feature of the *Cellulata*.

Three possible explanations for the presence of two types of *C. berlandieri* seeds are considered: (1) The thin-coated seeds are an immature stage in the development of thick-coated, wild-type seeds; (2)

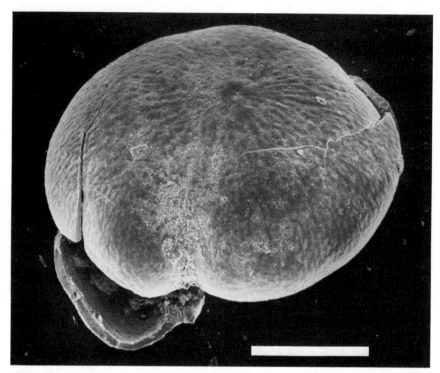

Figure 6.6. Scanning electron micrograph of wild-type *Chenopodium berlandieri* seed, Napoleon Hollow, Titterington Archaic occupation, Feature 23–01. Split in seed shows thickness of seed coat. Scale bar 0.5 mm. Provided by G.M. Caddell, University of North Carolina.

the presence of two prehistoric seed types reflects a natural dimorphism in wild forms of *C. berlandieri*; (3) the second seed type is a domesticated form.

In modern material that we have examined, the developmental trajectory toward mature, thick-coated seeds begins with an immature fruit that has a strongly concavo-convex cross-section. Before the perisperm is filled out to the extent that the concave dorsal surface becomes convex, the seed-coat wall has developed the biconvex margin found in the mature fruit. At no point in the developmental trajectory does a truncate margin occur.

The thin-coated, truncate prehistoric type at Smiling Dan does not have a concave dorsal surface. Notwithstanding the distortions resulting from carbonization, it appears that the perisperms of thin-coated prehistoric seeds are well developed. Also, as noted above, seed diameters of the thin-coated type are slightly greater than those of thick-coated seeds. These observations on modern and prehistoric material

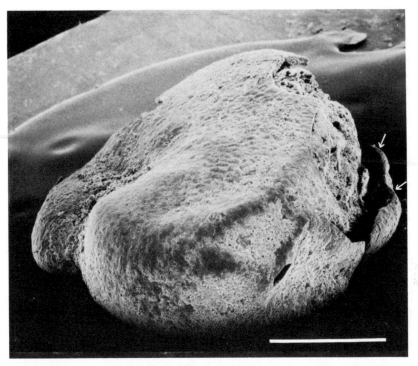

Figure 6.7. Scanning electron micrograph of domesticated *Chenopodium berlandieri* seed, Smiling Dan site, Feature 170–02. Arrows point to edges on broken seed coat where the thin wall is most clearly discernible. Scale bar 0.5 mm. Provided by Michael Veith, Washington University, St. Louis.

show that the morphological variation in Smiling Dan seeds is not due to variation in stages of maturity.

According to Harper, Lovell, and Moore (1970:340), "within the Chenopodiaceae, [seed] polymorphism seems to be the rule in species of *Atriplex* . . . and *Chenopodium* . . . . Individual plants produce both large brown and small black seeds. The brown are able to germinate at once whereas the black show some innate dormancy." Seed dimorphism in *Chenopodium* has been noted for *C. album* in Britain (Williams and Harper 1965) and for *C. rubrum* (Harper, Lovell, and Moore 1970:340). We have observed dimorphism in midwestern *C. missouriense* and described it for *C. bushianum* (D. Asch and Asch 1977).

The dominant morph of *C. bushianum* (and of *C. berlandieri* spp. *berlandieri*) is a thick-coated, deeply alveolate, biconvex, black type. The first Smiling Dan chenopod type defined above (which is like the Archaic seed illustrated in Fig. 6.6) clearly represents this "black morph." Most wild plants have at least a few seeds of a second type, here termed the "red morph." The red morph seed has a thin, reddish, relatively fragile seed coat (an outer epiderm) that is less prominently marked than the dominant type. Its seed coat, whose margin tends to conform to the truncate shape of the embryo and perisperm it envelops, is usually rounded or occasionally even truncate. Although developing seeds of the black morph type may also be reddish in color, the red morph definitely is not an immature stage in development of the black morph. This conclusion is substantiated, in part, from the fact that the red morph seed size is larger, on the average, than that of the black morph.

We once made a collection from small late germinating plants of *C. bushianum* on an Illinois River mudflat in which the red morph predominated, and we noted its resemblance to archaeological *Chenopodium* seeds from cave and rockshelter collections of Kentucky and Arkansas (D. Asch and Asch 1977:19–23). At that time it was our opinion that archaeological variability in midwestern *Chenopodium* could be accounted for by phenotypic, environmentally responsive variation in *C. bushianum*, i.e., that prehistoric selection to produce a domesticated form was not required to account for prehistoric seed characteristics (N. Asch and Asch 1980:158). More recently, we have rejected this hypothesis for reasons that are stated below (D. Asch and Asch 1982).

The conditions under which the red morph predominates in the wild are unusual ones. Since making our original mudflat collection, we have been able to document only one additional case (from a "stand" of just two plants) in which the red morph comprised most of the seeds. Thus, if *Chenopodium* fruits were collected prehistorically from wild plants, the red morph ordinarily should have constituted only a small percentage of the total. Instead, in Middle and Late Woodland archaeobotanical collections from west-central Illinois, thin-coated seeds are at least as abundant as thick-coated ones. There are no *a priori* grounds for expecting that cultivation of wild-type seed would cause a phenotypic response of red morph dominance.

Chenopodium seeds from Archaic contexts in west-central Illinois are the biconvex, thick-coated type. Thus, a shift from the thick-coated type toward the thin-coated type apparently occurred between Archaic and Woodland times. This lends further support to an interpretation that the prehistoric thin-coated type was a product of domestication.

Careful comparisons indicate that the thin-coated prehistoric type, although generally very similar to the modern red morph, is not identical to it. Almost all of the thin-coated Smiling Dan seeds have a truncate margin, whereas most modern red-morph seeds have rounded rather than truncate margins. The thin-coated prehistoric specimens from Smiling Dan appear to have smoother surfaces than does the modern red morph. Smooth seed coat surfaces are a character that also was noted for archaeological seeds from Ozark bluff shelter sites (D. Asch and Asch 1977:19–22). Thus, the differences between prehistoric thin-coated and thick-coated seeds probably were a product of genetic selection, as well as—or instead of—stemming from a phenotypically controlled variation.

What was the origin of the thin-coated domesticate from Smiling Dan? One possible explanation, which is borrowed from Wilson (1976a, 1981) and Smith (1984) is that domesticated *Chenopodium* was introduced into eastern North America from Mexico. Wilson (1981) discovered that the seed coat is lacking in *Chenopodium* from Holman rockshelter. More precisely, Holman *Chenopodium* has a very thin inner epiderm, but the outer epiderm of the seed coat, which is present in both black and red morphs of wild-type *C. berlandieri* seeds, is absent. Absence of the outer epiderm is a characteristic shared with the cultivar *huauzontle* of the Mexican domesticate *C. berlandieri* spp. *nuttalliae*, which remains in cultivation today. Wilson maintains that huauzontle probably was introduced prehistorically to the Ozark region from Mexico. He has also suggested that the Mexican cultivar *chia* of spp. *nuttalliae* may also have been introduced. Chia has a thin outer epiderm like that of the thin-coated seeds from Smiling Dan and other eastern North American sites. Wilson's hypothesis is attractively simple in that it proposes a single center of origin for the *Chenopodium* of North America.

An alternative hypothesis to account for the abundance of the thin-coated seed type at Smiling Dan is that an indigenous domestication of *C. berlandieri* occurred in eastern North America, independently of— but proceeding in a direction parallel to—the selection that produced domesticate *Chenopodium* in Mexico (D. Asch and Asch 1982). Distinguishing between an introduction of the domesticate and its local evolution is a problem made more difficult by the fact that spp. *nuttalliae* belongs to the *berlandieri* complex. Thus, the prehistoric *Chenopodium* from Mexico and midwestern United States was closely related biologically, whatever its origin.

The existence of the thin-coated red morph in modern wild populations of *C. berlandieri* suggests that large genetic changes would not have been required to bring a thin-coated type to dominance. Probably a minor shift in a plant's hormonal balance would suffice. Once cultivation of *Chenopodium* began, a process of "unconscious selection" may have become operative which favored plants that produced greater percentages of thin seed coats and which selected against those producing mostly thick-coated seeds. The process would not have been dependent on intentional selection of desirable seed. When plants are cultivated in dense stands on prepared ground, those which germinate promptly are able to shade out more slowly germinating seedlings. Thus, seeds of quickly germinating plants should be better represented in the harvest. Since germination inhibitors often occur in the outer structures of seeds and fruits, reduction in the thickness of the seed coat permits more rapid germination (Harper, Lovell, and Moore 1970:340–41; Wilson 1981).

One reason that cultivators might have attempted to maintain a thin-coated variety was to reduce the percentage of indigestible matter in a seed harvest. The percentage of fiber in wild *C. bushianum* fruits is Chenop—28% according to one determination by proximate analysis (D. Asch and Asch 1983). Almost all of the fiber is contained in the seed coat and pericarp.

If unconscious selection was the dominant process in domestication, then cultivation of locally derived *C. berlandieri* in Mexico and eastern North America conceivably could have produced a chia-like cultivar independently in both areas. The existence of the thin-coated red morph in wild populations makes such an outcome seem quite plausible. Even the huauzontle cultivar could have arisen separately in both areas. Evidence that elimination of the outer epiderm in cultivated *Chenopodium* seeds is a phenomenon that evolved more than once in the New World is provided in studies of the Andean domesticate *C. quinoa* spp. *quinoa*. Wilson and Heiser (1979:201) found that crosses between quinoa and huauzontle gave hybrids of "uniformly low fertility." Also, loss of the outer epidermi of quinoa and huauzontle appears to be controlled at different gene loci (Heiser and Nelson 1974). Wilson and Heiser, therefore, consider it most probable that quinoa and huauzontle are independent products of domestication.

The chronological record of *Chenopodium*'s utilization is consistent with the hypothesis of independent domestication. As was mentioned above, wild-type, thick-coated *C. berlandieri* was becoming more important economically in west-central Illinois at about 2000 B.C. If this represented the beginning of its cultivation in eastern North America, then there was subsequently a long period for unconscious selection to produce the changes in seed morphology. West-central Illinois lacks a good Early Woodland sample of *Chenopodium*. A sample of dimorphic *Chenopodium* loaned by Richard A. Yarnell and taken from an Early Woodland fecal specimen (SCU–9b) at Salts Cave, Kentucky, may exemplify an intermediate stage in domestication. One paleofecal seed type with 124 specimens averages 1.44 mm in diameter ($n = 15$); it is biconvex and has a thick, black alveolate seed coat. The other type, represented by 156 seeds, has a mean diameter of 2.00 mm ($n = 15$); it has a thin, often reddish, less prominently marked seed coat. The mixture of seed types from Smiling Dan Middle Woodland contexts provides another example of the hypothetical intermediate stage in domestication. At some other west-central Illinois sites, Woodland period collections contain the thin-coated type almost exclusively. One example is the John Roy collection dating to about A.D. 400–550 (D. Asch and Asch 1982). Such collections, like the *Chenopodium* recently described from Russell Cave, Alabama (Smith 1984), could document a further step in domestication of thin-coated forms.

The largest collections of prehistoric *C. berlandieri* from west-central Illinois are the carbonized seed masses from Newbridge site (N. Asch and Asch 1981). Radiocarbon dates for the occupation range from A.D. 480 to A.D. 660. We have tentatively concluded that many are a huauzontle-like type lacking an outer epiderm. Scanning electron micrographs of Newbridge specimens by Bruce Smith, Smithsonian Institution (personal communication, 1984), seem to confirm this impression. If our interpretation is correct, then the occurrence of huauzontle-like seeds in the East is not just a late prehistoric phenomenon of the Ozark periphery. Seeds like those from Newbridge also were present at Smiling Dan in association with the Late Woodland occupation there which dates to A.D. 850-900 (Stafford and Sant 1983).

Polygonum erectum, Knotweed

Knotweed has been documented as an economically important prehistoric species only from the upper Mississippi and Illinois valleys and may have been little used elsewhere in the East. However, in west-central Illinois *Polygonum erectum* is one of the quartet of starchy seeds which dominate in Middle and Late Woodland seed assemblages. Among 28 Middle and Late Woodland archaeological components whose plant remains have been analyzed by the Archeobotanical Laboratory, half had *P. erectum* as the most common seed (technically it is an achene) and the other one half had it as the second or third ranking species. Johannessen (1984) also reports a prominent position for *P. erectum* for Middle and Late Woodland components in the American Bottom.

Few achenes of the plant have been found in pre-Middle Woodland archaeobotanical assemblages. For instance, at Koster only two *P. erectum* achenes—3.5% of the specimens assigned to genus *Polygonum*—are from contexts older than 3000 B.C. For Archaic components at Napoleon Hollow, a single seed of *P. erectum* was identified out of 12 belonging to genus *Polygonum*. By comparison, almost all *Polygonum* from occupations dating to the past 2000 years is assignable to *P. erectum*. A new economic position for *P. erectum* beginning in the Middle Woodland period is implied by the change in species composition of the archaeological *Polygonum*, together with knotweed's much greater abundance at that time. The following paragraphs set forth arguments that this enhanced status reflects incorporation of the plant into the horticultural complex.

The achenes of *Polygonum erectum* are dimorphic. There is a slightly shorter, wider type with a thicker reticulate pericarp and a longer, narrower achene with a smooth thin pericarp. The two types occur on the same plant, with the percentage of smooth seeds increasing late in the fruiting season. Both kinds occur in prehistoric collections. No morphological differences have been noted in these seed types between prehistoric Woodland period collections and modern collections, except for an average 20% reduction (confirmed by experimental carbonization) in the length and width of carbonized prehistoric specimens.

Because changes in achene morphology are lacking and because the natural range of the species includes Illinois and adjacent states, a case for its former cultivation must rest on economic and ecological considerations. The strongest argument is that the abundance of *P. erectum* in natural or weedy stands would have been insufficient to support a harvest at the Woodland level of utilization. It is necessary, therefore, to describe the modern distribution and abundance of the species and to ascertain how these have changed since prehistoric times.

Struever (1968b) proposed that *Polygonum* seeds were harvested prehistorically from plants growing naturally on floodplain mudflats. That habitat, however, is occupied by smartweed species of the section *Persicaria* in the *Polygonum* genus, not by *P. erectum*. The absence of *P. erectum* is substantiated by our own searches for it, by a census of mudflat plants in the central Illinois Valley by Patrick J. Munson (n.d.), and by the absence of knotweed in stomachs of migratory waterfowl, which contain, rather, an abundance of less nutritious smartweed seeds (Anderson 1959).

Floral manuals describe *P. erectum* as a plant of waste places, and we have seen it only in habitats conspicuously disturbed by activities of man and his domestic animals. Euroamerican settlement has undoubtedly multiplied areas suitable for its establishment.

The term "waste place" is too inclusive to delimit adequately the habitats where *P. erectum* thrives. In searching for the plant from Kansas to Kentucky, we have noted three situations in which it may sometimes grow in a dense stand: (1) at the edge and in the center of dirt farmroads in floodplain fields; (2) in large hog lots and cattle pastures established in the bottoms of small valleys, where the concentration of livestock is too low to remove the plant cover completely but great enough that all of the knotweed stems have their tops cropped; (3) on the shoulders of certain paved highways in uplands (observed only in western Missouri) and in bottomlands. We have not seen *P. erectum* along Illinois highways.

Polygonum erectum flowers and fruits throughout the summer and into October, usually interrupted by one or more periods of dormancy in hot, dry weather. The small achenes develop on the plants in axillary locations. During the summer, only a few are ripe and ready to drop at a given moment, so that harvesting of the achenes for food is impractical. However, a synchronized period of flowering late in the growing season produces a quantity of ripe seed during October which can be harvested by pulling up the plants by the roots and shaking or stripping off the seeds into a container. At that time, all of the plants in a dense stand can be harvested. Since a single plant yields a very small amount of seed by weight, an effective harvest is possible only where the species is abundant.

Even in the kinds of disturbed locations described above, the occurrence of a dense, harvestable knotweed stand is the exception rather than the rule. In the Illinois Valley, for example, we have found only one stand where it was abundant enough to collect seed for a meal. It is impossible to reconcile the consistent occurrence of *Polygonum erectum* as a dominant or leading species during Middle and Late Woodland times in west-central Illinois with harvesting from wild or weedy plant populations that were no more extensive—or probably much less extensive—than those of today.

Knotweed is not a garden weed, at least as gardens now are tended. Therefore, it is unlikely that it became available prehistorically as a side effect of cultivating other species. If prehistoric gardens somehow provided precisely the kind of habitat for knotweed to flourish as a weedy plant, one would have to regard the most important product of that garden—knotweed—as a species whose reproduction was deliberately encouraged, whether or not seeds were actually saved for planting.

Could *Polygonum erectum* have been harvested from a rank growth occurring within the disturbed area of prehistoric habitation, thereby eliminating or reducing the element of intentionality in reproductive encouragement? It does occur today as scattered plants—never in harvestable frequencies—within stands of the smaller-seeded knotweed, *Polygonum aviculare*, which forms low mats on hard-packed, trampled ground around human habitations. *P. aviculare* sensu lato is a collective species including weedy taxa introduced from Europe (Mertens and Raven 1965; Savage and Mertens 1968). Could better adapted European knotweeds have displaced *P. erectum* from the most intensively trampled habitats?

If the speculation of habitat displacement (or any other perspective that accords to *Polygonum erectum* the position of an abundant weedy campfollower) were correct, it would introduce a new difficulty—accounting for its absence from Archaic sites. Sites such as Koster and Napoleon Hollow bear evidence of Archaic occupations as intensive and probably nearly as sedentary as those of Woodland times. If Woodland habitation areas were overgrown with knotweed, so too should have been some Archaic habitations. Evidence for Archaic harvesting of *Iva* and giant ragweed indicated some interest in utilizing small edible seeds (D. Asch and Asch 1982), and it is unlikely that an abundant camp following knotweed would be overlooked for exploitation.

Even if the hypothetical camp following knotweed was not collected at all during the Archaic, this economically most attractive species of the native *Polygonums* (see Murray and Sheehan 1984) would be, by hypothesis, the *Polygonum* species most likely to be naturally dispersed into campfires and accidentally preserved. In fact, as noted previously, *P. erectum* is poorly represented among the few *Polygonum* seeds that have been recovered from Archaic archaeobotanical assemblages.

To conclude, the hypothesis of a knotweed cultivation—beginning in west-central Illinois during the Middle Woodland period—is consistent with evidence concerning its prehistoric economic status and with information about its modern natural distribution and abundance. Alternative hypotheses of wild harvesting from mudflats, from weedy garden colonies, or from self-propagating plants with the habitation area are inconsistent with information about the plant's ecology, or else they cannot account for the differences between the Archaic and Woodland period archaeobotanical records.

Recently, we have studied an unusual collection of more than 1200 knotweed achenes from the Mississippian Hill Creek site, whose occupation dates to A.D. 1200 (N. Asch and Asch 1984; Conner 1984). The achenes differ in two respects from those of Woodland period collections: (1) their large size and (2) the exclusive occurrence of the narrow "late season" morph with thin smooth pericarp. With a correction of 20% for shrinkage due to carbonization, the mean length of the Hill Creek achenes, when fresh, would have been 4.2 mm. Corrected mean lengths of the comparable knotweed morph at Woodland period sites have ranged between 3.1 and 3.6 mm, which is consistent with the size of the morph from modern collections of *Polygonum erectum*.

Two alternative hypotheses have been proposed to account for the characteristics of the Hill Creek knotweed (N. Asch and Asch 1984:136–37):

1) The achenes were a domesticated form, potentially the product of unconscious selective pressure in a cultivated population. In a garden setting with intense competition for light in a dense growth of seedling knotweeds, there might be a growth advantage for seedlings that germinate from achenes having a larger than average store of food in the endosperm. Also, in the same manner that selective pressures promoting reduced dormancy in *Chenopodium* could result in thinner seed coats, the exclusive occurrence of thin pericarps in the Hill Creek knotweed might be a consequence of domestication.

2) The Hill Creek achenes are not *Polygonum erectum* but instead are *P. ramosissimum*, another indigenous species of the knotweed section *Polygonum* of genus *Polygonum*. Hill Creek achene lengths are compatible with those of the late season morph of *P. ramosissimum*. Even if the achenes are attributable to that species, it remains necessary to account for the exclusive occurrence of a single morph. Late season collections of *P. erectum* may have a predominance of the morph with a thin smooth pericarp, but ordinarily both morphs are present. Such may also be the case for *P. ramosissimum* (Savage and Mertens 1968:359–60; Brenkle 1946), although further documentation on this point is required. Conceivably, if *P. ramosissimum* was present at Hill Creek, it was a domesticated form of that species selected to produce only the thin-coated morph.

Phalaris caroliniana, Maygrass

Maygrass is one of the starchy-seeded annual species that are dominant in Middle Woodland and Late Woodland seed collections in west-central Illinois.

That maygrass was used as food prehistorically is most convincingly established by the abundance of seeds in Early Woodland feces from Salts amd Mammoth caves, Kentucky (Watson 1974). Bryant (1974:207) also identified chewed stems and leaves of maygrass in Mammoth Cave paleofeces. From west-central Illinois, there are at least two records of carbonized seed masses also providing indisputable evidence that maygrass was an economic species and not an accidental weedy inclusion in archaeobotanical samples. Several small clumps of maygrass caryopses were found in a pit (Feature 61) at the Smiling Dan site. These were clearly concentrations of cleaned seed, fused into a solid mass uncontaminated with sediment or other charcoal when they were burned. The fact that all of the seeds were lacking bracts, including those in the interior of the clumps, suggests that the bracts had somehow been removed prior to carbonization to make a more palatable and nutritious food. Feature 61 yielded a radiocarbon date of 1700 ± 70 B.P.: A.D. 250 (ISGS–958). A second unmistakable economic context was recorded from a pit (Feature 5) at the John Roy site. More than 50,000 carbonized seeds were present in a mass—mostly maygrass caryopses but also knotweed achenes and chenopod seeds. A prolonged storage of seeds at John Roy is implied by the joint presence of a spring food (maygrass) with fall foods (knotweed and chenopod). The seeds yielded a radiocarbon date of 1400 ± 70 B.P.: A.D. 550 (ISGS–971).

The near absence of maygrass from west-central Illinois sites older than Middle Woodland times, contrasted with its subsequent abundance, establishes that a major change occurred in its economic status about 2000 years ago. That the Middle/Late Woodland record of maygrass is a consequence of its cultivation is inferred from the discordance between the modern natural range of the species and its archaeological occurrence outside the limits of the present range. Under natural conditions, maygrass is basically a southern species, ranging across the United States from coast to coast (Hitchcock 1950:554).

Within the Mississippi Valley, in southern Arkansas, we have observed maygrass as an occupant of disturbed habitats—growing in dense stands along many roadsides, railroad embankments, and ditch spoils. Harvesting experiments indicate that it is feasible to collect the seeds for food in dense, naturally established stands. Maygrass becomes very rare north of central Arkansas. Cowan (1978:271) found herbarium records for the species as far north in the Mississippi Valley as the Bootheel of southeastern Missouri and a disjunct record along a railroad in St. Louis, Missouri. In western Missouri it extends northward to the Kansas City region where MacKenzie (1902:21) states that it is "rarely adventized along railroads." We have searched for maygrass unsuccessfully in the localities from which it has been recorded in Missouri and conclude that it must be very rare. East of the Mississippi River in Illinois it has never been recorded (Mohlenbrock 1972:189–90).

Because maygrass is a disturbed ground species that is especially likely to be found along railroads and highways, Euroamerican settlement can be inferred to have increased its abundance and probably to have favored recent range extension along the lines of transportation. As reconstructed from palynological data, the vegetation of Illinois one to two millennia ago was basically comparable to that of present times (J. King 1981). If one supposes that there was a climatic shift sufficient to extend the range of maygrass in abundant natural stands northward by more than 400 kilometers, it is surprising that an associated northward migration of other southern species has not been documented.

Thus, by elimination, intentional propagation remains as the only reasonable explanation why maygrass suddenly occurred about 2000 years ago as a common seed preserved at west-central Illinois archaeological sites. Cultivation of maygrass would not have been difficult. We have raised the plant with good success on a tilled plot in Kampsville from seed collected in southern Arkansas. Seed planted in the fall germinates in cool weather and overwinters, like winter wheat, to produce a crop the next spring in early June (one or two weeks later than in southern Arkansas). Alternatively, seed can be planted in very early spring.

The fact that maygrass germinates readily and is winter hardy at the latitude of west-central Illinois indicates that the northern limit of its natural range is not determined directly by climatic tolerance, but rather through competition with other weedy species which are better adapted at that latitude. The maygrass grown in Kampsville showed little tendency at all to invade adjacent tilled ground. Thus, it is not likely to have become naturalized simply by an introduction of seed to prehistoric campsites of the region. Planting and tilling appear to be essential to the maintenance of harvestable stands in the region.

By 1000 B.C., long before maygrass becomes prominent in the west-central Illinois archaeobotanical record, there is evidence that it was an important economic species in Kentucky (Watson 1974; Cowan et al. 1981). A range extension argument for cultivation is applicable for central and eastern Kentucky as well as for Illinois. Rare specimens have been identified as maygrass from apparently good Archaic contexts in west-central Illinois: at Koster as early as 6250 B.C. and at Campbell Hollow from a 5600 B.C. occupation (D. Asch and Asch 1984). Speculation concerning a long Archaic period of utilization— and cultivation, if one were to employ the range extension argument as well—seems unwarranted, however, until there is additional support for the validity of these records: (1) to demonstrate that they can be no other species than *Phalaris caroliniana* (*P. arundinacea*, a perennial species indigenous to Illinois is an alternative possibility); (2) to establish unequivocally the antiquity of individual maygrass grains, using linear accelerator technology for dating small radiocarbon samples.

Thus far, morphological changes in prehistoric maygrass stemming from selection in cultivated populations have not been established. Johannessen (1981:270–72) gave dimensions for caryopses from three components in the American Bottoms: Truck #7 (Middle Woodland)

= 1.1 mm L × 0.8 mm W; Julien (Early Bluff) = 1.5 mm L × 1.0 mm W; and Julien (Mississippian) = 1.5 mm L × 1.1 mm W. She suggested tentatively that the larger size of the later grains was a product of domestication. Woodland period collections that we have measured have mean grain lengths ranging between 1.4 and 1.6 mm. No collections have mean grain lengths as small as those reported by Johannessen from Truck #7 site, and no obvious temporal trends exist within the narrow range of variation occurring at the west-central Illinois sites we studied.

Comparisons with modern grains indicate that the prehistoric variability is due not to the presence of specimens that are larger than modern ones, but rather to the anomalously small size of the Truck #7 grains. Measurements on modern collections of Arkansas maygrass and from plants subsequently grown in our Kampsville garden give a mean mature grain length of about 2.1 mm. Maximum shrinkage of dimensions in carbonization experiments was approximately 10%. As noted by Cowan (1978:267), maygrass has an indeterminate type of influorescence, and the florets fall free as soon as the grain is ripe. Consequently, any collection of seeds from the compact panicle of maygrass will contain a substantial percentage of immature grains, which slightly reduces the mean grain size. Nevertheless, in Johannessen's prehistoric samples and our own there are only a small percentage of grains equalling or exceeding 1.8 mm in length, a length which is typical of mature, carbonized, modern maygrass. To conclude, prehistoric maygrass grains are if anything slightly smaller than expected if they were grown from populations like those of modern wild plants.

In modern wild collections of maygrass, the grain is tightly enclosed within a chaffy lemma and palea. However, carbonized archaeological maygrass almost always consists of the naked caryopses. Could prehistoric cultivators have selected for a naked grain? According to Cowan (1978:28), maygrass found in paleofeces from dry caves and rockshelters of eastern North America have the grains still enclosed in the lemma and palea. Thus, the absence of lemma and palea in carbonized collections probably is due to the differential potential for carbonization of the chaffy bracts and the caryposis.

Hordeum pusillum, Little Barley

For several years it has been recognized that the Woodland period complex of starchy seeds in eastern North America included goosefoot, knotweed, and maygrass. Now a fourth member of the complex—little barley—has been recognized in west-central Illinois where it probably was a cultivated plant (N. Asch and Asch 1979; D. Asch and Asch 1982, 1983). Little barley also was used by the Hohokam of Arizona by 2000 years ago (Bohrer n.d.; Gasser 1982). Gayle Fritz (Yarnell 1983:6) has identified little barley as an abundant seed type from the Spiro site in Oklahoma. Thus, its use prehistorically was geographically widespread.

Figure 6.8 illustrates a typical well preserved carbonized specimen of little barley. In earlier papers (N. Asch and Asch 1979; D. Asch and Asch 1982), we had tentatively identified this archaeological seed type as a fescue. However, in reviewing modern collections of numerous grass species and conducting experiments to determine the consequences of carbonization on the size and form of the caryopsis, it became clear that the archaeological material most closely resembles *Hordeum pusillum* (D. Asch and Asch 1983). Vorsila Bohrer, who has examined some of the west-central Illinois specimens, concurs in this identification (personal communication).

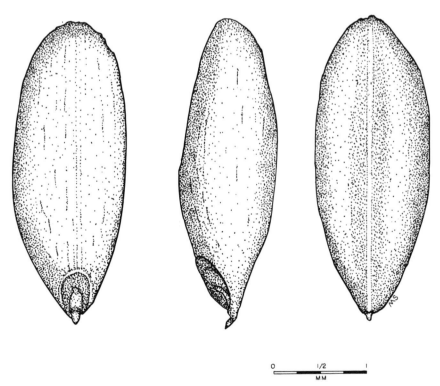

Figure 6.8. Carbonized caryopsis of *Hordeum pusillum*, Smiling Dan site, Feature 212–07P. Illustrated from left to right in ventral, lateral, and dorsal views.

Little barley is best represented in west-central Illinois from two recently studied sites: Smiling Dan and Kuhlman (D. Asch and Asch 1983). From Smiling Dan's Middle Woodland occupation, 15% of a collection of 14,000 identifiable seeds were little barley caryopses. It was the third most common seed type, ranking behind maygrass and knotweed and ahead of goosefoot. Little barley was present in 36% of 744 feature and midden flotation samples, so that it was more widely distributed than any other seed type except knotweed. At the Kuhlman habitation site, which was occupied by maize-growing Late Woodland groups between A.D. 600 and A.D. 1050, small horticultural seeds were quite well represented along with the maize. We found that little barley from Kuhlman constituted one half of a well dispersed seed sample of over 1000 identifiable specimens. Three other Late Woodland or Mississippian occupations have yielded the following record of little barley (as a percentage of identifiable specimens) in small collections of seeds (N. Asch and Asch 1979:125):

Worthy-Merrigan (late Late Woodland
    and Mississippian)   21% of 181 seeds
Carlin (late Late Woodland)   40% of 124 seeds
Deer Track (late Late Woodland)   33% of 122 seeds

Little barley may be less frequently a major seed type at Middle and Late Woodland sites of the region than other starchy cultivated seeds. Its frequency is somewhat underrepresented in seed summaries, however, because in the past it was not always sorted as a distinctive unidentified grass type. Despite this problem it is clear that temporal patterning in the occurrence of little barley at prehistoric sites is basically like that of the other cultivated starchy seeds—that is, it is present at sites younger than 2000 years but is absent or very rare at older sites. One possible exception to the generalization is provided by a small sample of plant remains from a preceramic Terminal Archaic occupation at the Gardens of Kampsville site. Several little barley caryopses were present in samples taken from the site's stratified preceramic midden, which underlies Middle Woodland and Mississippian strata. Little barley was present in two flotation samples whose charcoal was submitted for dating. The dates are 2770 ± 70 B.P.: 820 B.C. (ISGS–1153) and 2550 ± 70 B.P.: 600 B.C. (ISGS–1154).

Little barley is regarded as a native Illinois species, but human disturbance has contributed to its present abundance and aided a northward and eastward range extension (Pammel, Bell, and Lamson-Schribner 1904:304; Deam 1940:114). In *The Grasses of Illinois*, Mosher (1918:413) wrote that little barley "is becoming increasingly abundant over nearly all parts of the state. It is spreading rapidly along the railroad tracts and other waste places, growing in soil in which other plants grow with difficulty." It is also "a common invader on abused native ranges and in tame pastures of low vigor or fertility" (Phillips Petroleum Co. 1963:44). In Illinois and westward, little barley is common at the side of almost every highway.

According to Mosher (1918:413), little barley is usually a winter annual in Illinois, germinating in the fall and remaining green over the winter. It can also germinate in the spring. Among 53 sheets of *H. pusillum* collected in Missouri that we examined in the Missouri Botanical Garden herbarium, St. Louis, almost all of the plants had been collected during the last half of May or the first half of June. On these plants, inflorescences were present, but there usually were no mature caryopses or disarticulating spikelets. In west-central Illinois, we found that mature grains are present on the plants primarily during the second half of June.

A harvest of little barley would have been made two or three weeks after cultivated maygrass was collected. At that early summer season, no other cultivated foods would have been available, and there would have been no significant sources of starchy or oily seeds from wild plants. In processing little barley for consumption, it would be important to achieve a thorough separation of the bracts from the grain. The bristly awns can easily penetrate the mouth, as is the case when the flowering heads are grazed by livestock (Steyermark 1963:133). Bohrer experimented with several methods of removing the bracts of little barley and found the task to be "quite laborious when compared with the ease in threshing and harvesting other grasses" (Gasser 1982:220–21). According to Gasser, other experimenters were able to remove the bracts by parching.

What was the status of little barley in prehistoric Illinois? Because the species grows naturally in disturbed habitats, because the grain may be difficult to process for consumption, and because the grain has not been found in an unambiguous prehistoric storage context or identified in human feces, it is necessary first to consider the possibility that the prehistoric records have resulted from accidental carbonization of a noneconomic campsite weed. The disparity between the Archaic record of this plant and its Middle/Late Woodland record implies that a change did occur in its economic status—toward extensive utilization. As was mentioned in the discussion of knotweed, there were intensive and long-term Archaic occupations in the region during Archaic times which surely created disturbed habitats much like those associated with more recent occupations. Thus, if one were to suppose that little barley was a nonagricultural, noneconomic, campsite weed, it is not evident why there would have been a dramatic shift 2000 years ago in the rate at which its seeds were dispersed naturally into camp-fires. The great abundance and ubiquity of little barley caryopses at some Middle/Late Woodland sites is comparable with that of other cultivated starchy seeds and is far greater than for any other non-economic seeds whose presence could plausibly be due to a natural seed rain into campfires.

Since the prehistoric prominence of little barley in west-central Illinois coincided with the period of intensive horticulture, it is necessary to consider the possibility that it was an agricultural weed. The maturation of little barley does not occur at the season when other prehistoric crops would have been harvested. Thus, its archaeological presence cannot be due to occurrence as a harvest contaminant. Also, little barley presently is an invader of waste ground or degraded pastures. It is not a garden weed in Illinois.

If little barley was an economic plant in the Midwest, were the harvests made from self-propagating stands, or was it cultivated? Ecological/economic arguments for cultivation of little barley are not as strong as those developed for knotweed. Little barley grows densely in modern midwestern stands. At least in small patches it seems likely that wild seed production could equal that of an equivalent area under cultivation. Whether or not dense wild stands are large enough for an effective harvest of grain has not been investigated through harvesting experiments. Moreover, the degree of applicability of modern data on patch size and density to the prehistoric situation is uncertain, since the abundance of the plant is said to have increased after Euroamerican settlement.

Indirect arguments to support the plausibility of cultivation can be advanced. Little barley's use in west-central Illinois is associated with the period of intensive small-seed horticulture. The evidence for it from Smiling Dan and Kuhlman sites implies that it was economically important for some groups. Indeed, no other small, wild seed at Middle/Late Woodland sites has an abundance approaching that of little barley at Smiling Dan and Kuhlman. Finally, if we suppose that self-propagating stands were an attractive resource for Woodland groups, why would little barley have been ignored almost completely by Archaic harvesters who collected other kinds of small seeds?

Gasser (1982) cites an unpublished manuscript by Vorsila Bohrer (n.d.) in which Bohrer notes that carbonized little barley grains in Arizona Hohokam contexts lack hulls and tentatively suggests that a naked barley had been selected through domestication, as was the case with Old World barleys. The carbonized west-central Illinois specimens also are naked grains. We have proposed (D. Asch and Asch

1983) that differential preservation of bracts and caryopses during carbonization may be able to account for this phenomenon. These competing hypotheses to account for the prehistoric naked grains require further evaluation.

Nicotiana sp., Tobacco

Tobacco has been identified at two sites in the lower Illinois Valley. A single seed was present at the Mississippian Hill Creek site from an occupation dating to 1200 B.C. (N. Asch and Asch 1984). Five carbonized seeds were found in Middle Woodland contexts at the Smiling Dan habitation site (D. Asch and Asch 1983). One of the seeds was recovered from a pit feature for which a radiocarbon date of 1790 ± 80 B.P.: A.D. 160 (ISGS–1027) was obtained. The date is consistent with others associated with the site's Middle Woodland occupation (Stafford and Sant 1983).

The seeds of genus *Nicotiana* are of distinctive appearance, especially in the wavy reticulum of their seed coats (Gunn and Gaffney 1974). There are no native tobaccos in eastern North America. *N. rustica* was widely cultivated in the East at the time of contact. Ultimately a plant of South American origin, *N. rustica* is thought to have arrived in the East by way of Mexico, bypassing the Southwest where it seems to have been introduced only in post-contact times by the Spanish (Yarnell 1976:266, 1977:870–72; Ford 1981). Another species, *N. bigelovii* var. *quadrivalvis*, was cultivated historically by Plains tribes of the Missouri basin (Nuttall 1818:132–33, Gilmore 1919:61–62). It appears to have been introduced from California where it grows wild.

Haberman (1984) has classified carbonized archaeological tobacco from South Dakota to the species level on the basis of minor differences in seed form and patterning of reticulations. Goodspeed (1954:89) remarks that *N. rustica* is a "highly polymorphic species." In examining a few collections of North American *N. rustica* and *N. bigelovii* var. *quadrivalvis* from the herbarium of the Missouri Botanical Garden, St. Louis, we noted that seed variability from single plants seemed to be great as the level of variability on which Haberman has attempted to separate the species. In distinguishing these species by their seeds, Haberman may have generalized too broadly from a limited sample of modern comparative material and prehistoric seeds. The overlap between these species in seed form and patterns of reticulation is so substantial that it does not appear that one can reliably assign single seeds to one species or the other. Whether or not large samples of carbonized tobacco seeds can be classified reliably at a species level by the statistical tendencies of seed characters remains to be determined. On the basis of the geographic distribution of tobaccos used by historic Indians, it is most probable that the archaeological seeds from west-central Illinois are *Nicotiana rustica*.

The tobacco seeds from Smiling Dan represent the oldest securely dated occurrence of the plant north of Mexico. Elsewhere in Illinois, tobacco seeds are reported by Johannessen (1984) from Late Woodland and Mississippian sites in the American Bottom. The oldest of the American Bottom contexts for tobacco may date to about A.D. 500–600. On the northern Plains, tobacco has now been identified at several prehistoric sites (Haberman 1984:272–73). The oldest record from that region, from the Rainbow site in northwestern Iowa, probably dates between A.D. 450 and A.D. 650 (Benn 1981). One eastern North American record which could possibly predate the Smiling Dan tobacco is from Newt Kash rockshelter, Kentucky, where Jones (1936:156–57, 163) identified three tobacco seed capsules from among the uncarbonized plant remains. The predominant occupation at Newt Kash was Early Woodland, with radiocarbon dates of 700–650 B.C. (Griffin 1952:367). The association of this tobacco with the site's Early Woodland occupation was regarded by Jones as insecure.

Smoking pipes were used in eastern North America as long ago as Late Archaic times (Winters 1969:68–70), and it is plausible that flotation-aided recovery of plant remains may yet document the co-occurrence of tobacco with the earliest pipes. However, since plants other than tobacco have been used in smoking by eastern North American Indians (Yarnell 1964:85), an archaeological occurrence of pipes does necessarily imply that tobacco was being smoked.

Zea mays, Maize

In this section, we address two chronological questions concerning the incorporation of maize into the regional horticultural system: (1) the date of introduction, and (2) the time at which it became an important crop. It was once commonly postulated that the cultural complexity of Hopewellian and contemporaneous Middle Woodland groups of eastern North America required a productive, dependable subsistence base which was attainable only through maize horticulture (Willey and Phillips 1958:159; Griffin 1960). Numerous records of maize apparently dating to about 2000 years ago, or even before, have been reported from eastern North America (Ford 1979, 1981; Munson 1966, 1973; Yarnell 1964, 1983; Struever and Vickery 1973; Cutler and Blake 1973; D. Asch and Asch 1982). However, the number of such records and the quantities of maize recovered are far fewer than for later prehistoric times, and often the cultural associations of the purportedly early maize have been questioned. In west-central Illinois, intensive flotation sampling from many cultural components predating A.D. 600 have revealed a scanty inventory of possibly associated maize. Nor has Middle Woodland maize dependence been inferred from human skeletal studies (Buikstra 1976). Increases of the $^{13}C/^{12}C$ ratio in human bone due to consumption of maize, whose $^{13}C/^{12}C$ ratio is higher than in most plants, postdate Middle Woodland times (Vogel and van der Merwe 1977; van der Merwe and Vogel 1978; Bender, Baerreis, and Steventon 1981).

At one site in west-central Illinois, Koster East, the transition to intensive maize production may have occurred during a continuous span of Late Woodland occupation. Two Bluff cultural components are recognized at Koster East (Wettersten 1983), based on a distinction between earlier S-twist and later Z-twist pottery. Only one sample from an early component feature contained maize, whereas 24% of late component pits yielded maize. For the early component there is a ^{14}C date of 1330 ± 70 B.P.: A.D. 620 (ISGS–1024) from Feature 1100; the later component has a date of 1120 ± 70 B.P.: A.D. 830(ISGS–1020) from Feature 1040 (which contained maize). Johannessen (1984) found that in the American Bottom the frequency of maize became much greater for sites postdating A.D. 800 than for earlier occupations.

For the region of west-central Illinois north of the American Bottom, Table 6.3 lists all radiocarbon dates on charcoal from maize-containing cultural features of Woodland affiliation. These most stringently verified dates for maize indicate that the plant was introduced at least by A.D. 600.

Other discoveries of maize have been reported that were putatively or possibly associated with occupations prior to A.D. 600. These are enumerated in Table 6.4. Some have been discredited by directly dating the maize by the accelerator radiocarbon detection technique (Conard et al. 1984); others were in contexts that contained younger occupational material or where there was a reasonable probability of admixture with younger material; some of the maize was partially carbonized but came from contexts where such materials should have rapidly decomposed. Some of the maize was present as small fragments in very low frequency from very large flotation samples. Bulk extraction of plant remains by flotation has greatly increased the quantities of plant remains that are routinely analyzed by archaeobotanists, thereby increasing the likelihood that a contaminating specimen will occasionally be found, although perhaps not recognized as such. Because critical maize specimens from bulk samples are usually first identified in the laboratory, the possibility for more than routine inspection of field context is lost. Contamination during the processing

TABLE 6.3
RADIOCARBON DATES ON CHARCOAL FROM MAIZE-CONTAINING
CULTURAL FEATURES OF WOODLAND AFFILIATION

Site	Provenience	Age (B.P.)	Date (A.D.)	Lab. No.
Deer Track	F53	1370 ± 75	580	ISGS-785
Buffalo	F5	1350 ± 70	600	ISGS-1043
Scenic Vista	F42	1270 ± 70	680	ISGS-882
Kuhlman	F71/02–04	1190 ± 70	760	ISGS-864
Koster East	F1040/d–g	1120 ± 70	830	ISGS-1020
Deer Track	F46/00	1110 ± 75	840	ISGS-782
Loy	F19/a–d	970 ± 70	980	ISGS-1091
Loy	F64/b	960 ± 70	990	ISGS-1209
Kuhlman	F51/02–05	920 ± 75	1030	ISGS-805
Healey	F1	880 ± 80	1070	ISGS-1128

of samples for analysis probably is how small maize fragments became incorporated into flotation samples from deeply buried, 8000-year-old occupations at the Koster site (Conard et al. 1984).

Perhaps the most credible discovery among those listed in Table 6.4 is the Peisker site maize, which included carbonized partial cobs and smaller fragments. Some of the maize was said to have occurred in shallow cultural features (Struever and Vickery 1973:1200), and the midden area yielding the maize had primarily Middle Woodland ceramics along with a few early Late Woodland (White Hall) pottery sherds. Still, there are grounds on which a skeptic could question the cultural affiliation of the Peisker corn: (1) A complete inventory of cultural remains from the excavation area is not available, so that the possible presence of a minor late prehistoric occupation cannot be excluded. (2) There may have been brief occupation by historic Indians, since historic Indian burials were found in a mound adjacent to the excavated midden (Perino 1964). (3) There was once a Euroamerican house on another adjacent burial mound. (4) The maize came from a surface occupation area, whose sandy soil was virtually structureless—a situation in which material could easily be intrusive from the surface. (5) R.I. Ford (personal communication) has noted that some of the midden flotation samples contained carbonized European seeds.

Harlan and de Wet (1973) have cautioned that, in evaluating the quality of evidence for the origin and dispersal of cultivated plants, confidence in the authenticity of an association is reduced when the quantity of material is small, however secure the context may seem. This principle applies to the interpretation of evidence for maize in west-central Illinois prior to A.D. 600 when it was a minor subsistence element at best. A conclusive proof of the existence of maize in the region before that time should meet one of the following criteria:

1) A ^{14}C date (with correction for isotopic fractionation) made directly upon the maize, not on what is regarded as associated charcoal.

2) Ubiquitous occurrence of maize fragments in several undisturbed pit fills or in a sealed midden context. Excavations must be extensive enough to exclude the possibility of contamination from a minor late occupation.

In summary, maize clearly was not an important subsistence element in west-central Illinois before A.D. 600 and perhaps not even until after A.D. 800. For many interpretations this conclusion is sufficient, and the question of whether maize was entirely absent at earlier times need not be addressed. Nevertheless, determining more closely the date of introduction remains important for several questions concerning the development of cultivation.

Phaseolus vulgaris, Common Bean

The domesticated common bean was a late introduction to eastern North America, apparently at an A.D. 1000 time horizon (Ford 1981:17; Yarnell 1976:272). Domesticated beans seldom have been reported from Middle Mississippian contexts in Illinois. None were identified in the extensive flotation series from Mississippian sites of the American Bottom that were excavated in recent highway salvage projects (Johannessen 1984). Cutler and Blake (1973:20–22) cite two previous discoveries of common bean from the American Bottom that probably date to A.D. 1050–1150.

To the north in the lower Illinois Valley, the common bean has been identified at two of three Mississippian sites for which substantial archaeobotanical analyses are available: Hill Creek and Worthy-Merrigan (N. Asch and Asch 1984:141–42; Conner 1984; Wettersten 1983). At Hill Creek, a radiocarbon date on carbonized nutshell of 690 ± 75 B.P.: A.D. 1260 (ISGS–1157) was obtained from a refuse pit containing numerous bean cotyledons. Five radiocarbon samples from Hill Creek have an average date of A.D. 1190. Mississippian beans from Worthy-Merrigan are probably older than the Hill Creek beans, but radiocarbon dates are not available for this occupation.

CHRONOLOGICAL SUMMARY

Figure 6.9 provides a summary of the chronology of plants taken into cultivation prehistorically in west-central Illinois.

As early as 5500 B.C. nuts were a major wild plant resource of the

TABLE 6.4
POSSIBLE/PUTATIVE RECORDS OF MAIZE PRIOR TO A.D. 580

Site	Apparent context	Comments	References
Koster, Hor. 9D–9A	Deeply buried Archaic midden dating to 6200–5800 B.C.	Carbonized maize frags. from several flot. samples. Age determined as recent or modern by accelerator ^{14}C dating	Conard et al. 1984
Koster, Hor. 6	Deeply buried Archaic midden dating to 3800–2900 B.C.	3 pollen grains identified as maize	Schoenwetter 1979
Koster, Hor. 4A	Archaic midden, ca. 70 cm beneath LW-Miss. midden	Numerous carbonized maize frags. Age determined as late prehistoric or recent by accelerator ^{14}C dating	Conard et al. 1984
Kuhlman	Titterington Archaic pit at base of plow zone; pit limits ill-defined	Single carbonized cupule. For date on nutshell in pit see Table 6.1. Site also had LW occupation with abundant maize	Unpublished notes, CAA Archeobotanical Laboratory
Cypress Land	Unstratified, disturbed surface midden. Occupations primarily Archaic and EW; very light MW and LW scatter; 1 Miss. hoe recovered	4 carbonized maize frags. from two flotation samples. Carbonized wheat also recovered	N. Asch and Asch 1982:104
Macoupin	MW midden, 10 cm below plow zone	Partially carbonized cob. No maize identified by R.I. Ford in large flot. series	Rackerby 1969, 1982; Cutler and Blake 1973:27; Struever and Vickery 1973:1200; Ford 1979.
Macoupin	MW midden	Single maize pollen grain out of 50 samples analyzed by J. Schoenwetter	See above
Napoleon Hollow	Middle Woodland trash dump at surface on steep unplowed slope	3 carbonized maize frags. Age of one determined as modern by accelerator ^{14}C dating	Conard et al. 1984, N. Asch and Asch 1983

Site	Description	Findings	References
Loy	Surface habitation site. Occupations predominantly MW and LW (ca. A.D. 1000)	2 possible carbonized kernels in 2 MW pits; 2 kernel frags. in third MW pit in area of extensive LW disturbance. Maize abundant in site's LW contexts	Unpublished notes, CAA Archeobotanical Laboratory
Peisker	Surface occupations on sandy terrace. Mostly MW, some early LW	Several carbonized cob frags. and smaller frags. Some maize said to occur in MW pit	Struever and Vickery 1973, Cutler and Blake 1973, Ford 1979
Crane	Predominantly MW midden, small LW (Jersey Bluff) occupation	Carbonized maize frags. in 23 of 220 midden samples, none in definite MW pit assoc. Accelerator ^{14}C technique gave date of 1450 ± 350 B.P. (NSRL–302) on one maize sample	Conard et al. 1984, Carr 1982:184–191.
Smiling Dan	Stratified midden at contact between MW and LW (post-A.D. 800 levels)	Carbonized maize frags. in 4 midden samples	D. Asch and Asch 1983
Ansell-Knight	Pit containing MW,LW,Miss sherds	Charred kernels and cornstalk	McGregor 1958:169, Griffin 1960:23–24
Apple Creek	MW and early LW (White Hall) midden	Partially carbonized cob	Cutler and Blake 1973:26
Newbridge	Predominantly early LW (White Hall) midden; minor post-White Hall occupation after A.D. 600	5 carbonized maize frags. from 3 flotation samples	N. Asch and Asch 1981:288

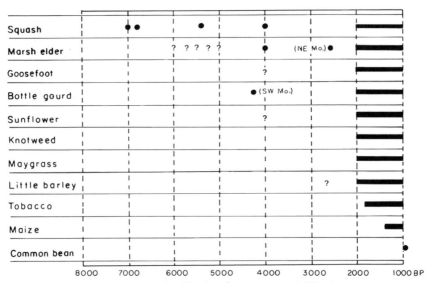

Figure 6.9. Chronology of cultivation for west-central Illinois.

region's hunters and gatherers. Minor wild foods included *Apios* tubers (groundnut), fruits, and—to a very minor degree—starchy/oily seeds such as giant ragweed. The first cultivated species, *Cucurbita* sp. (probably pepo squash), was introduced by 5000 B.C. It may have been more valued for technological purposes than as a food. Harvesting of marsh elder (*Iva annua*) achenes and the possible cultivation of this species began about 4000 B.C. By 2000 B.C. increases in the size of *Iva* achenes register that its development as a domesticate had begun. A nondomesticated form of *Chenopodium berlandieri* (goosefoot) also was utilized and may have been cultivated at 2000 B.C., and possibly common sunflower (*Helianthus annuus*) was cultivated then as well. Since bottle gourd (*Lagenaria siceraria*) had been introduced by 2300 B.C. to southwestern Missouri, it is possible (but unsubstantiated) that this cucurbit was another member of the 2000 B.C. horticultural complex in west-central Illinois.

The next two millennia mark a virtual hiatus in horticultural activity in the region, even though substantial dependence on crop plants had developed in other areas such as Kentucky by 1000 B.C. With the advent of the Middle Woodland period (certainly by A.D. 1), there is evidence of major horticultural dependence in west-central Illinois. Cultivated species included two cucurbits (squash, bottle gourd), tobacco, two domesticated oil seeds (*Iva*, sunflower), and four starchy seeds. The latter are domesticated goosefoot (*Chenopodium berlandieri*), a knotweed (*Polygonum erectum*), maygrass (*Phalaris caroliniana*), and very likely little barley (*Hordeum pusillum*). If maize was grown at this time in west-central Illinois, it was a very minor cultigen.

More adequate records for maize begin in the region at A.D. 600, and by A.D. 800 maize was a major crop of many groups. The common bean (*Phaseolus vulgaris*) was not introduced until the Mississippian period, presumably at about A.D. 1000. Use of the cultivated species that are indigenous to eastern North America continued into the Mississippian period. One of them, knotweed, may even show its first development as a domesticate at that late period.

By the historic period, the group of species introduced from beyond eastern North America had almost completely supplanted the native crops. Of the latter, only sunflower was maintained in cultivation by the historic Indians of Illinois.

ACKNOWLEDGMENTS

The recent botanical work for this study was funded primarily by the Illinois Department of Transportation and the Center for American Archeology. Marjorie B. Schroeder provided valuable assistance in archaeobotanical analyses and the final preparation of the report. Gloria M. Caddell also rendered important assistance in the analyses. This paper would not have been possible without the efforts of the many archaeologists who excavated and floated the plant remains. Among the excavation projects/project supervisors are Ambrose Flick and Bushmeyer (C. R. McGimsey, C. R. Stafford), Campbell Hollow (C. R. Stafford), Crane and Loy (K. B. Farnsworth), Cypress Land and Hill Creek (M. D. Conner), Deer Track (C. R. McGimsey), John Roy (A. L. Koski), Koster (J. A. Brown, S. Struever, R. K. Vierra), Koster East and Worthy-Merrigan (V. H. Wettersten, J. P. Nicholas), Kuhlman and Scenic Vista (H. Hassen), Lagoon (T. G. Cook), Macoupin (F. Rackerby, S. Struever), Napoleon Hollow (M. D. Wiant), Newbridge (S. Struever, B. W. Styles), Smiling Dan (M. B. Sant, B. D. Stafford).

Understanding the Evolution of Plant Husbandry in Eastern North America: Lessons from Botany, Ethnography and Archaeology

C. Wesley Cowan
The Cincinnati Museum of Natural History

At the present time we know a good deal about the order *in which various plants were domesticated in several areas. We still do not know why they were domesticated, and it will certainly be a long time before we do.*

[Flannery 1973:287]

Flannery's statement regarding the origins of agriculture in Mesoamerica adequately reflects the current picture of the evolution of food production in eastern North America. In 1968 Stuart Struever first advocated the use of flotation as a means of collecting information relevant to understanding past environments and subsistence economies. Since then, the archaeological community has admirably responded to his call to arms, and it is fair to say that annually tons of archaeological sediments are routinely "floated" for their contents. As a result, our information concerning past environments and subsistence strategies has taken a quantum leap in the past decade as more and more graduate and undergraduate students have made the decision to while away their time hunched over dissecting microscopes sorting through kilos of charred and uncharred plant remains. The resulting analyses have revolutionized our thinking regarding the origins of agriculture in eastern North America. Unfortunately we still know more about specific events than the processes involved.

With the discovery that squash and gourds were cultivated in several places in the east by 2000 B.C. (Chomko and Crawford 1978), for instance, we have seen our most cherished paradigms concerning the "Archaic" populations in the East utterly shattered. Caldwell's (1958) "primary forest efficiency" model has been discarded in favor of more multivariate models. Still, the question of *why* foraging populations in the East abandoned an economic pattern that had sustained them for almost 7000 years remains largely unanswered, and will likely remain so for years to come. Surely diffusion of an "idea" is not the sole anwer, and indeed there is probably no single answer.

This paper will present no new explanatory model to account for the evolution of plant husbandry in the East; I merely expand on one that has already been proposed. Because many readers may not be familiar with the Eastern Agricultural Complex, I begin with a brief review of its component plants. While many of these have received extensive treatment in recent publications, others have not heretofore been considered, and are discussed in some detail. In the second portion, I briefly discuss ethnographically documented hunting and gathering systems with an eye towards those factors which promote stability as well as those which disrupt the system and can lead to change. The third section examines the model which many archaeologists now use to help them understand the evolution of the Eastern Agricultural Complex, and presents a specific example from the Cumberland Plateau region of eastern Kentucky.

THE CAST OF CHARACTERS

Before launching into the evolution of crops and culture in the Eastern Woodlands, a review of the various species of plants that comprise the Eastern Agricultural Complex is perhaps in order. While technically squash and gourd are members of this group, they are not discussed here since neither is indigenous to eastern North America. At least three of the plants have received extensive treatment recently: goosefoot (Asch and Asch 1977), sumpweed (Asch and Asch 1978), and maygrass (Cowan 1978). In addition to the traditional members, the case for cultivation of several other plants is also briefly reviewed.

The Weedy Annuals

Five species of plants—sunflower (*Helianthus annuus*), sumpweed (*Iva annua* var. *macrocarpa*), goosefoot (*Chenopodium bushianum*), maygrass (*Phalaris caroliniana*) and giant ragweed (*Ambrosia trifida*)—have at one time or another been thought of as species that were cultivated by native eastern North Americans. Although members of three different families of plants, all share several common characteristics. They all complete their life cycles within the space of a single growing season, and are thus dependent on reproductive structures produced during one season to provide the basis for the next season's growth. Botanically, they are all "weeds" in that they are able to withstand a variety of habitat conditions, ranging from flood-deposited alluvium to sidewalk cracks in many of our cities. They are a major pest to our agricultural products because of their ability to invade cultivated fields, and are controlled only by the annual application of thousands of tons of commercial herbicide. In spite of efforts to eradicate these "problem" plants, they persist.

Helianthus annuus L. (Sunflower)

The origins of the domesticated sunflower in eastern North America are quite poorly understood. In part this is a result of the tremendous distribution of wild *Helianthus* species in North America, but also stems from the fact that archaeologically, sunflower remains are comparatively rare. The earliest securely dated sunflower achenes in the East (900 B.C. from the Terminal Archaic Higgs site in Tennessee) (Brewer 1973) are the domesticated *annuus* species, and *Helianthus* records prior to this time are virtually nonexistent. From a historical standpoint then, information regarding the evolution of the sunflower is woefully lacking.

Ford (1974, 1977) has stressed the role of allotoxins produced by the plant which inhibit stands from becoming permanently established in one area. While he has suggested that human populations could overcome this problem by breaking up the soil to prevent the buildup of these toxins, this does not constitute an explanation for the origins of its cultivation.

The sunflower is one of two members of the Eastern Agricultural Complex that apparently underwent a change in its genetic makeup. Its presumed wild ancestor (*H. annuus lenticularis*) produces achenes ranging in length from 4.5 to 5.0 mm (Heiser 1954) yet archaeological examples of the cultivated *H. annuus* have been recorded as large as 13 mm (Yarnell 1978). Unfortunately, almost all archaeological collections

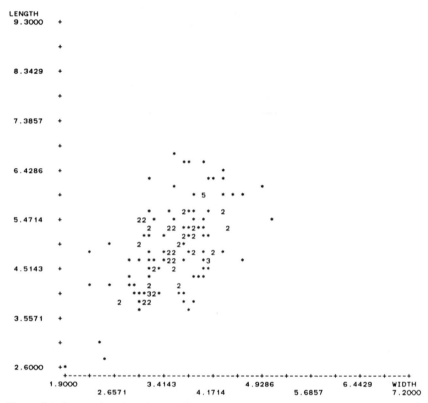

Figure 7.1. Scatterplot of Early Woodland *Iva annua* var. *macrocarpa* achene lengths and widths (*N* = 143) from the Cloudsplitter rockshelter, Menifee County, Kentucky (ca. 700–300 B.C.).

from the East are inadequate for statistical study, and all exhibit a tremendous range of variability. Consequently, it is difficult to identify an overall trend in the change of achene size through time.

Iva annua var. *macrocarpa* (Sumpweed)

This rather innocuous plant has received more attention than any other member of the complex because it underwent extensive genetic change as a result of the activities of prehistoric gardeners. The botanical characteristics of the plant, its natural availability, and harvesting potential, as well as its nutritive qualities have been recently reviewed (cf. Asch and Asch 1978; Yarnell 1978), and the reader should turn to these sources for a detailed description of the evolution of its use in eastern North America. There are, however, two points that I wish to make concerning the plant.

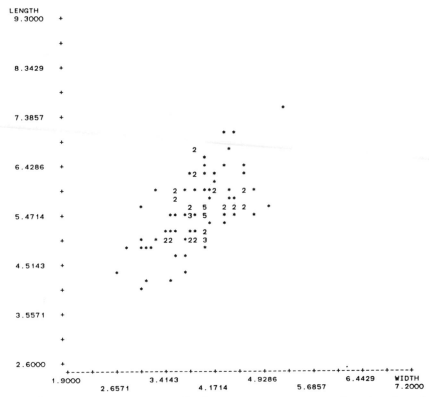

Figure 7.2. Scatterplot of Early Woodland *Iva annua* var. *macrocarpa* achene lengths and widths (*N* = 100) from the Newt Kash Hollow rockshelter, Menifee County, Kentucky (ca. 650 B.C.).

Through selection for larger and larger achenes, and probably by the removal of sumpweed from its preferred natural habitat, prehistoric human populations were able to drastically alter the size of the achenes. Yarnell (1978), for instance, has shown that length and width of achenes increases on the order of 1 mm/1000 years.

Apparently, however, prehistoric gardeners found it difficult to improve sumpweed to the point where a homogeneous crop could be harvested. Theoretically, because the plant is wind-pollinated, it would have been difficult to maintain genetically "pure" improved strains.

This phenomenon is also illustrated by the scatterplots of length versus width for dessicated *macrocarpa* populations from four archaeological sites ranging in age from approximately 700 B.C. to presumably quite late in prehistoric times. As the plots indicate, while achene size generally increases, there is a fairly strong tendency for the distributions to become more widely dispersed through time, suggesting

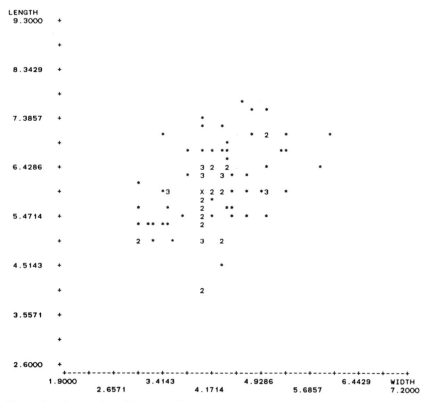

Figure 7.3. Scatterplot of Late Woodland *Iva annua* var. *macrocarpa* achene lengths and widths ($N = 117$) from the Rogers and Haystack rockshelters, Powell County (ca. A.D. 500).

that population variability was simultaneously increasing, rather than decreasing. Thus it may not always be possible to assign isolated achenes to a specific cultural/temporal period solely on the basis of size.

A second point that should be made concerns the present-day distribution of the wild ancestor of *Iva annua*, var. *macrocarpa*. A critical part of the original argument concerning its status as a domesticate (cf. Yarnell 1972) was the fact that large sumpweed achenes had been recovered in archaeological contexts far outside the natural distribution of the plant. Presumably, human populations were responsible for increasing the range of the plant. Two specific examples were cited: achenes from Salts Cave in central Kentucky, and those from the Newt Kash Hollow rockshelter in eastern Kentucky.

Recently, a wild population of sumpweed was located by members of

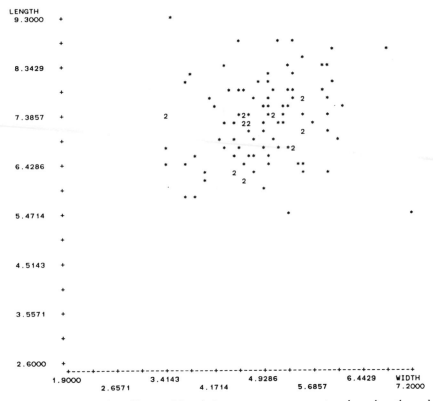

Figure 7.4. Scatterplot of late prehistoric *Iva annua* var. *macrocarpa* achene lengths and widths (*N* = 103) from the Alred bluff shelter, Benton County, Arkansas (ca. A.D. 1000–1200?).

the Shell Mound Archaeological Project in the Big Bend area of the Green River, a few short miles downstream from Salts Cave. An eastern Kentucky population has also been recently located in Pulaski County in the Cumberland River drainage. While this does not alter our conclusions concerning the domesticate status of sumpweed, it does indicate that initial cultivation of the plant could theoretically have commenced in any number of areas.

Chenopodium bushianum Aellen (Goosefoot)

Because the evidence for the prehistoric cultivation of this plant has been thoroughly reviewed in a recent publication (Asch and Asch 1977), the discussion here will be brief. At the present time there is little doubt that by the first millennium B.C. this large-seeded chenopod was an important part of the economies of prehistoric cultural groups ranging from the Mississippi River to the eastern slopes of the Appalachians. In spite of its widespread archaeological distribution, *Chenopodium bushianum* does not have a pan–eastern North American distribution. Furthermore, in several areas where we can document its archaeological occurrence, it does not seem to grow today (e.g., the Green and Red River drainages of Kentucky).

Even where *Chenopodium bushianum* occurs naturally, its economic potential is limited by the fact that it is not a common species. Regardless of its scarcity today, seeds of this goosefoot species are extremely common components of many archaeobotanical assemblages in the East. Our best direct evidence for the intensive use of the plant is exemplified by remains from Kentucky cave and rockshelter sites where human coprolites have consistently yielded large quantities of the small seeds (Jones 1936; Yarnell 1969, 1974a; Stewart 1974). Large masses of charred seeds have also been reported from Illinois and Ohio (Struever and Vickery 1973).

Initially it was thought that archaeological goosefoot identified as *C. bushianum* was little different from its modern counterpart. Recently, however, Smith (in press, 1984) has discovered there are significant differences in the thickness of the seed coat of archaeological and modern chenopods identified as *C. bushianum*. Goosefoot grains from a number of sites exhibit a thin, at times almost translucent, pericarp. This trait is not found in wild chenopods, but is characteristic of the contemporary Mexican domesticate *C. berlandieri* spp. *nuttaliae* cv. "chia." Smith feels this, along with other morphological differences, provides compelling evidence that a domesticated chenopod was being grown in some areas of the Southeast and perhaps Midwest by as early as 4000 years ago.

At the present time nomenclatural status of this seemingly distinct archaeological chenopod is unclear. While obviously a member of the subsection Cellulata, sharing a number of characteristics with both *C. berlandieri* and *C. bushianum*, it has yet to be decided whether the archaeological specimens warrant a new subspecies description. Whatever the taxonomic case, it seems clear that goosefoot may soon be added to our list of truly domesticated eastern agricultural plants.

Phalaris caroliniana Walt. (Maygrass)

Like *Chenopodium*, the cultigen status of this grass has recently been reviewed (Cowan 1978). Archaeologically, maygrass has been far north and east of its present distribution, often in contexts with other members of the Eastern Agricultural Complex. Although apparently a member of the complex, maygrass does not seem to have been genetically affected by its use by humans.

Maygrass is best described as an adventive weed that can tolerate a wide variety of habitats. The attraction of the plants to humans probably lies in the fact that its seeds (technically caryopses) are produced in a tightly packed terminal inflorescence. Nutritionally, maygrass seems to be on par with *Chenopodium* (cf. Asch and Asch 1978; Crites and Terry 1984).

The significance of maygrass in prehistoric economies in the East cannot easily be assessed. In general, the seeds are not often identified in flotation samples, but this may be more a factor of the manner in which it was prepared for consumption than an accurate reflection of the intensity of its use. However, at Salts and Mammoth caves, Kentucky, maygrass in dessicated coprolites was either extremely scarce, or present in great bulk (Yarnell 1969, 1974; Stewart 1974). This has suggested to Yarnell that large quantities of maygrass were not available for harvest or storage. It should be remembered, however, that the coprolites deposited in the caves by gypsum and mirabilite miners may not accurately represent the day to day diet of the human population.

Archaeological specimens of maygrass are no different from their modern counterparts, and there is little reason to believe that they were genetically different from present-day populations. Once again rockshelter data from eastern Kentucky may provide a partial answer. Virtually intact plants, but minus the seed-bearing inflorescences, are present in the materials from the Newt Kash Hollow shelter that are on file at the University of Michigan Ethnobotanical Laboratory, while scattered inflorescences have been found at many Kentucky and Ozark shelters. This suggests that maygrass, like *C. bushianum*, may have been harvested by pulling up the entire plant. Later the inflorescences may have been broken off in order to thresh the seeds.

Maygrass normally becomes available for harvesting by the latter part of May and early June. In eastern North America this is a time when plant protein is extremely scarce, and it has been suggested that maygrass may have been an important early spring commodity (Cowan 1978). Whenever found in eastern Kentucky rockshelters, however, maygrass *always* occurs in contexts with plant products that become available in the early fall. This raises the question of whether the natural period of availability of the plant could have been delayed by planting the seeds in the spring along with other garden crops.

Support for this hypothesis has not yet been assembled through experimental work with maygrass. Bye (1979) has reported a similar practice employed by the Tarahumara of northern Mexico who sow wild mustard seed (*Brassica campestris*) late in the growing season in order to stimulate increased vegetative growth of the plants. If it can be demonstrated that the natural availability of maygrass can be delayed in a similar fashion, then the case for actual planting of the seed will be considerably strengthened, and a thorny archaeological problem can be resolved.

Ambrosia trifida L. (Giant Ragweed)

Nearly a half century ago Melvin R. Gilmore (1931) suggested that giant ragweed was cultivated by prehistoric Ozark bluff dwellers. Gilmore based his judgment on several observations: (1) large quantities of ragweed achenes were found cached away with other cultivated plant foods, (2) many of the achenes appeared to be "4 to 5 times the size" of achenes he had observed from modern wild populations, and (3) all achenes were of a uniformly light color, as opposed to the dark brown color of achenes from wild populations. Later Payne and Jones (1962) restudied many of the Ozark ragweed achenes and demonstrated that the Ozark achenes were no larger than contemporary achenes, and were simply the result of clinal variation in modern populations.

With the publication of Jones and Payne's study, the cultigen status of ragweed was considered a dead issue. Their findings have, in fact, been supported by numerous recent analyses of archaeobotanical materials from other sites in the East. A single crushed achene was found in one fecal sample and in several levels of the Salts Cave vestibule (Yarnell 1969, 1974), but no other evidence for their use has ever been reported.

Recent excavations at the Cloudsplitter rockshelter in eastern Kentucky force us to reexamine ragweed's potential cultigen status. Giant ragweed achenes are entirely absent from the deposits before 3000 B.P. After this time, achenes occur throughout the Early Woodland deposits, in nearly every case in clear association with squash, gourd, sunflower, goosefoot, sumpweed and maygrass. They are not frequent, and always occur in low quantities in comparison to the other annuals, but nonetheless, this clear-cut association must be explained.

In order to partially assess the feasibility of the cultivation of ragweed, several experiments were conducted in the Big Bend of the Green River of western Kentucky during fall of 1979 to determine the practicality of collecting ragweed under prehistoric conditions.

A series of harvesting experiments was conducted in mid-October. By this time the plants were in various stages of senescence, and many of the tallest specimens had fallen over with their upper portions lying partially on the ground. Even so, many of the achenes had not yet fully matured, and their pericarps were noticeably light tan in color.

Two forms of plants were present—a tall, slender, unbranched form as tall as five meters, and a shorter, many-branched variety. Plants of the latter variety were located only on the edges of the stand; by far the majority were of the tall unbranched variety.

Achenes were harvested by hand stripping. Each harvester grasped the axial inflorescences, pulled them off the plant, and placed them into a large plastic bag. Three persons harvested achenes for a total of five minutes, and four such five-minute trials were conducted.

After the achenes had been stripped, they were air dried for several days and cleaned of floral bracts and stem fragments. Cleaning was accomplished by hand, and proved to be highly time consuming. In every case, nearly three to four times as much time was spent cleaning the achenes than had been spent in their actual harvesting.

The results of these harvesting experiments are presented in Table 7.1. Harvesting rates from individual to individual varied considerably, and probably reflect one or more of the following: maturity of achenes, interest on the part of the harvester, and intensity of collecting. It should be noted that harvesters were instructed *not* to collect achenes as rapidly as they could, since prehistorically harvesting was likely a highly social activity, and workers probably stopped frequently for rest and idle conversation. Thus the rates reported here are not strictly comparable with the average .5 kg/hr kernel collecting rate reported for sumpweed by the Asches (1978), who harvested at "top speed." On the other hand, the rates are probably lower than those achieved by prehistoric harvesters. Invariably hand stripping produced a considerable amount of waste materials (e.g., floral bracts, small leaves, and stems) that must be removed by hand. A more reasonable harvesting method probably incorporated a system like that used by native Americans in the Great Basin and California. Here seeds were beaten off the plants by means of a wooden club and collected in large baskets. By utilizing such a technique for ragweed, the harvesting rate might be lower, but would assure the collector of a harvest of fully mature achenes.

The ragweed harvesting experiments are important because they conclusively demonstrate that the seeds of this plant are the least efficient to harvest of any of the Eastern Complex plants, and that only in a dense field-type situation would it be practical.

Considering the fact that archaeological ragweed achenes from Cloudsplitter are no larger than their modern counterparts, the most plausible explanation for their presence in archaeological deposits

TABLE 7.1
HARVEST RATES FOR *Ambrosia trifida* ACHENES
IN THE BIG BEND OF BUTLER COUNTY, KENTUCKY

Trial Number	COLLECTOR 1		COLLECTOR 2		COLLECTOR 3	
	Kg. Kernel/hr.*	Kg. Kernel/day**	Kg. Kernel/hr.	Kg. Kernel/day	Kg. Kernel/hr.	Kg. Kernel/day
1	.09	.72	.06	.36	.20	1.60
2	.09	.72	.09	.81	.15	1.20
3	.11	.88	.20	1.60	.23	1.84
4	.07	.56	.14	1.12	.27	2.16

*Assuming 55% of the achene weight is composed of pericarp.
**Based on averages of 8 hours.

after 1000 B.C. is that achenes were collected from plants that sprang up as weeds in garden plots. That these plants were allowed to reach maturity speaks of a *form* of cultivation in itself since the young plants were not removed, but were encouraged members of a cultivated plant community. In "marginal" environments such as eastern Kentucky, they could have assumed a dietary importance not equalled by other richer food producing areas.

Minor Possible Cultigens

Polygonum erectum L. (Erect Knotweed)

By A.D. 500, the seeds of erect knotweed are the most common small seed in flotation samples in the lower Illinois River valley (D. Asch, personal communication). Yet today, this particular knotweed species is not present in large enough stands to warrant the extensive utilization that it seems to have experienced. Like all of the weedy annuals, its present distribution is almost certainly restricted by the use of modern herbicides, and hypotheses concerning its status as a cultigen must be viewed with caution.

Apios americana L. (Groundnut)

Beardsley's (1939) review of the use of the groundnut in eastern North America indicates that the small tubers of this plant were an extremely important early spring and summer resource of many historic Indian groups. In addition, she cites several authors (Rafinesque, quoted in Harvard 1895; Waugh 1916) who reported that groundnut was "cultivated" for both its tubers and seeds. Unfortunately, neither source mentions the method(s) of cultivation. Archaeologically the use of groundnut tubers is difficult to detect. Most historic accounts indicate that the tubers were prepared for consumption by boiling. Because of this, the chances that they could be included in the archaeological record are significantly reduced. Nonetheless, they have occasionally been reported (Cutler and Blake 1973). Perhaps groundnut, like many other plants, was "cultivated" more by protection than by extensive manipulation.

Arboriculture in the East

Arboriculture, the planting and/or tending of trees, is most often thought of as a European introduction to North America. Among non-Western societies today, it is especially important in tropical or subtropical areas among fully agricultural populations (cf. Yen 1974;

Conklin 1957). Since the annual masts of canopy-level trees provided the staple commodities to eastern North American populations for thousands of years, the question can be legitimately asked: Was arboriculture practiced in eastern North America *before* the first European settlers brought with them their retinue of Old World tree crops? The cases for two classes of tree crops in common prehistoric usage throughout eastern North America—nuts and fruit trees—are examined below.

Nut Trees

Long before the advent of the systematic collection of archaeobotanical remains began, eastern North American archaeologists surmised that nuts from a variety of forest trees were an integral portion of the economic systems of foraging populations, and recent paleoethnobotanical analyses have borne this out. Next to wood charcoal, carbonized nut shells are generally the single most common component of paleoethnobotanical samples from 7000 B.C. until the rise of field agriculture. Even after the advent of intensive maize cultivation, nuts continued to be an important collected resource. In fact, references to the utilization of nuts continues well into the mid-nineteenth century. At this stage, nuts were, of course, supplanted in importance by agricultural staples, but continued to be major hedges against the sort of environmental disaster that crops were subject to.

Were important nut trees cultivated? Bartram (1958), for instance, reports seeing shagbark hickory and black walnut trees in abandoned Indian fields in Georgia that suggested to him that "these trees were cultivated by the ancients on account of their fruits . . ."

The answer to this question is integrally tied to the biology and growth habits of most of our native eastern North American nut trees. All are wind-pollinated and can tolerate a bewildering array of temperature and edaphic regimes, and thus are not easily manipulated genetically. With the exception of pecan, numerous efforts by modern plant breeders have not produced important cultivars. Perhaps more importantly, most of our nut trees do not produce fruits until they are fairly old (Table 7.2), and even then, do not become really productive until much later.

Fruit Trees

When Hernando De Soto and his army marched through the southeastern United States in the middle of the sixteenth century, they were, for the most part, dependent for their livelihood on the stored prod-

TABLE 7.2
AGES OF FIRST MAST PRODUCTION
IN IMPORTANT EASTERN NORTH AMERICAN NUT BEARING TREES*

Genus/Species	Common Name	Earliest Date of Seed Bearing (in years)
Juglans nigra	black walnut	12
Juglans cinerea	butternut	20
Carya glabra	pignut hickory	30
Carya laciniosa	shellbark hickory	40
Carya ovata	shagbark hickory	40
Carya tomentosa	mockernut hickory	25
Carya illinoiensis	pecan	10–20
Quercus alba	white oak	20
Quercus coccinea	scarlet oak	20
Quercus macrocarpa	burr oak	35
Quercus rubra	red oak	25
Quercus velutina	black oak	20
Quercus prinus	chestnut oak	20

*From: Silvics of the Forest Trees of the United States of America. USDA Handbook No. 271, 1965.

ucts of the local inhabitants they subjugated. Besides maize, two other plants are consistently noted by De Soto's chronicler, the Gentleman of Elvas—"walnuts" (probably hickory nuts) and plums. Elvas describes the latter as being "finer than any grown in Spain", and "large quantities" of the dried fruits were found stored in several of the villages (Bourne 1904). Likewise, several early chroniclers mention quantities of persimmon "bread" (sun dried sheets of persimmon) as an important commodity among several of the southeastern groups (see Swanton 1946).

Both plum and persimmon trees are poor competitors with canopy-level trees, and do best in disturbed habitats. In general, seeds of these species are not often present in paleoethnobotanical assemblages in the East until quite late in the prehistoric record, where they are good indicators of the massive disturbance of the landscape by Late Woodland and Mississippian agriculturalists.

Considering Bartram's observations, there is little reason to doubt that some simple form of arboriculture was practiced by at least late prehistoric eastern North American populations. Simple weeding around young shoots and saplings, for instance, might have imparted an advantage to young plants by eliminating competitors. Protection of older trees in garden plots probably led to several beneficial results, not only to the plants, but also to the human groups who utilized their products. Young trees that became isolated in clearing might respond to the increased amounts of solar radiation by increasing their overall crown areas, opening the way for a larger crop than might normally be produced in a closed canopy forest. In addition, the fruits themselves would probably require less effort to collect since they would be easier to reach and more visible on the ground.

ECONOMICS AMONG HUNTERS AND GATHERERS

Before the appearance of *Man the Hunter* (Lee and DeVore 1968) and *Stone Age Economics* (Sahlins 1972), hunting and gathering was seen as a precarious way of life. Constantly on the move in search of food, foragers were seen as having little time for the "finer things in life" supposedly available to agricultural populations. Both of these works helped to dispel this anthropological myth by pointing out that in general, hunters and gatherers devote a relatively small amount of time in procuring the materials necessary to sustain them, and that in fact, foraging requires less labor, and is far less precarious than agriculture.

In an evolutionary sense, hunting and gathering can be seen as a remarkably stable adaptive pattern. In the Old World, foraging sustained human (or human-like) populations for millions of years; in the temperate forest region of eastern North America the record is, of course, not as lengthy, but truly agricultural societies did not appear for almost 8000 years. What then, are the mechanisms responsible for this stability?

As Keene (1979) and Winterhalder (1977) have suggested, hunters and gatherers organize their foraging activities around minimizing cost and risk. Cost can be defined as a "complex function of time invested (in procuring a specific resource), energy expended (in procurement effort), and risk incurred (in procurement)" (Keene 1979:21). While Keene defines risk along two dimensions, personal risk to the physical well-being of the forager as well as risk of failure in procurement of a specific resource, for our purposes risk may be defined as a probability function in which the probable success or failure of a particular foraging activity is weighed. Based on these definitions it can be predicted that hunters and gatherers select those resources that minimize time and effort spent in collecting and processing; they do not consciously seek to maximize their returns for time and energy invested. Since information about foraging activities in humans is in part transferred from one generation to the next, we can also predict that foragers select those resources that are culturally *perceived* to be stable and predictable.

Basically there are two types of resources utilized by foraging societies: fixed-place, or stationary resources, and mobile resources. Examples of the former would include such items as lithic resources used for chipped or ground stone tools, mussel shoals, and importantly, plants. The latter includes virtually all types of terrestrial, avian and aquatic fauna. Based solely on this definition, collection of fixed-place resources should be less costly to collect than mobile resources since their location within a given environment does not change, and they are more predictable in their annual yield. In fact, plant foods *do* constitute the bulk of the diet of most hunters and gatherers, with the exception of groups living in the Arctic.

This does not mean that fixed-place resources are collected to the exclusion of mobile resources. Virtually all plants are deficient in one or more essential proteins, vitamins, or amino acids that are necessary to maintain a human population, and these can only be obtained through the ingestion of animal flesh. Nor does this imply that all potentially edible plants are culturally perceived as important foods. While foragers frequently recognize a vast array of potentially edible plants within their territory, typically some ranking of these resources is made. Lee (1979), for instance, lists some 105 plant species that the !Kung San recognize as edible, but only 14 of these are regularly utilized. The remaining species are collected only in the event that the primary plant foods are unavailable, or are used as "snack" type foods.

Among the primary plant foods, a handful may assume an extremely prominent position in the decision making strategy of foragers. Familiar examples of such plants would include the mongongo nut utilized by the !Kung San of the Kalahari, the acorns of various species of oaks utilized by California groups, and as will be discussed later in this paper, nuts of various species of hickories utilized by Archaic foragers in eastern North America. While other resources are important, these plants are the staple commodities utilized on a daily basis, and are ones that in the long run, dictate many of the economic decisions made by hunters and gatherers.

In spite of the resiliency of foraging economic systems, they are by no means static. Dramatic changes in the populations of plants and animals to which foragers must adapt can seriously disrupt the human population. While hunters and gatherers do not live under the shadow of impending doom, they are fully aware of the consequences of a periodic failure of the commodities upon which they depend (Aginsky 1939; Colson 1979). As a result, numerous cultural mechanisms are maintained that are designed to buffer against failure of important subsistence commodities. Among these are: (1) conscious efforts to maintain or even increase the productivity of plant and animal populations, (2) social organization and group structure, and (3) ownership and distribution of food.

INCREASING THE PRODUCTIVITY OF
THE PLANT ENVIRONMENT

Anthropologists generally believe that hunters and gatherers are slaves to the natural productivity of the plant and animal resources upon which they depend for their livelihood. To the contrary, foragers possess extensive knowledge of the productive capabilities of plants and actively employ this knowledge to interfere with the life cycles of plants to improve their reproductive capacities. There are at least four areas we can turn to as examples of the manners in which hunters and gatherers actively seek to increase or maintain the productivity of their environment: (1) burning, (2) irrigating, (3) planting, and (4) ritual.

Burning

The effects of human induced fires on the natural landscape have been the subject of anthropological interest for many years (Stewart 1956; Sauer 1963; Lewis 1973; Mellars 1976; Guffey 1977, to list just a few). These and other sources document the extensive and conscious use of fire as a means of improving the biomass of an area by hunting and gathering populations. While we often equate the use of fire with swidden or "slash and burn" horticulturalists, preagricultural societies make extensive use of fire as well. Perhaps no areas better exemplify the importance of fire to hunters and gatherers than California and Australenesia.

The use of fire in aboriginal California has received monographic treatment by Lewis (1973), who assembled data from a diverse body of historic and ethnographic literature. Fires were routinely set in order to produce a variety of desired results. Burning off patches of seed bearing plants after a harvest stimulated rapid regeneration and was considered important in maintaining, and even increasing the productivity of the stand. Periodic burning of brushy chaparral reduced undergrowth and made bow hunting for game easier. The rapid regeneration of young shoots also invariably led to a temporary increase in plant diversity and productivity, which led to an increase in the numbers of hoofed browsers (deer in this case) in the area (see Mellars 1976 for a good discussion of this phenomenon). Hazel thickets were periodically burned in order to stimulate the production of young straight shoots which served as rods for coiled baskets. Vegetation under oak trees was removed by fire in order to reduce competition and to increase the visibility of fallen acorns.

Many of the same results are reported by Jones (1969) for Tasmania. Here the resultant increases in overall productivity of plants and animals in burned-over areas was so dramatic that Jones dubbed the practice "firestick" farming. Ironically, the extensive areas of grassland maintained through the prescribed burning of the aborigines was the primary factor in influencing the first white settlement of the island. The same grasslands that were maintained for hunting areas by the native Tasmanians were also attractive to European sheepherders; when the aboriginal population was exterminated, the grasslands were rapidly invaded by forests and were no longer suitable for grazing. Likewise, Harris (1977b) suggests that the large stands of edible cycads present in the open canopy woodlands of the Cape York peninsula are directly attributable to the use of fire by local aboriginal populations.

Irrigation

Although meagre in comparison with ethnographic accounts of the use of fire, there are occasional references which indicate that hunters and gatherers attempt to increase productivity, or maintain a certain level of productivity of plants and animals, through irrigation. A half century ago, Julian Steward (1929) published a brief note in which he outlined the irrigation of naturally occurring stands of important seed-bearing annuals by a Shoshonean band in the Owens Valley of southern California. Irrigation was accomplished by damming up a permanent stream and diverting the water through two ditches. The construction of the dam was a project that required considerable effort. Steward indicates that as many as 25 men were needed for its annual construction.

A similar form of water control was also practiced in Australia by the Aborigines of the Roper River drainage of southern Arnhem Land. Here small seasonal streams were dammed with logs, rocks, and bark slabs, not for the purpose of diversion onto any specific resource, but to maintain the growth of useful plants throughout the dry season (Campbell 1965:206–7).

Intentional Propagation of Plants

Records of the intentional propagation of food plants by foragers are also scarce, and are limited to examples from Australia. Campbell (1965) summarizes the evidence for the production of two classes of plant foods—tubers and seeds. Aborigines occupying the northwest coast routinely broke off and replanted the tops of wild yams after collecting the edible tubers, but besides this simple practice, the plants were not further cultivated. Inconclusive reports of several authors who observed the intentional planting of several species of grasses and weed seeds are also cited, and even if based on fact (as Campbell suggests), there is no evidence to suggest that this was an intensive sort of activity.

Ritual

Direct manipulation of plant and animal populations by foragers are conscious acts aimed at producing short-term benefits. Long-term stability of the same populations must be maintained through supplication of the spirit world. In virtually every origin myth of hunters and gatherers, plants and animals are the first occupants of the earth, placed there for the benefit of mankind. Plants are thus conceived of as living beings, with their own special needs. While plants were placed on earth to be used by humans, the relationships between these two life forms is not one-way. Since plants are recognized as living beings their use by humans is governed by reciprocal relationships designed to maintain both the survival of the plant as well as their continued availability to humans. These interrelationships are maintained through ritual observances and acts.

Ritual relationships between humans and plants take two forms: ritual behaviors between an individual human and a single plant or small group of plants, and those between the human community and the creative forces that govern the plant community. Typical of the first type are the simple apologies offered to the plant or plants by the individual who gathers its useful product. This type of supplication serves to assuage the feelings of the plant, thereby insuring its continued availability to humans.

Community-wide rituals, such as "first-fruits" ceremonies serve a similar function, but here the interaction between individual plant and human is transcended by those between the human population and the supernatural forces that govern life itself. Such rituals are designed to thank the creative powers for an abundant harvest and to insure that such abundance will be repeated in the future. Completion of these ritual obligations promotes a feeling of well-being among the human population, and is an important *culturally perceived* mechanism for reducing risk.

OWNERSHIP AND DISTRIBUTION OF PLANT FOODS
WITHIN THE POPULATION

Many anthropologists have commented on the general lack of concern for private property among hunters and gatherers (Fried 1967; Service 1962; Sahlins 1972). This extends not only to personal accoutrements such as tools and other implements, but to foods as well. In general, foods are considered "national resources" (cf. Lee 1979) that are available to all segments of the local group; but collection of plant foods is almost always the concern of the individual, or group of related individuals, and once back in camp, the resource remains the property of the individual who collected it. Patterned sharing of food along kinship ties serves to redistribute goods to individuals or families within the camp who have been been less successful in gathering activities.

Among the !Kung San, mongongo nuts are such national resources, and access to important groves of trees is unrestricted to members of the local band. Once collected, the nuts are brought back to the camp and placed near the door of the house ready for use. Siblings, parents, nieces and nephews of the married couple who occupies the house are free to come by at any time to sit down and crack nuts (*ibid*:200). Adults are more circumspect in this activity than are children, and obviously there is some unspoken limit to how much one may crack, but this seems to be more a function of etiquette than some rigidly enforced cultural rule.

While plant resources are seldom reported as being "owned" by particular individuals, there are exceptions to the general rule. In areas of high population density, notably in northern California, and in the Cape York peninsula of Australia, important food producing plants have been reported as the private property of individual families, or even individuals. Throughout California, acorns of a variety of oaks were the common staple of the state's 300,000+ population (Kroeber 1925; Baumhoff 1963). Only in the lower Klamath River drainage of northwestern California was the acorn surpassed in importance. Here anadromous fish were only "slightly" more important (Baumhoff 1963). For the most part, oak groves were communally owned, but there are numerous records that indicate that groves of trees, individual trees, and important seed producing patches were owned by families or even individuals (see Heizer 1978 for a detailed listing). Importantly, ownership was not limited to solely the lower Klamath where the Hupa, Karok, and Yurok have long been recognized as being obsessed with the accumulation of personal wealth (cf. Goldschmidt 1951; Kroeber 1925).

Records from the Cape York peninsula also shed light on the concept of personal ownership of plant resources. Before the introduction of Western commodities, tubers of a number of species of wild yams were the principal starchy staples of the population (Harris 1977b:434). The places where wild yams grew were well known to all of the inhabitants of the peninsula, and when the leaves and vines of the plants withered at the end of the wet season, individuals would mark the buried tuber with a broken stick or snapped branch. This served as a sign of ownership, and assured that no one else would harvest the yam.

DEFENDING AGAINST A CRASH: THE ROLE OF SOCIAL ORGANIZATION AND GROUP STRUCTURE IN RESPONDING TO ENVIRONMENTAL FLUCTUATIONS

Hunters and gatherers generally have little problem procuring enough food to meet basic nutritional needs, and failure of important resources can usually be buffered by social mechanisms. In many cases, availability of important plant foods can be determined long before they become available for consumption; since plants are stationary, their annual production can be monitored throughout the growing season by examining the production of flowers, or later, the development of the fruits themselves. This sort of environmental information can then be used to adjust patterns of seasonal movement. If the hunting and collecting territory of a group is large enough, when it becomes apparent that important resources are likely to produce a poor crop, or even fail, it is often possible to simply move to another alternative collecting area.

Another means of defending against periodic crashes is through the conscious storing or caching of food. Storage of plant foods serves a number of functions, and has several important consequences. Short-term fluctuation in the seasonal availability of food can largely be evened out through storage. By concentrating food in one place, search time and travel to and from collecting areas is reduced, allowing for longer periods of occupation in one place. Finally, stockpiling of resources in one place provides a surplus that can be used for nonsubsistence activities such as interband exchange.

In traditional anthropological thinking, hunters and gatherers do not stockpile food, or for that matter any sort of material goods. But once again, the hunters and gatherers of California and Australia provide examples which challenge such traditions.

In most areas of California (and not just the coastal areas of the northwestern portion of the state), acorns were routinely stored in carefully constructed above-ground granaries or in large open baskets (see Kroeber 1925, and Heizer 1978 for specific examples). Aborigines in the Darling River drainage of southeastern Australia likewise practiced a form of storage by mounding up large quantities of grass plants with their ripened inflorescences, and by caching small seeds in clay encased packages (Allen 1974).

Direct storage of plant foods serves as a form of "banking" against fluctuation in the annual productivity of important resources, but has important constraints. Most foods cannot be stored indefinitely without infestation from pests or molds, or loss of nutritional qualities. An alternative means of "banking" is through accumulation of more durable goods that can be exchanged directly for food in times of need. In California, shell and magnesite beads, woodpecker scalps, albino deer skins and large obsidian bifaces all had standardized values, and were commonly used in bride-wealth payments, fulfilling debts, and importantly, to "buy" foods during periods of shortage (Loeb 1936; Barrett 1952; Vayda 1966).

Cultural mechanisms, however, provided the ultimate safety valves to offset the effects of periodic environmental perturbations. While most foragers inhabit culturally recognized territories that might be defended from trespass, territorial restrictions are commonly lifted in times of want, and access to neighboring groups may often be granted after consultation with the local family or lineage head (Lee 1979). Kinship ties established between neighboring bands through exogamous marriage patterns, as well as fictive kin relations between trading partners also provide outlets for certain segments of the band experiencing hardship. If resources fail within one's own territory, then a possible response is to move to another territory where one has relatives or alliances.

CHANGE IN THE FORAGING ADAPTIVE STRATEGY

As was suggested earlier, hunters and gatherers organize their activities around reducing risk or cost incurred in foraging for specific resources. Risk is reduced by developing a subsistence regime based on a careful mix of predictable fixed-place resources, and less predictable, mobile resources. Stability of this system is maintained through a variety of mechanisms, ranging from active interference in the life cycles of plants and animals to institutionalized ritual acts designed to appease the spirits responsible for continued productivity. Far more significant, however, are patterns of resource ownership, interband marriage, and exchange between members of other groups; these provide the means by which foragers can forestall change due to food shortages.

Given the fact that the foraging adaptive strategy is apparently quite stable, what factors can we point to that promote long-term change? More importantly, what factors lead to plant husbandry? Many hypotheses regarding the origins of food production have been proposed over the years, and to discuss them all would easily fill many pages. Suffice it to say that most have sought simple univariate explanations, and none have withstood careful scrutiny. In the past few decades there has been a trend towards the development of multivariate explanatory models in which a number of factors are seen as playing important roles. Basically, however, most of these models incorporate some sort of "stress" of one kind or another as a "prime mover" in instigating change. Although most authors never precisely define the meaning of "stress," it is clear that some imbalance in the population/resource ratio is the implied result of stress.

For eastern North America, the model that has gained favor in recent years is one which incorporates two key variables as "prime movers"—reduction in population mobility and subsequent population pressure. A synopsis of this model follows.

THE CURRENT "STRESS" MODEL

In this section I briefly review the "stress" model that many now use as a heuristic device in understanding the origins of plant husbandry in eastern North America. For a more detailed discussion of specific events, the reader is urged to consult the several papers in which the model has been more fully articulated (cf. Ford 1977, 1974; Asch et al. 1972).

As currently envisioned, the Eastern Agricultural Complex is seen as a result of nearly 10,000 years of human adaptation to an evolving postglacial landscape. The first human populations that entered eastern North America some 10,000 to 12,000 years ago were adapting to deteriorating full-glacial plant and animal communities. In many areas, forests dominated by jack pine and spruce were being replaced by broadleaf deciduous taxa. The Pleistocene megafauna that had inhabited these coniferous forests were rapidly becoming extinct, and were likewise being replaced by the Holocene fauna that we see today. The first humans were dependent for their livelihood on mobile resources such as whitetailed deer and other small game; while fruits and berries may have been seasonally collected (cf. Kaufman 1977), they probably played minor roles.

Because these Paleo-Indian hunters were dependent on mobile prey, numerous movements within presumably large territories were a necessity. Low population densities were maintained through a number of biological mechanisms such as spontaneous natural abortion and prolonged lactation. Essentially identical projectile point style spread over vast areas of the East indicating that interband contact was frequent during this period. Based on these factors—a rapidly changing environment, numerous seasonal moves, and low population density—we can predict little human impact on the evolving postglacial landscape.

By 9000 years ago important deciduous taxa had reached the central Mississippi and Ohio River drainages, and immediately became important components of the Early Archaic economies. Charred hulls of pecan, hickory, black walnut, butternut, and acorn are present in numerous sites dating between 9000 and 8000 B.P. (cf. Broyles 1971; Asch et al. 1972; Chapman 1975; Collins 1979; Cowan later in this paper), as are nutting and milling stones. This reflects the beginnings of human dependence on fixed-place resources that will steadily increase in the next five millennia. While seasonal population movements were perhaps alleviated by these new food resources, the trees themselves were still invading new niches and the eastern North American forests had not yet reached maturity. Deer remained the single most important source of animal protein, and continued to be a prime factor in promoting seasonal redistribution of the human population. Although certain projectile point types are quite widespread, we can begin to see regional differentiation of the human population at this time—stemmed and notched points occur west of the Ohio River, stemmed and bifurcate-based points occur to the east.

The economic pattern that first became established in the Early Archaic intensified during the succeeding Middle Archaic as a result of the stabilization of the forests by about 6000 B.P. Nut utilization in particular probably increased as the various nut producing trees became more firmly established and their numbers within the forests increased. In some areas we begin to see the intentional collection of seeds from weedy annuals such as sumpweed and *Chenopodium* (Asch and Asch 1978). Still, the Middle Archaic tool kit expands to include the grooved axe and groundstone pestle, reflecting an increasing dependence on the products of the maturing deciduous forest.

Ford has suggested that the increasing stability of the eastern plant communities may have resulted in a more structured seasonal round of activities for human populations. This "scheduling" of activities within a yearly cycle may have led to a decrease in the number of moves a group might have to make. A critical consequence of decreasing movement may have been a reduction in biological "stress" on women of childbearing age, and population may have begun to increase.

The population growth that is postulated as beginning in the Middle Archaic is seen as continuing into the succeeding Late Archaic. By now the forests in eastern North America were probably not much different than those that we see today. Human groups were relying more than ever on nuts as a staple resource, and as a consequence became more susceptible to periodic fluctuation in the availability of the masts of these trees. Ford has suggested that with an increase in the human population access to alternative collecting locales may have been restricted. In turn, a decreasing amount of exploitable territory set in motion a series of cultural mechanisms designed to buffer against the periodic shortage of *preferred* resources.

These cultural mechanisms designed to guard against a crash are reflected in the archaeological evidence from the late Archaic. An increase in intergroup contact and exchange is seen in the appearance of items manufactured from exotic shell, metal and stone in some Late Archaic burials. Recalling our California example, it is highly plausible that such goods had recognized values, and were thus valuable hedges against short-term fluctuations in the availability of foodstuffs.

Community-wide ritual designed to insure productivity or to appease the spirit world is difficult to detect archaeologically, but suggestive evidence of this sort of activity may be present at several of the large Late Archaic sites in southern Ohio. Earth ovens as large as three meters in diameter and more than a meter deep have been found at the DuPont site in Hamilton County (Kent Vickery, personal communication 1975), and several have burial platforms cut into the wall of the pit. Both the oven and burial platforms seem to have been covered over at the same time, perhaps consummating some sort of community-wide ritual.

As we have seen, another alternative to periodic fluctuation in food resources is storage. Storage pits appear for the first time in many Late Archaic sites and probably reflect an attempt to buffer against perturbations in the availability of nut crops.

Finally, Late Archaic groups expanded their diets to include a number of less preferred foods. Fish and shellfish use for instance, seems to dramatically increase at this time throughout eastern North America. Importantly, shell mounds are not restricted solely to the Green River area of western Kentucky, or the Tennessee-Cumberland drainages of the Midsouth. Extensive shell heaps are scattered up and down the Ohio River trench from West Virginia (Mayer-Oakes 1955) to the mouth of the Wabash (Janzen 1977; Collins 1979), that is perhaps indicative of some regional trend towards expanding the food base. Other stationary resources were also now exploited. At the Carlston Annis shell mound in western Kentucky, for instance, acorns dramatically increase in the upper portion of the mound, although hickory continues to be intensively utilized (Crawford 1979, 1982). At the Koster site in Illinois, there is an increased utilization of seeds from annuals such as sumpweed (Asch and Asch 1978).

This final mechanism—expansion of the food base—seems to be the most important for our consideration here. Intensification of the use of small seeds, particularly sumpweed and goosefoot, begins here and is a process that continues on an upward spiral in the succeeding millennia. Small seeds have distinct advantages over many of the other fixed-place resources noted above. Because they complete their life cycles in the course of a single year, they can produce an immediate payoff. All are able to adapt to a wide variety of habitats and may thus be taken out of their natural habitat and still produce a good crop of seeds. Many of the weedy annuals also produce their seeds in convenient "packages" that makes collection easier. The sole factor inhibiting their utilization seems to be their scarcity in the natural environment. However, intentional broadcast sowing of their seeds in habitats such as seasonally flooded stream or river banks, or burned over areas could easily lead to an expansion of the natural populations.

By the Early Woodland, the Eastern Agricultural Complex seems to be fully developed in many places in eastern North America. Two of the species, sumpweed and sunflower, were by now fully domesticated, while the other important members may never have become true domesticates. Our discussion of the current model can, for all practical purposes, end here. The main mechanisms that are seen as promoting an expansion of the food base seems to be a postulated population growth in the Late Archaic that resulted in a constriction of exploitable collecting territories for the human populations. Faced with decreasing alternatives in collecting areas, small seeds became an important means of expanding the diet without expanding the total area of exploitable territory. Once a trend towards seed utilization began, it continued unabated until the advent of maize agriculture.

AN EXAMPLE FROM THE CUMBERLAND PLATEAU

As we have seen, by at least 4000 B.P., the major river drainages of the midcontinent were heavily populated by groups probably occupy-

ing fixed territories. Nuts, deer, aquatic resources, and beginnings of
the Eastern Agricultural Complex were the most important factors in
allowing a stable adaptation to these large drainages. What was hap-
pening in the small upland drainages? What, if any, cultural transformations were occurring here? What was the role of incipient
horticulture? To partially answer these questions, an example is presented from the Red River drainage in the Cumberland Plateau region
of eastern Kentucky. The information presented below is the result of a
half century of sporadic research in the drainage (Funkhouser and
Webb 1929, 1930; Webb and Funkhouser 1936; Fryman 1967; Cowan
1975, 1976, 1979; Cowan and Wilson 1977; Cowan et al. 1981; Wyss
and Wyss 1978; Turnbow and Duffield 1978). I begin by briefly describing the physiography of the area and its floral and faunal resources, and then move on to describe the human adaptation to the
region from roughly 9000 B.P. to the birth of Christ. Although important cultural transformations occurred in the drainage after this time,
they are too lengthy to describe within the context of this paper.

Physiographically, the area of the Red River which I examine below
lies wholly within the dissected western edge of the Cumberland
Plateau (Fenneman 1938). From the air, the Red River area appears as
a rugged, maze-like tableland. Here the Red River and its tributaries
have cut downward through resistant Pennsylvanian sandstones and
Mississippian aged shales and limestones to produce a complementary
series of narrow, winding ridges and steep V-shaped valleys. The valley
walls rise abruptly from the floodplain and most of their margins are
rimmed with vertical sandstone cliffs, or series of cliffs. A profusion of
natural stone arches, isolated sandstone pinnacles, and literally thousands of sandstone and limestone rockshelters add to the distinct fla-
vor of the area. The rugged relief and vertical cliffs make travel from
one valley to the next difficult, with access afforded most often by
natural "gaps", or small breaks between the valley walls.

In contrast to the broad floodplains of the major river valleys to the
west, that of the Red River is almost nonexistent. In much of the 25
km-long study area, the floodplain of the river is not more than a few
hundred meters across; only near its juncture with the Middle and
South forks of the Red River does the North Fork valley widen appreciably. Small tracts of relatively flat bottomland areas are present in
several of the larger tributaries of the North Fork, but in general, level,
arable land is at a premium.

Today the area supports a complex mosaic of diverse floral communities adapted to the array of temperature regimes produced by differential exposure to solar radiation and to an equally diverse complex of
soil associations. All of the drainage lies wholly within Braun's (1950)

mixed mesophytic forest association, with floral communities dominated by beech, yellow poplar, white basswood, sugar maple, red and white oaks, and hemlock. This simple classification unfortunately masks the variability of the forest communities present in the drainage, however, and further amplification is required.

Although late nineteenth and early twentieth century lumbering activities have severely disturbed the original forests, since 1939 most of the drainage has been managed by the United States Forest Service as part of the Daniel Boone National Forest, and relatively stable communities are once again establishing themselves.

Recent botanical fieldwork has described a rich and varied flora; over 800 species of vascular plants have so far been recorded in the drainage (Higgins 1970; Weintrub n.d.). A simple description of the various communities and the factors which have led to their development could take pages, and is beyond the scope of this paper. The paragraphs that follow then should be viewed as a highly synthesized account, and emphasize those plants that were of critical importance to the human populations who adapted to them.

A basic division of plant communities can be made on the basis of three variables: (1) elevation, (2) position on slope, and (3) exposure. The generally flat ridgetops support three community types. Where the substrate is shallow, mixed pine-heath communities grow to the margins of the cliff-rimmed valleys. Further back from from the valley margins, where the soil is deeper, a mixed oak-hickory-chestnut forest dominates. Mixed oak and pine communities are often present in intermediate areas. For the most part oaks account for as much as 50–70% of ridgetop oak-hickory forests, with hickories ranging from 6% to as high as 20% on more favorable sites.

Below the cliffs, the forests take on a more mesic character. Though dry upper western and southern slopes support forests with relatively high admixtures of oaks and hickories, they are dominated by yellow poplar, sugar maple, beech, hemlock, yellow buckeye, and various magnolias. In most places, this sort of mixed forest grows to the edge of the tributary streams of the river. Where small floodplains are present black walnut, butternut, and thick shellbark hickory trees become minor components of an otherwise mixed mesophytic forest.

A narrow band of floodplain forest, consisting of various birches, sycamores, and silver maples, occupies only the widest portions of the Red River floodplain, but otherwise, mixed mesophytic forest dominates.

The weedy annuals that comprise the Eastern Agricultural Complex are exceptionally scarce in the North Fork Drainage. Small scattered stands of giant ragweed and isolated clumps of *Chenopodium mis-*

souriense occur in floodplain areas disturbed by modern agricultural practices, but are absent in other habitats. On the whole neither of the plants could be considered present in quantities sufficient enough to permit an intensive harvest, and maygrass, sumpweed, and *Chenopodium bushianum* have not been recorded in the area today.

To the untrained observer, the lush forests of the Cumberland Plateau seem to offer everything a normal human being could ever desire. Indeed, to many of the million-plus annual visitors to the area, the North Fork is a veritable "heaven on earth". But here lies the paradox, for natural beauty does not automatically connote productivity. While over 100 species of potentially edible plants presently grow in the drainage (Cowan 1979) much of the richness seems to be the result of disturbance through logging and forest fires. In spite of the lushness of the forests, the plant foods that were most critical to the cultural groups who inhabited the area are widely scattered, often difficult to reach because of the rugged terrain, and unpredictable in their annual variability. Unlike the forests to the west, hickory species are not major components of any of the plant communities, but are instead minor members of forests dominated by admittedly beautiful, but in the eyes of a hunter and gatherer, perfectly worthless trees.

Likewise we can predict that important game species must have been quite low in the closed canopy forests. Although Barbour (1973) reports a diverse fauna for the area, only four species—deer, turkey, black bear, and box turtle—are consistently found archaeologically. Significantly, the Red River itself does not harbor large numbers of fish and is not on the flyway of any migratory waterfowl. Mussel shoals, while present, are so small that a single group of collectors could wipe out the entire population in a matter weeks.

Initial Human Occupation in the Early Archaic

At the present time we can definitely fix the arrival of the first human populations in the Red River drainage sometime before 9000 years ago. The distinctive notched and bifurcate based projectile points of these early groups have been located at several floodplain sites, and at least two rockshelter sites. Radiocarbon dates of 9215 ± 290 B.P. and 8200 ± 225 B.P. are the earliest dates from the Cloudsplitter rockshelter (Cowan et al. 1981). LeCroy (Broyles 1971) and Kirk (Coe 1964) types provide our best evidence of these transient populations, and their almost exclusive manufacture from exotic cherts testifies to the extensive hunting territories of what must have been a small population. The tool kit of the Red River populations is not well known, but elsewhere in the Appalachians and in the Ohio Valley proper includes a diverse number of cutting, piercing and scraping tools as well as small pitted cobbles for processing nuts (Broyles 1971; Chapman 1975; Collins 1979).

Unfortunately, no hint of the Early Archaic diet has been preserved in the acidic soils of the Red River floodplain, but the earliest deposits at the Cloudsplitter shelter provide important insights into their adaptation to the early postglacial landscape. A few small surface hearths and remnants of a possible windbreak marked by a single charred spot and several postmolds suggest the site was probably used on occasion as an overnight camp or resting spot.

Black walnut and butternut, both probably late invaders of the area, seem to have been the most important nuts collected, although hickory nuts rank a close third. No other definite plant foods have been identified in the earliest deposits, but we can assume that fruits and greens must have been important seasonal commodities.

Deer and elk seem to have provided the bulk of the meat utilized by the Early Archaic occupants of the site, though aquatic resources, including mussels and fish, are also present. Bones of water snakes and a large aquatic amphibian (mudpuppy?) indicate that almost any animal food was collected when encountered.

The early postglacial plant and animal communities to which the Early Archaic populations adjusted to were probably not too dissimilar to what we can observe in the area today. Wood charcoal and other plant macro-fossils from the earliest levels at Cloudsplitter indicate a mixed forest of various oaks, southern pines, hemlock, elm, chestnut, walnut, butternut, and hickory with an understory of holly, mountain laurel, rhododendron and huckleberry was present by at least 8000 years ago. However, early Holocene pollen records from eastern Tennessee indicate that the forests of the Cumberland Plateau had not yet stabilized and still contained remnants of a Pleistocene spruce–jack pine forest (Delcourt and Delcourt 1979). Based on this observation we can predict that the forest of the Red River drainage likewise must have harbored similar northern elements.

These first transient occupants of the drainage probably had little effect upon the changing postglacial landscape. Plant and animal communities in flux dictated low human population density, and large collecting territories were necessary to provision the human population. Numerous moves within a single year were necessary in order to exploit available plant and animal populations as well as to maintain the human population through marriages contracted between other groups. Considering the apparent short-term utilization of most sites in the drainage we can predict little influence on local plant and animal communities.

Middle Archaic

The succeeding several millennia apparently saw little change in the human utilization of the drainage. Scattered dart points recovered from several of the floodplain sites point to the presence of small human populations, but overall, a continuation of the Early Archaic lifeway is indicated. As we shall see, however, this pattern was to change significantly in the the following Late Archaic period.

The next few millennia witnessed a stabilization of the plant and animal communities, and probably by 6000 B.P. the forest communities we see today were present.

Late Archaic

As we have seen, the Late Archaic populations in the main river valleys to the west were by now well established in presumably fixed territories considerably restricted in size from the earlier Middle Archaic period. As a result of lessened seasonal movement the biological factors regulating population growth may have been lessened, and population may have begun to increase.

This postulated population increase to the west is reflected in the Red River drainage by the first appearance of substantial floodplain sites. Although small in comparison with their counterparts to the west and north, nonetheless these sites signal a measurable change in the utilization of the drainage. Only one of the Late Archaic sites has been examined through excavation, but all are characterized by the presence of an expanded inventory of material culture, and substantial earth ovens and middens containing large quantities of fire-cracked rock. These date suggest more than just a short-term utilization of the area. Large quantities of waste from the manufacture of stone tools, as well as numerous projectile points, cutting and perforating tools indicate expanded activities, and the addition of grooved axes, pestles, and multiple-pitted nutting stones perhaps indicate an increasingly efficient technology designed to exploit the resources of the now stabilized forest.

Contact with neighboring populations to the west is perhaps reflected in the chipped stone tools and debitage from the Skidmore site, and other Late Archaic floodplain locales. All projectile points, and the majority of the waste flakes are manufactured from high quality Boyle chert which outcrops on the outer edge of the Bluegrass approximately 40 to 50 km west of the site. Heavy bifacial tools on the other hand are made almost exclusively of locally available Haynie chert.

The lack of the abundant aquatic resources that characterized the major midwestern river systems meant that human populations in the Red River were still hampered by a scarcity of animal protein and seasonal shifts in the population continued to be the major cultural means by which human groups adapted to the seasonal availability of wild plant and animal populations.

Faunal materials have not been preserved in the acidic floodplains of the valley, but presumably fish, limited amounts of mussels, and deer were exploited. Plant remains recovered from flotation samples from the Skidmore site provide important clues to the pattern of Late Archaic plant utilization at these floodplain sites. Nuts from three species restricted to the floodplain in the Red River valley—black walnut, butternut, and thick shellbark hickory—suggest that plant collecting took place close to the site, to the exclusion of more abundant slope species.

With the advent of fall, the population seems to have dispersed into smaller groups to exploit the seasonal mast of upper slope and ridgetop hickories. Deer and turkey, attracted to the annual acorn and chestnut masts would have been densest in these areas. Sites are difficult to locate on the heavily forested ridgetops of the area, but their presence can be predicted by our knowledge of the distribution of important nut bearing trees.

Rockshelters continued to be occupied, particularly those associated with western and southern exposures. Although some have suggested such exposures were chosen because of the solar radiation they received during the fall and winter months, more likely they were occupied because of their proximity to important hickory populations.

Once again we can turn to the deposits at the Cloudsplitter shelter to provide information on the seasonal activities of the Late Archaic populations in the drainage. Judging by the paucity of chipped stone tools in these deposits, procurement of game did not seem to be a major fall activity, although deer was apparently taken whenever encountered. Hickory nuts, collected from the dry upper slope forests, were intensively collected and processed at the site. Their cracked shells are abundant in all Late Archaic deposits, and in one area an almost solid lens of shell fragments ranging from 5 to 15 cm thick, and covering an area of almost four square meters has been radiocarbon dated to 3060 ± 225 B.P. (Cowan et al. 1981). Black walnut, butternuts, and small amounts of chestnut and hazelnut are also present, although they are secondary to hickory.

For the first time we can begin to measure the effects of a presumably larger population on the natural landscape. Needles of eastern red cedar, a successional species that is restricted to limestone-derived soils in the drainage are present just prior to 3000 B.P., as are the culms of bluestem grass and seeds of pokeweed and sumac, indicating that small garden plots may have been invaded by these species.

Small amounts of squash rind are present in the Late Archaic deposits, and small amounts of seeds of weedy annuals appear just prior to 3000 B.P., marking the beginning of a process that will markedly increase for the next few millennia. Goosefoot (*Chenopodium bushianum*), and the cultivated variety of sumpweed (*Iva annua* var. *macrocarpa*) are also present but are probably intrusive from later occupations.

Early Woodland

The processes set in motion during the Late Archaic were intensified after 3000 B.P. In contrast to the preceding Late Archaic period, however, no Early Woodland floodplain village sites are present on the North Fork, and virtually all evidence for utilization of the drainage comes from rockshelter sites. This lack of evidence for the seasonal aggregation of the Early Woodland population is puzzling, but may indicate a real shift in land use patterns during this time. Unfortunately, interpretation of the regional settlement pattern is hampered by a lack of an intensive site survey in upland areas, and suggests a significant area for future research.

In part the answer to the question of Early Woodland population distribution may also lie in developments in the Bluegrass region immediately to the west of the mountains. The middle of the first millennium B.C. saw the Bluegrass populations transformed into societies with new mechanisms for cultural integration. Burial mounds probably served as monuments to local lineages, and the inclusion in tombs of artifacts manufactured from a wide array of exotic materials suggests the development of an elaborate trade network, perhaps manipulated by local headmen.

What effect the evolution of this new system that we now call the Adena culture had on the indigenous mountain populations remains unclear, but the Bluegrass chert that had been so important to Late Archaic toolmakers seems to dramatically decrease at this time, with a concomitant increase in the use of locally available cherts. In the nearby Bluegrass, the pattern reverses. A collection of projectile points from the pre-mound deposits beneath the larger of the two classic Adena Wright mounds (Webb 1940) in nearby Montgomery County contains small but significant quantities of mountain cherts; all of the classic Adena type points and leaf-shaped blades recovered from the mound fill and log tombs are made exclusively of high quality locally available Boyle chert.

One fact is clear, however. The Red River drainage was not extensively utilized by Bluegrass Adena populations. While Webb and Baby (1957) sought to show a substantial Adena utilization of the eastern Kentucky rockshelters, the recent spate of intensive archaeological research in the area has failed to support their hypothesis.

While Early Woodland floodplain sites are almost nonexistent, rockshelter utilization is comparatively abundant. Once again the Cloudsplitter shelter can serve as an example for the Early Woodland utilization of the area, but other sites, notably Newt Kash Hollow (Webb and Funkhouser 1936) and Hooton Hollow (Haag 1974) also seem to have experienced their most intensive utilization during this period.

At Cloudsplitter, the Early Woodland deposits are visibly distinguishable from the earlier layers by their extremely high ash and organic content. Numerous features riddle these deposits, and the distribution of hearths, major ash lenses, wooden posts and postmolds suggest that a social grouping of two families utilized the site during a portion of the Early Woodland period.

Nuts are still important components of the deposits but there is a dramatic increase in the use of small seeds, and several important additions to the garden complex are indicated. Sumpweed and goosefoot seeds are ubiquitous, and maygrass, sunflower, and giant ragweed make their first appearance in the deposits. Squash and gourd rinds and seeds become more abundant, reflecting the increasing importance of these tropical cultigens. The squash rinds are thick and woody and indicate that the fruits were still being grown primarily for their use as containers.

The kernels of all Eastern Complex plants are not easy to extract from their surrounding pericarps, and the Early Woodland groups seem to have solved this difficulty by developing a technology to deal with this processing problem. Bedrock mortars, erroneously termed "hominy holes" (Webb and Funkhouser 1929), are consistently associated with Early Woodland sites in the drainage, and may have been used to dehusk the seeds and achenes of the new garden complex.

Even with the intensive utilization of a wide range of cultivated plants, the Early Woodland groups must have found it difficult to maintain permanent settlements, and seasonal redistribution of the population was likely still an important means of meeting basic nutritional requirements. Faced with continued restriction placed on their seasonal movements, the Early Woodland groups finally developed a strategy similar to that which had occurred in the major midwestern river valleys a thousand years earlier.

Storage pits appear for the first time, which when filled with food could be used to buffer against a system crash caused by what was probably an increasing population-resource imbalance. Two types of these facilities are present at the Cloudsplitter shelter. Large circular pits almost a meter and a half in diameter and over a half meter deep are present on one end of the site. Lined with slabs of pitch pine bark, filled with nuts, and covered with large rocks, they would hold several bushels of high energy food that could be counted on during periods of the year when gatherable resources were scarce. One of these pits at Cloudsplitter, for instance, could hold something on the order of 30,000 hickory nuts (based on ca. 120 nuts/liter × 247 liter capacity of the pit). This represents a 30-day supply of nuts for 10 persons utilizing 300 nuts/day per person. In terms of caloric intake, this would provide roughly 1800 cal/day/person (assuming an average weight of 4 gms/nut and 1 gm edible portion/nut). These figures of course assume that the pits were used exclusively for the storage of nuts. Unfortunately, none retained their original contents.

At the present time we do not think that the larger pits were used for the extensive storage of cultivated plants. The large pits are located in a portion of the site that did not serve as the main occupation area, and although care was taken to protect the stored commodities from insects and marauding animals, their treatment can only be described as casual when compared to the care taken to protect stored cultigens. Only one storage pit designed for cultivated plants was found at Cloudsplitter, but it is located in the heart of the main occupation area. It consists of a small circular pit excavated down until a large roofblock was encountered, and then carefully lined with small slabs of sandstone. The interior fill contained large quantities of sumpweed achenes, sunflower disks and achenes, goosefoot seeds and plant fragments, small amounts of maygrass inflorescences, *Polygonum erectum* achenes and wild bean loment segments.

The natural landscape was being transformed on a new scale during this period as a result of increasing clearance of canopy level trees for Early Woodland garden plots. New wild plant foods were incorporated into the diet and included such species as honey locust, *Polygonum* and wild bean. It is not known if the *Polygonum* was cultivated by the Early Woodland occupants, but achenes are almost totally absent from the general deposits at the site. It is interesting, however, that the achenes *are* quite concentrated in the rock-lined feature containing other members of the Eastern Agricultural Complex. *Polygonum erectum* is uncommon in the drainage today, and perhaps these achenes were collected from encouraged plants. The wild bean loment segments are, in fact, quite common in the deposits, and probably were intensively collected.

Today wild bean is an extremely common member of the understory of disturbed second growth forests in the drainage.

Although these new additions probably provided relief from a monotonous diet of nuts and seeds, they were hardly present in quantities sufficient enough to be considered important resources, and alternative food sources were necessary. As we have seen, a similar process took place in the midwestern river valleys. Here the process is reflected by an increasing utilization of mussels and other fixed-place resources such as acorns. In the Red River, the process of territorial restriction led to an increase in the use not of acorns, but of chestnuts. Like acorns, they are rich in carbohydrates.

Because we are interested solely in the development of the Eastern Agricultural Complex, my discussion of the prehistoric cultural developments in the Red River drainage will end here. Regardless of later developments, several important points emerge which are relevant to the evolution of plant husbandry in eastern North America.

First, it should now be apparent that the rockshelter area of eastern Kentucky was never in the mainstream of the developments that led to the Eastern Agricultural Complex. With the exception of squash, and probably gourd, all other members of the complex do not appear in quantity in the rockshelter deposits until after 3000 B.P. No convincing data can be marshalled to support a gradual increase in the utilization of weedy annuals through the Archaic, but instead all make a sudden appearance in the area.

Since the Complex seems to have been introduced to the area, we can legitimately wonder why the cultigens were incorporated into an economic strategy that had supported local human populations since the early Holocene. Obviously, trade with neighboring groups cannot provide the sole answer, and here Ford's model may supply an explanation.

Throughout the Archaic, but particularly during the Late Archaic, contact with the Bluegrass region to the west is reflected in the overwhelming number of chipped stone tools manufactured from Boyle chert. Yet during the Early Woodland period this pattern changes, as locally available chert seems to dominate local assemblages. Although not discussed in the context of this paper, the pattern reverses again during the Late Woodland, as once again the Bluegrass chert becomes an important source of material for the manufacture of stone tools. Although speculative at this point, this may indicate some change in the territory size of the Red River Early Woodland populations, or some change in their relationships with neighboring Bluegrass Adena societies. If the latter is the case, the Early Woodland societies may have *had* to expand their diet in a new way—through the introduction of the Eastern Agricultural Complex.

A CHALLENGE FOR THE FUTURE

The development of plant husbandry in the Eastern Woodlands was a gradual process that seems to have taken place over many thousand years. While the past decade has provided us with a general historical framework of the particular *events* in this process, we still do not fully understand the *mechanisms* that transformed Archaic foragers into Woodland horticulturalists. It seems likely that some form of the "stress" model that Ford has outlined may indeed help us to understand the process, but it is clear that we cannot yet point to a specific archaeological example which fits his general outline.

With the exception of the lower Illinois Valley, where apparent intensive collection of sumpweed may have begun as early as 5500 B.P., there are no other areas where a similar level of intensity can be demonstrated for other wild members of the Eastern Agricultural Complex. Even in the lower Illinois, however, the process did not continue, since a basic "Archaic" subsistence pattern seems to have persisted until the Middle Woodland (Asch and Asch, this volume). Certainly we cannot point to the eastern Kentucky rockshelter area, or the western Kentucky shellmounds as locales where the complex first developed. Given this fact, it seems that in eastern Kentucky there is little to be learned about the *incipient development* of plant husbandry in the interior Midwest. If we accept the "stress" model proposed by Ford, then we must look for evidence in new areas.

One critical area that is a virtual archaeological void before the Early Woodland period is the lower Mississippi Valley and its tributary drainages. Unlike the other areas I have discussed within the context of this paper, all of the wild members of the complex occur here naturally. Unfortunately, there are few references to plant utilization for the region; we find ourselves in the unfortunate position of lacking data from what may have been one of the most important areas in regard to the evolution of plant husbandry in eastern North America.

It should also be apparent that the transformation of Archaic foragers to Woodland gardeners involved more than just a change in subsistence patterns and strategies. The shift to heavy dependence on cultivated plants required a drastic reorganization of the world view of the eastern hunters and gatherers, requiring a replacement of a world structured by events in the recent past, to one structured in the past but geared towards the future.

Likewise, it can be predicted that the rise of plant husbandry was also accompanied by a marked change in the conception of personal property and territorial boundaries. As we have seen, most foraging societies show little concern for personal property, and even the territory they exploit may on occasion be utilized by adjacent groups. These attitudes are entirely incompatible with the concept of horticulture, where rules of land tenure and inheritance rights serve to insure that plots of fertile agricultural land will be handed down from one generation to the next, and that a community of individuals can maintain rights to a given piece of property.

Another important transformation involved the position of the weedy annuals within the cosmography of the human populations. As the economic position of these plants gained increasing importance, we can predict that the mythical histories and rituals surrounding their use likewise grew. Such an assumption may be difficult to detect archaeologically, but nonetheless may receive partial confirmation by finding the remains of plants in such nonsubsistence contexts as burials and ritual structures.

I make these points only to emphasize that it is not possible to understand the origins of plant husbandry in eastern North America by a simple review of the historical events represented by flotation samples. While we must rely on such materials to provide the direct evidence on the evolution of the Eastern Agricultural Complex, structural changes in the ideological and social systems of the human populations are equally important considerations.

Admittedly, the wealth of exciting new data provided us by analyses of flotation samples has increased our knowledge of the evolution of specific members of the Eastern Agricultural Complex. Unfortunately, our understanding of *societal* evolution has not kept pace.

Domestication and Diffusion of Maize

Walton C. Galinat
University of Massachusetts Agricultural Experiment Station
Suburban Experiment Station, Waltham, Massachusetts

INTRODUCTION

By the time of Columbus, maize had already become the staff of life in the New World. It was distributed throughout both hemispheres from Argentina and Chile northward to Canada and from sea level to high in the Andes, from swampland to arid conditions and from short to long day-lengths. In becoming so widespread, it evolved hundreds of races, each with special adaptations for the environment including special utilities for man.

Yet, up until the early 1900s, only a single race, Maiz-de-Ocho, predominated in a broad zone from the Dakotas to New England and to the northernmost limits for its growth such as the Gaspé Peninsula in Canada. The limited variability in the early maize of this area resulted from a delay by several thousand years in its spread northward from its short-day homeland in Mexico and Central America. The first domesticates must have been short-day in flowering, like teosinte and most tropical maize. This preadapted them for an early spread southward into northern South America but limited their movement northward into areas of longer day-lengths and shorter growing seasons. In addition to the photoperiod factor, a zone of arid conditions and poor soil in the U.S. South and Southwest, as well as the thick prairie sod in the area of the present-day U.S. Corn Belt, required the development of both adaptations by the maize and technological agriculture.

245

In order to come to a real understanding of the symbiotic relationship between man and maize, the problems of improving the maize ear, the use of introgression and the loss from genetic erosion, we need a profound understanding of the evolutionary roots of maize. It is toward this goal that the present paper is directed.

THE ORIGIN PROBLEM

The historical "Tripartite Theory" for the origin of maize was described by Mangelsdorf and Reeves in 1939. Although accepted in textbooks for about 30 years, objections to it continued to mount, especially under examination by George Beadle. By 1983 even Mangelsdorf admitted the necessity to adjust one of its three parts to the discovery by Iltis et. al. (1979) of a perennial diploid teosinte (*Zea diploperennis*). These parts now claim as follows: (1) As previously described, there was a wild maize, apparently now extinct, with a diminutive soft cob that was the direct ancestor of domesticated maize. (2) Annual teosinte can be dismissed as this ancestor because it is just a derivative from the hybridization of domesticated maize and the recently discovered perennial diploid teosinte. Mangelsdorf and Reeves had originally dismissed teosinte as just a maize-*Tripsacum* hybrid, but now no one supports this (Mangelsdorf 1974). (3) Teosinte introgression into maize in North America and probably *Tripsacum* introgression in South America played a major role in the evolution of modern maize. While there is little or no controversy about the third part, the first two parts are no more acceptable in the revised tripartite than in its original version. For example, the greater number of chromosome knob positions in the annual teosintes than in either of these putative parents indicates a long predomestic age for annual teosinte (Kato-Y 1975; McClintock et al. 1981).

In contrast to the wild maize hypothesis, the teosinte-to-maize hypothesis occurs in two forms that have not as yet been compromised by consensus agreement. The problem is that the archaeological record available so far seems to have some missing links between teosinte and maize. Iltis (1983) suggests that the gap was jumped by a "catastrophic sexual transmutation" in teosinte by which the target area for expression of the secondary male traits came to include the female spike, a new theory readily accepted by Gould (1984). Beadle (1980) and Galinat (1983) hold that the transformation was step-wise since the key-trait genes segregate from maize-teosinte hybrids (*Pd:pd*, paired vs single female spikelets; *Tr:tr*, many-ranked vs two-ranked spike) and there is no genetic evidence of a single macromutation separating them. In fact, the rate of recovery of parental types in the F2 indicates a

4 or 5 unit difference rather than just a single difference (Collins and Kempton 1920; Mangelsdorf and Reeves 1939; Beadle 1980). We believe that someday the problem of sampling error in the archaeological record may be overcome with discovery of the connecting links as often happens in so-called examples of "punctuated evolution."

In a discussion of the controversial evidence for and against an origin of maize (*Zea mays* L. ssp. *mays*) from teosinte (*Zea mexicana* or now *Zea mays* L. ssp. *mexicana* Iltis), Beadle (1980) concludes, "It now seems quite likely that a teosinte of some 8,000 to 15,000 years ago was the direct ancestor of modern corn and was transformed into a primitive corn through human selection." The condensed forms of teosinte with triangular fruit cases and spikes borne in fascicles, as described later, may themselves be indirect products of human selection. Starting with such a condensed teosinte, the transformation to a botanically correct ear of maize may have been going on simultaneously in many places and have transpired relatively rapidly, in perhaps 100 years (Galinat 1983).

The oldest archaeological maize from Bat Cave, New Mexico, with an age now reassessed at 500–700 B.C. (Berry 1980; Mangelsdorf 1974) from an earlier estimate of 2000 B.C. (Mangelsdorf and Smith 1949) and also the much older maize from Tehuacán, Mexico dated at about 5000 B.C. (Mangelsdorf, MacNeish, and Galinat 1967a) was a tiny eight-rowed soft-cob popcorn. Because it was more primitive and 5000 years older, the Tehuacán specimens were judged in their first studies to be from a now extinct wild maize. At both sites the maize appears to carry a weak form of the pod or tunicate trait in which soft, elongate glumes partially enclose each kernel rather than having the glumes slightly reduced so that the upper half of each kernel is exposed as in modern corn. Also, at both sites, the oldest corn cobs are much more compacted (condensed) than their counterpart in the spike of teosinte.

Both the tunicate and the condensation traits are at the heart of the controversy on the origin of maize. Mangelsdorf (1974, 1983) considers that the tunicate gene of primitive maize stems from a hypothetical wild pod popcorn. Beadle (1980) suggests that there never was a wild maize per se and the tunicate trait of primitive maize is presumed to be descended from a tunicate mutation in an ancestral form of teosinte. According to this hypothesis, the tunicate mutant of teosinte was discovered and selected by man, because of its increased threshability, during an early step in the pre-domestication process leading toward an origin of maize. The tunicate gene converts the hard fruit cases of teosinte into shallow softer cupules carrying elongate soft glumes that enclose and protect the kernels. The domestic advantage of tunicate teosinte is its ease of free threshing as a cereal. Because the tunicate alleles are dominant over the normal nontunicate condition, Beadle considers that the selective transfer of the gene to domestic teosinte populations would be rapid. In subsequent stages of domestication of a condensed cob-like rachis in early maize, man would find it advantageous to select back for the original nontunicate condition, readily available through introgression from teosinte. The tunicate trait would be removed from the better types of cobs by selecting for ears with naked kernels, which could be easily removed by shelling. A weak tunicate allele does appear to persist in some selections of the primitive race, Chapalote. This is possible because an evolutionary elongation of the kernel will elevate most of its outer surface above the chaff. Use of the tunicate allele from Chapalote has economic value in sweet corn as a modifier for the expression of the vestigial glume gene (Galinat 1966).

THE INFLORESCENCES

The male and female floral structures in maize and teosinte are carried in separate flowers on different parts of the plant. A brief description of the morphological structures involved has been adapted from Galinat (1975) to help those unfamiliar with these specialized inflorescences and their botanical terms.

The tassels of these relatives are usually exclusively male (staminate) and they usually terminate the main stalk as well as any long tillers (usually basal branches or suckers). The tassel of maize is a modification upon that of teosinte. In maize the uppermost spike has strong apical dominance over the lower spikes as it forms a so-called "central spike." The central spike becomes many-ranked while the lower spikes, commonly called "tassel-branches," remain two-ranked. These lower spikes usually occur in pairs (binate) at the base of the tassel and in whorls approaching the central spike. In teosinte all of the spikes are usually binate, except in cases of multiplication (proliferation), and the uppermost spike has weak apical dominance and it is like the lower spikes in being two-ranked. Staminate spikelets of both teosinte and maize have two functional florets and the spikelets are binate, one being sessile and the other usually pedicellate (stalked). The term "binate" is being used here to mean more than just paired. Its suggested usage is in the sense of unequal pairs in which one member has the potential to become pedicellate.

The ears of maize and teosinte are usually exclusively female. They may terminate (maize) or be axillary (teosinte) at the nodes along lateral stalks. The spikes are enclosed by one (teosinte) or more (maize) of the uppermost husks that are borne on the shank. The spikes are binate (teosinte) or solitary (maize). The other characteristics of the female spikes represent the definitive criteria that separate the species (Fig. 8.1).

In teosinte, the female spike has two ranks of solitary spikelets, although sometimes the pedicel, as a rudiment from the second spikelet, is present along one margin of the cupule. Each female spikelet is enclosed on all sides but one by an elongate cupule. The cupule is a specialized cavity in the rachis, with lateral wings (flaps) that clasp a specialized outer glume of its enclosed spikelet, forming with it a protective device for individual kernels termed the cupulate fruit case. Above each cupule within a rank is an interspace representing the back side of the alternate fruit case from the other rank oriented at 180°. Recognition of the interspace is meaningful in terms of revealing condensation and the degree of cupule development, especially in forms that are intermediate between teosinte and maize. On either side at the base of the glume is a hairy root pore, or pulvinus notch, which allows water to enter, and the primary root to emerge during germination. At maturity the fruit cases become highly indurated and abscission layers that develop between the fruit cases cause their disarticulation and allow shattering.

The teosinte fruit case protects the seed's viability even after ingestion by animals and birds followed by dispersal through the manure droppings (Wilkes 1967:63). It may be almost invisible upon the ground because of its camouflaging coloration and small pebble-like shape (Beadle 1980). Furthermore, a dormancy substance in the freshly shed mature fruit cases delays germination until conditions are appropriate for successful growth (Wilkes 1972 and others).

Condensation (compaction from a reduction or failure of internode elongation) differences in the rachis change the shape of the teosinte fruit case. Under relaxed condensation in Nobogame teosinte, the shape is usually trapezoidal although sometimes it is triangular, as illustrated by Wilkes (1967). Under tighter condensation in Chalco teosinte, the shape becomes triangular, as compared in Figure 8.2. Differences in condensation within the shank affect the floral habit. Under relaxed condensation, the binate spikes are spaced out by elongate internodes in a manner adapted for seed dispersal. Whip-lashing in the wind of the slender stalks (canes) throws the disarticulated fruit cases out through the open top side of the husk. Under tight condensation in the shank, the binate spikes are held in fascicles (clusters) that are preadapted for harvesting.

In maize, the cob (female spike) is unique in its part of the grass

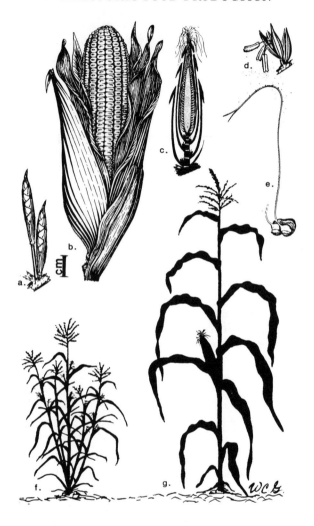

Figure 8.1. *a.* The female spikes of teosinte are binate, one pedicellate and the other sessile. Each spike is enclosed in its own husk. The spike has two alternating ranks of fruit cases each enclosing a spikelet with one kernel. *b.* The solitary female spike (ear) of maize is enclosed in many layers of husks. It has many ranks of binate spikelets. *c.* As shown in longitudinal section, the rosette of husks in maize is formed by a condensation of the internodes in the shank. The styles must extend up beyond the top of the husks in order to become exposed to the pollen. *d.* The male spikelets of both teosinte and corn are binate with one member pedicellate and the other sessile. Three anthers are dangling from the upper floret in the pedicellate spikelet. The lower floret also carries three anthers. The sessile spikelet also totals six anthers in the same arrangement. *e.* The female spikelets of maize are binate, each pair being carried by one cupule. *f., g.* The plant habits of teosinte (left) and maize (right) showing the differences in size, shape and tillering. In teosinte the energy is dispersed into many small spikes. In maize it is concentrated into one or a few large ears.

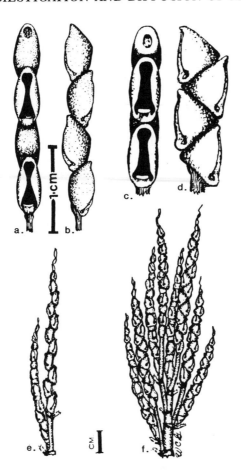

Figure 8.2. *a., b.* Front and profile views of four successive fruit cases borne in two ranks in Nobogame teosinte. Low (relaxed) condensation results in elongate trapezoidal fruit cases. *c., d.* Front and profile views of four successive fruit cases borne in two ranks in Chalco teosinte. High (tight) condensation results in compressed triangular fruit cases as well as a thicker and shorter rachis. Note that the degree of condensation cannot be measured as the length of the cupule at its opening, but rather as the average internode length. *e.* The spikes of teosinte are binate, shown here with husk removed in order to reveal a trapezoidal-shaped fruit case. *f.* The shank carrying binate spikes in teosinte is condensed producing here a fascicle of spikes. The husks have been removed in order to reveal a triangular-shaped fruit case. The scale between *a.* and *b.* applies for *a.* through *d.* The scale for *e.* and *f.* lies between them.

family in having many ranks (polystichous) of binate spikelets with the number of ranks depending upon the degree of condensation. Each pair of spikelets is borne outside of a condensed cupule. Because the binate spikelets and their kernels have twice as many rows as the ranking of cupules, the kernel row-number is usually even. The high condensation in the maize ear eliminates the cupulate interspace, collapses the cupules floor to roof and creates a rigid rachis. The result is a dependency upon humans for the shelling and dispersal of seed.

THE TAXONOMY OF THE GENUS ZEA

Although at one time *Zea* was thought to be a small genus with maize (*Zea mays* L.) as its only species, it is now apparent that it is an ancient, relatively large and complex genus. This is now correctly reflected in the taxonomic system chosen for the genus by Iltis (1972) and modified recently in companion papers by Doebley and Iltis (1980) and Iltis and Doebley (1980). Their morphological data is deliberately based on tassel structure in order to avoid the artifacts due to human selection on the ear for increased yield and harvestability. Their conclusions seem justified to this author on the basis that they do the least damage to the evolutionary hypotheses involved and still reflect the biological differentiations.

According to this system, the taxonomic context of the genus *Zea* is divided into two sections with specific, subspecific and racial groupings as follows:

Section: LUXURIANTES.
    Species: *Z. diploperennis*; perennial; 2n = 20; Jalisco, Mexico
            Z. perennis; perennial; 2n = 40; Jalisco, Mexico
            (possibly an autotetraploid of diploperennis)
            Z. luxurians; annual; 2n = 20; Jutiapa-Progresso,
            Guatemala; Honduras.
Section: ZEA
    Species: *Z. mays*
      subspecies *parviglumis*; annual; 2n = 20
        var. *parviglumis*; Guerrero, Michoacan, Jalisco, Mexico
        var. *huehuetenangensis*; Huehuetenango, San Antonio Huixta,
          Guatemala
      subspecies *mexicana*; annual; 2n = 20
        race Chalco; Los Reyes, Amecameca, Valley of Mexico
        race Nobogame; Chihuahua
        Central Plateau, Durango, Guanajuato and various others
      subspecies *mays*; annual; 2n = 20; corn or maize, only known as
        a cultivated plant

CANALIZED CONDENSATION AND THE
TEOSINTE-MAIZE RELATIONSHIP

The cytogenetic similarity of maize and teosinte indicates that their relationship cannot be more distant than a parent-progeny one (Galinat 1971:466). The evolutionary roots of Chalco teosinte reach back through other more primitive subspecies of teosinte such as Balsas teosinte and the recently discovered perennial diploid (*Zea diploperennis*) into the Sorghum tribe (Andropogoneae). The sequential steps continue to extend farther back within the Sorghum tribe to include types now loosely represented by the genera *Manisuris* and *Elyonurus*, as described by Weatherwax (1935) and Galinat (1956, 1974) and shown here in Figure 8.3.

This evolutionary series leading to a formation of the teosinte fruit case is based on canalized increases in condensation representing a suppression of internode elongation and other reductions such as that of the pedicellate female spikelet, bisexual flowers and in the rhizomes of perennialism. Thus, when we realize that the oldest known cobs of corn from Tehuacán, Mexico, have a higher level of condensation than that of teosinte and that they have a reduced teosinte fruit case such as can be produced by the tunicate trait also apparent in these cobs, we see there is important evidence supporting a teosinte origin for corn (Galinat 1970, 1975; Beadle 1980).

RECIPROCAL SWITCHING OF BINATE VS. SOLITARY
FEMALE SPIKES AND SPIKELETS

If we assume that maize was derived from teosinte during domestication, as most of the evidence seems to indicate, then two of the changes seem to represent reciprocal differences. That is, when the solitary female spikelets of teosinte became the binate female spikelets of maize, simultaneously the binate spikes of teosinte became the solitary spikes of maize. In the change to binate female spikelets, there would be a reactivation of the pedicellate member of the pair. In the simultaneous change to the solitary spike, apparently it is the sessile member which is suppressed. Thus, when the pedicellate spikelet is reactivated, the same gene action gives dominance to the pedicellate spike and thereby suppresses the sessile spike. The level of energy storage in the ear appears to remain about the same just before and after the switching in morphology.

There is almost no information available yet on the inheritance of these relationships. When the single recessive gene for solitary female spikelets is transferred to the solitary-eared type of modern corn, it has

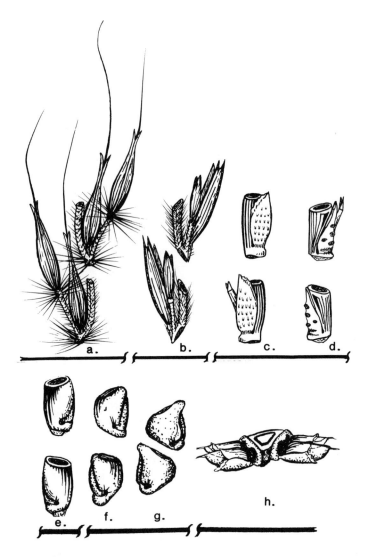

Figure 8.3. A series of representative types leading to formation of the cupulate fruit case and culminating in the rachis of maize. *a–d*. Andropogoneae. *a. Erianthus coarctatus* Fernald. *b. Elyonurus tripsacoides* Humb. and Bonpl. *c. Manisuris cylindrica* Kuntze. *d. M. tuberculosa* Nash. *e–h*. American Maydeae. *e. Tripsacum dactyloides* L. *f. Zea mexicana* Kuntze (var. Guatemala). *g. Z. mexicana* Kuntze (var. Chalco). *h. Z. mays* L. (Mexican type). [Galinat 1974]

an unstable expression (Galinat 1978). Attempts to transfer the binate spikes from teosinte to maize are usually unsuccessful or unstable. Theoretically, a combination of solitary spikelets plus binate ears in maize would be both stable and successful. This is currently under study.

THE GATHERING PROCESS AS UNCONSCIOUS SELECTION

Assuming here and in subsequent sections that maize originated from a domestication of teosinte, the following sequence of events seems probable. The gathering of wild plants for food has been recognized as predisposing them for domestication (Darwin 1868; Darlington 1969; Hawkes 1969, 1977; Bray 1977) and teosinte should be no exception. The fascicle form of floral habit, such as was observed in about 15% of the plants of Guerrero teosinte, preadapts them for easy harvesting without the loss of abscission layers across the rachis (Galinat 1975). The resistance to seed loss through shattering is derived from the mutual support of the overlapped spikes within each fascicle. When these plants are uprooted and the whole plant is inverted and/or beaten, perhaps onto an animal hide, their fruit cases spill forth from the open tops of the husks. In contrast, harvesting by the picking of individual fascicles or the dominant spike within a fascicle would favor the nonshattering trait via a suppression of abscission layers, but this was probably a later step in the predomestication process.

Fascicles of spikes do occur in other related grasses such as *Manisuris rugosa* but without the physical intervention of a husk around each spike as in teosinte. If genes for condensation into fascicles in teosinte do have less fitness for natural seed dispersal than the elongate type, some other balancing factor such as increased bird protection must maintain it in the Guerrero teosinte. If it was a result of introgression from corn, one would expect other corn cob traits to be linked with it and this was not the case in the Guerrero material. Some of the variation for fascicles now present in teosinte probably is derived from corn introgression because it has a more acceptable level of fitness in the wild than any of the other corn cob-like floral traits.

CAMPSITE COLONIES AS CRADLES OF MAIZE EVOLUTION

Assuming again that maize originated from a domestication of teosinte, the scenario continues as follows:

That the process leading toward the evolutionary emergence of maize started as an unintentional by-product from the gathering of seed by man is evident from the selective pressure for harvestable types of teosinte with their spikes condensed into fascicles. The fascicle type of teosinte would become established by accident near campsites from the unintentionally selected samples of teosinte seed that were harvested in the wild and then lost or discarded in disturbed soil of an open habitat created by man. Like other weedy campfollowers that were emphasized by Anderson (1952), annual teosinte would find an ideal habitat in the campsite dump heaps. But, more important, these colonies would automatically diverge in the direction of higher condensation and greater domestic-type variation from which humans could select the most useful types.

The simple tending of these colonies by the removal of the competing vegetation may have been the first deliberate act toward cultivation. As attention to these plants increased, humans became the planting as well as the harvesting agents. When they selected just the more useful types to plant, the female spike became genetically canalized down a pathway leading toward maize.

As various genetic factors for increased condensation in the shanks accumulated and recombined in the campsite populations, perhaps for hundreds of years, it seems plausible if not probable that the method of harvesting would change to the obvious one of picking the tightened fascicles as units. Under amplified condensation, only the uppermost spike would have adequate space for development. Under such conditions, selection would favor mutations that gave apical dominance to the uppermost pedicellate spike. Studies of modern maize–teosinte hybrids show that the uppermost spike can have various degrees of dominance in which first just the sessile member of binate spikes is reduced and then with stronger apical dominance all lower binate spikes are suppressed. This step-wise reduction from the multiple spikes of teosinte to the monocephalic ear of maize would differ from the early reports of a parallel but single gene mutation from the many small lateral heads of the wild sunflower to the monocephalic head and stout single stem of the cultivated sunflower (Heiser 1978; Iltis 1973) although Heiser (this volume) now feels that the reduction in branching in sunflower was also step-wise.

Cultivation and fertilization as part of the simple tending of semiwild populations of teosinte at the campsites would be followed by attempts to enlarge these colonies by the deliberate sowing of seed selected from the most desirable types. This second stage represents the invention and eventual perfection of agriculture. It is presumed that these permanent gardens at the campsites would sometimes be located near a water source which would stimulate increased growth and lead to the deliberate irrigation of such gardens. Although the early domestic forms of teosinte may have been no more productive than wild teosinte, they were easier to harvest and the continuing process of domestication was set in motion.

STAGES IN THE APPARENT TRANSFORMATION FROM TEOSINTE TO MAIZE

The various stages in condensation, switching in binatism, reduction to a solitary spike and its enclosure in multiple layers of husks are illustrated in Figure 8.4*a–e*. Overall, the sequence illustrates that the longer the branch (tiller) the more male its terminal inflorescence. The stages shown represent only trends and two or more adjoining stages may occur on different branches of the same plant. The individual husks, each of which encloses one spike, have been partially dissected away in order to reveal the changes within the spikes at each stage. A preliminary stage with a soft cob (rachis) resulting from the tunicate (pod) gene is not represented here. Tunicate teosinte is more threshable than normal teosinte and it was probably the form of teosinte that was ancestral to the Tehuacán soft-cob types. Because the normal teosinte fruitcase is still usable as a cereal if given special treatment (Beadle 1980), the presence of a tunicate stage, while helpful, was not essential to attract domestication. A brief description of these stages adapted from my earlier paper (Galinat 1983) follows:

Stage I (8.4*a*). Long canes (tillers) borne near the base of the plant are terminated by an all male panicle (tassel) with binate branches similar to the terminal inflorescence of the main stalk. The upper lateral spikes are largely male, while lower spikes graduate to a female condition.

Stage II (8.4*b*). As the branches and their internodes become shorter and borne higher on the plant, the femaleness increases including a penetration into the lower portion of the terminal inflorescence. Each node carries binate spikes with elongate fruit cases.

Stage III (8.4*c*). Increased condensation in the branch produces a loose fascicle in which the uppermost spike is larger due to slight apical dominance and the fruit cases slightly triangular. Stages I–III may be found in wild populations in Guerrero, Mexico.

Stage IV (8.4*d*). The uppermost spike has clearly acquired apical dominance. Increases in condensation within the spike cause the fruit cases to triangulate and thicken as the interspace between fruit cases disappears exemplified by Chalco teosinte. Condensation may cause a fusion between rachis segments (cupule apex to glume cushion) and, thereby, prevent abscission. This, in turn, required the intervention of man for seed dispersal and changed the vascular anatomy of the rachis.

Figure 8.4. The various stages in an apparent transformation from teosinte to maize.

Stage V (8.4*e*). Continued increases in condensation, together with increases in apical dominance of the uppermost spike, result in a reduction of the lower spike, and, as a result, the husks become an enclosure for the ear. There has been a switching from binate spikes to binate spikelets. At this stage, expression of two independent genes that control the key-traits of maize become fixed (homozygous). These genes, *Pd:pd* (paired vs. single female spikelets) and *Tr:tr* (many-ranked vs. two-ranked spike) stabilize the maize ear phenotype.

When the harvesting process increased the condensation in the teosinte, accidentally introduced at the campsites, a semidomestic type of teosinte emerged (Fig. 8.2). When man began selective harvesting and planting of this transitional form of teosinte, its reproductive strategy changed to dependency upon the intervention of man. A genetic revolution followed in which attributes that further facilitated its harvesting and use as human food had a selective advantage.

THE ARCHAEOLOGICAL RECORD ON INTERMEDIATE FORMS

The near lack of the various intermediate forms that would be expected between teosinte and maize in an archaeological context proven from a pre-maize period, might be explained if the transformation took place relatively rapidly, or in about 100 years. Also, at the time of the early stages of the presumed transformation, the open campsites and the dump heaps left by small mobile groups of plant gatherers would not provide much opportunity for the preservation of plant materials. Nevertheless, the archaeological record is not completely silent on the occurrence of the transitional forms postulated between teosinte and maize.

Some of the oldest maize cobs, on the one hand, and archaeological teosinte gathered by man, on the other, still bear a mark left by their more ancient transformation. There were several two-ranked and partially two-ranked cobs among the oldest specimens from Tehuacán, some or all of which may have been lateral members in a fascicle. One of these specimens (Tc50, S2E12, Zone XI, Level 9, Feature 42' 6000 years) approaching the oldest ones in age (ca.7000 years), is especially significant because its partial abscission layers across the rachis and partial reduction of the pedicellate member of the binate female spikelets approximate the intermediate condition of a primitive corn–teosinte hybrid (Fig. 8.5). Since there is no known teosinte today or archaeological remains of it in the Tehuacán Valley that could have produced such a hybrid, the specimen is regarded here as a degenerate form that is relic from its more ancient teosinte ancestor tracing through its first introduction as a domesticated plant from outside the valley.

There are various remains of teosinte that were harvested and processed with maize from prehistoric habitation sites that tend toward maize in that they are highly condensed in comparison to the truly wild teosinte. Several of these condensed types of teosinte come from southwestern Tamaulipas (Mangelsdorf, MacNeish, and Galinat 1967b), another from the domestication cradle of the Valley of Mexico (Lorenzo and González-Quintero 1970) and numerous specimens from Oaxaca (Ford, n.d.). Although none of this is pre-maize in age and thereby sufficiently old to represent a test of the teosinte-to-maize

Figure 8.5. *Upper and lower left*: Two-ranked cob from Tehuacán, Mexico (Tc50 [Coxca-tlán] S2E12, Zone XI, Level 9, Feature 42). *Upper and lower right*: Cob from an F_1 hybrid of Confite Morocho maize crossed by Guerrero teosinte. In the lateral view shown above in each specimen note that abscission layers extend only partway across the rachis be-cause condensation of the adjoining internodes has partially overlapped the cupules. In the lower front views note that in each case there is a partial reduction of the pedicellate spikelet on the left-hand side of the cupules. The archaeological specimen is about 6000 years old. It appears to have softer tissues than its modern phenotypic counterpart, possibly because of a weak tunicate allele.

hypothesis, it does demonstrate that teosinte was gathered for food. To this day it is used as a distress cereal in times of famine, as first recorded by Lumholtz (1902), and ground teosinte seed was once used as a cure for dysentery (Hernandez 1790 in Wilkes 1967).

At the Canyon Infiernillo in Tamaulipas (Manglesdorf, MacNeish, and Galinat 1967b), the earliest teosinte was represented by a fruit case fragment in a human coprolite dated at 1850–1200 B.C. Other teosinte specimens in later phases (900–400 B.C.) at this site include a tight fascicle of spikes with triangular fruit cases, representing the condensed form of teosinte that is harvestable and semidomesticated.

In the Valley of Mexico at the Tlapacoya site (Lorenzo and González-Quintero 1970), there were two teosinte fruit cases that were also of a triangular shape. Thus, here again the harvested teosinte was condensed, and like the present-day Chalco teosinte from the same area, it may be considered as an indirect by-product of the domestication process. The age of this Tlapacoya teosinte $(7,000 \pm 115$ B.P.) approaches that of the oldest remains of maize at Tehuacán, Mexico.

TRANSFORMATION OF THE CUPULE BY CONDENSATION AND A PAIRING OF SPIKELETS AS EVIDENCE OF A TEOSINTE ORIGIN FOR MAIZE

Progressive increases in condensation together with a pairing of the female spikelets result in several changes in the shape, spacing and function of the cupule in a sequence from teosinte to maize. Some of these changes are illustrated in Figure 8.6*a–e*. First, the shape of the teosinte cupule, with its greatest dimension as the internode length (vertical axis of the rachis) in *a*, undergoes vertical condensation (*b*). In order to accommodate the switch from the solitary spikelets of teosinte to the binate spikelets of maize, there is a horizontal expansion resulting in a triangular-shaped cupule in cobs of the oldest archaeological maize (*c*). Maize–teosinte hybridization deepens the cupule which becomes circular in outline (*d*). Increased condensation has a horizontal outlet in which the wings of the cupule flare out to either side, as in the primitive race Chapalote (*e*) of the American Southwest and Mexico. In Chapalote the width (w) of the cupule is about equal to the internode length (i) (usually the same as kernel thickness) so that the w/i ratio is equal to or less than 1. The interspace between cupules within a vertical row that corresponds to the back of the alternate fruit case in teosinte is reduced in primitive maize and completely suppressed in modern maize. Further increases in condensation produce a strong horizontal force for expansion. The result is the cupules become wider than the internode length (*f*). In Maiz de Ocho this results in a w/i ratio

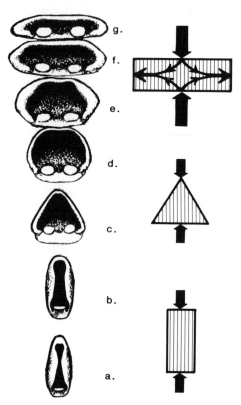

Figure 8.6. Some of the cupule shapes involved in the postulated transformation of the cupulate fruit case. The spikelets have been cut away and the hairs in the pulvinus notch are omitted to reveal the cupule. The diagrams at the right show how the forces of condensation change the vertical cupule of teosinte into the horizontal cupule of maize. *a*. The vertical cupule of Nobogame teosinte is a highly specialized component of the cupulate fruit case. An apical shoot pore and basal root pores are well developed. Enlarged cupule wings infold and clasp tightly the outer glume of the enclosed spikelet. *b*. Chalco teosinte. The infolding of the cupule wings is relaxed and the embrace of the enclosed spikelet less secure. *c*. A triangular-shaped cupule in primitive archaeological maize is associated with paired spikelets. The cupule wings project straight outward from the rachis and no longer clasp the spikelets which are borne outside of the cupules (Selected Coxcatlán Cave Zone H, 1600–300 B.C.). *d*. The cupule of a hybrid between modern maize and teosinte approaches that of primitive maize. *e*. In Chapalote maize, the cupule wings usually flare out on either side as the cupule widens. *f*. The wide and condensed cupule of modern maize as represented by Maiz de Ocho or its hybrid descendant, the Corn Belt Dent, has lost most of its resemblance to the cupule of teosinte. *g*. The collapsed cupule of the Corn Belt Dent. [Adapted from Galinat 1970]

greater than 1. The two races that are common in Southwestern archaeological maize, Chapalote and Maiz de Ocho, may be identified from cob fragments on this basis.

THE DIFFUSION AND ISOLATION OF MAIZE AS A FACTOR IN ITS EVOLUTION

The explosive evolutionary consequences of isolating a subpopulation by genetic drift (Wright 1931) and founder principle (Mayr 1942) leading to specialized novelties (Darwin 1859 and others), as well as to heterosis when the divergent populations reconverge and hybridize, has long been recognized (Wright 1931 and others).

The rapid spread of the first maize-like cultivars of teosinte from the area of southern Mexico and Guatemala is presumed to have occurred at an early time although the exact date for the oldest maize at Bat Cave, New Mexico, is uncertain (for a discussion of the problem see Berry in this series). Regardless of how ancient, the first immigrants of maize at Bat Cave, New Mexico, and at Ayacucho, Peru, are at opposite extremes of geographic isolation. It is clear that there was an initial diffusion by thousands of miles of a primitive eight-rowed maize with soft glumes. This common ancestral corn is represented by the "Early Cultivated" race from Tehuacán, Mexico, dated at about 7000 years ago. The pre-Nal Tel and pre-Chapalote of 5000 B.P. at Tehuacán that evolved from the earlier types are the counterparts of the oldest Bat Cave and Ayacucho corn. The subsequent derivatives of the Ayacucho corn, such as modern Confite Morocho, that evolved in South America under one set of natural and agriculturally selective conditions are different from the other derivatives of the same basic maize, such as modern Nal Tel and Chapalote, that evolved in the presence of teosinte under the dictates of other selective pressures in Mexico.

The low condensation of Confite Morocho and its related races in South America had certain adaptive advantages in terms of a slender cob type that would mature and dry rapidly without the onset of destructive molds. But such low condensation corn is highly intolerant of introgression from the even lower condensation that occurs in teosinte. That is, hybrids of Confite Morocho and teosinte produce an array of nonagronomic derivatives that would ordinarily be cast out by man. In contrast, the high condensation of the maize ear of Mexico allows a heavy load of teosinte introgression, at least in the heterozygous condition, and as a result it may benefit from increased genetic variability and hybrid vigor associated with the presence of heterozygous teosinte germplasm.

THE DIFFUSION OF MAIZE TO SOUTH AMERICA

The archaeological evidence, including the distribution of fossil pollen from the Panama Canal Zone (Bartlett et al, 1969) and the corn phytoliths from coastal Equador (Pearsall 1978), supports the hypothesis of the southern diffusion of the first domesticated form of *Zea* (proto-maize) from within an area of southern Mexico and Guatemala in contrast to the hypothesis of multiple domestication from six or more races of a presumed wild maize widely scattered in both North and South America (Grobman et al, 1961; Mangelsdorf 1974). There is a lack of confirmatory evidence from pollen profiles south of Mexico that there ever was a wild *Zea* with a wide range of distribution extending from Mexico into South America.

Recognized evolutionary processes will satisfactorily account for the anomalous wider range of races in South America than in Mesoamerica and thus require only one common wild ancestor rather than independent domestication from a number of hypothetical wild races from South America. The transportation and isolation of primitive forms of maize into areas beyond the range of wild teosinte, such as into the Tehuacán Valley of Mexico and somewhat later into South America and the United States Southwest, allowed a more extreme divergence from the wild type and the early fixation of the essential traits that separate maize and teosinte. While the isolated forms lost certain advantages from continuous introgression with the wild, their potential for divergence was increased by no longer having to cope with the stabilizing effect of gene flow from the wild teosinte on kernel enlargement and a counterbalancing effect on condensation level. In South America, the raw material for specialization came from the genetic variability available in the founder stock plus any subsequent introductions and mutations. The numerous narrow geographical and ecological niches based on altitude, temperature, water stress, daylength, etc., promoted diversification in local races of maize in South America.

THE DIFFUSION AND EVOLUTION OF MAIZE IN UNITED STATES

The spread and subsequent isolation of races of maize into geographical and ecological niches has been basic to the evolution of maize and to the benefits of heterosis when the divergent populations reconverge and hybridize. This is dramatically illustrated by the origin of the Corn Belt Dent in the mid-1800s from a convergence and hybridization of the New England Flint Corn and the Southeastern Dent Corn in the area we now call the U.S. Corn Belt (Fig. 8.7). In the

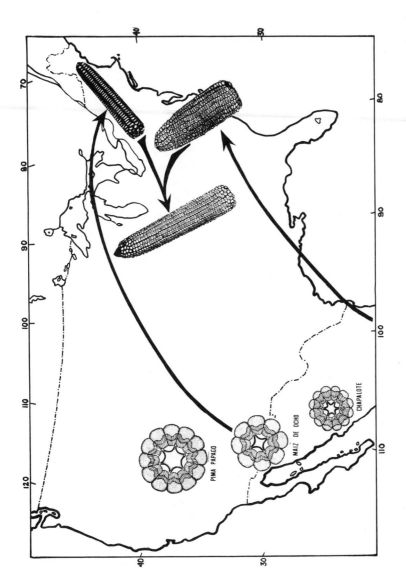

Figure 8.7. The geographic spread of the eight-rowed maize (Maiz de Ocho or Northern Flint) and Southern Dent (gourd seed) and their eventual movement into the area of the U.S. Corn Belt where they hybridized to produce the modern Corn Belt dent corn. In the Southwest, cross-sections of ears of the ancient Chapalote, of the introduced Maiz de Ocho and their hybrid, Pima Papago, are shown.

greatest success story of modern agricultural research, we continuously reconstitute the heterosis of this original hybridization through the commercial process of hybrid seed production. This requires repeated crossing between a Southern Dent-like inbred (e.g. B73) with a modified Northern Flint-like inbred (e.g. Mo17), frequently with important increases in yield. While the inbreds are usually developed from inbreeding races of the Corn Belt Dent such as Reid's Yellow Dent or Lancaster Sure Crop, for raw material to increase their combining ability the inbreds may be backcrossed to their more ancient racial ancestors or their inbred derivatives (Anderson and Brown 1952; Wallace and Brown 1956).

The New England flint corns (Maiz de Ocho) are thought to have originated from a reconstitution of eight-rowed germplasm derived from an earlier hybridization of Chapalote and Harinoso de Ocho producing the so-called Pima-Papago race in the Southwest. Its modified eight-row derivative diffused out of the Southwest along multiple pathways. One of these was probably across the Central Plains in the riverine areas. While not the classic type of Northern Flint as described by Brown and Anderson (1947), its eight-rowed ancestor or relative identified as Harinoso de Ocho (Wellhausen et al, 1952) carried genes for preadaptation to higher elevations and/or more northern latitudes. The Maiz de Ocho that stayed behind in the Southwest evolved tight husks as a means of earworm and second brood corn borer protection and this in turn changed the shape of the ear giving it a more tapered tip and butt than its northern derivative. Harinoso de Ocho was first identified at A.D. 200–850 in Canyon Infiernillo located in southwest Tamaulipas, Mexico (Mangelsdorf, MacNeish, and Galinat 1967b).

The Maiz de Ocho from the Southwest had a broad genetic base involving various amounts of Chapalote germplasm derived through its hybrid, Pima Papago. The large broad kernels of the southwestern eight-rowed maize are an evolved trait that appeared suddenly at about the same time (A.D. 200–850) as that in southwest Tamaulipas. Thus, this new maize combined the evolved trait of large kernels with the primitive one of only eight rows of kernels. The origin of the large kernels is an unsettled problem. Some suggest they were introduced from the highlands of Guatemala, perhaps from the race Serrano (Brown 1974) and others prefer the highlands of Colombia, perhaps from the race Cabuya (Wellhausen et al. 1952). South American maize has demonstrated a capacity to diverge toward increased kernel size, perhaps because of its isolated freedom from stabilizing introgression by teosinte, a carrier of small kernels.

Not all eight-rowed maize had either the broad genetic base or the large kernels of that in the Southwest. The original Bat Cave maize

(700–500 B.C.) considered to be "pre-Chapalote" was similar to the earlier Nal Tel dated at 4445 ± 180 years ago at LaPerra Cave in Tamaulipas in having a small eight-rowed ear bearing small kernels (Mangelsdorf, MacNeish, and Galinat 1956). These primitive eight-rowed type were adapted to lower elevations and more humid conditions (Wellhausen et al. 1952) than the large kerneled Maiz de Ocho. The early remains of eight-rowed maize in the southeastern United States probably stem from the Nal Tel of Tamaulipas rather than the Maiz de Ocho of the Southwest.

One avenue of spread of Maiz de Ocho to the eastern slopes of the Rocky Mountains was up through the Rio Grande valley of New Mexico, as evidenced by dates of A.D. 370 ± 168 for it at Boca Negra Cave and A.D 1 ± 138 for its hybrid at site BR45, both near Albuquerque (Galinat, Reinhart, and Frisbie 1970). Expansion out of the canyons of northeastern New Mexico and southeastern Colorado may have followed a northeasterly route through Chacuaco Canyon to the Pirgatoire River leading to the Arkansas River area and eventually along all the major river valleys which have abundant sites with eight-rowed maize, especially those of the Mississippi, the Missouri, the Platte and the Ohio rivers, as plotted out by Galinat and Campbell (1967). Suitable agricultural sites at that time did not include the area of the present Corn Belt because its agricultural exploitation had to wait for almost a thousand years until another civilization introduced technological agriculture, especially the steel plow that could break and cultivate the thick prairie sod. The dates of A.D. 1140 ± 125 at the Medina site and A.D. 1135 ± 85 at the Pyeatt site for Maiz de Ocho in the Chacuaco Canyon are not quite as old as the A.D. 780 date once estimated for an eight-rowed type from the Davis site in Texas (Jones 1949). There are now a number of more recent dates for the Davis site. One date on the maize itself is A.D. 1307. Subtracting a correction factor for maize of 250 years makes the date ca. A.D. 1050 ± 75. The Texas site could have been reached by a southeasterly route from northeast New Mexico as represented by the Albuquerque area sites through the Panhandle area into Texas. Eventually it would spread up the Mississippi Valley and eastward into the Woodland sites. Most of the archaeological remains of eight-rowed maize have been on the western side of the Rocky Mountains in Utah and Arizona. These were not earlier than A.D. 700, as discussed by Galinat and Gunnerson (1963).

The southwestern strain of Maiz de Ocho as well as the form at the Davis site in Texas were not preadapted without modification for a translocation to the northern and northeastern U.S. The eventual role of this race as the principal, if not the exclusive, race to be cultivated in a broad zone from the Dakotas to New England and to the northern limits for the growth of maize in Canada up until the early 1900s was achieved only after introgressive hybridization allowed it to pick up certain traits from its more primitive predecessor that helped in its adaptation to the cooler spring conditions. Traits that probably introgressed from the earlier Chapalote race include the flinty endosperm and the tillering plant habit. Not only was selection relaxed for the tight husks adapted for earworm and borer resistance but loose husks had an adaptive advantage in allowing drying of the mature ear under cool rainy fall conditions in the U.S. Northeast. The result was that the butt of the ear and its basal shank became enlarged and the looser husks developed blades (flag leaves) such as typify the Northern Flints. The classic type of Northern Flint had become sorted out in adaptability at the Blain site in Ohio by A.D. 1040 (Galinat 1970) and at several sites in upstate New York at about the same time (Brown and Anderson 1947).

The adoption of Maiz de Ocho as a staple food plant by non-agriculturally oriented people as it spread to the northeastern United States must have been slow and intermittent. Sometimes maize that was planted had to be abandoned before the harvest due to an unanticipated exodus by man. If this maize survived on its own to another generation, it was because nature selected a feral derivative. These escapes might be redomesticated at one or more generations later. The combination of the primitive traits of an eight-rowed ear with a tillering habit creates a potential to occasionally escape by readaptation for survival in the wild. Under stunting conditions, including competition with other vegetation, eight-rowed maize may develop two-ranked spikes that are capable of self propagation. Survival of such a domestic escape would be fragile in that it could be wiped out by a deer or flock of birds intent on consuming its unprotected seeds.

The race Chapalote or pre-Chapalote was the earliest maize in the Southwest. Chapalote is a 12- to 14-rowed popcorn with brown kernels. It still carries a weak pod corn or tunicate allele in which each kernel is partially enclosed in long glumes, a trait remnant from the first maize. The present day remnants of Chapalote are probably like the original form of this race in being adapted to warm growing conditions at low elevations (Wellhausen et al. 1952). Before the differentiation of diverse races, apparently Chapalote became more adaptable in occurring widely in Mexico and parts of the United States Southwest and Midwest. Before its retreat and/or replacement by Maiz do Ocho, Chapalote had left its genetic mark on its successor. The tillering habit which resulted in a rosette of shoots under the cool conditions of April in the north, allowed a form of drought escape later on in the summer in that secondary stalks provided more options for pollen shedding and ear development under later and possibly wetter seasonal conditions.

The importance of teosinte introgression in the evolution of southwestern maize has probably been overestimated. It seems reasonable to account for at least part of the so-called teosinte introgression in the archaeological cobs from Tonto Cave and Richards Cave in Arizona (Galinat et al. 1956) and Cebollita Cave in New Mexico (Galinat and Ruppé 1961) by other means. Maize stunted by drought may develop nubbin ears, sometimes on tillers, that are indurated, shorter and of lower kernel row numbers. The result may be only a phenocopy of teosinte introgression rather than the actual thing. In contrast to maize, teosinte never overcame the day-length barrier to its northward spread although day-neutral strains of teosinte have been developed through plant breeding initiated by Galinat. Wild populations of the teosinte race Nobogame nearest to the United States Southwest come from southern Chihuahua. These have been modified in the direction of becoming day-neutral during their spread to northern Mexico in that they require fewer short day–long night cycles (ca. 14 days) for floral induction than the teosinte from southern Mexico or Guatemala (ca. 21 days) (Wilkes 1967).

The case in favor of sporadic introductions of teosinte introgression in the Southwest and other areas far outside the natural range of teosinte must be given. Teosinte-contaminated maize may produce large ears due to hybrid vigor from heterozygous teosinte chromosome segments (Sehgal 1963). Such "prize" ears might be selected for transport from areas with teosinte in the South. Subsequently under isolation in the Southwest, inbreeding would result in some of the teosinte germplasm becoming homozygous with its more obvious effects on reduced ear size and increased induration. Such deleterious effects would tend to result in the selective elimination of the teosinte germplasm involved. Meanwhile, the effects of Maiz de Ocho germplasm, both on reducing kernel row number and on increasing cob induration was broadening the germplasm base and complicating its understanding. Continued introductions of Mexican maize in historic times under the influence of the Spanish, such as with the race Cristalino de Chihuahua, resulted in the giant eared Pueblo race of maize (Galinat and Gunnerson 1963).

The origin of the Southeastern Dent Corn which was to become one parent of the Corn Belt Dent is complex and not well documented archaeologically. Because there is no archaeological evidence of high row number cobs in the Southeast prior to A.D. 1500, it is probable that this race of dent corn was introduced to the area through trade by

Spanish shipping from Mexico. There are several races of dent corn from southeastern United States that have almost exact counterparts in Mexico. Tuxpeno from along the Gulf coast of Mexico is the same as Tuxpan of the Southeast. Vandeño from the west coast of Mexico may also be part of the southeastern dents. The best known of the southern U.S. dents is Gourdseed or Shoepeg. Its Mexican counterpart is called Pepitilla.

The Southern Dents are dissimilar from the Northern Flints in almost every plant and ear character. The Southern Dents have a late flowering, tall, single stalked plant that carries a short thick ear with many rows of thin, deep kernels. The Northern Flints have an early flowering, short, much tillered plant that carries several long, thin ears with few rows (eight) of thick, shallow kernels.

The amalgamation of these diverse races into a new super race, the Corn Belt Dent, and the controlled regulation of heterosis in modern hybrid corn is now the economic backbone of American agriculture.

The question might be asked that if an eight-rowed race was already present in the Southeast when the dents from Mexico arrived, why didn't we get the massive heterosis that was to occur later in the mid-1800s in the area of the present U.S. Corn Belt? The answer is that the early eight-rowed maize of the Southeast was a more primitive version without the evolutionary experience of having spread to the north and northeast of the United States where the divergence necessary for significant heterosis on reconvergence could accumulate.

THE CYTOGENETIC EVIDENCE ON CORN'S ORIGIN

While this is not the forum to present details of the cytogenetic evidence and to discuss the inheritance of the individual mutational steps in the apparent evolution of maize from teosinte (Galinat 1978), the important conclusions and processes are summarized as follows.

In the Mexican teosinte that was sympatric with maize, disruptive selection between nature and man allowed these species to undergo coevolution. Yet their germplasms undergo exchanges. In order to tolerate near freedom of hybridization with maize that carries deleterious genes for the maize-type ear, teosinte must benefit some from the relationship in order not to evolve means to completely shut it off. Natural selection to cope with introgression among the segregates from maize–teosinte hybrids would favor the grouping of genes essential to the teosinte-type of female spike rather than their recombination resulting in nonfunctional intermediate types of ears of no value to either man or natural survival. The integrity of the genes essential to the teosinte spike was maintained by becoming locked into blocks through inhibitors to crossing over (review of Kato 1975). The mechanisms involved include chromosome knobs, small inversions, gametophyte alleles for preferential fertilization and/or close linkage. The presence of four or five of these blocks in segregating progenies from hybrids of maize and Mexican teosinte has been demonstrated repeatedly (Collins and Kempton 1920; Beadle 1972; Mangelsdorf and Reeves 1939). This was not the case with the Guatemalan teosinte which was more isolated from maize (Galinat 1973).

The comparative cytogenetics of maize and teosinte is presumed to reflect their relationship. While genes controlling the major floral differences between these close relatives are locked up in four or five blocks, there are a few quantitative differences, including the degree of compaction (condensation) and induration (hardness) as well as productivity. While such polygenic traits are usually indicative of natural speciation and have been used as evidence by Mangelsdorf that maize was not derived by domestication of teosinte, they do arise under domestication.

Increased productivity is the best known example of a polygenic trait that may be assembled under domestication. In maize it may take the form of advances in the size of individual seeds (*Cuzco giganti*) or increases in kernel row number (*Conico fasciado*) or the size of individual ears (*Jala*) or various levels of all three components. These effects of human selection are usually contrary to those of natural selection. In the early products of domestication, as with annual teosinte or weedy annuals in general, the strategy for survival is based on the production of an enormous number of small seeds borne in many small inflorescences.

High condensation and its effect on increasing kernel row number in maize are known to be of quantitative inheritance (Anderson and Brown 1948; Emerson and Smith 1950). The high condensation level and correspondingly high kernel row number of maize in genetic exchange with teosinte allow it to carry heterozygous teosinte germplasm and, thereby, to benefit from maize–teosinte heterosis. The essential teosinte segments have an effect of lowering kernel row number in maize (Sehgal 1963).

While induration of the rachis and outer glume in teosinte may be polygenic, the switch to the softer tissues of maize may be monogenic (the tunicate gene). A diversion of energy from the rachis to the extra kernels from paired female spikelets and many ranks of spikelets may in itself result in a lowering of rachis induration.

While the separation of maize and teosinte may be artificial in being due to human intervention, their taxonomic recognition is clear-cut. Maize appears to be the only example of a new species or subspecies created directly by human selection. If by speciation we mean a maize that is capable of survival as a domestic escape by readaption to the wild, no such form of feral maize has been reported. While such a type of maize would have a fragile existence, perhaps with some of the more primitive eight-rowed races, it would bear only on the adaptability of maize rather than its origin.

REMAINING QUESTIONS FOR THE ORIGIN OF MAIZE

The question has been raised as to the significance of the recently discovered perennial diploid teosinte (*Zea diploperennis* Iltis, Doebley and Guzman) to the origin problem. It appears that teosinte and maize exemplify a recognized tendency in the evolution of plants for the perennial habit to be primitive and the annual one derived and specialized such as with weedy and/or domestic plants. Many grasses which have become food plants, such as wheat, barley, rice and sorghum, have both annual and perennial species and it is almost always the annual one that has been domesticated, sugar cane being an exception because it is the stalk or its sugar that is used as food. Hawkes (1969) has pointed out that the annual habit appears to be part of the nature of ancestral prototypes which made it possible for them to be brought into cultivation. Annuals can be grown as row crops and are highly productive of seed. Perennials fail in both of these attributes. Beadle (1980) has suggested that perhaps the perennial trait allowed a mutant type to survive in spite of a handicap to natural seed dispersal, but that became important under domestication by facilitating harvesting. Once humans learned to plant the seed of an emerging maize ear, the perennial trait would lose its value and selection would favor the annual habit. But the perennial species were probably not involved in the domestication process because they are placed in the *Luxuriantes* section by Iltis and Doebley (1980) rather than the *Zea* section of the genus.

The recombination of the perennial trait in derivatives of hybrids between either annual maize or teosinte and the perennial teosinte is only to be expected. The suggestion of Collins (1921) that the annual trait of annual teosinte was derived from introgression with maize has no more bearing now on the origin problem than when first proposed. Since the perennial tetraploid is an autotetraploid, it was expected to have a perennial diploid ancestor. The perennial diploid, like the Guatemalan teosinte, may have special utility in corn breeding because it has not been under selective pressure to develop block inheritance of its definitive traits such as characterize the co-evolved teosinte partners of maize (Galinat 1973). Perennials in general evolve a higher level of insect and virus disease resistance than their annual counterparts. Thereby, perennial teosinte is a better source of genes for such resistance than annual teosinte.

One question still unresolved at the present state of knowledge is why modern teosinte, that is sympatric with maize, has pollen that is smaller than that of modern maize. Because of this fact, one group of researchers (Mangelsdorf, Barghoorn, and Bannerjee 1978) feels that the large size of some very ancient pollen proves that the ancestor of cultivated maize is a wild maize and not teosinte, based on this one trait.* Studies are underway to measure pollen tube competition between maize and teosinte pollen in the styles of teosinte which is where any differential growth of the tubes would have to operate in order to protect teosinte from swamping by maize. The data so far available (Aquirre-González 1977) only involve maize styles. It indicates that in a shortened maize style (2.5 cm), the pollen tubes of teosinte have about the same growth rate as those of maize but at greater distances in the maize style, the maize pollen tubes rapidly outgrow those of teosinte. The problem may also involve the style. Teosinte is known to have a thinner pericarp and an apparently thinner style (silk) consisting of fewer and smaller cells. It seems probable that the thinner pollen tubes from the smaller pollen of teosinte would worm their way more rapidly between the thinner, smaller cells of the teosinte style than the thicker tubes from the larger maize pollen. Morphological comparisons of the styles of teosinte and maize are planned. The pollen tube competition experiment will apparently have to be repeated with teosinte styles despite the greater technical difficulties. These morphological or physical considerations are intended to explain why teosinte that is sympatric with maize has evolved smaller pollen. Other partial barriers of a probable chemical nature in style and/or pollen grain between the species are postulated and are a separate problem (Pfahler 1978).

Another important problem that remains to be worked out is the inheritance of the essential traits separating maize and teosinte on a teosinte background. All previous studies have involved segregations from hybrids between teosinte and modern maize. The essential traits of maize such as paired female spikelets and a many-ranked spike should be transferred to teosinte through repeated backcrossing and their inheritance studied within teosinte in order to attempt a recrea-

---

*Sears, P.B. (*Science* 216:932–934,1982) has removed the oldest Bellas Artes pollen as evidence of wild maize by now concluding it came from a sinking lake bed of only Archaic age (2000 years) rather than from a Pleistocene deposit (80,000 years).

tion of the original situation. To study the corresponding traits of teosinte in a maize background is to presume that maize came first. Furthermore, the results of using teosinte and modern maize that are separated by many thousands of years of evolution since the original divergence are often confusing and equivocal, as reviewed by Galinat (1978). The inheritance of the key taxonomic traits of maize on a teosinte background, if they do represent the mutational steps leading to maize, is the only meaningful way to evaluate their inheritance and mode of expression. For example, it is possible that increasing the kernel row number in a pure teosinte background would eliminate most of the lignification without adding a tunicate allele because the energy would be diverted into increased kernel development rather than a lignification of the rachis. The reverse of this procedure has obscured the picture when teosinte traits are studied on a modern maize background involving a highly vascularized rachis and a high energy sink in the ear. Since we have developed day-neutral inbred strains of teosinte, this is a realistic project to undertake in the United States.

Modern maize, including the so-called ancient, indigenous races in Mexico (especially Palomero Toluqueño), is highly condensed in comparison to teosinte and this condensation results in an unstable type of expression or low penetrance of the essential genes from teosinte. In breeding for a stable expression of the gene (*tr*) for a two-ranked (distichous) spike in maize, Galinat (unpublished) had to lower the condensation to a level approaching that of teosinte. When recombined with the paired female spikelets of maize, the two-ranked ear becomes four-rowed or square. When the solitary female spikelets of teosinte are added, the ear becomes two-ranked or flat.

While more questions than answers remain on the origin and diffusion of maize, the available time and the state of knowledge are inadequate to attempt a more comprehensive treatment here.

SUMMARY

Credit to the early natives of the New World for their role in the origin and descent of maize should be recognized. This achievement would be much greater and its understanding more challenging if the wild ancestor were its extant close relative called teosinte (Beadle 1980) rather than an extinct hypothetical wild maize with the same essential botanical traits as cultivated maize, as postulated by Mangelsdorf (1974). The cytogenetic, morphological and linguistic evidence does in fact favor the possibility that the more profound transformation from teosinte to maize took place under domestication.

If the domestication process did start with teosinte in many places and at different rates, then the sequel of events may have been as follows: In gathering the harvestable forms of teosinte during a pre-maize period of nine to ten thousand years ago, these early natives predisposed the collected seed into a canalized pathway leading toward maize. In harvesting teosinte with its spikes condensed into fascicles, gene pools for increased condensation were accidentally introduced into evolutionary cradles near the campsites. As a result, the genetic base changed to condensed races of semidomestic teosinte comparable in this respect to Chalco teosinte. Deliberate selection within these semidomestic forms for increased productivity of seed per ear resulted in fixing the mutational steps of binate female spikelets and many- ranked spikes, both of which became key taxonomic traits in the formation of maize. Other changes, including the selection of a weak tunicate allele, increased its threshability during these early stages of evolutionary emergence. Much later, at still higher condensation levels, the tunicate factor was discarded when the grain was "shelled" instead of threshed. These final steps from a condensed spike or tight fascicle of spikes in teosinte to a botanically correct ear of maize was probably relatively rapid, occurring in perhaps 100 years.

The result over the millenia has been the creation of a new, great cereal so clearly superior to any other food that it has been the "staff of life" in the New World for over 2,000 years and it has now assumed great agricultural importance around the world. By A.D. 1492 when Europeans arrived on the scene, the first native peoples had already developed hundreds of true breeding races of maize that were specialized for particular uses, thus demonstrating the effectiveness of their plant breeding techniques.

That most of the oldest archaeological remains of the maize ear had the essential botanical characteristics of maize at 7000 B.P. at Tehuacán, Mexico, does not constitute proof that the ancestor of maize is maize. It takes a far greater degree of speculation at a low level of plausibility to imagine such a spike as being from a wild plant than to accept the possibility that the first Tehuacán specimens were derived from an earlier domestication of teosinte outside the valley.

Teosinte is neither imaginary nor extinct. It is a highly successful wild plant that is cytogenetically identical to maize and it crosses freely with maize, giving fully fertile hybrids. It represents an ancient genus (*Zea*) that culminates certain evolutionary trends in this part of the grass family. The great antiquity of the several wild species and subspecies of the genus *Zea*, collectively called teosinte, in contrast to the single domestic subspecies called maize is shown by the greater taxonomic differentiation of teosinte, whose species have annual and perennial habits, diploid and tetraploid forms, a far greater number of chromosome knob positions and various other plant and floral traits, excluding the ear, that are more diverse in the wild than in the cultivar (for taxonomy see Doebley and Iltis 1980; Iltis and Doebley 1980).

The steps described in the transformation from teosinte to maize are largely a result of imagination that is based on cytogenetic and morphological clues combined with analytical reasoning. This does not reduce the high credibility of the re-creation. Creative imagination is based on an analysis of all of the relative facts. The mind can become a time machine that reveals the past and, thereby, opens a portal to reach back. Through the window of the mind, we have seen how teosinte was transformed into maize by human selection, unconsciously at first and then deliberately over the millenia. Through the portal we may reach to extant populations of teosinte in order to retrace the mutational steps in corn's origin and to recapture germplasm once dropped by the evolutionary wayside. Thus we may reconstruct and utilize types of maize that became extinct thousands of years ago but which now have a specialized niche in modern civilization. We may go to the wild populations that are constantly filtered for genes to resist diseases and insects to find the raw material for survival of our genetically eroded modern derivatives.

The Time Factor in the Spread of Maize

The first domesticates from teosinte were undoubtedly like teosinte and also most tropical maize in being short-day in flowering response. This preadapted them for an early spread with the southward movements of man into northern South America where certain primitive short-day races such as Confite Morocho became stabilized and isolated from the mainstream of maize evolution under domestication. Their primitive ear traits retained partly for use as a whole-ear soup-corn has led to confusion about the geographic location of corn's origin.

The first domesticates were not preadapted to spread northward out of Mexico and the American Southwest into areas of longer day-lengths and shorter growing seasons. Also as a limiting factor to the northward spread into the United States was a zone of arid conditions and poor soil in the South and Southwest. This required both special farming technology as well as maize adaptations other than to day length. For example, the capacity to grow a greatly elongated meso-cotyl that permits deep planting has evolved as a drought-resisting adaptation in seedlings of Hopi maize (Collins 1914). The spread of maize into most of the area now called United States and southern

Canada was delayed by thousands of years until preadapted, day-neutral varieties of the eight-rowed race, Maiz de Ocho, became available (Galinat and Gunnerson 1963; Zevallos et al. 1977).

After productive white dent corn was introduced into the U.S. Southeast from Mexico by the Spanish explorers, the spread northward was again delayed until introgression from Maiz de Ocho occurred. The present-day Corn Belt Dents did not evolve until the mid–1800s from hybrids of the Southeastern Dents with the Northeastern Flints (Wallace and Brown 1956).

The diffusion and subsequent isolation of random samples of maize into special geographical or ecological niches has contributed to the evolution of maize and to the degree of heterosis when divergent populations eventually reconverge and hybridize. The history of the U.S. Corn Belt dent corn exemplifies the process. The genetic distance and potential for heterosis between its parents, namely the Northern Flints and Southern Dents, continued to increase during adaptation to New England in one race and to the Southeast in the other. Later in the mid–1800s these races converged and hybridized in the area now called the Corn Belt after this intermediate habitat opened up by the plowing of its prairie soils. The recombination and heterosis resulting from this interracial crossing produced a new super race, the Corn Belt Dent. The heterosis not only increased productivity, but it also preserved some of the genetic diversity necessary for continued improvement, especially in the hands of the corn breeder.

The eight-rowed race (Maiz de Ocho) first appeared in the Southwest about A.D. 200 to 700 after having spread from either highland Guatemala or highland Colombia, a problem yet to be resolved. In either case, it was preadapted to high altitudes and northern latitudes. It gradually spread along the riverine areas toward the Northeast, arriving in New England about A.D. 1400. Maiz de Ocho became almost the exclusive race to be cultivated in a broad zone from the Dakotas to New England and to the northernmost limits for the growth of maize in Canada up until the early 1900s.

There remains a question of how much Chapalote germplasm was captured and retained in the various varieties of Maiz de Ocho. It probably settled at different levels depending upon its contribution to adaptability. The Maiz de Ocho that stayed behind in the Southwest acquired the tight husks of Chapalote as an adaptation for ear-worm and borer protection. This in turn constricted the shape of the ear and resulted in a more tapered tip and butt than its northern descendant.

The southeastern dent corns were from several races that came chiefly from the coastal areas of eastern and western Mexico. These include at least three races known in Mexico as Tuxpeño, Vandeño and Pepitilla. The latter was known in the United States as Gourdseed or Shoepeg. The dents probably spread to the Southeast in historic times with Spanish trade from Mexico.

Our knowledge on the origin of maize is far from complete. The morphological and cytological identity of maize and teosinte is undeniable and the implications of this for the descent of maize are inescapable.

Maize is a morphological loner without any connecting links to the rest of the grasses except through teosinte. The presumed teosinte origin of maize is a conclusion based on solid evidence. This evidence is sufficient to discuss how teosinte became maize, starting with the morphology and harvestability of teosinte. The only selective forces that could account for its derivation from teosinte are those of domestication. Maize is not only highly specialized for harvesting, consumption and planting by man, but it is dependent upon its relationship with man. That is, it is so ill-adapted for natural survival that it would soon become extinct if it were not for the intervention of man.

Our stewardship of this wild ancestor of maize is as much a responsibility as that for maize itself.

ACKNOWLEDGMENTS

This paper was adapted from Paper No. 2720 from the Mass. Agric. Exp. Sta., University of Massachusetts at Amherst, by W. C. Galinat, presented at the advanced seminar of the School of American Research, entitled "The Origins of Plant Husbandry in North America," March 5, 1980.

The author is greatful to his colleagues, friends, students and family for their discussions which made this paper possible.

This research was supported in part from the University of Massachusetts Agricultural Experiment Station Hatch Project No's. 556 (NE-124) and 558, as well as a USDA/SEA/CRGO Grant (82-CRCR-1-1024) under Genetic Mechanisms for Crop Improvement.

The Age of Maize in the Greater Southwest: A Critical Review*

Michael S. Berry

We will not be in a position to say anything very informative about the processes involved in the introduction of maize to the American Southwest until the relevant spatio-temporal variables are much better controlled than they are at present. As it now stands, virtually any plausible model might be imposed upon the available evidence without fear of falsification. While the arguments that follow do not remedy the situation, they do underscore deficiencies in the extant data base and point to some potentially productive lines of investigation.

THE EVIDENCE FOR EARLY SOUTHWESTERN MAIZE

According to current orthodoxy, the time and place of the introduction of maize are fairly well established archaeological facts:

> The early corn in Bat Cave, on the St. Augustine Plains of west-central New Mexico, was associated with a stone assemblage that differs little from Chiricahua Cochise. Radiocarbon dates from corn bearing levels in the cave run as early as about 4000 B.C., but data on the association of the corn and the charcoal samples dated have not yet been published. The earliest Bat Cave corn is exceedingly primitive—it cannot be said with certainty that it is not a wild variety—but reliable

---

*From *Time, Space and Transition in Anasazi Prehistory*, by Michael Berry, published and copyrighted in 1982 by the University of Utah Press.

evidence of domestication comes early in the sequence, and we can infer that it was well advanced by 2000–3000 B.C. [Willey and Phillips 1958:128]

The earliest appearance of maize in the greater Southwest . . . has been determined in the order of 3000 B.C. by radiocarbon means. The places are Bat Cave (Mangelsdorf and Smith 1949), Tularosa and Cordova Caves (Martin et al. 1952) in New Mexico, all in altitudes over 6,000 feet; and at Point of Pines, Arizona (Ariz. W:10:112), in a valley floor geological context of first, possibly second, millenium B.C. age (Martin and Schoenwetter 1960). . . [Haury 1962:113].

To the small scattered bands of the Desert Archaic food collectors, specifically to those of the Cochise group, there came a series of new and, eventually, revolutionary traits. First, and ultimately the most important, maize—appearing in southwestern New Mexico more than four thousand years ago . . . [Reed 1964:177]

The chiricahua period was a crucial one in Southwestern development for during its time agriculture was introduced from Mexico. On of the first indications of corn in the Southwest in the form of pre-Chapalote pod appeared in Bat Cave, New Mexico about 2,000 B.C. . . . [Whalen 1971:91]

The first evidence of corn in and around Arizona occurs during the Desert culture stage. Corn pollen was recovered from sediments at the Cienega Creek Site in southeastern Arizona (Martin and Schoenwetter 1960, pp. 33–34). This pollen was deposited at 2000 B.C. or earlier. Corn dating to 2000 or 3000 B.C. was found at Bat Cave in west-central New Mexico. [Martin and Plog 1973:277]

As previously noted, domesticated plants were being cultivated on a small scale in the Southwest by 2000 B.C., if not earlier, and the Late Archaic was also a time of gradual population growth and increasing complexity. [Lipe 1978:341]

These statements, while not exhaustive, are an accurate reflection of the prevalent view that maize was first introduced between 4000 and 5000 years ago in the Southern Basin and Range province of New Mexico and Arizona. Arranged in chronological order, they demonstrate that this belief has remained essentially unchanged for at least two decades. In fact, it has persisted for a longer period of time than the list of quotations indicates since, excepting Jelinek (1965) and Jennings (1967), no one has seriously questioned the validity of the Bat Cave chronology or cultural sequence as first set forth in the late 1940s and early 50s by Mangelsdorf and Smith (1949), Dick (1952, 1954) and Libby (1955). Nor has anyone openly criticized the interpretations of Bat Cave's "companion sites," i.e., the handful of sites and locales that purportedly have yielded maize remains nearly as old as the Bat Cave complex. These include Cienega Creek (sometimes referred to as the Point of Pines alluvial site) in east-central Arizona (Haury 1957; Martin and Schoenwetter 1960), LoDaisKa in north-central Colorado (Irwin and Irwin 1959, 1961), and the Arroyo Cuervo region of northwestern New Mexico (Irwin-Williams and Tompkins 1968; Irwin-Williams 1973). I will argue that (1) the evidence for 4000 to 5000 year old maize at each of these sites is, at best, inconclusive, and that (2) a careful reading of the data yields a much more conservative age estimate. The implications of these conclusions will be considered in the final section of this paper.

Bat Cave

Bat Cave is located on the southern fringe of the Plains of San Augustin, approximately ten miles southeast of Horse Springs, New Mexico. The large main chamber contained very little evidence of human occupation and the bulk of the cultural materials came from four much smaller tunnel-like caves.

Though the site was excavated in 1948 and resampled in 1950 (Dick 1952, 1954) the descriptive monograph did not appear in print until 1965 (Dick 1965). In the interim, the site and the interpretations of its excavator became firmly fixed in the tradition of southwestern archaeology. Jennings' (1967) review of the monograph and, to a lesser extent, Jelinek's (1965) critical assessment of the status of southwestern radiocarbon dating cast doubt on the credibility of the Bat Cave data. However, it seems clear that few students were influenced by these criticisms. Indeed, Jennings himself apparently has reversed his position on the matter (Jennings 1974:291). This is unfortunate since the points he raises in his review article pertaining to excavation techniques and the nature of the radiocarbon samples constitute adequate grounds for rejecting the Bat Cave data as essentially meaningless; at least insofar as the age of maize is concerned. It will be useful here to discuss and further elaborate the two major features of Jennings' critique and to draw attention to a few additional problems.

First, Jennings noted that the site was excavated in arbitrary horizontal levels. Given the complexity of the midden deposits shown in Dick's Figures 10 (Dick 1965:14) and 17 (Dick 1965:20), it seems obvious that the imposition of arbitrary levels must have had the dual effect of (1) obliterating the actual association of contemporaneous materials by artificial segregation into different levels, and (2) creating fictitious associations by lumping distinct strata within the same level. Hence there is nothing at all certain about the supposed association of maize and the charcoal samples that yielded fourth millenium B.C. radiocarbon dates.

Even if it could be argues that Dick's arbitrary excavation units closely approximated the actual stratigraphic situation, two additional sources of uncertainly deserve our attention: the lack of provenience control in the 1948 excavations and the questionable sampling techniques of the 1950 excavations.

Radiocarbon samples were collected during both 1948 and 1950 excavation seasons (see Table 9.1). According to Dick, these were

> . . . selected by Mangelsdorf and Smith from the botanical specimens they were studying at the time. This material was sent to Libby without being checked by me so I cannot vouch for its exact provenience in the cave deposits. [Dick 1965:18]

So, even given the tenuous assumption that excavation in arbitrary levels is an appropriate procedure, there is no way to ascertain which of the 1948 samples came from what levels. The 1950 excavations were designed primarily to rectify this problem of provenience control. Six additional samples were obtained, each of which consisted of

> . . . small pieces of charcoal, picked by hand throughout a twelve-inch level in a five-by-six block. It was necessary to use this method to obtain enough charcoal, and this might well account for some of the discrepancies in the dates. [Dick 1965:18]

"Necessary" or not, the practice of taking composite radiocarbon samples is of questionable utility even when stratigraphic excavation techniques are employed, but the composite sampling of arbitrary levels is a completely unacceptable procedure which is likely to produce fictitious radiocarbon dates. A hypothetical example will make this clear. Suppose a site has two distinguishable strata, A and B. Stratum A constitutes the refuse of the first occupation which ceased 3000 years ago. The site then remained unoccupied until 1000 years ago, at which time the deposition of stratum B was initiated. Now, if this site were excavated in arbitrary levels and one of these levels happened to bracket the stratigraphic break between A and B (as it almost certainly

TABLE 9.1
BAT CAVE RADIOCARBON DATES*

1948 EXCAVATIONS			1950 EXCAVATIONS		
Material	Level	Date	Material	Level	Date
cobs	0–12"	1752 ± 250			
wood	12–24"	1907 ± 250	Charcoal	11–15"	1610 ± 200
wood	24–36"	2239 ± 250	Charcoal	24–36"	2816 ± 200
cobs & wood	36–48"	2249 ± 250	Charcoal	36–48"	2048 ± 170
wood	48–60"	2862 ± 250	Charcoal	48–60"	5605 ± 290
Extrapolation	60–66"	$3000 - 3500$	Charcoal	60–66"	5931 ± 310

*After Mangelsdorf, Dick and Camara-Hernandez 1967:4. Dates are given in radiocarbon years before present (B.P.).

would), a composite radiocarbon sample from the level in question would, if collected by the method Dick describes, give the date of (3000 years + 1000 years)/2 = 2000 years B.P. Hence the level would be dated to 2000 B.P. even though the site was actually unoccupied at that time. Needless to say, this line of argument could easily be extended to encompass the association of maize with early dates at Bat Cave.

Given the likelihood that the relevant associations are spurious, the only possible means of demonstrating the great antiquity of the Bat Cave maize would be to date it directly. But, as Jennings noted, ". . . the earlier dates come from apparently associated charcoal, *not* from the corn specimens themselves" (Jennings 1967:123). And this brings up an interesting point which I do not believe is a matter of general knowledge, since Dick failed to include adequately detailed information on the type of material dated in his table of radiocarbon dates (Dick 1965:17). As a later, albeit, infrequently cited, article entitled "Bat Cave Revisited" (Mangelsdorf, Dick and Camara-Hernandez 1967) clearly shows, only one date was run on a sample consisting solely of cobs, and one more date was run on a mixed sample of cobs and wood. These yielded dates of 1752 ± 250 B.P.: A.D. 198 (C-165) and 2249 ± 250 B.P.: 299 B.C. (C-164; C-171) respectively.[1] This is a far cry from the 3000 to 4000 B.C. temporal provenience originally suggested by Dick (1965:95). It is also considerably more recent than the "guess date" postulated by Mangelsdorf, Dick and Camara-Hernandez (1967) on morphological grounds. I quote the argument at length since it is of fundamental importance and I have not seen it referenced elsewhere.

> One of the most important questions to be answered is the date of the [maize] remains. The radiocarbon determinations (Libby, 1951; Arnold and Libby, 1950) of samples of charcoal and other materials from the several levels are set forth in Table I [Table 9.1 above]. The data from the two excavations are fairly consistent for the three uppermost levels but differ widely for the two lower levels. There is reason to believe that the date of 5605 for the charcoal in the 48-60" level is not valid for the associated earliest maize.
>
> On the basis of the characteristics of the cobs, especially those which represent evidence of teosinte contamination, we have concluded that the maize from the 48-60" level of Bat Cave is later than the maize of the Abejas phase in the Tehuacan caves and earlier than that of the Ajalpan phase. This would date it at between 2300 and 1500 B.C. A similar correlation with the remains of maize in Romero's Cave, Tamaulipas, Mexico, excavated by Dr. Richard S. MacNeish . . . makes it contemporary with the Guerrero phase dated by radiocarbon at 1800–1400 B.C. These correlations suggest that the earliest Bat Cave maize is probably not earlier than ca. 2300 B.C. and may be several centuries later. [Mangelsdorf, Dick and Camara-Hernandez 1967:4–5]

Here we have an apparent recantation of Dick's earlier pronouncements, but note that the proffered temporal placement is based on morphological comparisons with the Mexican maize sequence (which itself is imprecisely dated) and ignores completely the Bat Cave radiocarbon data. Obviously, morphological dating is a pretty hazardous business and, as shown in Table 9.1, none of the dates fall anywhere near 2300 B.C. (4250 B.P.). If we ignore the 3655 B.C. (5605 B.P.) date, as the authors suggest, then the next oldest dates in the sequence fall around 850–900 B.C. (2800–2850 B.P.). Of course, there is no way of knowing whether or not these dates mean anything for reasons discussed earlier, i.e., composite sampling and excavation in arbitrary levels.

Finally, all of the dates from Bat Cave were determined using the solid carbon method. It has since been recognized that this technique is unreliable due to the effects of airborne radioactive contamination (Crane 1956) and self-absorption (Ralph 1971).

In summary, there is no reason to place much confidence in the Bat Cave data. It was a poorly excavated site that can be interpreted nearly any way one pleases by juggling the data and picking and choosing from the list of questionable dates those that fit a given hypothesis. It would seem that the only prudent alternative is to tentatively accept the ^{14}C determinations on samples that contain maize and ignore the rest. This may seem overly conservative but I think the approach is justifiable. The burden of proof for "ancient maize" falls on the shoulders of those making the claims. Clear-cut and well documented evidence is not too much to ask for, nor is it that difficult to obtain. Unfortunately, the Bat Cave data are not of the required quality and, as will be seen in the arguments that follow, evidence from the other southwestern sites boasting "ancient maize" is similarly inadequate.

Cienega Creek

The Cienega Creek site, located in east-central Arizona, was excavated in 1955–56 by Emil Haury and reported the following year in *American Antiquity* (Haury 1957). It frequently is alluded to in the same breath as Bat Cave as yet another site that demonstrates the very early occurrence (in this case, prior to 2000 B.C.) of maize in the Southwest. The basis for such claims is a paper entitled "Arizon's Oldest Cornfield" (Martin and Schoenwetter 1960) in which Martin and Schoenwetter report the recovery of possible maize pollen from Bed D-1 of the site which was at that time thought to date as early as 2200 B.C. (Haury 1957). However, there were major inconsistencies in the original radiocarbon dating that had not been resolved at the time of Martin and Schoenwetter's publication, and a subsequent series of ^{14}C determinations did little to clarify the situation. The relevant data are summarized in Table 9.2. Figure 9.1 is a schematic profile of the site as published in Haury's (1957) article. At the time the article appeared, only the University of Arizona solid carbon series (Wise and Shutler 1958) and the University of Michigan gas dates (Crane and Griffin 1958a) were available. These are listed in stratigraphic order in the second and fourth columns of Table 9.2. As shown, there is a glaring discrepancy between the Arizona solid carbon and Michigan gas determinations on samples recovered from Bed D-1. The Michigan dates are contemporaneous[2] ($F = .196 < 3.00$: $df = 2, \infty$) with a weighted average of 2493 ± 132 B.P.: 543 B.C. The three Arizona dates are also statistically contemporaneous ($F = 1.99 < 3.00$: $df = 2, \infty$) but their weighted average is 4238 ± 91 B.P.: 2288 B.C., indicating an age for Bed D-1 roughly 1700 years older than the Michigan series. Haury, of course, had no way of knowing that the solid carbon method was soon to be discarded in favor of the gas counting technique by all major labs and chose to accept the older Arizona solid carbon series because the artifact complex of D-1 apparently was related to ". . . the Chiricahua stage, though admittedly the identification had to be made on only a few traits" (Haury 1957:24). Since the Chiricahua complex had been elsewhere dated (also by the solid carbon method) between 2000 and 2500 B.C., the Arizona series was a reasonable choice. In their attempt to assign a date to the earliest maize pollen-bearing stratum (Bed D-1), Martin and Schoenwetter (1960) mention the 1700 year discrepancy between the two sets of dates and accept the earliest on the basis of Haury's argument.

In 1959 the University of Arizona laboratory converted to the carbon dioxide gas-proportional counting method (Damon and Long 1962). During 1960 a number of repeat analyses were conducted on samples previously utilized in solid carbon determinations. Those from the Cienega Creek site are shown in column three of Table 9.2. Dates marked with an asterisk are recombustions of the solid carbon used in the original dating. The others represent new runs on duplicate samples of charcoal, wood, and carbonaceous material. Also included in Table 9.2 is a La Jolla laboratory date (L-432B), originally run as a cross-check on M-540 (reported in Damon and Long 1962).

The interpretation of this evidence is fairly clear-cut for Bed D-1. The recombustion of sample A-29 yielded a date of 2430 ± 150 B.P. which is compatible with the Michigan dates and invalidates the earlier solid carbon determination of 4400 ± 150 B.P. Samples A-25B and A-25 bis, as well as L-432B, are also in agreement with the Michigan series. In fact, the seven gas dates for D-1 from the Michigan, La Jolla and Arizona laboratories are statistically contemporaneous ($F = .84 < 2.1$: $df = 6, \infty$). Such strong concordance allows for the une-

TABLE 9.2

RADIOCARBON DATES FROM THE CIENEGA CREEK SITE

Provenience	Arizona Solid Carbon Series (Wise and Shutler 1958)	Arizona Gas Series (Damon and Long 1962)	Michigan Gas Series (Crane and Griffin 1958)
Pit 3, originating from the surface of C-2	2515±300 B.P. (A-28) carbonaceous material	1900±160 B.P. (A-28)*	1140±300 B.P. (M-462) fragmented solid charcoal
Pit 3, originating from the surface of C-2		2100±150 B.P. (A-20, A-23) charcoal (composite sample)	
Pit 7, originating from the surface of C-2	2150±200 B.P. (A-48) charcoal		
Pit 8', originating from the surface of C-3	3250±200 B.P. (A-50) 3025±200 B.P. (A-52) two runs on same sample of wet, charred wood	2720±150 B.P. (A-50 bis)*	
Within C-3	2610±200 B.P. (A-49) 2080±200 B.P. (A-53) 3380±200 B.P. (A-51) three runs on same sample of wet, rotten wood	3190±160 B.P. (A-51 bis)*	
Within C-3, above Cremation 36	3280±200 B.P. (A-26) carbonaceous material	2490±170 B.P. (A-26 bis)* 2900±150 B.P. (A-26B) organic material (rootlets removed before analysis)	

Pit 6, originating from the surface of D-1	3070 ± 150 B.P. (A-27) charred, waterlogged pine branch	3190 ± 150 B.P. (A-27 bis)*	
Within D-1	3980 ± 160 B.P. (A-21, A-22) fragmented charcoal (composite sample)	2440 ± 160 B.P. (A-25B) wood	2400 ± 200 B.P. (M-540) fragmented charcoal (composite sample)
	4310 ± 160 B.P. (A-19) fragmented charcoal	2700 ± 160 B.P. (A-25 bis)*	2530 ± 250 B.P. (M-541) fragmented charcoal
	4400 ± 150 B.P. (A-29) fragmented charcoal	2430 ± 150 B.P. (A-29 bis)*	2600 ± 140 B.P. (M-461) fragmented charcoal
		2200 ± 140 B.P. (L-432B) charcoal	

*indicates recombustion

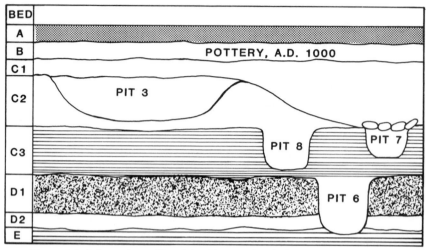

Figure 9.1. Schematic profile of the Cienega Creek site. [After Haury 1957]

quivocal rejection of all three of the D-1 Arizona solid carbon dates. The weighted mean of the seven gas dates is 2442 ± 66 B.P.: 492 B.C.

A somewhat different situation arises for Bed C-3 in that the recombustion and same-sample analyses agree quite closely with the solid carbon determinations, excepting A-26 bis which Damon and Long (1962) argue was probably contaminated by modern rootlets. The weighted average of the three contemporaneous C-3 gas dates is 3104 ± 92 B.P.: 1155 B.C.

As Jelinek (1965) has already noted, these results are anomalous since they indicate that Bed C-3 was deposited roughly 600 years earlier than the underlying Bed D-1. Damon and Long tentatively suggested that the D-1 dates were in error as a result of silica and limonite replacement.

> Although it is difficult to imagine contamination causing fortuitous agreement of all the D-1 layer dates, it is even more difficult to reconcile young ages with the cultural assemblage in D-1 and the older dates above it. [Damon and Long 1962:243]

This line of argument is unconvincing for two reasons. First, the suggestion of fortuitous agreement as a consequence of replacement stretches credibility since the sample materials involved (unburned wood and wood charcoal) have considerably different contamination potentials. Second, the identification of D-1 cultural assemblage as "Chiricahua" is, as mentioned earlier, tenuous at best since few diagnostic artifacts were recovered. Hence, a 500 B.C. temporal placement for the D-1 deposits is not necessarily contradicted by the associated items of material culture. If we accept the D-1 dating, we are left with the problem of explaining why the C-3 determinations are older than expected. Two solutions come immediately to mind, the most obvious of which is the ever present possibility of some mix-up in provenience assignments during the transfer of samples from field to laboratory to museum storage, etc. The only suggestion that this sort of error might have occurred is the discrepancy in published C-3 sample descriptions wherein Haury describes A-27 as "fragmented solid charcoal" (Haury 1957:22) and the radiocarbon analysts describe it as a "charred, water-logged pine branch" (Wise and Shutler 1958:73). Apparently, the specimen bearing the A-27 provenience label in the laboratory was not the same specimen described in the field. It seems unlikely, however, that provenience errors can be held to account for the inversion problem as a whole since no less than seven mistakes would have to have occurred in order to produce results of the type indicated.

Alternatively, the dating inversion might be attributable to the origin(s) of the sample materials and the depositional processes by which they entered the site record. Apparent reversals in the stratigraphic ordering of well dated ceramic types are commonplace in southwestern alluvial settings. Hack (1942), for example, describes an inversion of Anasazi Pueblo III and Pueblo IV ceramics within the Naha formation of the Jeddito Wash alluvial sequence.

> . . . the (a) member of the Naha formation was deposited, then cut by an arroyo, and the (b) member deposited, all between Pueblo III time and 1700 A.D. That the unconformity actually exists is proved by the assemblage of pottery fragments found in the two members. Member (a) (the oldest) yielded only 1 piece of Pueblo III pottery and 24 pieces of Pueblo IV pottery. Member (b) (the younger) on the other hand yielded 30 pieces of Pueblo III pottery and 6 pieces of Pueblo IV pottery. In other words the younger of the fills yields the highest proportion of the older pottery . . . Both members must be dated by the youngest potsherds in them, so they are both Pueblo IV or later. The situation may be explained by assuming that during the deposition of the (b) member a portion of a Pueblo III ruin was being actively eroded by the wash. [Hack 1942:53]

An analogous process could account for the anomalous dating of Cienega Creek. Referring again to Table 9.2, three of the four contemporaneous radiocarbon determinations from within Bed C-3, as well as the older than expected (i.e., older than D-1) date from intrusive Pit 8, were derived through recombustion of solid carbon originally prepared by Wise and Shutler from waterlogged timbers. The possibility exists that all of these were transported to the site by the same floods responsible for the laminated C-3 deposits. The similarity in ages of the specimens easily could have been the product of natural agency, e.g., alluvial burial or a forest fire, several centuries prior to redeposition at the Cienega Creek locale. In fact, death by forest fire would account for the charring reported for three of the four specimens (Wise and Shutler 1958). This is admittedly speculative, but no more so than the assumption that the age of the timbers equates with the age of Bed C-3 and the associated artifacts. If the wood *was* culturally introduced, why wasn't it subsequently burnt to exhaustion in campfires? In contrast, the radiocarbon samples from Bed D-1 are, with one exception, all fragmented charcoal associated with a great abundance of hearthstones. This leaves little doubt that the D-1 sample material was deposited as a result of human activity. If this interpretation of the chronometric evidence is correct, the basal occupation of the Cienega Creek site occurred at approximately 500 B.C.

As for the association of maize pollen with the earliest deposits, only 48 of the 51,170 grains analyzed from the preceramic levels were identified as *Zea*. These may in fact indicate that maize was being grown during D-1 and C-3 times. However, contamination from the overlying Mogollon occupation cannot be ruled out. This seems all the more likely in view of the numerous deep aboriginal pits, some of which originated in the Mogollon levels and were intrusive into Beds D-1 and C-3 (Fig. 9.1). Schoenwetter (personal communication) has suggested that the vertical distribution of corn pollen argues against contamination since the relative percentage drops between the Mogollon and San Pedro levels, then increases in the next level, a possible Chiricahua level. However, this objection finds little statistical support. For one thing, the pollen sample comes from a single vertical column in this extensive and complex site. There is absolutely no way of knowing whether or not the relative pollen frequencies are representative of the site as a whole. Second, the percentages of corn pollen are so minuscule (Mogollon level = .081%, San Pedro level = .044%, Chiricahua level = .13%) that the differences are not demonstrably significant. The case for association would be much stronger if cobs, kernels, stalks or husks had been recovered from the early deposits. But none were found even though such normally perishable items as basketry, plant parts and wild seeds were preserved in the bog-like C-3 deposits (Haury 1957).

In sum, despite the use of stratigraphic excavation techniques and the concern shown by Haury and others (Damon and Long 1962) for the accuracy of the absolute dating methods, there are major anomalies in the Cienega Creek record that cannot be resolved without additional excavation. The assertion that maize was being grown at the site as early as 2000 B.C. may not be discounted as wholly unsupportable. If we accept Damon and Long's argument and reject the D-1 dates, then the earliest dated occupation level is Bed C-3 with a mean determination of approximately 1150 B.C. If we accept the alternative interpretation offered above and reject the C-3 dates, then the most probable beginning date for occupation of the site is around 500 B.C. The presence of maize cannot firmly be demonstrated in either case due to the possibility of contamination.

The LoDaisKa Site

The LoDaisKa site is located in the foothills of the Rocky Mountains roughly 15 miles west of Denver, Colorado. It was excavated in the late 1950s by Henry and Cynthia Irwin (Irwin and Irwin 1959, 1961). According to the authors, the site was occupied by four distinct, perhaps temporally overlapping, prehistoric cultures: Desert Archaic (Complex D), McKean (Complex C), Plains Woodland (Complex B), and Fremont (Complex A). Nelson (1967) and Breternitz (1970) have disputed this latter assignment, noting that the ceramics are probably Shoshonean rather than Fremont. In the following argument, I have substituted "Shoshonean" for Irwin and Irwin's "Fremont" in order to acknowledge this generally accepted revision. Again, according to the authors, maize was first utilized at the site by approximately 2000 B.C. As was the case with Martin and Schoenwetter's (1960) interpretation of the Cienega Creek site, Irwin and Irwin accepted the Bat Cave evidence as valid and pointed to the Bat Cave maize complex as the probable progenitor of the early LoDaisKa maize.

> Since corn was present at Bat Cave (Dick, 1952), a site with certain Chiricahua Cochise affinities, it is not unreasonable to assume corn diffused to LoDaisKa from New Mexico or Arizona. [Irwin and Irwin 1959:143]
>
> Maize cobs of Chapalote type and what is probably maize pollen occur earliest at LoDaisKa from 78 to 82 inches below baseline . . . this level falls between 1140 and 2800 B.C., roughly 4000 years ago. This maize is morphologically very similar to maize of about the same age from Bat Cave in New Mexico. [Irwin and Irwin 1961:115]

There are a number of reasons for questioning Irwin and Irwin's interpretations. First and foremost, the site was excavated in arbitrary horizontal levels. Hence, for the same reasons discussed in connection with Bat Cave the presumed association of maize with any particular radiocarbon date or, for that matter, any particular cultural complex, is far from certain. In this case it would appear that the excavators had no choice but to employ arbitrary excavation units since the bulk of the deposits consisted of homogeneous, undifferentiated colluvium derived through chemical and mechanical weathering of the sandstone outcrop which forms the overhang and extends upslope above the site (Rodden 1959). The base of the site is well above the level of the local, late Holocene alluvium, hence the culture-bearing deposits were never subject to the kind of rapid, intermittant inundation that typically produces strong stratification and simplifies the excavation process. As a consequence of the slow accretion of fill material and the resultant potential for mixing of artifacts from adjacent time horizons, interpretation of the cultural sequence is subject to certain ambiguities which Irwin and Irwin were unable to resolve.

> From the available material it is not possible to determine whether groups of divergent affiliation ever inhabited the area synchronously. The considerable overlapping of culture units seems to point in this direction; but, as indicated above, this phenomenon may be partially due to the telescoping of stratigraphy. This plus certain traditional continuums provide possible evidence of the influence of these groups on each other. [Irwin and Irwin 1959:147]

Nowhere in the monograph do the authors make an unequivocal analytic decision as to how much of the typological overlap should be attributed to depositional factors and how much to cultural contemporaneity. This being the case, how much confidence can one attach to either their proposed cultural reconstructions or the purportedly early temporal placement of maize at the site?

Some idea of the onerous nature of the interpretive task that faced Irwin and Irwin is conveyed in Table 9.3 which summarizes the distributional data from LoDaisKa. For convenience of presentation, the various tables scattered through the monograph have been juxtaposed. The projectile point data were taken from Irwin and Irwin's Table I (p. 37). Their types A through L are lumped together under the heading of "Dart Points" while types aa through xx make up the "Arrow Point" category. The ceramic distribution originally appeared in Irwin and Irwin's Table II (p. 57) and the maize data were taken from Galinat's "Plant Remains from the LoDaisKa Site" published in the same volume. The radiocarbon dates were not available at the time the monograph was published but were the subject of a later article in *American Antiquity* (Irwin and Irwin 1961). In preparing Table 9.3, I have taken the liberty of collapsing the four-inch arbitrary levels to twelve-inch units in the interests of clarity and space. This produced no substantial alteration in the data patterning.

In retrospect, Irwin and Irwin's equivocation regarding the "overlap problem" should have been put to rest by the results of the radiocarbon analyses. As shown in Table 9.3, the region of greatest overlap of cultural complexes and artifact categories is *also* characterized by inversion and intermixture of radiocarbon dates. This strongly suggests that the apparent contemporaneity of cultural complexes was artificially produced through (1) severe mixing due to "trampling" of deposits and aboriginal reuse of tools, (2) the imposition of arbitrary,

TABLE 9.3
DISTRIBUTION OF ARTIFACT TYPES, CULTURAL COMPLEXES AND RADIOCARBON DATES AT THE LODAISKA SITE

Arbitrary Levels	Dart Points	Arrow Points	Ceramics	Maize	Radiocarbon Dates (years before present)	Desert Archaic	McKean	Plains Woodland	Shoshonean
0–12"									X
12–24"	3	7	4	1 Kernel					X
24–36"	1	7	7					X	X
36–48"	16	50	32		970±150 B.P. (M-1003) 1260±150 B.P. (M-1002)			X	X
48–60"	34	36	21	1 Cob	1150±150 B.P. (M-1005)	X	X	X	
60–72"	32	7	2		3400±150 B.P. (M-1004) 1150±150 B.P. (M-1008)	X	X		
72–84"	23			1 Cob & Fragments	3150±200 B.P. (M-1006)	X	X		
84–96"	12					X			
96–108"	4				4840±250 B.P. (M-1009)	X			

horizontal excavation units on sloping deposits, or (3) some combination of these two factors. Whatever the case may be, virtually every instance of overlapping artifact types and complexes evidenced at the LoDaisKa site is demonstrably anomalous in light of what is now known about the prehistory of the region. For instance, a face value reading of Table 9.3 indicates that the McKean complex lasted from some time prior to 1450 B.C. (3400 B.P.) to some time after A.D. 800 (1150 B.P.) and was partially contemporaneous with the Plains Woodland occupation. However, the twenty-four radiocarbon dates listed by Reeves (1973) for the McKean and closely related Oxbow complex of the central and northern Great Plains all fall between 3250 and 1200 B.C. There is no evidence that the McKean complex survived beyond 1200 B.C. nor is there any evidence that Woodland populations entered the Great Plains prior to A.D. 1 (Symms 1977). In fact, Woodland ceramics in the vicinity of the LoDaisKa site do not appear to date any earlier than A.D. 200 (Breternitz 1969), so it is highly unlikely that the two complexes actually overlapped in time. Quite to the contrary, they were most likely separated by 1500 years or more. The absolute values of the radiocarbon dates from the site are consistent with this interpretation though their relative positions within the deposits are out of sequence.

As another example, there is general agreement that the bow and arrow was not introduced to the Great Plains until the inception of the Avonlea complex during the second or third centuries A.D. (Kehoe 1966, 1973; Wood 1967; Reeves 1973; Symms 1977). However, Table 9.3 suggests that arrow points occur as early as 1450 B.C. (3400 B.P.) in association with the Desert Archaic and McKean complexes. Again, a face value reading of the distributional data produces at least a 1500 year anachronism.

It is interesting in this regard that Irwin and Irwin saw fit to reject the early occurrence of arrow points as intrusive (Irwin and Irwin 1959:140) and I presume that they similarly rejected the ceramics from the same levels since no claim was made for the occurrence of pottery at 1450 B.C. Why, then, should a single corn cob and a few fragments recovered from a Desert Archaic "level" be accepted as a valid association? I strongly suspect that all of the maize remains from LoDaisKa, along with the ceramics and arrow points, are attributable to the Woodland and Shoshonean occupations. This is a testable proposition since the Chapalote specimen in question could still be submitted for radiocarbon analysis. If the above arguments are valid, it should yield a date well into the Christian era.

Whether or not such a test is ever conducted, I think it is clear that the evidence for "ancient maize" at LoDaisKa leaves much to be desired. It is certainly not the kind of data that will support higher level constructs regarding the introduction and diffusion of maize farming.

The Arroyo Cuervo Region

From 1964 through 1970 Eastern New Mexico University conducted an extensive program of survey and excavation in northwestern New Mexico under the direction of Cynthia Irwin-Williams (Irwin-Williams and Tompkins 1968: Irwin-Williams 1967, 1973). This research inspired Irwin-Williams' definition of, first, the Picosa culture and, a few years later, the Oshara Tradition. The Picosa culture

> . . . is defined as a continuum of similar closely related preceramic cultures existing in the southwestern United States during the last three millenia before Christ. It is seen as representing the elementary period of the development of the Southwest as a discrete culture area and is believed to be the result of a cultural synthesis of uniform developments originating as early as 8000 B.C. [Irwin-Williams 1967:441]

The Oshara Tradition was formulated for the "northern Southwest" and was based solely on data from the Arroyo Cuervo region. It purportedly represents

> . . . an unbroken sequence of preceramic cultural development beginning in the sixth millenium before Christ and culminating in the early phases of the local Anasazi-Pueblo culture. [Irwin-Williams 1973:2]

Both constructs are rather extreme statements of the gradualist school of evolutionary thought, presupposing as they do the slow-paced accretion of increments of culture change and implying biological and ethnic continuity within fairly restricted geographical domains for millenial periods. The gradualist perspective is quite compatible with the notion that maize farming was introduced to the Archaic hunter-gatherers of the Arroyo Cuervo region prior to 2000 B.C. but that it had no significant effect until the Basketmaker II-III period during the first few centuries A.D. More properly, gradualism demands that the problem be framed in this manner. While I disagree totally with the tenets of gradualism, my intent in broaching the subject is not to initiate a theoretical debate but merely to point out that Irwin-Williams' Picosa and Oshara constructs rely more on theoretical assumptions than they do on any archaeological data. With respect to the current topic of investigation, what data allow the inference that maize has a 4000 year history of utilization in the Southwest? The evidence marshalled by Irwin-Williams is less than convincing.

> The one subsistence feature which sets the Southwest Picosa area off from all contemporary western Archaic cultures is the early presence and growing impor-

tance of horticulture. Probably introduced through the medium of the Cochise culture, its occurrence by about 2000 B.C. is documented in Arizona, New Mexico, and Colorado (Cienega Creek, Arizona, Haury 1957; Bat Cave, New Mexico, Dick 1965; Armijo Shelter, New Mexico, Irwin-Williams 1967a; LoDaisKa Shelter, Colorado, Irwin and Irwin 1959). [Irwin-Williams 1967:443]

The list of citations would be impressive if not for the fact that three of the four sites named have been reviewed above and, in each case, the evidence was found wanting. The fourth, Armijo Shelter, was excavated by Irwin-Williams as part of the Arroyo Cuervo, Anasazi Origins Project. However, the preliminary descriptive report cited above was for some reason never published and the relevant data cannot be evaluated. In fact, of the seven major excavations carried out in conjunction with the Anasazi Origins Project, only one site, En Medio Shelter (Irwin-Williams and Tompkins 1968), has been described in print. In that brief publication we learn that the evidence for the very early occurrence of maize consists solely of maize pollen recovered from alluvial and eolian deposits dating from 1500 B.C. to 10 B.C. (laboratory numbers, material dated and standard errors not given). Schoenwetter (personal communication) informs me that the 1500 B.C. date was on charcoal from a hearth, the "top" fill of which contained maize pollen. Maize pollen was also present in a sediment sample from the level of origin of the hearth and in seven of the samples between 7 cm and 82 cm above the hearth. It is Schoenwetter's view that this constitutes strong evidence for the 1500 B.C. occurrence of maize. I would argue, on the other hand, that these data leave much to be desired. For one thing, the dating of the hearth is based on a single uncorroborated radiocarbon determination. For another, the current evidence does not sufficiently establish the contemporaneity of pollen deposition and hearth ignition. In principle, the sediments containing the maize pollen could have been deposited subsequent to the hearth "event" following an interval of time ranging from a few minutes to several centuries in duration. Obviously, many more radiocarbon samples would be necessary to resolve these difficulties. Finally, as suggested for the Cienega Creek situation, the "early" occurrence of maize pollen may well be attributable to contamination from the overlying Basketmaker-Pueblo levels which contained both maize pollen and macrofossils.

Schoenwetter (personal communication) also notes the presence of maize pollen in Archaic contexts at a number of other sites in the Arroyo Cuervo region. Since there are no published descriptions of these sites, any assessment of these proposed associations would be inappropriate at this time.

As I have tried to show in previous sections, Bat Cave and its "companion sites," individually and collectively, comprise a very weak body of evidence for early maize. Hence, appeal to these data does nothing to enhance the probablility of the early use of maize in the Arroyo Cuervo. Irwin-Williams' evidence must stand or fall on its own merits, but these cannot be evaluated until the results of this important project are made available in published form. As it now stands, little can be said about the age of maize in the Arroyo Cuervo region or Irwin-Williams' gradualist formulation of Anasazi origins.

Other Sites

In addition to the traditionally cited loci of ancient maize discussed above, there are a number of other sites that occasionally surface in the literature for which similar claims of great antiquity are made. Minnis (this volume) has discussed a number of these and, in general, summarily dismisses the supporting evidence as trivial or inconclusive. Included in this category are the Chaco Canyon alluvial sequence (Hall 1977), the County Road site (Plog 1974), Double Adobe (Martin 1963), Fresnal rockshelter (Human Systems Research, Inc. 1973), O'Haco rockshelter (Bruier 1977), and Sand Dune Cave (Lindsay et al. 1968). I agree with Minnis's assessment since, in each case, the data are scant and far less convincing than the evidence for early maize at the sites I have criticized in detail above.

Recently, Simmons (1981) has reported the association of maize pollen and radiocarbon dates in the 1700 to 2000 B.C. range from two hearths in northwestern New Mexico. Unfortunately, the hearths were located in sand dunes and the certainty of the association, is problematical. The possibility of post-depositional mixture is strongly suggested by the fact that one of the two hearths also yielded a date of A.D. 1700.

Finally, it bears mention that Haury (1976; see also Gladwin et al. 1937) dates the beginning of the agricultural Pioneer Hohokam at 300 B.C. This temporal placement has been soundly criticized by Bullard (1962) and, more recently, by C. Berry (1980), Haynes and Long (1976), Plog (1980), and Wilcox (1979). The consensus of opinion seems to favor a beginning date in the A.D. 300 to 500 range.

THE AGE OF MAIZE: A CONSERVATIVE ESTIMATE

Direct dating of maize specimens provides the most secure form of evidence though even that approach is subject to an uncertain degree of error due to isotopic fractionation in maize that produces anomalously high $^{14}C/^{12}C$ ratios and, hence, radiocarbon dates that are too recent. The amount of ^{14}C enrichment has been estimated indirectly through mass spectrometric analysis of $^{13}C/^{12}C$ ratios by Bender (1968) and Lowden (1969). Bender's work with both prehistoric and modern specimens suggests that a correction factor of 210 years is appropriate (Bender 1968:471). Lowden's analysis of modern maize suggests a correction factor of 234 years (Lowden 1969:392). Following Haynes and Long (1976), 250 years will be used herein as a rough approximation of the correction for fractionation.

Table 9.4 is a compilation of the earliest directly dated maize samples in the Southwest. The 250-year correction factor has been added to all but three of the dates. The three in question (C-585, C-612, C-164, 171) consisted of mixed samples of maize and other organic materials. There is no way of knowing what percentage of these samples was maize and I have simply assumed a $^{50}/_{50}$ split and added 125 years to the uncorrected radiocarbon dates. All of the dates are from the Southern Basin and Range province except those from Cowboy Cave and Clyde's Cavern, both of which are located in southeastern Utah.

Obviously, these dates do not support the notion that maize was introduced to the Southwest prior to 2000 B.C. The earliest date is 740 B.C. (2690 B.P.) on maize from Jemez Cave described by Volney Jones as ". . . of generalized Bat Cave character (Crane and Griffin 1958)." His description is of more than passing interest in light of the arguments offered earlier since the date overlaps the earliest directly dated maize from Bat Cave within one standard error. Ford (1975) has recently conducted additional excavations at Jemez Cave and confirmatory dating of 2410 ± 360 B.P. (Arizona) is now available.

Admittedly, this is a very small sample upon which to base any farreaching conclusions. But if maize dates earlier than Table 9.4 suggests, it is surprising that none of the really ancient specimens have been submitted for radiocarbon analysis in the quarter century that the method has been available. This is especially true when we consider the great amount of interdisciplinary attention that this particular topic has attracted.

Another secure means of dating maize is by association with clusters of radiocarbon dates recovered from discrete architectural proveniences in open sites containing only one or two cultural components. In such contexts, the chances for significant mixture are negligible and, so long as we insist on tight clustering of radiocarbon dates, aberrant determinations, such as might be caused by the aboriginal use of dead trees, can readily be identified and rejected. The three earliest sites that meet these rather stringent requirements are Ariz D:7:152 (Gumerman and Euler 1976; J.A. Ware, personal commu-

TABLE 9.4
EARLY RADIOCARBON DATED MAIZE SAMPLES

Site	Provenience	Uncorrected Radiocarbon Date (B.P.)	Corrected Radiocarbon Date (B.P.)	Reference
Jemez Cave	Square IX; Levels 7 to 9	2440±125 (M-466) / 2410±360 (Arizona accelerator)[4]	2690±125	Crane and Griffin 1958 / Long
Tularosa Cave	Square 2R2; Level 10	1810±200 (M-716)	2060±200	Crane and Griffin 1960
Tularosa Cave	Square 2R2; Level 10	2145±160 (C-585)[1]	2270±160[2]	Libby 1955
Tularosa Cave	Square 2R2; Level 13	2300±200 (C-612)[1]	2425±200[2]	Libby 1955
Tularosa Cave	Square 2R2; Level 14	2223±200 (C-584)[1]	2473±200	Libby 1955
Bat Cave	0 to 1 ft. level	1752±250 (C-165)[1]	2002±250	Libby 1955
Bat Cave	3 to 4 ft. level	2249±250 (C-164, 171)[1]	2374±250[2]	Libby 1955
Bat Cave		2340±420 (Arizona accelerator)[4]		Long
Cowboy Cave	Unit IVc	1865±70 (SI-2422)	2115±70[3]	Stuckenrath, personal communication
Clyde's Cavern	Level 2	1490±100 (RL-175)	1740±100	Winter and Wylie 1974

[1] Solid carbon determination.

[2] Mixed sample of maize and other organic material (see text).

[3] SI-2422 was originally corrected to 2075±70 B.P. on the assumption of 12 per mil δ^{13}C for fractionation (Stuckenrath, personal communication), and is probably closer to the true date than the value used here. I have increased the correction factor to 250 years for the sake of consistency.

[4] These dates were obtained by R. I. Ford after this article was originally submitted for publication.

nication), NA14646 (Marmaduke, personal communication), and the Hay Hollow site (Martin 1967; Martin and Plog 1973; Bohrer 1972; Fritz 1974). Relevant radiocarbon dates are listed in Table 9.5. A brief description of the sites and the context of the radiocarbon samples will, here, be useful.

Ariz D:7:152

Ariz D:7:152 is located on Black Mesa northeast of Redlake, Arizona. It was excavated in 1974 in conjunction with the Black Mesa Project under the general supervision of George Gumerman (Gumerman and Euler 1976) of Southern Illinois University. The site is a single component pithouse village with abundant remains of maize cobs and kernels (J.A. Ware, personal communication). The radiocarbon samples selected were either carbonized twigs and small branches from pithouse hearths or the outer ten rings of pithouse support posts or other structural timbers. The nine radiocarbon determinations are statistically contemporaneous ($F = .70 < 1.94$: $df = \infty$ and have a weighted mean of 2136 ± 27 B.P.: 186 B.C.

NA14646

Site NA14646 was excavated in 1977 by the Museum of Northern Arizona. It is located in Hardscrabble, Washington, near St. Johns, Arizona. Pithouse 1 was the earliest structure at the site. Maize macrofossils were recovered from the roof fall. Four radiocarbon dates were run on support posts and roofing material. These are statistically contemporaneous ($F = 1.22 < 2.60$:$df = 3,\infty$) with a weighted mean of 2135 ± 31 B.P.: 185 B.C.

Hay Hollow

The Hay Hollow site is an agricultural pithouse village located in the Hay Hollow Valley near Snowflake, Arizona. It was excavated by John Fritz in conjunction with an extensive program of survey and excavation under the general direction of Paul S. Martin (Martin and Plog 1973). Maize pollen and macrofossils were recovered from the floors of several of the dated pithouses (Bohrer 1966, 1972). The twenty-three radiocarbon dates for the site range from 470 B.C. to A.D. 305 (Fritz, personal communication) and published estimates of its age range from 200 to 400 B.C. (Martin 1967, 1972; Martin and Plog 1973). However, the earliest dates are on samples from external pits rather than pithouses and are well outside the range of the architectural dates. This seems to be a fairly clear-cut case of "driftwood" effect. The dates shown in Table 9.5 are from the three earliest pithouses at the

TABLE 9.5
RADIOCARBON DATES FROM ARCHITECTURAL FEATURES
ASSOCIATED WITH MAIZE MACROFOSSILS

Site	Provenience	Date (B.P.)		Reference
Ariz D:7:152	Feature 9	2210 ± 80	(I-8402)	Ware, personal communication
Ariz D:7:152	Feature 6	2000 ± 80	(I-8403)	Ware, personal communication
Ariz D:7:152	Feature 15	2180 ± 80	(I-8404)	Ware, personal communication
Ariz D:7:152	Feature 24	2120 ± 80	(I-8405)	Ware, personal communication
Ariz D:7:152	Feature 4	2205 ± 80	(I-8406)	Ware, personal communication
Ariz D:7:152	Feature 18	2170 ± 80	(I-8407)	Ware, personal communication
Ariz D:7:152	Feature 3	2150 ± 80	(I-8408)	Ware, personal communication
Ariz D:7:152	Feature 16	2090 ± 80	(I-8409)	Ware, personal communication
Ariz D:7:152	Feature 5	2100 ± 80	(I-8410)	Ware, personal communication
NA14646	Pithouse 1	2180 ± 60	(UGa-2101)	Marmaduke, personal communication
NA14646	Pithouse 1	2145 ± 60	(UGa-2102)	Marmaduke, personal communication
NA14646	Pithouse 1	2185 ± 65	(UGa-2103)	Marmaduke, personal communication
NA14646	Pithouse 1	2040 ± 60	(UGa-2104)	Marmaduke, personal communication
Hay Hollow	House 17	2095 ± 105	(GX-0540)	Fritz, personal communication
Hay Hollow	House 17	1995 ± 100	(GX-0580)	Fritz, personal communication
Hay Hollow	House 17	1895 ± 110	(GX-0798)	Fritz, personal communication
Hay Hollow	House 32	2030 ± 80	(GX-0799)	Fritz, personal communication
Hay Hollow	House 32	1920 ± 75	(GX-0797)	Fritz, personal communication
Hay Hollow	House 25	2030 ± 80	(GX-0792)	Fritz, personal communication
Hay Hollow	House 25	1845 ± 95	(GX-0727)	Fritz, personal communication

site. The weighted averages are 1998 ± 60 B.P.: 48 B.C. (F = .28<3.00: df = 2,∞) for House 17, 1953 ± 61 B.P.: 3 B.C. (t = .20<1.96) for House 25, and 1972 ± 55 B.P.: 22 B.C. (t = 1.0<1.96) for House 32. Published accounts notwithstanding, it would appear that the Hay Hollow site was first occupied in the second half of the first century B.C.

Summary

Figure 9.2 is a graphic representation of the nine directly dated maize specimens and the three adequately dated pithouse villages discussed above. Each date or weighted mean is depicted as a horizontal bar the length of which indicates the plus-and-minus one standard error range. The values shown for maize dates incorporate the corrections for fractionation (see Table 9.4). Dates for architectural features are the weighted means of contemporaneous radiocarbon determinations. I should point out that five of the nine maize dates were derived using the solid carbon method. This factor may, however, not be as debilitating as it seems since all of these were run by Libby at the University of Chicago laboratory (Libby 1955), and Libby's determinations are demonstrably more consistent with modern gas dates than any of the other pioneering solid carbon laboratories, e.g., Michigan (Crane 1956) or Arizona (Wise and Shutler 1958). The data shown in Table 9.4 suggest that a modest degree of confidence in the solid carbon dates may be warranted in the present case. The three solid carbon determinations for Tularosa Cave all overlap within one standard error and, after correction for fractionation, the three means of these dates occur in the appropriate "stratigraphic" order. In addition, the solid carbon date from Level 10 (C-585) is statistically contemporaneous with the Michigan gas date (M-716) from the same level (t = .82<1.96). A certain, if considerably weaker, degree of support can be mustered for the Chicago maize dates from Bat Cave (C-165 and C-164/171) since they are at least in the correct order suggested by their gross provenience levels.

Considering all the possible shortcomings and sources of error, the data of Figure 9.2 present a fairly coherent picture. The situation is clearest for the Colorado Plateau where both the earliest directly dated maize and the earliest maize-associated domestic architecture appear shortly after 200 B.C. The estimate for the Southern Basin and Range depends on whether or not we are willing to accept the solid carbon maize dates on equal footing with the gas dates. If we do, the probable beginning date for maize, based on the clustering of the earliest Tularosa, Bat, and Jemez Cave dates, could then be placed at approximately 500 to 750 B.C. If we do not, then the very early dates from

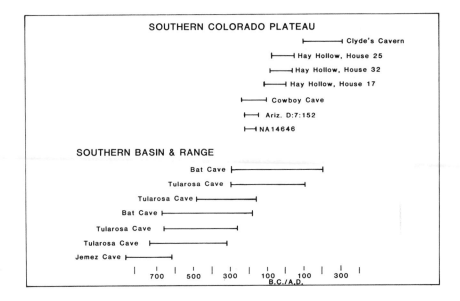

Figure 9.2. Directly-dated maize and dates from maize-associated houses.

Jemez Cave would have to be rejected as aberrant, leaving only the lone gas date from Tularosa Cave of 110 ± 200 B.C. (M-716, corrected for fractionation) to serve as an estimate. This cannot be ruled out but it seems a bit too conservative given the current state of the data and the latest accelerator radiocarbon dates. For the time being, a "looser" estimate of 500 B.C. give or take 200 years is probably appropriate.

CONCLUSIONS AND IMPLICATIONS

There is no longer any reason to believe that maize had made its initial appearance in the Southwest by 2000 B.C., much less 3500 B.C. In fact, there has *never* been any very good reason to believe such claims. The notion has its roots in the pioneering interdisciplinary efforts of the Bat Cave project. With two notable exceptions (Jelinek 1965; Jennings 1967), no one has ever seriously questioned the Bat Cave evidence, and subsequent workers have transformed Dick's highly speculative interpretation into archaeological fact through the continual citation of that work in standard text books and professional journals. Obviously, the data are no better now than they were in 1948 and it is unfortunate that the myth of "ancient" maize has been perpetuated in this manner.

The realization that maize did not enter the Southwest until a few hundred years B.C. entails certain shifts in perspective with regard to the spread of maize north of Mexico. For one thing, we need no longer concern ourselves with the question of why it took so long for maize to appear in the midwestern and eastern United States after its initial occurrence in the Southwest. Struever and Vickery (1973) date the inception of maize in the Midwest riverine area at around 500 B.C. In a somewhat more critical assessment of essentially the same data, Yarnell (1976) concludes that maize was first introduced to the Midwest region by 200 ± 100 B.C. Regardless of which of the two estimates ultimately proves correct, it is, in light of the arguments presented earlier, quite conceivable that maize was introduced to the Southwest and Midwest at about the same time from a common Mexican source area.

A second issue of concern centers on the type(s) of models used to characterize the introduction of maize to the Southwest. It is generally held that maize farming was adopted by indigenous Archaic populations and, further, that the initial impact on these hunting and gathering groups was negligible. The process initiated by the addition of maize to the local resource base typically is envisioned as a slow shift from primary dependency on wild resources to primary dependency on domesticates. Acceptance of this view has been fostered by both the prevalence of gradualism as a theoretic orientation and the belief that maize had been present in the Southwest for thousands of years without producing any perceptible evolutionary consequences. The supposed great antiquity of maize has, I believe, been adequately refuted. The gradualist model and the related notion of negligible initial impact may, in like manner, be disposed of on empirical grounds. Figure 9.3 shows the relationship between the postulated introduction dates of maize (as indicated by the Xs) and the relative intensity of cultural activity (as indicated by the radiocarbon probability bar charts[3]) for the southern Colorado Plateau and the Southern Basin and Range provinces. In both regions, there is a rapid, perhaps immediate, increase in the number of dated cultural events coincident with the probable inception of maize farming. The meaning of these increases is admittedly open to conjecture, but it no longer seems reasonable to speak of a gradual transition from hunting and gathering to agriculture in the Southwest. The transition was clearly abrupt and the impact immediate and profound.

In closing, it will be useful to offer a few speculative interpretations of the data patterning evident in the bar charts:

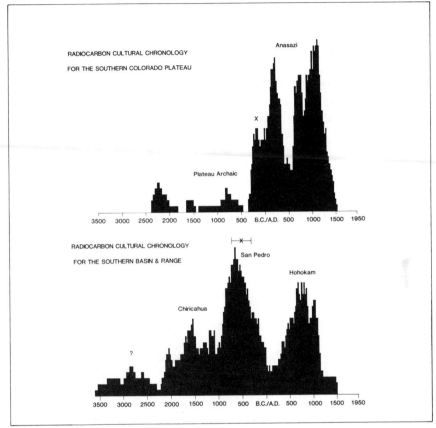

Figure 9.3. Radiocarbon bar charts for the southern Colorado Plateau and Southern Basin and Range provinces.

1) The introduction of maize in the Southern Basin and Range province corresponds with the emergence of the San Pedro stage of the Cochise culture. The San Pedro cultural assemblage is sufficiently distinct from the preceding Chiricahua stage to suggest an intrusion into the area by immigrating populations. The primary cause of this early agricultural dispersal may well have been the widespread "Fairbank Drought" which lasted from approximately 950 B.C. to 650 B.C. (Haynes 1968). All of the sites that have yielded evidence of very early maize (750 B.C. to 500 B.C.) are located in the Mexican Highland section of the Southern Basin and Range province at elevations between 6000 and 7000 feet (cf. Haury 1962). This is consistent with the notion of climatically induced population movement since these high

elevation sites would have served as excellent drought refugia for small farming groups. Unfortunately, the source area(s) for this postulated migration cannot, at the present, be identified.

2) Following the San Pedro peak, there was a rapid decline in cultural activity in the Southern Basin and Range as indicated by the trough in the radiocarbon bar chart centered at A.D. 100 to 200. This corresponds precisely with the Basketmaker II peak for the Colorado Plateau. The complementary distribution of radiocarbon dates combined with the fact that western San Juan dart points of the Basketmaker II period (Morris and Burgh 1954) are indistinguishable from San Pedro points, strongly suggests that Basketmaker II represents a migration from the Southern Basin and Range to the Plateau. This demographic shift began shortly after 200 B.C. for reasons that are not entirely clear. One possibility is that the trend toward moister and cooler climate following the Fairbank Drought may have drastically shortened the growing season in the high elevation refugia while simultaneously increasing the potential for agricultural productivity on the Plateau.

3) Following the Basketmaker II peak, the southern Colorado Plateau was virtually abandoned due to deteriorating climatic conditions (Berry 1980). That abandonment corresponds to the onset of the Mogollon and Hohokam traditions. The beginning of the Pioneer period of the Hohokam sequence at A.D. 300 to 500 (C. Berry 1980; Bullard 1962; Plog 1980) is of considerable significance since it constitutes the first evidence of agricultural settlement in the Sonoran Desert section of the Southern Basin and Range.

If the above reconstruction is correct, there was no lineal, in situ relationship between Chiricahua and San Pedro, nor between the Plateau Archaic and Basketmaker II. In both cases, the introduction of maize farming was accomplished through sociocultural intrusion rather than through diffusion of agriculture to indigenous hunter-gatherer populations. I suspect that this is true of the dispersal of maize agriculture in general throughout the Desert West. That is, there is no reason to expect that a successfully adapted hunting and gathering culture would voluntarily adopt a practice that imposes so many constraints on mobility and whose seasonal maintenance and harvest requirements conflict with the seasonality of so many productive wild resources, e.g., pine nuts, Indian rice grass, amaranth, etc. The gradualist model alluded to earlier apparently was devised to accomodate this very problem. But the model errs in failing to acknowledge the all-or-nothing nature of maize agriculture. It is impossible to sustain a plant that is not self-propagating for any length of time without a total commitment to its planting, maintenance and harvesting on a year to year basis. And that commitment minimally entails semisedentarism and a considerable reduction in wild resource exploitation during the growing season. There is no evidence to indicate that this sort of transition ever occurred in the Southwest. Rather, everything seems to point to colonization by small groups of farmers whose cultural ties are ultimately (though probably not directly) traceable to Mesoamerica.

NOTES

1. All dates are reported in years before present (B.P.) using A.D. 1950 as the reference year and calculated on the basis of a ^{14}C half-life of 5568 years. No calibration for variation in atmospheric ^{14}C was attempted since there is no general agreement as to which of the various calibration curves is most nearly correct (Olsson 1970; Watkins 1975).

2. Tests for contemporaneity and the method of determining weighted means of radiocarbon dates are those outlined by Long and Rippeteau (1974). Results of t-tests and F tests are shown in parentheses in the text. For example, a case in which the null hypothesis for three dates is accepted because F = 1.00 and the region for rejection at the .05 level with two and infinite degrees of freedom is any value greater than 3.00, will be written as $(F = 1.00 < 3.00 : df = 2, \infty)$.

3. These bar charts were constructed by first plotting all the radiocarbon dates on graph paper as plus-and-minus one sigma horizontal bars. Then the number of bars falling within each 25-year increment were counted and plotted as the ordinate value for that increment of the final graph. The result is a display of the relative probability of cultural activity at any given time. It may also be thought of as a crude measure of the relative intensity of aboriginal activity.

Not all of the available radiocarbon dates were used in the bar chart. Solid carbon determinations were eliminated as well as dates run on shell, bone, soil and other questionable materials. In addition, dates clearly unrelated to cultural events and those that were demonstrably inconsistent with clusters of dates from the same site or stratum were not considered. No adjustments for variation in atmospheric ^{14}C were made, but 250 years was added to each maize date to allow for isotopic fractionation (Haynes and Long 1976). The southern Colorado Plateau bar chart was constructed from 151 dates published in M. Berry (1980). The Southern Basin and Range bar chart contains 137 dates which have been evaluated and summarized by C. Berry (1980).

Domesticating People and Plants in the Greater Southwest

Paul E. Minnis
University of Oklahoma

INTRODUCTION

Most recent archaeological research on the origins of agriculture focuses on places and time periods where cultivated plants were first domesticated (pristine domestication). Comparatively less research has studied the first use of domesticates and agricultural strategies by populations which did not actually domesticate the plants used. Yet such circumstances have been more frequent that pristine domestication. These situations will be termed *primary crop acquisition* to differentiate them from pristine domestication and secondary domestication (new plants domesticated by groups already practicing cultivation).

As Harris (1977a), Flannery (1973), and others have pointed out, crop domestication is an "outcome" of processes which could have involved different factors. That is, the principle of equifinality applies to agricultural origins: different processes may lead to the same result. It may be useful to consider primary crop acquisition as simply another alternative pathway to agriculture, the study of which can provide insights into the causes and consequences of agriculture and which can be compared with the processes of primary domestication. Many of the factors (natural environmental change, anthropogenic environmental change, fluctuating human population densities, and sociocultural processes) involved in pristine domestication also may be important in primary crop acquisition. As well, primary crop acquisition involves a whole set of factors which were not important in pristine domestication. Such unique factors may include established neighboring agriculturalists, the presence of already altered plants, the knowledge of plant manipulation skills, and the possible presence of an already available extractive technological complex and may have altered the economic value of crop cultivation compared with pristine domestication (LeBlanc 1982). Therefore, the study of primary crop acquisition can provide case studies which compliment studies of pristine domestication, as well as provide examples of the initial use of domesticated plants which involve factors unique to primary crop acquisition.

This paper examines the Greater Southwest (American Southwest and northern Mexico) as an example of primary crop acquisition. A few plants may have been domesticated in the Greater Southwest: a native barley (*Hordeum* sp.), tepary bean (*Phaseolus acutifolius* var. *latifolius* Freeman), devil's claw (*Proboscidea parviflora* [Wooton] Woot. & Standl.), *Panicum sonorum* Hitchc., and perhaps beeweed (*Cleome serrulata* Pursh.) and other plants. If these plants actually were first domesticated in the Southwest, then their domestication occurred after the introduction of Mesoamerican-derived crops. The most important of these were corn (*Zea mays* L.), common bean (*Phaseolus vulgaris* L.), various cucurbits (*Cucurbita* spp. and *Lagenaria siceraria* [Mol.] Standl.), and cotton (*Gossypium hirsutum* L.).

The primary thesis of this paper is that the initial introduction of domesticated plants into the Southwest was a monumental nonevent with little *immediate* impact on native human populations. For at least a millenium, if not longer, the use of cultigens was incorporated into a hunting-gathering economy without wide ranging or immediate changes in the environment, economy, or sociocultural context of the Archaic period population. If we understand that hunter-gatherer populations often actively manipulate their natural environment, then we can see how the introduction of domesticates could have been a minor change. The most important change was increasing reliance on agriculture. It was not until later, probably between A.D. 200–700, that many prehistoric Southwestern societies became dependent on agriculture for a large percentage of their diet, thus substantially changing the ecological relationships of the prehistoric Southwesterners, both for agriculturalists and nonagriculturalists. This paper, then, utilizes Bronson's (1977) distinction between cultivator (those for whom crops are not necessarily major economic items) and agriculturalist (those dependent on cultivated plants) and discusses the reasons for becoming the former.

In order to understand the processes and context of cultigen introduction into the Greater Southwest, background discussion of hunter and gatherer economies, plant husbandry, and Southwestern prehistory and environment are presented. Then a summary of the dating and the locations of earliest cultigen remains is considered. Had this paper been written ten years ago, there would have been little question about the time/space coordinates of early domesticates. However, within the last few years, reevaluation of early Southwestern cultivated plants, particularly that of Berry (1982, this volume), has called into serious question assumptions held by Southwestern archaeologists for thirty years.

A NOTE ON PLANT HUSBANDRY

All human groups manipulate and affect plants, but the types and intensity of these effects differ widely. Plant husbandry involves manipulating the life cycle, habitat, and genetics of plants. It can be as simple as the Cahuilla of California who prune mesquite trees to make legume harvest easier (Bean and Saubel 1972), or prehistoric Mesa Verdeans who manipulated the growth characteristics of timber sources (Nichols and Smith 1965). At the other extreme is the clearing of thousands of square kilometers to be planted with human-made and human-maintained crops such as maize. While agriculture is the best known manipulation, it is only one type. Even the same plant can be manipulated in different ways. *Cucurbita*, for example, has been raised for food (seeds, fruit, and flowers) and for containers.

Too often we think of hunters and gatherers as passive users of their natural environment, but many cases document how they actively alter their botanical environment. A common effect of hunters and gatherers is to change the distribution of plant populations. The San have extended the range and density of mongongo (Lee 1973), and the Siriono have done the same for papaya (Holmberg 1950). There are examples of such changes from prehistoric eastern North America (Asch and Asch 1977; Yarnell 1976; Cowan 1978). Habitat enrichment for useful plants is well documented for hunter and gatherer societies. The Owens Valley Paiute irrigation of stands of wild plant resources is perhaps the best known example (Steward 1938; Lawton et al. 1976). Although not as well studied as necessary, many foraging groups alter plant and animal habitats by intentional vegetational burning (e.g.,

Lewis 1973). I would suggest that hunter and gatherer manipulation is more widespread than has been reported.

If plant manipulation by hunters and gatherers is more common than reported, then we should not be surprised if Southwestern Archaic societies also actively manipulated plant populations. Bohrer (1983) provides an illustrative example of Archaic manipulation of squawbush (*Rhus trilobata*). By burning these bushes, unnaturally elongated branches were produced, and these were used to produce twig figurines. Careful analysis of environmental changes during the Archaic period may well document substantial anthropogenic environmental change. As natural burning of native Southwestern vegetation is has been common (Wright and Bailey 1983) and as native populations in adjacent regions such as California manipulated resources by burning, it would be improbable that Southwestern groups were unfamiliar with the effects of fire on plant and animal populations.

If the conclusion that Southwestern Archaic groups were activity manipulating nature biotic communities by such methods as burning is correct, then the step to minimal cultivation of domesticates would have represented a minor change in ecological interactions between humans and plants.

A NOTE ON ARCHAIC ECONOMIES

The old stereotype of hunters and gatherers as brutish savages living on the brink of extinction has been replaced with the notion that they enjoyed a leisurely and abundant lifestyle. Castetter and Opler (1936:10), ahead of their time, characterized the Western Apache in the following manner.

> Of all this [environmental] variety the Apache was the master. He moved with the seasonal changes of weather, and followed the wild food harvest as they occurred. His adaptation and responses to the ecological region in which he lived was sensitive and *complete*. [emphasis added]

Surveying modern hunter and gatherer societies, Sahlins characterized them as the "original affluent society" and "free from market obsession of scarcity, hunters' economies may be more consistently predicated on abundance than our own" (1972:2). Sahlins' conclusions are echoed by others (Lee and DeVore 1968; Lee 1973). One wonders whether this view is predicated on as much an "antibourgeois ethnocentrism" as the savage characterization is based on "bourgeois ethnocentrism." Sahlins is correct when he suggests that the demands of mobility constrain the quantity of material culture, but perhaps he is being slightly romantic when he states that "scarcity is the judgment decreed by our economy" (1972:4). As he suggests, but tends to ignore, there are relatively rigid nutritional demands to be met if humans are to survive and reproduce. The modern view of hunter and gatherer abundance trivializes the process of food acquisition. If we consider the problem of seasonal and yearly variation in food availability and the strategies used to cope with this variation, then I believe we will have a better understanding of Archaic economies than if we simply characterized them as leisurely and abundant. It may well be that the contradictory descriptions of hunter and gatherer affluence and deprivation by nineteenth century explorers, missionaries, and incipient social scientists reflect actual variation in food availability and are not solely the result of ideological biases as Sahlins suggests.

Some of the examples of modern hunter and gatherer societies used to illustrate the bucolic life of these peoples present severe analytic problems. The effects of colonial policies on population movement and dislocation, technological changes, and economic and political inducments to alter lifestyles have not been taken into sufficient account. For example, the San of Botswana represent the most widely cited examples of hunter and gatherer adaptations and have become an anthropological "type." On one hand, we are told how secure the San economy is (Lee 1968), and on the other hand, it is pointed out that only about five percent of the San remain hunters and gatherers (Lee 1973). Removing the vast majority of San from an Archaic pattern of resource exploitation may have relieved any pressure on the resource base to supply an adequate food supply for the remaining San. Hitchcock (1978) discusses the effects of food supply variation on the San, an approach which will only increase our understanding of human economic and ecological relationships.

The obvious solution for understanding human food provisioning behavior is simply to recognize that these strategies vary, and that such simple normative characterizations as hunting and gathering or agricultural mask critical variation in human economic behavior. For example, the highly agricultural groups of the American Southwest, such as the early historic Pueblos and Pimas, relied on domesticated foods for 50–70% of their diet. However, in some years they consumed little or no cultivated foods, and during others the cultigens were staples. Natural environmental and sociopolitical factors influenced the types of subsistence strategies employed. For example, during periods of sustained crop failure, the Hopi broke up into family foraging groups which would live off of naturally available foodstuffs (Thomas 1932).

The Western Apache of Arizona provide an example of the use of a variety of food acquisition strategies as "only" 20–25% of their food supply is derived from plant domesticates. In addition, the Western Apache inhabit the same area as some of the earliest users of cultigens in the Southwest and thus may provide a specific analogy for understanding the role of the cultigens in Southwestern Archaic society. While many of the factors affecting the subsistence practices of the Western Apache are much different from the prehistoric Archaic, there seems to be a general similarity between their patterns of seasonal movement, exploitable natural resource structure, and agricultural environment.

Data on Western Apache subsistence patterns can be found in a variety of sources (Goodwin 1935; Castetter and Opler 1936; Reagan 1929; Gallagher 1977; and especially Buskirk 1949). The ethnographic present as used in this paper is the nineteenth century. The Western Apache lived in east-central Arizona and were divided into five major social divisions ("super-bands") which were then subdivided into smaller groups. The irreducible social unit was the relatively autonomous household. Individual households could shift residence from one group to another, although members of each group tended to be from the same clan.

The Western Apache were quite mobile during their yearly cycle, and they exploited habitats ranging from 1500 to 3300 m in elevation. Hunting contributed about 35–40% of their food supply, gathered plants yielded about the same as hunting, and agricultural products provided approximately 20–25% of the diet. Winter camps were located in the southern areas of their range where they hunted and foraged. In March or April they moved their residences to the farming sites which were located at higher elevations than the winter camps. There they planted crops, hunted, and collected various resources such as pinyon, acorns, and juniper berries. Crops were harvested in late August to October. The bands then moved back to their winter residences.

Maize was their principal crop, and other aboriginally available crops included gourds, squash, and beans. European-introduced crops were also tended. The main introduced crops were wheat, watermelons, tobacco, sunflowers, chili, some fruit trees, and a variety of garden vegetables. Two plants, devil's claw (*Proboscidea parviflora*) and goosefoot (*Chenopodium* sp.) were also planted although they were not true domesticates. Cotton may have been cultivated by the Western Apache in the past.

Fields were small. Goodwin (1935:163) estimated that they were "about half an acre or so, often less." Each household owned four to six fields, but usually only two or three were planted each year. Several types of field locations were farmed. Easily irrigated floodplain sites were the most common locations for fields. Fields watered by springs and seeps were also planted, as were *akchin* sites (places where alluvial fans from small drainages widen and are occassionally watered by runoff). At higher elevations some dry farming was practiced. Buskirk (1949) emphasized that adequate water was the primary constraint on the selection of field locations, although care was taken to minimize vulnerability to flooding.

Fields were planted from late March to July, but April to early May were the preferred planting times. Planting times depended on the location of the field. Lower elevation fields could have been planted earlier than higher elevation locations, because the threat of early frost damage was less at lower elevation fields. Field maintenance consisted of preparing the soil, irrigating the fields a few times, and one or two weedings. After the crops were large enough to compete with weeds, the fields were left alone until harvest. Less mobile household members often stayed with the crops to protect them from animal predation. Goodwin (1935:63) summarized the agricultural cycle:

> Preparation of the fields and planting took about a month. All members of the family were expected to help if needed. When the corn was about three feet tall, most of the people moved away for the summer to harvest the various wild plant foods. In September they returned to harvest and store the crops, this again taking about a month's time.

There was substantial variation in subsistence practices. Households in some local groups did not farm at all, whereas in others nearly all households cultivated plants. Several factors contributed to this variation. Buskirk (1949) recognized that there were environmental constraints. Some groups lacked adequate field locations, and others had an abundance of good agricultural sites. Among the northern Western Apache, Navajo raiding precluded a substantial investment in agriculture. Sociopolitical motivations were another factor encouraging agricultural activity mentioned by Buskirk. Prestige was gained by growing crops in excess of the household's needs and giving the surplus away. Other unreported factors probably also were important in creating variation in Western Apache subsistence strategies. As well, there are no data available on long term trends in the varying use of agriculture by these people.

Why did the Western Apache practice agriculture if it supplied a relatively small part of the diet? Unfortunately, this question has not been addressed adequately. However, Buskirk (1949:425) provided a clue: "farm lands gave added *economic security* and prestige to their owner" (emphasis added). While the 20–25% of the diet contributed by cultivated foods may seem small, agriculture may have represented an efficient and inexpensive buffer against the failure of important naturally available foodstuffs. Because much of the maize was stored, it was readily available in times of nutritional stress. Cultivation was inexpensive because it did not conflict with other food acquisition strategies, and the time spent in farming—a month or two—may not have represented major energy expenditure. Major plant foods used by the Western Apache, such as mescal, pinyon nuts, cactus fruits, and juniper berries were most available at times which did not conflict with agricultural work. As women did most of the farming, the bulk of farming labor did not interfere with hunting (Buskirk 1949). The value of the "low cost" of agriculture among the Western Apache is further heightened by the fact that farming under these conditions was relatively reliable. Fields were small, so only the best agricultural locations, those with greater soil fertility and water availability, were farmed. Similarly, crop pests may not have been a major problem because the small, scattered, polycultural fields did not provide a dense enough host population for outbreaks of serious pest infestations. Also, the fields were not used every year, thus reducing the effects of decreased soil fertility. Therefore, the patterns of Western Apache agriculture may have been a relatively inexpensive and reliable subsistence activity which did not interfere with the traditional cycle of resource exploitation.

The Western Apache example also may provide an insight into the role of cultigens in resource ownership. The Apache, like most hunters and gatherers, had a very flexible patterns of natural resource ownership (Sahlins 1972). Resources were often used on a first come, first serve basis. However, fields among the Western Apache were owned and the farming rights to fields were widely known and respected. This Apache example may illustrate that the practice of plant husbandry, particularly agriculture, has significant ramifications in terms of resource ownership and use and may signal a change in the ethos of resource ownership among Archaic peoples. The increasing demarcation of resources will have affected patterns of mobility, economic security, and intergroup relationships.

This example of one group's subsistence regime illustrates the major point raised about Archaic economies. It is not useful to think in terms of dichotomies, such as hunter and gatherer as opposed to agriculturalist, particularly in regard to the study of the earliest use of agriculture. Rather, it is more useful to concentrate on the variation in the use of various food acquisition strategies. Whether we think of the Western Apache as agriculturalists or hunters and gatherers is unimportant. What is important is an understanding of how populations obtain an adequate and reliable food supply. Furthermore, this example suggests that even in an arid to semi-arid environment such as the Greater Southwest, agriculture can be a low-effort, reliable subsistence activity.

SOUTHWESTERN ARCHAIC ENVIRONMENT AND PREHISTORY

The Greater Southwest is too often thought of as a good place to visit but a poor place to secure a living from the naturally available food resources. However, hunting and gathering societies have extracted an adequate livelihood in this region for thousands of years, much longer than agriculturalists or pastoralists. While there are Southwestern areas depauparate in native foodstuffs, other areas provide a rich resource context. The former is characterized by vast stretches of the San Juan Basin where low densities of various animals, grasses, and some shrubs which produce edible goods are the majority of the edible biomass. The latter regions include the lower Sonoran Desert with its abundance of cactaceous, agavaceous, and leguminous foods, and areas where woodland-covered mountains intersect with lush river valleys.

The diversity in the richness in locally available resource structure within the Southwest provides a valuable variable for understanding the cause and context of cultigens use by Archaic peoples, a situation quite similar to the Near East with its marked regional changes in environmental diversity.

The composition of the Southwestern environment has not been constant, and modern biotic patterns are not necessarily those present during the Archaic. Modern human activity such as grazing, fire suppression, and excess water use, has dramatically changed vegetational composition particularly in the deserts (Hastings and Turner 1965; York and Dick-Peddie 1969). As well, natural fluctuations in climatic parameters have altered the Southwestern environment.

The environmental history of the Southwest for the time period under consideration here, 2000 B.C. to A.D. 1, has not been satisfactorily established. By this time the vegetation of the Southwest had undergone a transformation from a Pleistocene pattern to its present-day configuration, but the nature of changes within this time period is not agreed upon (Martin 1963). For example, Irwin-Williams and Haynes (1970) provided a model of long-term precipitation conditions. They divide Southwestern post-Pleistocene climatic history into five periods: 9500–9000 B.C., period of greatest precipitation; 9000–6000

B.C., decreased effective moisture; 5500–3000 B.C., low effective moisture; 3000–300 B.C., more abundant moisture; and around A.D. 700, decreased effective moisture. Others provide somewhat different chronological schemes. Still others have argued that the climate and vegetation of the Southwest have remained relatively stable during the Late Archaic period. Van Devender et al. (1979), based on the analysis of wood rat middens, suggested rather insignificant vegetational changes in the Southwest for the last 4000 years. Whatever climatic changes occurred and whatever their effects on vegetation, fauna, and human populations, these climatic periods are very broad and cannot be well correlated with changes in the patterns of human behavior.

In addition to long-term changes in climate, there are also relatively short-term changes. The type of short-term fluctuations with the greatest impact on human populations seems to be precipitation, as even minor variation in precipitation in an arid to semi-arid region can dramatically affect biotic communities (Tuan et al. 1973). Unfortunately, dendroclimatologically-generated patterns of short-term precipitation changes do not extend beyond 300 B.C.. Given the poor understanding of pre-A.D. climatic and biotic changes in the Southwest, we cannot easily or with confidence document the relationships between climatic change and culture change.

The Southwestern Archaic period represents many thousands of years of relatively stable hunter and gatherer societies scattered throughout all areas of the Southwest with the introduction of cultigens occurring only during the last part of this period. The general similarity between the archaeological remains from Archaic contexts throughout the Southwest (typically lithic scatters with some groundstone and perhaps various features such as small pit structures, hearths, and pits), may mask substantial differences in the organization of social relationships and patterns of geographic movement. Nevertheless, they all were probably small groups with flexible patterns of populational aggregation and a foraging economy.

The first chronological divisions for the Archaic was that of Sayles and Antev (1941), and these divisions are still used for southeastern Arizona and southwestern New Mexico. As slightly revised by Whalen (1971, 1973), this chronology is divided into three phases: Sulpher Springs (7000–3500 B.C.), Chiracahua (3500–1500 B.C.), and San Pedro (1500–200 B.C.). Archaic chronologies have been established for other southwestern regions, but the best known of these, Oshara, (Irwin-Williams 1973) has not been supported in print with substantial documentation. Compared with other time periods in the Southwest, the temporal divisions available for the Archaic are very broad. This reflects an apparent general stability of Archaic lifestyles as well as the paucity of research on the Archaic.

Some time toward the end of the Archaic period, cultigens were first used by these people. The introduction of cultigens does not correlate with obvious or substantial changes in other aspects of Archaic life-style. The earliest date proposed for a relatively sedentary agricultural adaptation in the Southwest is not until A.D. 200–300 (LeBlanc 1982), assuming the initial dates for the Hohokam are A.D. 300 not 300 B.C. (Plog 1978). Thus we have a period of no less than 800 years, and probably much longer, when the cultivation of domesticated plants coexisted with a basic hunting and gathering economy.

DATING AND LOCATION OF EARLIEST CULTIGENS

Berry (1982, this volume) discusses the major examples of early Southwestern maize remains which were the basis for concluding that the introduction of maize into the Southwest occurred at approximately 2000 B.C. He clearly shows how unreliable these examples are and how uncertain we now are about the chronology of early cultigens in the Southwest. Fortunately, the use of new radiocarbon dating techniques allows archaeologists to directly date organic artifacts (such as maize cobs) which previously were too small to date except in their stratigraphic contexts. By avoiding the pitfalls of stratigraphic context which is particularly unreliable with cave deposits, we will soon have a wealth of reliably dated cultigens.

Four cultigens may have been introduced into the Southwest before A.D. 1: maize, common bean, squash, and gourd. All other prehistoric cultigens grown in the Southwest appear to have been introduced later. These four crops do not appear to have been introduced as a coherent complex, often one or more of these four cultigens is missing from sites with early domesticated plant remains. Therefore, we will discuss the dating and location of each separately.

Berry considers the major Southwestern sites with maize remains reported to have been early (pre-A.D. 1). There are many other such sites. Table 10.1 lists many of these, and Figure 10.1 shows their locations. From the comments presented in Table 10.1, it is obvious that most of these examples are ambiguous evidence of early maize. Problems with dating based on stratigraphy and artifactual association present the greatest problem. In addition, many of these sites, despite their possible significance, have no comprehensive site report so that we cannot evaluate the archaeological context of the possible Archaic

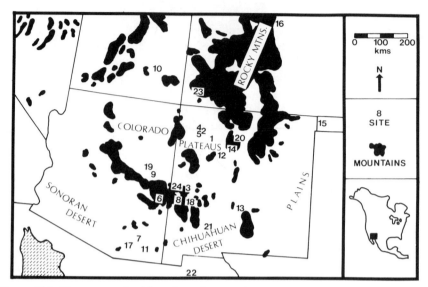

Figure 10.1. Sites reported with early maize remains. *1)* Armijo rockshelter; *2)* Atlatl Cave; *3)* Bat Cave; *4)* Chaco alluvial site; *5)* Chaco Archaic sites; *6)* Cienega Creek site; *7)* Cienega Creek site, Empire Valley; *8)* Cordova Cave; *9)* County Road site; *10)* Cowboy Cave; *11)* Double Adobe site; *12)* En Medio rockshelter; *13)* Fresnal rockshelter; *14)* Jemez Cave; *15)* Kenton Caves; *16)* LoDaisKa rockshelter; *17)* Matty Wash site; *18)* O Block Cave; *19)* O'Haco rockshelter; *20)* Ojala Cave; *21)* Placitas Arroyo site; *22)* Swallow Cave; *23)* Tabeguache Cave; *24)* Tularosa Cave.

maize. The sites with maize pollen present the greatest interpretive problem. In many cases, the number of maize pollen grains recovered is small so that vertical transportation of the grains down through the deposits cannot be ruled out. None of the maize pollen was from contexts (such as sealed deposits) where this problem can be ruled out. At this point, the directly dated maize macroplant remains from Jemez Cave are the most reliable early maize from Southwestern sites. Correcting the date of B.C. 490 for isotope fractionation difference in maize will provide a date of B.C. 700 (Bender 1968; Lowdon 1969; Ralph 1971). Therefore, a date of 1000 B.C. is a more justified estimate of the introduction of maize into the Southwest than 2000 B.C. As yet unpublished research in the Chaco Canyon area may have dated maize earlier than 1000 B.C., but I have not seen any reports (Donaldson, personal communication, 1984).

All examples of pre-A.D. and early post-A.D. cultivated beans are the common bean (*Phaseolus vulgaris*). Other beans cultivated in the prehistoric Southwest (*P. acutifolius* var. *latifolius, P. lunatus, P. coccineus,* and *Canavalia ensiformis*) were later additions to the inventory of prehistoric cultigens.

TABLE 10.1

SUMMARY OF SITES WITH EARLY MAIZE REMAINS

Site	Location	Dating	Comments
Armijo Rockshelter	Arroyo Cuervo region, New Mexico	1050–550 B.C.	Maize pollen was recovered from one of four profiles. This is an ambiguous example of early maize for four reasons: (1) no site report has been published, (2) dating of the maize is indirect, through stratigraphy, (3) little maize pollen was recovered, and (4) vertical movement of maize pollen is possible. References: Schoenwetter, personal communication 1979; Irwin-Williams, personal communication 1979.
Atlatl Cave	Chaco Canyon, New Mexico	2900 B.C.	The shallow (25 cm) deposits of this cave yielded maize macroplant remains, as well as the remains of beans and squash. The shallow deposits, the wood rat disturbance, and the lack of a full report of the excavations limit the reliability of Atlatl Cave as an example of early maize. References: Mathews and Neller 1979.
Bat Cave	San Augustin Plains, New Mexico	460–800 B.C.	Much controversy surrounds the maize remains from Bat Cave. See Berry (this volume) for a discussion of the maize from the original excavations. Recent re-excavation by the University of Michigan produced directly dated maize dating to 800 B.C. ± 90 (A–4166). References: Smith 1950; Dick 1954, 1965; Mangelsdorf 1954, 1974; Mangelsdorf and Smith 1949; Mangelsdorf and others 1967.

TABLE 10.1
CONTINUED

Site	Location	Dating	Comments
Chaco alluvial site	Chaco Canyon, New Mexico	5050–3850 B.C.	One maize pollen grain was identified from this site. This is an unreliable example of early maize because of the small amount of maize pollen, the possibility of vertical movement of the pollen in the deposits, and the problems with alluvial deposits as pristine pollen traps. References: Hall 1977.
Chaco Archaic sites	Chaco Canyon area, New Mexico	approx. 2000 B.C.	Two projects directed by Alan Simmons claim both maize pollen and macroplant remains. Some of the macroplant is the earliest reliable example of maize in the Southwest. I have not yet seen the limited distribution reports. References: Donaldson, personal communication, 1984.
Cienega Creek Site	east central Arizona	unclear	See Berry (this volume) for a discussion of the maize pollen from this site. References: Haury 1957; Martin and Schoenwetter 1960.
Cienega Creek, Empire Valley	southeastern Arizona	older than 50 B.C.	Seven pollen grains out of 64,000 were identified as maize. Because of dating uncertainty, the fact that few maize grains were identified, and the possibility of vertical pollen movement in the deposits, this is an unreliable example of early maize. References: Martin 1963.
Cordova Cave	Pine Lawn Valley, New Mexico	300 B.C.	The radiocarbon dating used for this pioneering excavation may not be reliable, and there is no tabular summary of maize remains by level. Therefore, it is difficult to judge the validity of this example. References: Cutler 1952; Kaplan 1963.

Site	Location	Date	Comments
County Road Site	Hay Hollow Valley, Arizona	1000 B.C.	This site has not been published, so that it is not possible to evaluate its significance. References: Plog 1974; Reals n.d.
Cowboy Cave	Canyonlands National Park, Utah	A.D. 300	The cache of maize from this site was originally dated to 2000 B.C. based on material cultural similarities with other dated sites. However, Jennings (personal communication to Joseph Winter, 1977) reported that the maize was radiocarbon dated to A.D. 300. Adding a 200 year correction factor for isotope fractionation makes this example date to A.D. 100. References: Jennings 1975.
Double Adobe Site	southeastern, Arizona	older than 1900 B.C.	As Martin suggests, the single maize pollen grain from this site cannot be considered a trustworthy example of early maize. References: Martin 1963.
O Block Cave	Pine Lawn Valley, New Mexico	see comments	Two radiocarbon dates (830 B.C. and 650 B.C.) are reported for this site. There are no published descriptions of the maize macroplants other than notation of their presence. Therefore, it is unclear if the maize remains are earlier, later, or contemporary with these dates. References: Martin and others 1954.
O'Haco Rockshelter	Chevelon Creek drainage, Arizona	3000–100 B.C.	The earliest stratum with maize (stratum III) cannot be dated more closely, and the shallowness of the deposits makes stratigraphic control difficult. References: Briuer 1977.
Ojala Cave	near Los Alamos, New Mexico	670–590 B.C.	This small cave yielded two maize kernels, both of which came from the 240 to 250 cm level. Two radiocarbon dates from this stratum were 670 B.C. and 590 B.C. Although a final report on this excavation has not been prepared, this example appears to be promising. References: Traylor and others 1977.

TABLE 10.1
CONTINUED

Site	Location	Dating	Comments
Placitas Arroyo Site No. 5	near Hatch, New Mexico	80 B.C.	Pollen and macroplant remains of maize have been reported from this site, but no detailed site report is available. References: Morenon and Hays 1978.
Swallow Cave	near Casas Grande, Chihuahua, Mexico	unknown	Maize was recovered from deposits which appear to predate the ceramic Mogollon levels. No clear dating has been established for Swallow Cave, nor has a comprehensive site report been published. References: Mangelsdorf 1974; Mangelsdorf and Lister 1956.
Tabeguache Cave	Montrose County, Colorado	older than 10 B.C.–A.D. 10	The maize macroplant remains have not been dated, but recent dendrochronological dates for the upper level suggest a possible pre-A.D. date for the maize remains. References: Hurst 1940, 1941, 1942; Hurst and Anderson 1949; Dean, personal communication 1980.
Tularosa Cave	Pine Lawn Valley, New Mexico	approx. 300 B.C.	Maize macroplant remains were present in the lowest level dating (on the bases of early radiocarbon dates) to 300 B.C. References: Cutler 1952.
En Medio Rockshelter	Arroyo Cuervo region, New Mexico	1550 B.C.	The data from this site is yet to be published in detail so that the integrity of the maize pollen cannot be assessed. References: Irwin-Williams, personal communication 1979; Irwin-Williams and Tompkin 1968; Schoenwetter, personal communication 1979.

Site	Location	Date	
Fresnal Rockshelter	Tularosa Basin, New Mexico	1665 B.C.	Maize macroplant remains have been recovered from this site. The single radiocarbon date cannot be directly correlated with the occurrence of the cultigens. Study of the plant remains from this site is continuing. References: Human Systems Research 1974; Bohrer 1982.
Jemez Cave	Jemez Mountains, New Mexico	700 B.C.	Maize macroplant remains from the 1930s excavations were directly dated to 490 B.C. Adding 200 years as a correction yields a date of about 700 B.C. However, early radiocarbon dating is not as reliable as modern dating. References: Alexander and Reiter 1935; Ford 1968, 1975.
Kenton Caves	Cimarron County, Oklahoma	unknown	This series of caves in the extreme western part of the Oklahoma panhandle produced macroplant remains of maize which Mangelsdorf characterized as like those from Bat Cave. However, the deposits were not excavated in a manner that allows temporal placement of the cultigens. References: Renaud 1929, 1930; Lintz and Zabawa 1984.
LoDaisKa Rockshelter	near Denver, Colorado	unclear	See Berry (this volume) for a discussion of the six macroplant remains of maize from this site. References: Irwin and Irwin 1959, 1961.
Matty Wash Site	southeastern Arizona	270 B.C.	Three maize pollen grains out of 8000 identifications were noted at this site. As with other sites where only a few maize pollen grains were recovered, this example is an ambiguous occurrence of early cultigens. References: Martin 1963.

The most reliable early example of beans from the Southwest is from Tularosa Cave (Cutler 1952; Kaplan 1956). These beans date to 300 B.C. Some early beans have been reported. The best known example is Bat Cave. Smith (1950) reported that seven beans were recovered during the first season's excavation. He stated that the earliest beans were from Level III, but in his tabular summary of bean remains he showed that the earliest beans were from Levels IV and V. Further confusing the interpretation of Bat Cave beans is the fact that Dick (1965) mentioned beans recovered from Levels I through VI. Therefore, the stratigraphic placement of beans is unclear. An additional problem is that the seven beans noted by Smith are very similar to a cache of several quarts of beans found in a leather bag from Level II. Were the seven beans originally from this cache and somehow redeposited in lower levels? Another possible example of early beans is Fresnal rockshelter. Wimberly (personal communication, 1979) stated that; "we found both maize and beans in the lowest levels of the cultural material." Vorsila Bohrer is currently analyzing the plant remains from this site so confirmation of the chronology of Fresnal beans must await her report.

There is reasonable evidence that beans were present in the Southwest by 300 B.C., but all evidence is quite ambiguous. These limited data suggest that beans were a later introduction into the Southwest than maize.

All *Cucurbita* specimens from possible Southwestern Archaic contexts are the common squash (*Cucurbita pepo*). Other prehistorically cultivated squash (*C. mixta* and *C. moschata*) were later introductions.

Like beans, *Cucurbita* remains have a low probability of archaeological preservation. The earliest example of *Cucurbita* from the Southwest is from Tularosa Cave and dates to 300 B.C. (Cutler 1952; Cutler and Whitaker 1961). Other possible examples of pre-A.D. *Cucurbita* remains have been reported. Squash was reported from the earliest levels of Bat Cave (Smith 1950), which is difficult to date. Squash fragments were found in all levels at Fresnal rockshelter, but they may be from the native wild gourd, *C. foetidissma* (Bohrer, personal communication, 1980). Ford (1975) reported the presence of *Cucurbita* remains from the reexcavation of Jemez Cave, but no dating is yet available. Very early squash remains have been found in the Chaco Canyon area, but I have not seen the documentation of this (Donaldson, personal communication, 1984).

Cultivated squash appear to be an Archaic cultigen in the Southwest. On the current data, squash and beans probably were later than maize, and we cannot determine whether the introduction of beans and squash occurred about the same time or at different times.

The earliest relatively reliable example of gourd (*Lagenaria siceraria*) are fragments from Tularosa and Cordova Caves (Cutler 1952; Kaplan 1963; Cutler and Whitaker 1961) and dates to 300 B.C. No gourd remains are reported from Bat Cave, Jemez Cave, or Fresnal rock-shelter (Bohrer, personal communication, 1980). Therefore, gourds appear to have been first introduced into the South by late Archaic times, perhaps at the same time as beans and squash.

It is difficult to discuss the location of the earliest Southwestern cultigens given the dating problems with most examples. Further-more, very few examples of Archaic beans, squash, and gourds are available, and their distribution will not be further considered. A quick glance at the distribution of sites in Figure 10.1 shows that sites with possible early maize are located throughout the Southwest except in the higher mountainous zones and the plains of eastern New Mexico and western Texas. Excluding the sites with little pollen remains (many of which concentrate in southeastern Arizona), sites with possible early maize tend to be found in the mountainous regions between 1525–2100 m in elevation. Most of these sites are also within a short distance of lower elevation plains. As will be discussed, the distribution of early sites with maize in relatively high elevations may not be a function of a lack of drought resistance in early maize but rather due to the nature of seasonal movements by Archaic peoples. Any discussion of the distribution of early cultigens must recognize the poor quality of the chronological control. I suspect that when this map is redrafted in five years with more reliable data we will be able to draw important inferences from the patterns present. For example, were early cultigens as widely distributed as Figure 10.1 superficially suggests? Were early maize and other crops really absent from desert regions?

CONTEXT OF ARCHAIC CULTIGEN USE

Discussion of the role of domesticates in the Southwestern Archaic economy includes consideration of the use and dietary importance of cultigens, the spatial patterning of farming locations and the scheduling of cultivation, and changes in cultigens. Because of the lack of a consistently good data base, the points raised here must be viewed as suggestions which are open to further data acquisition, analysis, and theory building.

Use

The four early cultigens—maize, beans, squash, and gourd—could have been used in a variety of ways, and there is little evidence for documenting cultigen use. It is fair to assume that maize was grown to be eaten, as green fruits and/or as mature kernels. There is evidence of popped maize kernels from Bat Cave (Mangelsdorf 1974) and Tabeguache Cave (Hurst 1940, 1941, 1942). Evidence of green maize consumption is unlikely to be recovered archaeologically. Early Chapalote-like maize was used as a popcorn and also could have been used as green maize and the mature kernels ground into meal or boiled whole. While pottery was not available, mature maize kernels may have been prepared by stone-boiling, an effective but inefficient technology (Driver and Massey 1957). If, on the other hand, mature kernels of maize were not used, and most maize was consumed in the milk stage, then the nutritional value of maize would have been reduced significantly (Ford 1968b). *Cucurbita pepo* probably was used in several ways. The seeds and fruits were probably eaten, and the hard shelled varieties were made into containers. Obviously, squash fruit eaten for their meat would have a low probability of being preserved in archaeological sites. Several examples of *Cucurbita pepo* rinds used as containers have been recovered from early sites in the Southwest (e.g., Tularosa and Bat Caves). Gourds were probably used solely as containers, although the seeds and flowers may have been consumed. Beans must have been grown for food. Kaplan (1956) indicated that dry beans do not require the use of pottery as Carter (1945) suggested.

The presence of pottery and efficient grinding implements (trough metates) would have made the use of these resources more efficient, and dependence on agricultural products, such as maize, correlates with the use of efficient technological complex. Nevertheless, Archaic peoples with only stone-boiling, roasting pits, and basin metates could have processed and consumed large quantities of cultigens.

Wetterstrom (1978) argued that new foods are integrated into existing food technologies and consumption patterns. Foodstuffs already consumed by Archaic populations provided food analogies which may have "preadapted" these people to the use of cultigens. In fact, there are a number of wild resources similar to the early cultigens which were available to the Archaic population and which were consumed. Wild gourds, legumes such as mesquite, and grass seeds are the most common of these resources. Given variation in the availability of various resources in the Greater Southwest, we might expect that different cultigens were differentially incorporated by different Archaic groups. For example, if Winter (1976) is correct that grasses were not used before the introduction of maize in southern Utah, then the patterns of cultigen use may have been different in this area compared with areas where grasses may have been a major Archaic food resources (e.g., in the San Juan Basin).

Dietary Contribution

The dietary importance of cultigens to Archaic groups is unknown. It has been assumed that these people used wild resources for the bulk of their diet and that cultigens were a small part of their diet, (Whalen 1973; Ford 1968a; Lipe 1978; Martin and Plog 1973; Irwin-Williams 1973). In a gross quantitative sense this may be true. Even the ethnographically known Southwestern groups considered heavily agricultural, such as the Puebloans and Pimans, probably rarely relied on cultigens for more than 50–75% of their diet (Ford 1968b; Castetter and Bell 1941; Stephens 1936), and this appears to have been the case archaeologically (Stiger 1977; Minnis 1981). There are historic Southwestern groups where agriculture contributed a small (less than 30%) portion of the diet, such as the Papagos (Castetter and Bell 1941), Yumans (Gifford 1932; Castetter and Bell 1951), and the Western Apache.

Dietary importance should not be considered solely on caloric contribution. As was discussed for the Western Apache, plant cultivation may have provided a relatively efficient form of insurance against failure of one of the major collected resources. A similar situation may have been true for the Archaic use of domesticates. This is not to say, as has been suggested by Irwin-Williams (1973), that maize cultivation was unique in allowing a surplus build up. Most likely during times of normal resource abundance, other resources could have been collected in large enough quantities to collect a surplus.

The role of other cultigens probably was different from maize. Gourds and squash provided easily acquired containers. In the absence of pottery, durable, watertight containers must have been a valuable material cultural item. Other *Cucurbita* varieties and beans added to the variety of the diet, and, in combination with maize and other resources, provided a nutritionally sound diet.

Resource Scheduling

There is some question as to how well cultivation would fit into the pattern of Archaic resource exploitation and mobility. Archaic sites have been found in a wide range of environmental settings from desert plains up to higher elevations in the mountains. While Archaic remains are conspicuously absent from some regions such as Cedar Mesa (Matson and Lipe 1978), and the Long House Valley (Dean et al. 1978), Archaic remains are common in most areas of the Southwest. Whalen (1971), on the basis of survey in the San Pedro drainage in southern Arizona, suggests that the Cochise Archaic residence pattern consisted of lowland sites and mountainous camps. This pattern of movement between diverse, altitudinally segregated life zones would allow flexible exploitation of major resources such as various animals, acorns, pinyon nuts, mesquite, cactus fruits, herbacious seeds, and agavaceous plants.

The majority of early maize remains have been recovered from sites at high elevations, about 1800 to 2200 m. Assuming that water availability was the primary limiting factor for field selection and that Archaic horticultural technology did not include complex irrigation, most suitable field locations would have been in the mountains. Some sites must have been so high that the length of the growing season must have been a problem, if the crops were grown near where they were recovered. For example, the frost-free period around Bat Cave is between 100–130 days (Dick 1965; Tuan et al. 1973). This length of time is very short to insure successful crop harvest. However, topographic variability can be manipulated to increase solar radiation and thus increase the frost-free period. The use of south-facing slopes to increase the growing season appears to have been used by some later Puebloan groups living at higher elevations (Minnis and Ford 1976). Nevertheless, there is only so much field location manipulation one can do, and it is probably true that the length of the growing season was the limiting factor on high elevation cultivation.

The fact that fewer early maize remains have been recovered from sites in the desert regions of the Southwest does not mean that there were no suitable field locations in these areas, although they would not have been as abundant as at higher elevations. The lack of early agricultural sites in the desert may have been a function of resource scheduling conflicts (Flannery 1968). By planting at higher elevations, one would be in the area in the fall to harvest the crops. This is the time of year when important mountainous resources such as pinyon, acorns, and juniper would have been available. If one were to plant in the desert field locations then harvest might conflict with collection of the mountainous resources.

This point does not necessarily mean that maize harvest itself had to present serious scheduling conflicts with major resources. Unlike most natural resources, maize harvest does not depend on the vagaries of seed and fruit dispersal, which can limit the time available for collection. Further maize probably was harvested in September and October and earlier if green corn was desired. Most resources would be available at times not in conflict with maize harvest. Mesquite, acorns, many herbacious seeds, agavaceous resources, and cactus fruits would be available earlier than maize. Pinyon nuts and probably juniper berries would be available after crop harvest. The main conflict would be with some herbacious seeds. Therefore, few important resources conflicted with crop harvest from small scale farming, and if there was a conflict, the group could forgo crop harvest in favor of the more abundant wild resources. Few significant plant resources would be available at the time of planting so that scheduling conflicts between natural resources and crop planting may not have been important.

It appears that limited plant cultivation could fit well within a seasonal pattern of resource collection. The necessary minimal time spent planting, tending, and harvesting crops in small fields probably did not take a significant amount of time away from other subsistence pursuits except for hunting. However, there is no reason to assume that hunting could not have occurred during the time spent with the field; this is particularly true if the agricultural effort was undertaken by women and the young. This further reinforces the conclusion that limited agriculture could have provided an inexpensive form of insurance against subsistence failure during the Archaic period.

An understanding of resource scheduling must be placed within a specific regional perspective. For example, the resource structure of the desert regions of southern Arizona is much different from other regions in the Southwest. Edible legumes and cacti are more abundant in this area. Therefore, resource scheduling may have been very different in this area, as is the case with the Papago as compared with the Western Apache or the Utes of the northern Southwest.

Changes in Cultigens

Several trends in the morphology and role of cultigens during the Archaic period have been noted. The first is the supposed evolution in maize from a small unproductive resource which was not well adapted to Southwestern growing conditions to a productive resource. The second trend is an increase in the dietary contribution of maize. Each of these will be discussed briefly.

One of the most widely reported results of the excavations at Bat Cave was the presence of an evolutionary sequence in maize morphology (Mangelsdorf 1954, 1974; Mangelsdorf and Smith 1949). Mangelsdorf (1974) summarizes these changes as an increase in the cob length, increased rachis diameter, change in kernel size and shape, degree of tripsacoid contamination, decrease in husk length, and a decrease in row number. However, it was reported that there was no real change in the maize in the lowest three levels at Bat Cave. Therefore, there is no good evidence for changes in Southwestern maize during the Archaic. In fact, it is not clear if changes noted between archaeological collections of Southwestern Archaic maize represent populational differences or variation within a single population of maize growing at the upper limits of its tolerance. Cutler (1952:466) did note for the lower and middle level maize from Tularosa and Cordova Caves that there was an unusually high occurrence of aborted spikelets which he suggests, "usually occurs when environmental conditions are unfavorable and the vigor of the plants is reduced." Whether this occurred because of infrequent field maintenance or growing at high elevations is not clear. Similarly, the presence of small cobs at the lower levels at Tularosa, Cordova, and Bat Caves may be a function of horticultural techniques which allowed tiller cobs (unusually small cobs) to mature.

There were significant changes in Southwestern maize during the prehistoric period, but there are no clearly documented significant changes during the Archaic. Cutler (1952) found a decrease in the row number from higher to lower numbers, but this change occurred sometime after the Archaic around A.D. 700. Other maize collections from the Southwest have noted this change. As well, there were changes in the endosperm characteristics; early maize was a popcorn, and later prehistoric maize included flour, flint, dent, and popcorn endosperm.

It has been suggested that with increased teosinte contamination of the maize gene pool, the drought resistance of Southwestern maize was increased. For example, Whalen (1973) sees the lack of drought resistance as a key factor limiting the spread of maize use in the Southwest. If, as Galinat (as discussed in Beadle 1980 and this volume) suggests, there is a steady progression from more teosinte-like to modern maize-like morphology in prehistoric Southwestern maize, then the question of teosinte-introgression becomes open. Further, modern Chapalote maize is best grown at lower elevations (Wellhausan et al. 1952) so that its drought resistant characteristic may be better than originally supposed. However, compared with other races of Mexican maize, Chapalote is "adapted to a wide range of altitudes" (ibid:56). Therefore, it is not clear if the growing requirements of prehistoric Chapalote-like maize precluded its cultivation in the desert regions in the Southwest.

There were definite changes in maize in the prehistoric Southwest, but there is no good evidence for changes in the Archaic maize population. What changes occurred seem to have been relatively gradual transitions suggesting that:

> the races of maize are not sharply differentiated entities, but rather peaks which rise from greatly varied populations. Almost certainly the corns reaching the Southwest already had some heterogeneity, and it is not necessary or wise to postulate a separate arrival of each influence. [Jones and Fonner 1954:115]

The general changes in maize morphology which occurred in the Southwest mirror the changes in Mesoamerican maize although the timing of the changes is different. While the Southwest and Mesoamerica probably represented a single broad maize gene pool, it cannot be said that all of the changes which occurred in Southwestern maize simply represent the importation of new races of maize from the south. Given a similar genetic heterogeneity in Mesoamerican and Southwestern maize, similarities in the changes in maize seen in Mesoamerica and the Southwest may reflect similar selective pressures by farmers in both regions as much as the diffusion of maize races.

Unlike maize, there is no evidence for changes in the other early cultigens in the Southwest. This is most likely a function of the fact that so few remains of early squash, beans, and gourds have been recovered and the fact that certain types of cultigens such as soft shelled squash have a low probability of being recovered from archaeological sites. There is some evidence of varietal selection of *Cucurbita* in some areas of the Southwest after the Archaic period (Cutler 1966). While it is probable that the prehistoric Southwesterners were selecting for certain characteristics in early cultigens other than maize, there is little evidence for it.

The discussion of the context of cultigen use by Southwestern Archaic peoples has been based on a thin empirical foundation. We simply have very little evidence for plant food resources used by the Archaic populations and for the organization of food acquisition strategies. The evidence which we have used to infer one context of Archaic cultigen use for the last twenty years does not hold up to the demands of recent archaeological interpretation and model building. Most evidence of Archaic ethnobotany now available came from cave sites excavated over thirty years ago. Not only are cave sites only a part of Archaic settlement patterns, but most provenience and chronological control from these sites is inadequate. The recent trend in reexcavating and/or reanalyzing these sites will add substantial new information about the cultigen use during the Archaic.

TWO MODELS OF PRIMARY CROP ACQUISITION IN THE SOUTHWEST

That Archaic cultivation of domesticates fit well within the already established subsistence, settlement, and social organizations is not necessarily an explanation of why these people began to use domesticated plants. Two explanations for the origin and spread of agriculture in the Southwest will be discussed here. The first type of explanation is a "stress model" ("Model of Necessity" in Table 10.2). This model has been used to explain pristine domestication worldwide (Binford 1968; Cohen 1977; Glassow 1972). A necessary characteristic of hunter and gatherer economies (particularly in an arid to semi-arid environment with a relatively low edible biomass and substantial fluctuations in factors critical to resource abundance) is to assure a steady food supply. Therefore, Archaic economies must have a number of potential responses or strategies to assure an uninterrupted food supply. Under low human population densities, a major option is simply to use a wider sustaining region. With a larger population or a decrease in the edible biomass (due to natural or anthropogenic environmental change and fluctuations), the exploitable area may well decrease, the resource base would need to be more intensively exploited. Use of low preference foods, environmental manipulation, and use of cultigens are three forms of more intensive food acquisition strategies. This model is presented in Figure 10.2. The early Archaic period may have been a time when population densities were low enough that use of a wider catchment area could have been an adequate response to cope with a fluctuating food supply. The late Archaic may have been the period when more intensive strategies, such as environmental manipulation and/or nonintensive agriculture, were used. Only later, during the post-Archaic period, did agriculture become a major food acquisition activity.

The second explanation is a modification of LeBlanc's (1982) model ("Model of Opportunity" in Table 10.2) He suggested that the introduction already established domesticated plants and the associated technology for planting, harvesting, storage, and consumption may

TABLE 10.2
COMPARISON OF TWO MODELS OF THE ORIGINS
OF ARCHAIC CULTIGEN USE

Characteristic	Model of Necessity	Model of Opportunity
Speed of the spread of cultivation	slower	faster
Correlation with population density	higher	lower
Correlation with resource abundance	higher	lower
Correlation with resource stability	higher	lower
Areal extent of cultigen use	smaller	larger
Probability of plant manipulation before cultigen use	higher	lower

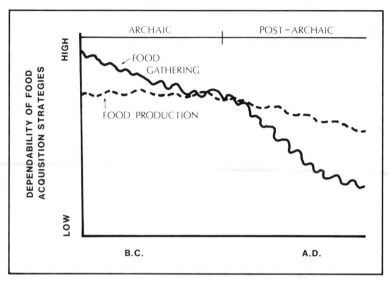

Figure 10.2 Hypothesized comparison of the dependability of food gathering and food production in the greater Southwest. Under some circumstances (probably human population increase and perhaps decrease in edible biomass) the increased dependability of food production encourages increased reliance on agriculture.

have provided a more secure livelihood than only hunter and gatherer strategies regardless of any stresses due to increasing population and/ or deteriorating resource abundance. That is, primary crop acquisition may be very different from pristine domestication. This idea is not directly applicable to the first use of cultigens in the Southwest as pottery and other parts of an agricultural technology were not present when domesticated plants were first introduced into the Southwest. However, LeBlanc's argument can be extended (although he may not agree with this extension) to say that the presence of domesticated plants themselves offered a more secure food acquisition strategy than only foraging. As discussed with the Western Apache example, low intensity farming in the Southwest may have been a very dependable and low cost activity so that a model of opportunity deserves consideration.

These models are not mutually exclusive. If late Archaic groups were having increasing difficulty provisioning themselves (for example, because of an expanding population), then the advantages of using relatively dependable farming techniques may have become more apparent. Nevertheless, these two explanations suggest different implications of the dynamics of Archaic prehistory.

Table 10.2 presents contrasting expectations derived from each of these two models. If the model of opportunity is correct, then we should see a very fast spread of cultigen use, whereas with the stress model we would expect a slightly slower spread, assuming the population densities within the Southwest were not the same. With the stress model we would expect a high correlation between the use of early agriculture and regional carrying capacity (as measured by such variables as human population density, resource abundance, and the stability of resource availability). If low intensity agriculture is such an economic advantage, we would expect cultivation to be used regardless of population density, resource abundance or stability. Similarly, with LeBlanc's model we would expect a wide use of agriculture, whereas a stress model would predict that Archaic agriculture would be found in a smaller area, those with food provisioning problems (again, assuming that human population densities varied throughout the Southwest). Finally, if there were imbalances between the dietary needs of Archaic groups and the resource base, then we might expect to find evidence of various forms of environmental manipulation to increase naturally available foods before the first use of cultigens. The same is not as likely with the model of opportunity.

There are other exceptions which might be used to contrast these two models. For example, if domesticated plants provided an opportunity for greater subsistence stability, then we would expect that the first introduction of crops into the Southwest would have occurred "soon" after their development as effective food sources in Mesoamerica. In fact, there is approximately a 3000 year lag for maize and perhaps longer periods for the other four Southwestern Archaic cultigens (Flannery 1973). This temporal difference is consistent with the model of opportunity only if there were substantial blocks in the flow of communication between Mesoamerica and the Greater Southwest during the Archaic period, a condition which I doubt existed.

The data base for currently testing these potentially contrasting models is not now available. While there is some evidence of increasing population during the Archaic period in the Southwest (Whalen 1973), we do not know what effect this increase may have had on the security of the Archaic economy. Similarly, we cannot correlate late Archaic cultural dynamics with environmental changes. As well, these expectations are more quantitatively than qualitatively distinct so that it will be difficult to compare the two models by an analysis restricted to the Southwest. Rather, a comparative research strategy which contrasts several examples of pristine crop acquisition with several examples of pristine domestication should help understand if models of agricultural origins (most of which were developed to account for pristine domestication) are applicable to the more common process(es) of primary crop acquisition.

CONCLUSIONS

Most models of agricultural origins have emphasized pristine domestication. Although more common than pristine domestication, primary crop acquisition (first use of cultigens by populations which did not develop the crops) has not received sufficient attention. This situation is unfortunate as the causes of and factors involved in primary crop acquisition may be different from pristine domestication. The Greater Southwest can provide an analytically useful example of primary crop acquisition, as the earliest and most important cultivated plants in the prehistoric Southwest were first domesticated in Mesoamerica and then spread into the Southwest.

The first use of cultigens by Southwestern Archaic peoples did not immediately nor dramatically alter their economies or social relationships, and it appears that, for at least 800 years and probably for much longer, cultigen-using Archaic groups continued a pattern of mobility and material culture similar to that of their ancestors. Several reasons account for the apparently smooth introduction of cultigens into Archaic lifestyles. First, like many hunter and gatherer societies, Southwestern Archaic peoples actively manipulated their environment for their economic benefit. Low cost agriculture, as probably practiced by the Archaic peoples, may not have been a much greater investment of energy or time than other forms of ecological manipulation. Second, the foods produced by the earliest Southwestern cultigens had analogies in the edible products of naturally available resources. Maize kernels are after all grass seeds, beans are a legume and the Southwest has a rich assemblage of naturally produced legumes, and cultivated cucurbits are similar to native cucurbits. Therefore, no major transformations in food consumption patterns or processing technology were necessary to use these early domesticated plants. Third, the location of farming sites and the seasonal timing of cultivation labor requirements probably fit well into already established patterns of resource exploitation for many Archaic groups in the Southwest. As the Western Apache example shows, nonintensive agriculture can require minimal labor and time and can easily adjust to seasonal population movement.

The fact that early plant cultivation was easily integrated into the Southwestern Archaic economy is not an explanation of the cause of first plant husbandry. Two models of the causes of primary crop acquisition in the Southwest have been examined. The first, a model of necessity, is similar to models proposed for pristine domestication, and this model suggests that Archaic cultivation was adopted because of imbalances between the dietary needs of the human population and the ability of their resource structure to supply an abundant and stable food supply. A model of opportunity was then proposed (LeBlanc 1982). This model argues that the presence of already domesticated crops and the reliability of low intensity agriculture provided an opportunity for a more secure food supply. Although both models can be integrated, contrasting implications from each model were presented.

We do not know very much about the ecological and economic characteristics of Archaic cultigen use, and in fact we may know less than we previously thought. For example, the supposed evolution of maize during the Archaic from a very small-cobbed plant to a more drought resistant larger cobbed, teosinte-introgressed plant is not consistent with modern research on the origin of maize and has much less theoretical justification than in the past. As Southwestern collections of very early maize (particularly from Bat Cave) were used as the empirical support for a now outdated model of maize origins and evolution, the need for a reanalysis of early Southwestern maize in light of recent research on maize origins and genetics is clear. The situation for the other cultigens is even less favorable; we not only have little data, but much less research has been conducted on the Archaic use of squash, gourds, and beans.

When cultigens were first used in the Southwest, and the speed of their spread, requires further empirical documentation. Within the last few years accelerated radiocarbon dating has allowed direct dating of individual cultigen remains, thus bypassing the problems of cultigen dating by stratigraphic context. On the basis of currently available data, the date of 2000 B.C. is not well supported, and 1000 B.C. seems a more reasonable date. Again, on the basis of ambiguous evidence, maize seems to have been established throughout the Southwest by A.D. 1. The first occurrences of other cultigens is even less well known than maize. Squash may be as early as maize or a slightly later introduction. We know almost nothing about the dating of early gourds. Beans were most probably later introductions into the Southwest than maize and perhaps squash. All of these four cultigen types probably were present in the Southwest by A.D. 1. Dating the first appearance of cultigens in the Southwest is critical to understanding the role which these plants played in Southwestern prehistory. However, an obsession for finding the earliest cultigens without also trying to understand the environmental and sociocultural context and causes of their introduction reflects nineteenth century archaeological interest.

ACKNOWLEDGMENTS

Many scholars offered necessary unpublished data for this paper: Vorsila Bohrer, Jeffry Dean, Marcia Donaldson, Cynthia Irwin-Williams, Christopher Lintz, Thomas O'Laughlin, James Schoenwetter, Mark Stiger, Mark Wimberly, and Joseph Winter.

Patricia Gilman read various drafts. The staff of the School of American Research and the other conference participants, particularly the organizer, Richard Ford, provided a stimulating seminar. A "thank you" is an inadequate expression of my gratitude for their help.

NOTES

1. Standard deviations of modern *Iva annua* populations were obtained from those reported by Asch and Asch 1978, Table 2. Archaeological populations include the achenes recovered from three Illinois River valley sites (Late Archaic Koster Horizon 6, the Middle to early Late Woodland Macoupin site, and the early Late Woodland Newbridge site [Asch and Asch 1978, Table 9]), three Eastern Kentucky rockshelter sites (the Early Woodland Cloudsplitter and Newt Kash shelters, and the early Late Woodland Rogers and Haystack rockshelters), and the Alred shelter in Benton County, Arkansas. While few of the Arkansas shelters have been chronometrically dated, the perishable materials from most are presumed to be quite late. Alred samples on file at the University of Michigan Museum of Anthropology Ethnobotanical Laboratory were apparently borrowed by Melvin R. Gilmore from the Museum of the American Indian, Heye Foundation, and retain the following Heye catalogue numbers: 11/7597 and 11/7380. With the exception of the achenes from Koster Horizon 6, all other archaeological populations appear to be *Iva annua* var. *macrocarpa*.

Patterns of Prehistoric Food Production in North America

Richard I. Ford
Museum of Anthropology, University of Michigan

The manipulation of plant species by humans for many purposes undoubtedly dates back to the entry of humans into the New World. Unfortunately, specific details about interactions with most taxa are lacking from the archaeological record. As the papers in this volume have demonstrated, deliberate plant food production is confirmed at archaeological sites by the actual remains of tropical cultigens, by seeds that differ from their putative wild ancestors, and by quantities of seeds found outside their known range of distribution. There is indirect evidence based upon assemblages of plants that suggest gardens, larger fields, or other forms of anthropogenic habitat modifications.

Individual species of plants diffused by several mechanisms from Mexico into what is now the United States arriving at different times and along corridors widely separated in space. These introduced domesticates were integrated into previously existing economies and often had an history in human subsistence quite different than in their Mexican font. Similarly, several plants were independently domesticated long after the introduction of Mesoamerican domesticates in both the eastern and southwestern United States. Despite the individual origin of each cultivated and domesticated species, several do cluster to form distinctive patterns in the archaeological record and history of the United States.

These patterns form an agricultural or crop complex. The concept of a prehistoric crop complex implies a group of species with an apparent common geographic origin and a mutual environmental and cultural association in the area where the complex develops. However, after the inception of a complex an individual species may later experience a separate geographical distribution and history. The idea for geographically-based complexes originated with Linton (1924) but received a continental application by Carter (1945). He distinguished an Eastern Mexican Corridor which was the source of agriculture in the East and these plants then diffused westward to form the Plateau Complex and a West Mexican Corridor that terminated in the Southwest as the Gila-Colorado Complex (Carter 1945:12). Although the history of each crop area in Linton's and Carter's formulations has changed, nevertheless, their insights are apparent in the revised agricultural complexes previously identified by Ford (1973, 1981). The papers in this volume have further expanded and elaborated upon the diversity of crop plant origins north of Mexico.

1) *Gourd Crop Complex*. Present evidence suggests that the first domesticated plants in the prehistoric United States originated in eastern Mexico, probably diffused across Texas (Story, this volume), and then were conveyed into the Southeast and the major river systems of the Midwest (Watson, this volume). The earliest identified plant in this complex is a small squash, (*Cucurbita pepo* perhaps *ovifera*) that has been dated to 7000 years ago in Illinois (Asch and Asch, this volume). Several millennia later the bottle gourd (*Lagenaria siceraria*) arrived. Large and small varieties of pepo gourds were bred over time. The two species had hard shells, that were used for containers, and edible seeds. While the antiquity before the domestication of each is unresolved, Heiser and King (this volume) have outlined the known botanical and archaeological history of this complex.

2) *Eastern Agricultural Complex*. Linton proposed this appellation, but it was Gilmore who, in 1931, applied it to enlarged seeds of several indigenous species found in the Ozark shelters which he interpreted as prehistoric domesticates. Jones (1936) further developed this theme with material from Newt Kash Hollow, Kentucky, and suggested a possible independent origin of agriculture in the East. Although it is now clear that Mexican gourd cultigens preceded these local domesticates by several millennia, several native species did undergo a series of genetic changes resulting in their domestication, and others were cultivated in the Eastern Woodlands and up the Missouri River drainage. In this volume Asch and Asch and Cowan have discussed the domestication of the sunflower (*Helianthus annuus*) and the sumpweed (*Iva annua*) and to these Smith (1984) has added *Chenopodium*. Maygrass

(*Phalaris caroliniana*), a lamb's-quarter (*Chenopodium berlandieri*), knot-weed (*Polygonum erectum*), and little barley (*Hordeum pusillum*) were cultivated. Subsequently, many were introduced beyond their modern range without recognizable genetic modifications, however.

3) *Upper Sonoran Agricultural Complex.* Sometime about 3000 years ago crops from western Mexico diffused from band to band into the Southwest. They first became established in mountain valleys above 2000 m in southwestern New Mexico and southeastern Arizona where sufficient precipitation permitted dry farming. This region coincides with the Upper Sonoran Life Zone in the Southwest and in the Sierra Madre Occidental of northern Mexico. The crops in this complex, as Berry and Minnis (this volume) explain, are corn (*Zea mays*), squash (*Cucurbita pepo*), the bottle gourd (*Lagenaria siceraria*), and common beans (*Phaseolus vulgaris*). These crops correspond to Carter's Plateau group, although he incorrectly derived them from the eastern United States (Carter 1945:222). There is no evidence for corn or beans in the East before they were grown in the Southwest.

4) *Lower Sonoran Agricultural Complex.* The crop plants constituting this group are tolerant of high temperatures but generally require supplemental moisture from irrigation. They were brought, perhaps by traders or visitors from more complex cultures in Mexico, between A.D. 500 and 1200 through the Sonoran Basin and Range phys-iographic region of western Mexico into the Sonoran Desert and Lower Sonoran Life Zone of southern Arizona. Despite its limited distribution, this complex, which is the same as Carter's Gila-Colorado group, has the greatest number of species. The earliest recognized plants in the complex were cotton (*Gossypium hirsutum* var. *punctatum*) and tepary beans (*Phaseolus acfolius*). Later additions included two or three beans—the jackbean (*Canavalia ensiformis*), lima bean (*Phaseolus lunatus*), and perhaps the scarlet runner bean (*Phaseolus coccineus*)—and two squashes (*Cucurbita mixta* and *C. moschata*). The least well known and most limited in occurrence was a grain amaranth (*Amaranthus hypochondriacus*).

5) *Southwest Agricultural Complex.* The only possible domesticated indigenous plants in the Southwest are late in the prehistoric record or of recent origin. Two grasses are potential candidates. Sonoran panic grass (*Panicum sonorum*) was cultivated in the historic period by Cocopa Indians and has been found in a possible prehistoric seed cache (Nabhan and de Wet 1984). Little barley grass (*Hordeum pusillum*) from several archaeological sites has phenotypic characters suggesting the early stages of domestication (Adams 1984). A third native species, devil's claw (*Proboscidea parviflora*), is a domesticate today providing decorative fibers for baskets and edible seeds.

Other plants were possibly cultivated outside their known range. An agave (*Agave parryi*) has been proposed and perhaps the native tobaccos, *Nicotiana attenuata* and *Nicotiana trigonophylla*, received special attention.

6) *Hispanic Agricultural Complex.* All European explorers introduced crop plants from one geographical area to another. In the United States the Spanish had the most profound impact during the first 100 years of colonization. They brought Eurasian and African plants to the New World and moved many cultigens from one New World continent to another. It was the Spanish, for instance, who first carried domesticated tobacco (*Nicotiana rustica*) and chili peppers (*Capsicum annuum*) from Mexico to the Southwest and who brought two Mexican squashes (*Cucurbita mixta, C. moschata*) to the eastern United States and one South American domesticated squash (*C. maxima*) to both the Southeast and the Southwest. The early introduction in Florida and the Southwest of watermelons and peaches can be attributed to Spanish contacts as well. In retrospect the Spanish had a profound impact on the distribution of crop plants in a very short period of time.

7) *Late Eastern Mexican Crop Complex.* This is the most artificial of the previously discussed agricultural groups. Three plants were introduced from eastern Mexico sometime after 2000 years ago, but there the association ends. The earliest was a yellow-flowered smoking tobacco (*Nicotiana rustica*). This is the tobacco the first European explorers found under cultivation throughout the East and in southern Ontario, but not anywhere in the Southwest. The other two plants are represented by the edible seeds of a chenopod (*Chenopodium berlandieri* var. *nuttaliae*) and an amaranth (*Amaranthus hypochondriacus*). Both have been found desiccated in the latest prehistoric levels in several Ozark bluff shelters (Fritz 1984).

Not all plants can be forced into crop complexes, even for analytical purposes. Some food plants were cultivated on a limited local basis but never had their ranges extended or phenotypic characters selected from one generation to the next. Medicinal and ritual plants were protected and transplanted to assure their availability but not every member of a single community necessarily engaged in this activity. Finally, there were weedy campfollowers that spread as human inhabitation created disturbed areas or as gardens and fields made new habitats available for their colonization.

GOURD CROP COMPLEX

The bottle gourd (*Lagenaria siceraria* [Mol.] Standl.) is the earliest agricultural plant in the Old World tropics as well as the New World.

In South American and Mexico its remains are associated with the oldest domesticated remains. It was domesticated independently in all these areas of the world, and its primary use was the same: containers. Although the seeds are edible, they usually have a bitter taste which render them a low preference food, but the hard shell is durable and light, qualities that make it ideal for carrying or storing things.

The report of water-saturated bottle gourd and squash seeds and rind fragments from the anaerobic wet environment at Phillips Spring radiocarbon dated to 2300 B.C. (Chomko and Crawford 1978; Kay 1979) resolved that these tropical cultigens preceded any domesticated indigenous plants. Their occurrence this far north of Mexico still left open the time for their entry.

Although *Lagenaria* rind fragments were found with three seeds of *Cucurbita pepo* in the Infiernillo phase, estimated to date 7000–5000 B.C., from southwestern Tamaulipas (Mangelsdorf et al. 1964:430), the first evidence of gourd north of Mexico is identified as a small variety of *Cucurbita pepo* (Asch and Asch, this volume). Bottle gourd is not present until several thousand years later (King, this volume).

The exciting possibility for squash as early as 6000–7000 years ago was raised by Asch and Asch (1979) based on charred rind fragments from deep levels at the Koster site, Illinois, with radiocarbon dates in this time period. Since then squash rinds have been dated directly by the accelerator radiocarbon method from three midwestern sites. The Koster specimen has a date of 7100 ± 300 B.P. (Rochester; Conard et al. 1984) and of 6820 ± 240 B.P. (Arizona; Austin Long, personal communication) on a specimen from the same level. The nearby Napoleon Hollow site has been dated to 7000 ± 250 B.P. (Conard et al. 1984). Carlston Annis in Kentucky has a date of 5730 ± 640 (Arizona; Austin Long, personal communication).

As exciting as these discoveries are, there is a possibility that they are not domesticated (King, this volume) and, if they are, their ancestry must be examined (Heiser, this volume). The buffalo gourd (*Cucurbita foetidissima* H.B.K.) does extend into the Southeast and may have had a more northerly range. Asch and Asch (this volume) have measured the thickness of rinds from Koster and Napoleon Hollow and they are on the average outside the range of the wild gourd. They suggest that the earliest cucurbits were of a size similar to the egg gourd (*C. pepo* var. *ovifera* Alef.). In light of this there is another small, hard-shelled cucurbit that is known from southern Texas and the Edwards Plateau that must be considered. Morphologically, the rind of early cucurbits in the Midwest and the Texas gourd (*Cucurbita texana* Gray) would be difficult to separate. However, assuming its range 7000 years ago was as limited as it is today, it would not grow in Illinois. Heiser (this

volume) suggests that there still may be an ancestral connection between the Texas gourd and the domesticated pepo. In fact, no pepo
gourd ancestor has been identified in Mexico and assuming that the
Texas gourd did not derive from pepo, it may be the direct genetic
parent. Until further research is conducted, the prospect that cucurbit
domestication took place in Texas or the East and spread southward
remains an intriguing hypothesis.

If northeastern Mexico was the geographic origin of *C. pepo* as is
now assumed, archaeological evidence for its diffusion north and why
it was accepted at the exclusion of the larger and harder container
fruit of the bottle gourd which was associated with it in Tamaulipas is
unexplained. Story (this volume) has discussed the cultural situation of
nomadic hunters and gatherers and the absence of plant evidence
when the pepo gourds would have been introduced along the Gilmore
Corridor from Mexico. No archaeological *C. texana* has been found in
any prehistoric context. Although Story has established an easy geographic and cultural connection with Mexico, no domesticate of any
gourd has been excavated in eastern Texas.

Watson (this volume) provides an excellent overview of Archaic adaptations from the time of the introduction of gourds and their diffusion in the Midwest. The pepo seeds were edible, and even the small
size of the gourds may have still rendered the durable, hard shell of
the fruit a useful container and led to a widespread preceramic trade.
Archaeologically, there is no evidence for extensive clearing of the
landscape to plant these pepo gourds, no obvious changes in the
settlement pattern or seasonal round, but by the Late Archaic cucurbit
gourds were found from eastern Tennessee to Kentucky and Missouri.

The Phillip Spring site is very significant for understanding the
range of variation in the pepo cucurbit and for our first appreciation
of the bottle gourd. By 4300 years ago a range of pepo gourds up to
the size of the Mandan variety was grown. During the Archaic larger
fruits with bigger seeds were selected for planting. The bottle gourd
provided a complementary fruit that could be deliberately shaped
while it grew to yield special containers or utensils.

Squash and/or bottle gourd are found in numerous Early Woodland
sites. Both are recovered from shelters in Kentucky (Cowan, this volume; Jones 1936). In the northern areas squash has been dated to 870
B.C. at Meadowcroft rockshelter in western Pennsylvania (Cushman
1982:216), at Leimback in northern Ohio, at 500 B.C. (Shane 1967),
and at the same date from Schultz near Saginaw, Michigan (Ozker
1982). The Schultz remains consist of large seeds within the range of
the Mandan variety and the cast of a egg gourd seed within an Early

Woodland pottery sherd. Remains of egg gourd have also been identified from Cloudsplitter, Kentucky (Cowan, this volume).

The gourd crop complex was the earliest in North America. A small variety, *Cucurbita pepo* var *ovifera*, appears first but during the Archaic a larger variety is selected. By 4300 years ago the bottle gourd has diffused northwestward to Missouri, and the gourd complex continued in the East until the contact period. The major undocumented change is the selection for a fleshy, edible rind that became the familiar squash or pumpkin. It is possible that the breeding of these varieties began with the extensive use of bottle gourds for containers or with pottery formed into vessels of several shapes. With the availability of functional equivalents, pepo gourd containers would not be required, and simple mutations for a thick flesh were favored. In either case the edible fruit expanded the dietary significance of cucurbits in prehistory.

EASTERN AGRICULTURAL COMPLEX

The collection for food and the eventual domestication of some plants native to the eastern United States followed the introduction of the Gourd Crop Complex from eastern Mexico by several millennia. At Cloudsplitter evidence of squash precedes all indigenous small seed cultigens (Cowan, this volume). At Koster a few archaeological wild sumpweed date back 6000 years but show no demonstrative phenotypic seed changes until long after its first intensive foraging and even cultivation (Asch et al. 1972; Asch and Asch, this volume). By the Late Archaic and through the Middle Woodland periods this group of plants manifests a number of cultivation techniques and stages leading to domestication. The detailed studies on these plants from west-central Illinois conducted by Asch and Asch (this volume) is the best case study available for any region in the East.

By the end of the Late Archaic three plants had been domesticated in the eastern United States. The sumpweed (*Iva annua* var. *macrocarpa* Jackson) was derived from its ancestor *Iva annua* (Blake 1939) and is recognized by its large achenes. Evidence for its collection is found at Koster and for its Late Archaic domestication in Kentucky and Illinois about 4000 years ago. It continued to be grown and larger achenes were selected until the Mississippian period (Yarnell 1981). It was abandoned as a domesticate at the time of European contact. Black (1963) has described its archaeological distribution beyond the modern range of *Iva annua*. Yarnell (1972, 1978, 1981) has clarified the archaeological stages of its domestication and the enlargement of its achene. Asch and Asch (1978) have discussed its ecological requirements and its potential nutritional contribution to the prehistoric diet. The actual subsistence importance of this annual seed remains to be determined. Certainly by the Late Archaic it had been moved from wet bottomlands to plots where it could be planted in larger stands. These may have been sizable gardens consisting of *Iva* and other domesticated and cultivated species. The importance of sumpweed must not be minimized. It spread westward to eastern Kansas by A.D. 200 (Adair 1984:149) and efforts were made to increase its quantity by collecting wild achenes even when the domesticated variety was available.

The domesticated sunflower (*Helianthus annuus* L.) evolved in the eastern United States and has become one of the major oil seed crops in the world today. Its beginnings are remote with a few possible achenes from Koster almost 8000 years ago and 4000 years in time at Napoleon Hollow where they were directly associated with domesticated *Iva* (Asch and Asch, this volume). Yarnell (1978) has reviewed the domestication of the sunflower in the Late Archaic. The first evidence for its 3500 years of development is from the Higgs site in Tennessee and Salts Cave and Mammoth Cave in Kentucky. Larger achenes were selected throughout the prehistory of the Midwest with the largest attained in Mississippian times (Yarnell 1981). Asch and Asch (this volume) have reviewed the variation in achene size from several sites in Illinois. Kernel dimensions may depend upon the number of flower heads on a plant. In all likelihood domesticated, cultivated, and even volunteer wild plants in Woodland gardens or in Mississippian corn fields yielded harvests of edible seeds.

The status of goosefoot in the East was ambiguous until Asch and Asch (1978) provided the systematics for most archaeological examples and conclusively eliminated *Chenopodium album* as the seed archaeologists were reporting. They showed that *Chenopodium bushianum* Aellen was intensively collected. Continued reevaluation has led them to recognize all the chenopods in their region as *Chenopodium berlandieri* Moq. This species was domesticated sometime ago in the East. It has been found in Archaic sites but with a thick seed coat. By 2000 years ago, however, Smith (1984) has identified domesticated *C. Berlandieri* from Russell Cave in Alabama. About the same time Asch and Asch recognize the domesticated form at Smiling Dan in Illinois (this volume). This is the third irrefutable domesticated native plant in the East.

Four additional plants contributed small, starchy seeds to the Late Archaic or Woodland economy, but while they were moved to new habitats and sown, evidence for actual domestication has not been recognized. Maygrass (*Phalaris caroliniana* Walt.), as assessed by Cowan (1978; this volume), was spread by prehistoric farmers beyond its now basically southern range into the Midwest and became a deliberately planted garden crop in the Late Archaic in Kentucky. Knotweed (*Polygonum erectum* L.) was collected in quantity and has been found in a small cache deposit with cultivated maygrass and chenopod at Cloudsplitter suggesting storage for future planting (Cowan, this volume). In west-central Illinois knotweed was not common until the Middle and Late Woodland. Asch and Asch (this volume) suggest further its possible domestication at the Mississippian Hill Creek site. Many grass seeds have gone unidentified in the archaeobotanical literature. Only recently has charred maygrass been recognized more universally than a decade ago. Similarly, little barley (*Hordeum pusillum* Nutt.) is now acknowledged as a cultivated grass in Illinois (Asch and Asch, this volume). Gilmore (1931) thought that ragweed (*Ambrosia trifida* L.) was domesticated in the Ozarks, but Payne and Jones (1972) demonstrated that the enlarged seeds found there were actually the natural hybridization where clines of different achene sizes converge. The presence of ragweed achenes at Cloudsplitter with other cultigens raises again the question of whether it might not have been cultivated as a garden plant as well, but without suggesting domestication. All these species became part of the horticultural system recognized in Kentucky by 1000 B.C. and in Illinois by the Middle Woodland.

The region where sumpweed, sunflower, and the chenopod were domesticated and where this assemblage of plants first emerged is unresolved. At Cloudsplitter the complex arrives at once without precedent (Cowan, this volume). In western Illinois a local *Iva* may have been domesticated but the same process probably occurred elsewhere as well. Based on phytogeographical evidence the lower Mississippi River delta is the most reasonable area to search according to the authors in this volume. Here wild ancestors of all these plants grow in abundantly large stands but without archaeobotanical evidence. North of this region they are either less frequent or unavailable. The *processes* leading to their cultivation and eventual domestication still require archaeological investigation. Despite the necessity for continuing research, the emergence of a constellation of native domesticated and intensively cultivated food plants to form the Eastern Agricultural Complex has been a significant contribution of paleoethnobotany to American archaeology.

UPPER SONORAN AGRICULTURAL COMPLEX

Corn (*Zea mays* L.) is the most critical of the four groups in this higher elevation complex. It originated in the southern highlands of Mesoamerica from teosinte parents (Galinat, this volume). The development of a full cob of kernels still has not been documented with archaeobotanical evidence, however. For most of its evolutionary history maize was grown by seasonally nomadic hunters and gatherers. It was spread from one social band to another until it reached northern Mexico and the mountainous regions of the Southwest some 3000 years ago. Unfortunately, the best evidence from northern Mexico is a Chapalote-type maize from an undated preceramic horizon in Swallow Cave (Mangelsdorf and Lister 1956).

The question of the dietary impact of maize on the eventual cultural development of the Southwest depends upon a chronological answer. Berry (1983, this volume) has assessed the evidence for dated corn from throughout the Southwest and has concluded that its introduction was quite late. Certainly the published date of 2200 B.C. for maize from Bat Cave is woefully too early, and the so-called "primitive" diminutive cobs from the same site associated with these unreliable early dates have been reanalyzed as the unfertilized terminal portions from larger cobs (Mangelsdorf 1974:Figs. 14.1, 14.2). An accelerator date on the earliest stratigraphic cob excavated by the University of Michigan in 1981 from Bat Cave has an uncorrected date of 2340±420 B.P. (Arizona; Austin Long, personal communication). Additional dates from the 1983 excavation only extend the chronology of maize in Bat Cave back a few centuries. A single corn kernel from a nearby porcupine midden has been accelerator dated to 2420±170 B.P. (AA-679; Julio Betancourt, personal communication). Elsewhere, the Sheep Camp shelter in Chaco Canyon, has yielded maize dated directly to 2250±280 B.P. (300 B.C. corrected) and 2150±170 B.P. (200 B.C. corrected) (Simmons 1984:215). Before these accelerator dates became available, Berry (this volume) maintained that Jemez Cave with its published date of 2440±250 B.P. was the best dated early maize in the Southwest. A new accelerator date on maize from the same unit in the shelter of 2410±360 B.P. (Arizona; Austin Long, personal communication) continues to support his contention. While other claims for maize pollen and maize fragment dating earlier than 1000 B.C. have been made, no accelerator date is that early, and this date is a convenient chronological placement for the diffusion of maize into the Southwest.

If, indeed, corn was such a late arrival as current evidence suggests, it must have had a revolutionary impact rather than a long evolutionary integration into the pre-existing foraging economies (Minnis, this volume). Corn was a more reliable carbohydrate source than any indigenous plant in the prehistoric economy. Certainly this was recognized along with its greater dependability from year to year than naturally occurring plant food products (Ford 1984). A rapid spread and a reorientation of dietary preferences, even on a seasonal basis, should not be surprising for archaeologists to find.

Further human selection for a productive, enlarged cob maize customary to the later pueblo sites requires continued research. By 300 B.C. sufficient genetic variability was present in the Southwest to account for all varieties that were eventually bred (Galinat, this seminar). Claims for teosinte introgression in the Southwest (cf. Richard's Cave near Montezuma Castle in Arizona [Galinat et al. 1956] and Cebollita Cave near Acoma, New Mexico [Galinat and Ruppé 1961]) are questionable. Not only does teosinte not grow within the Southwest (Galinat, this volume) but a more likely explanation is heat stress during pollination that will produce a similar morphological cob to one with teosinte genes (Galinat, this volume). Early maize was a Chapalote-series maize with about 12-kernel rows and small, globular flint kernels. Through interbreeding larger ears with more kernels were grown, although not until a sedentary lifestyle developed, and nevertheless a range of cob sizes continued. At one time it was believed that Fremont Dent corn came from the diffusion of a Mexican race, Conico Norteño (Anderson 1948; Cutler 1966:16). Winter (1973) has refuted this explanation by demonstrating that selection in situ can account for this distinctive maize. This does not preclude any genetic additions from Mexico, however. Such a source may account for 8-rowed maize in the latest preceramic levels in the Southwest (Jones and Fonner 1954) and perhaps floury kernels (Cutler 1966). Selective breeding and the growth in new environments produced local varieties, and cultural changes in food preparation would result in crop selection from flint to flour kernel preferences.

In the Southwest the first squash (*Cucurbita pepo* L.) is as early as maize. It was found in the bottom midden level at Bat Cave (Dick 1965), in Jemez Cave, and with the possible exception of Cordova Cave (Kaplan 1963:355), it is in all preceramic sites where corn has been recovered. At the Sheep Camp shelter there is a single early date on squash of 2820 ± 220 B.P. and a later one of 2130 ± 280 B.P. (Simmons 1984:215). This is the only site where squash is dated before maize. Just as in the East, its hard rind was initially used for containers and the seeds were consumed for food. By A.D. 900 several varieties were grown and a fruit with a thick edible flesh became important. Along with maize it was the first crop in the Lower Sonoran area, evidently diffusing from the Mogollen area, and these plants were even found at Casas Grandes (Bohrer and Fenner 1974). In contrast to the East, no *C. pepo* var. *ovifera* has been found in the Southwest.

The bottle gourd (*Lagenaria siceraria*) was apparently transmitted into the Southwest after corn and squash. A date of 300 B.C. from Tularosa and Cordova caves is generally used for its arrival. It was not present in the preceramic levels of Bat Cave (Smith 1950) or Jemez Cave (Ford 1975). It does not grow well where temperatures are cool and the availability of water is a problem. These environmental factors limited its eventual distribution in the Southwest. Although gourd rind fragments have been found in many later sites throughout the Southwest (Cutler and Whitaker 1961:473), the absence of peduncles and seeds suggests that it may not have been grown so widely especially at higher elevations and that trade for containers and rattles may account for its presence in some localities.

The appearance of the common bean (*Phaseolus vulgaris* L.) in the Southwest followed the previous three plants, but a date for its arrival is uncertain. Part of the chronological confusion results from an inadequate date for Level IV in Bat Cave in which beans are found and from the poorly dated Tularosa and Cordova caves where beans occur in all levels (Cutler 1952). Common beans are found initially in the Mogollen area, probably after 300 B.C. and Kaplan (1956) defines the greatest number of his types from this cultural area. At the higher latitudes they reach the Durango Basketmaker II after A.D. 400 and then are found several centuries later in western pueblo sites. At most pueblo sites they were the only beans raised (Kaplan 1981). Common beans were grown by the Hohokam before later species of beans (discussed below) arrived (Bohrer 1970), and they continued to be grown near Sonoran Desert sites into historic times (Cutler 1956). Beans undoubtedly were grown in fields, perhaps with or along side corn and squash and added a vegetable proteins to the prehistoric Southwest.

Because squash and gourd husbandry was widely practiced in the East, the only Upper Sonoran Agricultural Complex crops that are obvious introductions there from the Southwest are corn and the common bean. Available evidence continues to support the established contention that they diffused independently of each other (Yarnell 1964).

The process by which corn diffused across the Plains remain unsolved. The route of transmission appears to be south of Kansas. In a recent survey of botanical remains from that state, Adair (1984) finds maize, squash, and *Iva* at A.D. 200, presumably coming from the East, a hiatus, and then an A.D. 800–1000 introduction of a larger and more productive 8-rowed maize, typical of later Plains sites with sunflower, bottle gourd, and beans again with a probable Eastern origin. Sites in Oklahoma and Texas with maize are too late and have different varieties than found dominant by A.D. 1 in the Southwest.

The actual time period when corn was added to the established gardens in the East is unresolved. No Archaic corn has been found (Conard et al. 1984). Corn remains are associated with dates of 340 B.C. and 375 B.C. at Meadowcroft rockshelter (Cushman 1982:216) and of 280 B.C. from Daines II Mound near Athens, Ohio (Murphy 1971). Dates of 80 B.C. have been applied to cobs from Jasper Newman in Illinois (Struever and Vickery 1973:1200), but they could be intrusive from later occupations on the site (Conard et al. 1984). The Ohio Hopewell sites including McGraw (Cutler 1965), Hopeton Square, and Edwin Harness Mound (Ford 1979) have yielded undated cob fragments and they are Chapalote-like. Middle Woodland corn is also reported from Renner and Trowbridge near Kansas City dated about A.D. 250 (Johnson 1976:14) and the Peters site in southern Tennessee (Ferguson 1978:760). If the evidence from Meadowcroft and Daines II were dated by the accelerator, the dating problem would be clarified. In west-central Illinois maize is improbable before 2000 years ago (Conard et al. 1984:445) and may best be placed between A.D. 600 and 800.

In a Middle Woodland context, maize would be added to well established, mixed horticultural gardens and its full potential not necessarily recognized immediately. The transformation of agricultural activities from mixed crop gardens to larger corn fields after A.D. 800 was based on cultural interaction and not simply maize. It is not necessary to postulate more than one entry of maize into the East. Jones (1968:85) has stated that ". . . all aboriginal corn types of North America north of Mexico were derived from a highly diverse gene pool in the Southwest." The many varieties found in the East after A.D. 1000 could have been developed from this genetic base.

The common bean was the only domesticated bean to reach the prehistoric eastern United States, and it did so by a still undefined route from the Southwest after A.D. 800 (Yarnell 1976:272). By A.D. 1000 beans have been identified from as far away as Mitchell in South Dakota (Benn 1974:66), Blain Village in Ohio (Kaplan 1970:228), and Roundtop near Binghamton, New York (Yarnell 1976:272). With the addition of the common bean the trinity of corn, squash, and beans was completed in the East. Together they provided complementary amino acids for a complete vegetable protein and could be grown together in a field agriculture mode of production (Ford 1974).

LOWER SONORAN AGRICULTURAL COMPLEX

This crop complex was brought from western Mexico to the sedentary canal irrigation farmers of the Sonoran Desert by a second route of transmission through the Basin and Range physiographic province at lower elevations. Although precise Mexican regions for its origins remain unidentified, formal contacts, most likely traders, resulted in the transfer of cotton, grain amaranth, and several species of beans and squash to the hot desert and river valleys occupied by the Hohokam and their neighbors. Most of these plants were limited by their ecological requirements to southern Arizona, although the green striped cushaw squash and cotton did become important in some areas where the Upper Sonoran Agricultural Complex was already well established.

Dating the introduction of each of these crop plants is difficult until radiocarbon accelerator dates become more frequent. A simple association with Hohokam or Hohokam-related sites is inadequate because the chronology for this desert culture is under debate. An inaugural date of 300 B.C. for Snaketown proposed by Haury (1976) has lost credibility with further analysis. Plog (1980:22) argues for a date no earlier and most likely later than A.D. 350. More recently, Schiffer (1982:336) has reduced the inception of the Hohokam as a distinctive culture to A.D. 700. Initially the Hohokam subsistence pattern depended upon Upper Sonoran Agricultural complex plants and not those from Mexico. When the latter did arrive, however, is not a trivial question because many did have an ecological advantage and eventually greater dietary importance than did those from higher elevations (Gasser 1980).

Cultivated cotton (*Gossypium hirsutum* L. var. *punctatum* [*Gossypium hopii*]) and loom weaving first appeared in the Hohokam area at an unresolved date but certainly not before A.D. 500. The first recognized cotton is from Snaketown but by the eighth century cotton products were in the Kayenta region. An absence of seeds and bolls outside southern Arizona supports the hypothesis that cotton textiles and cordage were traded northward to the Anasazi and eastward to the Mogollen long before cotton was grown in the other culture areas. Outside the Hohokam, seed evidence for actual local cotton cultivation is dated after A.D. 1100. Antelope House in Canyon de Chelly has been proposed as a production center (Magers 1975). It was also grown in the Mimbres area after A.D. 1100 (Minnis, this seminar), and it may have been raised as far north as Glen Canyon. The southwestern variety became well adapted to local conditions to the degree that it was grown in the short growing season on the Hopi Mesas. Where it was raised, the seeds were consumed by humans, but because of the fiber's ritual and practical importance, throughout its history trade in cotton occurred all through the Southwest. The demand for cotton fabrics and cordage gave this original Lower Sonoran plant the widest distribution of any plant in the complex.

The adaptation of the tepary bean (*Phaseolus acutifolius* Gray. var. *latifolius* Freeman) to arid environments has been reviewed by Nabhan and Felger (1978). Its taxonomic history is confusing because wild forms extend from southern Arizona throughout western and southern Mexico. Kaplan (1956) recognizes eight varieties in the Southwest, indicative of endemism, and they suggest to him multiple origins for its domestication possibly including western Mexico and the Southwest. In the Southwest the cultivation of tepary beans probably began as early as cotton. By A.D. 760 it was in the Durango Basketmaker area (Kaplan 1963a:47). As expected it has been found in several Hohokam sites and at Tonto (Bohrer 1962), Tuzigoot and Montezuma Castle (Kaplan 1956), and Babocomari (Jones 1951:16). After A.D. 1100 it occurred as far east as El Paso (Ford 1977a), in the Mogollen area (Cosgrove 1947), and northward to Kiet Siel and Zion (Kaplan 1956). Tepary beans have not been found in the upper Rio Grande Pueblos, Mesa Verde, or Glen Canyon.

The small lima bean or sieva bean (*Phaseolus lunatus* L.) was domesticated in Mesoamerica independent of its larger relative in South America (Kaplan 1971:418). It was recovered in northern Durango, Mexico, after A.D. 600, although the type L-6 from there has not been found in the Southwest (Brooks et al. 1962:359). Only five Lower Sonoran sites have yielded identifiable sieva beans and they date after A.D. 1000. However, a Pueblo I site (D:11:2030) from Black Mesa near Kayenta, Arizona, has provided confirmed lima beans (Lawrence Kaplan, personal communication) before this date, and this evidence suggests that lima beans entered southern Arizona by A.D. 850, if not earlier. Although they were grown on the Hopi Mesas from prehistoric times to the present, this bean had a limited distribution in the Southwest.

Sauer and Kaplan (1969) concluded that the jack bean (*Canavalia ensiformis* [L.] D.C.) was first domesticated in tropical southern Mesoamerica, and its high water requirement restricted its distribution to areas where irrigation was practiced. The earliest examples are from the Hodges site and Punta de Agua (Bohrer et al. 1969:5) near Tucson and Pueblo Grande (Gasser 1980:23) in Phoenix and date, after A.D. 1100. Aside from a Pueblo III cave near Flagstaff, jack beans had a distribution limited to the Lower Sonoran area.

Although the scarlet runner bean (*Phaseolus coccineus* L.) was identi-

fied from the Rio Zape in Durango (Brooks et al. 1962:364), no uncon-
tested example has been found north of Mexico. This observation
sustains Nabhan's (1977:147) conclusion that evidence for prehistoric
runner beans is lacking for the Southwest, and those grown by the
Hopi were probably a historic introduction.

The green striped cushaw squash (*Cucurbita mixta* Pang.) appeared
in southern Arizona by A.D. 900, perhaps as early as A.D. 700 (Cutler
and Blake 1976:365). Unlike the previously discussed beans in this
complex, this squash spread well beyond the Lower Sonoran Life
Zone. As long as its water requirements can be met, it produces abundant, large fruits. By A.D. 1100 it was grown as far east as El Paso (Ford
1977a), the Reserve area (Cutler and Whitaker 1961:472), and northward to Glen Canyon. At high elevations such as Glen Canyon and
Mesa Verde where bottle gourds fail to mature, thick rind varieties of
this squash were used for containers (Cutler and Meyer 1965). Eventually it was raised as far north as southern Nevada and Utah and the
Gallina area in northern New Mexico (Cutler and Blake 1973:51). *C.
mixta* is still grown in the Pueblos, and it has now become the most
widely cultivated Lower Sonoran crop.

The warty squash (*Cucurbita moschata* Poir.) apparently was the last
squash brought into the Hohokam area and its eventual distribution
was quite restricted until Hispanic times. It was the most abundant
botanical squash remain at Montezuma Castle and Tonto (Bohrer
1962:103), but is known from only six other sites.

Grain amaranth (*Amaranthus hypochondriacus* L.) has been identified
from Tonto (Bohrer 1962:107) and from Pot Creek south of Taos, New
Mexico (Woosley and Baker 1984). Both date after A.D. 1100 but their
contrasting environmental settings and the distance between them
raises several interesting questions. At both sites the light colored seeds
of a domesticate were not charred. Amaranth seeds are commonly
found carbonized in southwestern sites. Using known criteria it would
not be possible to determine if any of these were domesticated.
Amaranthus powellii is considered its ancestor, and it grows widely in
Arizona and New Mexico. Although *A. hypochrondriacus* is regarded as
a Mesoamerican introduction, it has been confirmed only from
Tehuacán (Sauer 1969), and a late prehistoric indigenous domestication should not be discounted.

The Lower Sonoran Agricultural Complex is a later development in
southern Arizona. The plant assemblage is best represented in the
fourteenth century archaeobotanical remains from Tonto (Bohrer
1962). However, it is associated with sedentary Hohokam derived
cultures which practiced various forms of water control and maintained complex long distance trade networks including northwestern

Mexico. The full dietary significance of these plants in Sonoran Desert archaeological cultures is not known, and until recently the fact that this region had received the greatest number of Mesoamerican domesticated species received scant attention (Ford 1981; Nabhan and de Wet 1984).

SOUTHWEST AGRICULTURAL COMPLEX

Despite the possible domestication of grain amaranth and the tepary bean in the Sonoran Desert region, the existing archaeobotanical remains are fully domesticated and no antecedent developmental stages for these plants have been uncovered. Nonetheless, the possibility of the domestication of native southwestern plants must be anticipated. Certainly a number of wild species were intensively cultivated by ethnographic people (cf. Castetter and Bell 1951). Archaeologically, the extensive recovery of beeweed (*Cleome serrulata* Pursh.) seed from prehistoric sites may point to its encouragement by prehistoric people. Similarly, the wild tobaccos may have been cultivated or at least dispersed by human agency for easier access. *Nicotiana attenuata* Torr. leaves and capsules have been found widely in the Southwest and often in ceremonial "cigarettes" or sucked quids (Jones and Morris 1960:116). *Nicotiana trigonophylla* Dunal. was sought out by ethnographic groups in the Sonoran Desert (Castetter and Bell 1942:108) and it should be found in Hohokam archaeological sites.

Bohrer (1975) and Doebly (1984) have discussed the importance of native grasses in the Southwest and the extent to which they have been recovered from archaeological sites. Currently, little barley (*Hordeum pusillum* Nutt.) is being investigated as a possible domesticate because several features, including naked seeds, have been observed on archaeological specimens (Adams 1984). A reassessment of Sonoran panic grass (*Panicum sonorum* Beal.) has led Nabhan and de Wet (1984) to conclude that it is probably an indigenous domesticate. It was cultivated by historic Cocopa Indians (Castetter and Bell 1951:170) and sown by the Warihio in northern Mexico. Its only archaeological occurrence is in a cache bag with *Cucurbita mixta* seeds and tepary beans from the Trigo Mountains near Yuma, Arizona. The grass seed was dated directly by conventional radiocarbon methods to 603 ± 140 B.P. (Kaemlein 1963). The association of these seeds suggests intensive collection and perhaps storage for later planting. While the evidence clearly points to domestication, more archaeological examples are necessary to clarify the changes leading to historic botanical collections.

Devil's claw (*Proboscidea parviflora* Woot. and Standl.) pods are sources of edible seeds and decorative fibers for baskets. Equally distinctive is a white seeded variety raised by Papago and Moencopi villagers which differs from the black seeds in most untended examples. Castetter and Bell (1942) argue that this is a domesticated form which was selected for in the historic period by the Pima and Papago as a response to a commercial demand for baskets. In a thorough review Nabhan et al. (1981) conclude that the white seeded variety is undergoing the process of domestication but it still is able to reproduce annually without assistance from humans. Prehistoric remains of a white seeded, enlarged pod variety have not been found.

Extending the range of native plants is another process that must be considered. Minnis and Plog (1976) have reported the disjunct association of living agave (*Agave parryi* Engelm.) in central Arizona with archaeological ruins. They suspect prehistoric inhabitants may have increased its range northward intentionally or accidentally. Archaeological evidence for its utilization at these sites does not exist, but its absence does not negate the potentially active role southwestern Indians had in spreading this and other species beyond their contemporary range.

More controversial is a large, purple achene sunflower (*Helianthus annuus* L.) that is raised by the Hopi for food and a dye. Sunflower seeds are known from southwestern archaeological sites and in particular from the Black Mesa Archaeological Project north of the Hopi villages. Unfortunately, no seed is as large as the Hopi variety nor are they outside the modern dimensions of wild achenes. It appears that this cultivar was introduced to the Hopi in historic times and its distinctive characteristics have been selected for by cultural dictates. The Hopi sunflower is not a prehistoric domesticate.

Until further research is conducted and new plant evidence is forthcoming, it must be concluded that a true Southwestern Agricultural Complex of indigenous domesticated plants has not been found in an archaeological context. Those examples presented above that have been intensively cultivated, transplanted, and even domesticated do not form a region-wide crop complex. On the other hand, the Southwest is a very diverse geographical area. When examined critically, the Sonoran Desert area does have a tradition of extensive interference in the life cycle of numerous economic plants, a long history of using water conservation measures, and a number of distinctive varieties bred from introduced domesticates. The historic pathway to domestication of the devil's claw is a continuation of a process begun in prehistoric times with Sonoran panic grass, for the time being, the only known example. Further archaeobotanical investigations may reveal a Sonoran Desert Agricultural Region (Nabhan and de Wet

1984:80) and a separate Colorado Plateau Agricultural Region distinct from a Greater Southwest crop complex. The exciting point at this time is that native plants were manipulated and perhaps domesticated for food in the Southwest.

HISPANIC INTRODUCTIONS

Spanish missionaries and colonists introduced more plants to areas outside their place of origin than did any other Europeans. Orchard, garden, and field plants were brought to the Catholic missions and the first settlements. In the sixteenth century, southwestern Indians adopted wheat, barley, peaches, apricots, plums, peas, chickpeas, broadbeans, grapes, watermelons, and melons from Spanish contacts. Many of the same plants came to the Southeast, but were discontinued for environmental reasons. Equally significant were the plants of New World origin that were transported between the continents.

Surprisingly, it was the Spanish who brought the chili pepper (*Capsicum annuum* L.) and domesticated tobacco (*Nicotiana rustica* L.) to the Southwest. Both plants were grown in central Mexico, but despite claims by some archaeologists, no archaeological evidence for either in unambiguous precontact contexts, not even at Casas Grandes, has been found. Both plants were accepted immediately by the Indians after the Spanish introduced them. Chili seeds and stems appear in New Mexican seventeenth century mission-pueblos. Domesticated tobacco was quickly adopted as evidenced by the identification of *Nicotiana rustica* from a Pueblo Rebellion (A.D. 1680) reoccupation of the Bandelier cliff dwellings (Volney H. Jones, personal communication). In Pueblos today it is used as a leisure time cigarette, but in rituals it has a complementary relationship with *Nicotiana attenuata,* the indigenous wild tobacco that pioneers human-disturbed habitats or fields, which is cultivated there and collected. *N. rustica* will reseed itself for a year or two after initial planting in gardens or edges of fields, but then must be replanted. Introduced tobacco and chili are indispensable in the economic and ritual lives of southwestern Indians.

The Spanish brought several varieties of corn from Mexico into both the Southwest and the Southeast. Cristalina de Chihuahua, which evolved in northern Mexico, was introduced by them to the Southwest. The Spanish carried Tuxpeño, a dented kernel maize, by sea to the Southeast where it crossed with prehistoric maize to produce the modern Corn Belt dent. Another Mexican dent first appears at Picuris in post-Rebellion deposits (Cutler and Blake 1969b). Together highland Mexican dent and Cristalina de Chihuahua were bred by the Rio

Grande pueblos to produce the extremely large semi-dent cobs found growing there today.

The Spanish also favored fleshy vegetables and fruits. They carried the watermelon with them from Africa via Europe and disseminated it across the southern United States. Its acceptance by the southern Woodland Indians was so rapid that it spread faster to the Plains than did direct European contact leading Gilmore to believe mistakenly that it originated in America (Blake 1981). Likewise watermelon and cantaloupe became important sweet fruits in the Southwest by A.D. 1630. They brought *Cucurbita maxima* from South America to Mexico, the American Southwest, and the East where the only authenticated find is from Fort Berthold Village, North Dakota (Cutler and Blake 1973:53). From Mexico they introduced *Cucurbita moschata* to the Southeast as early as the 1700s at the Fatherland site in Mississippi (Cutler and Blake 1973:37) and it eventually diffused as far north as the Hidatsa Rock Village site in North Dakota (Cutler and Blake 1973:53).

The repertory of Spanish-introduced crops rapidly revolutionized native food plant production across the continent from Florida to California. The Spanish taught the Indians new techniques for raising these and traditional domesticates. Gardens, orchards, and plow agriculture were employed to assure a successful harvest. Indian plant names and legends acknowledged most of these plants as post-European arrivals and as a group they were usually treated separately in rituals from aboriginal cultigens.

The Hispanic Agricultural Complex augmented the diet of the American Indian in the historic period and increased the productivity of the land. These species, in fact, were so numerous and so easy to raise that they transformed the indigenous economics to a degree unparalleled since maize first appeared in the Southwest.

LATE EASTERN MEXICAN CROP COMPLEX

For lack of a better term this description at least expresses both the place of origin and the time of the introduction of the last three plants from Mexico into the East. Tobacco, another cultivated chenopod, and a grain amaranth were late additions.

The Tamaulipas cave plants are instructive but do not resolve the Mexican history of these plants. Tobacco (*Nicotiana rustica* L.) is noted there after A.D. 300. An unspecified *Amaranthus* goes back to 2200 B.C., and no chenopodium was recovered. However, by A.D. 1 the same sites had chili peppers, cotton, an additional species of bean and one of squash, and four distinctive races of maize. Why only a few plants diffused northward is unknown.

It could be that highland Tamaulipas had nothing to do with the spread of tobacco. It was grown along the Gulf of Mexico and coastal traders may have found it there. In North America tobacco has been found in the Midwest and the Missouri River drainage. Its earliest appearance is charred seeds from the Smiling Dan site dated to A.D. 160 (Asch and Asch, this volume). Farther south three sites from the American Bottom area near St. Louis have also yielded seeds: the Mund site dates between A.D. 400–600 and the Late Woodland Range and Fish Lake sites (Johannessen 1984:196). Elsewhere, they are recognized by A.D. 1000 at Mitchell (Benn 1974:56) and Brewster (Stains 1972). By the time of European contact it was grown from the coast to the Plains and up to southern Ontario. Technically, it is not a food plant but it continued the garden tradition begun millennia earlier in the East.

Haberman (1984) has summarized evidence for tobacco in the Plains and the East and proposes, based upon scanning electron microscope analysis, that *Nicotiana bigelovii* var. *quadrivalvis* came eastward through contact with western people. This plant originated in California and the Great Basin but was recorded grown by Prairie groups in the historic period. *Nicotiana* seeds are quite variable in surface sculpture and the seeds illustrated (Haberman 1984:278) are not convincingly different from *N. rustica*. For the prehistoric period the only authenticated tobacco in the East is *Nicotiana rustica*.

The cultivated chenopod (*Chenopodium berlandieri* spp. *nuttalliae* Standl.) of Mexico has an origin independent from *Chenopodium quinoa* in South America (Heiser and Nelson 1974). Gilmore (1931) first identified it from the Ozark bluff shelters by its large pale seeds. Wilson (1981) has restudied the taxonomy of the Mexican chenopods and their history and has confirmed the identification of this plant. Fritz (1984:564) has re-examined the archaeological evidence from two Ozark rockshelters in Arkansas and concludes that this subspecies was not derived from the domesticated species identified by Smith (1984) and Asch and Asch (this volume) but was brought late in prehistory from Mexico. Without additional evidence, as Fritz acknowledges, its significance to the late occupants of the bluff dwellings remains unknown. Its contributions to the diet may have included the leaves as well as the seeds but even this method of "double-harvesting" which is typical of other chenopods and seed annuals is unverified.

Amaranth seeds have been identified from several Eastern sites but in neither a context nor quantity to suggest their place in the Eastern

Agricultural Complex. However, Fritz' (1984:559) investigation of Ozark desiccated botanical remains has recognized the domesticated grain amaranth (*Amaranthus hypochondriacus* L.). It, too, is late and of equally limited distribution. It seems independent of the same species in the Southwest, and an eastern Mexican origin is posited for it. Again, the dietary contribution of this domesticate must await future research.

CULTIVATION OF OTHER PLANTS

Several food plants were undoubtedly of local importance and received special attention from prehistoric Indians. The Jerusalem artichoke (*Helianthus tuberosus* L.) spreads into old fields and is easy both to maintain and to propogate through simple harvesting methods and the elimination of competitors. Others like purslane (*Portulaca oleracea*) may have been a "campfollower" from Mexico whose seeds were disseminated by accident while gathered as a potherb (Chapman et al. 1974). Even tree species were introduced beyond their range by human foragers (Black 1978).

Ethnographically, medicinal and ceremonial plants require the same cultivation techniques as food plants. Only a few, however, follow the broad pattern of protection, sewing, and transplanting exhibited by tobacco. The trade and planting of rootstock of sweet flag (*Acorus calamus*) by historic Indians probably had prehistoric antecedents if we interpret its modern distribution correctly (Black 1978). In the Southeast the yaupon (*Ilex vomitoria*) associated with corn production was also transplanted inland from its coastal plain habitat to serve as a ready ceremonial purifier (Hudson 1979). Most other ritual plants were more limited in their cultivation, if at all, and only a few persons in a society would care for them. This generalization contrasts with food production where, at least, one gender would practice food production and common uses could be found over large geographic areas in prehistory and across ethnographic linguistic boundaries (e.g., Munson 1973).

CONCLUSION

Prehistoric food production north of Mexico was as diverse as any place in the world. While some 11 domesticated plants diffused from Mexico at different times, a comparable number of native plants were domesticated or intensively cultivated. The cultural importance of each depended upon when it was introduced and upon associated plants in the economy. The grouping of food plants into complexes reflects temporal and functional similarities.

For most of prehistory the East and the Southwest were independent from each other. The first domesticate in the eastern United States was a small gourd cucurbit introduced from Mexico, unless it was domesticated from the Texas gourd more than 7000 years ago in Texas. The use of cucurbit seeds did not transform the foraging economy immediately nor did the idea of domestication lead to obvious manipulation of indigenous plants. The bottle gourd came several millennia later also from an eastern Mexican source. By 4000 years ago cultural contacts, demography, and probably social relations in the Late Archaic changed sufficiently that native annual plants were used more extensively relative to tree nuts and three—sumpweed, sunflower, and a chenopod—actually were domesticated. Several others were sown outside their natural habitats. These changes in human-plant relation show that new plant domestication was not inevitable, after all gourds had been present for 3000 years previously, that domesticated plants were additive in the diet, and that the subsistence impact of native domesticates was not synchronous in the East. Certainly expanded horticulture of small starchy seeds was earlier in Kentucky than in Illinois.

The Southwest witnessed an initial introduction from highland west Mexico of a large gourd cucurbit and corn about 3000 years ago. Shortly later bottle gourd and common beans completed a new subsistence base for high elevation foragers. Here, however, the economic transformation favoring domesticated crops was quite rapid and was not accompanied by domestication of native plants.

Corn and later beans were transported eastward by unknown means and following an unspecified southern Plains corridor. Corn was present several centuries before its dietary staple potential was realized in the Late Woodland and Mississippian cultures of the Midwest. Beans arrived after a large field horticulture for corn was already established.

A second Mexican crop complex presumably was brought by traders to the Hohokam-related cultures of the Sonoran Desert region. The cotton, beans, squashes, and amaranth of this group expanded the agrarian diet of sedentary people and were maintained by elaborate water control. With the exception of cotton and the cushaw squash, this crop complex was limited in its distribution. However, dependence upon a field agriculture and the need for options during seasons of want may have led to the manipulation and perhaps domestication of several native grasses. Other plants were given special treatment as well.

The East never benefited from any of these Lower Sonoran crops until the Spanish introduced them. But, it did receive three more plants from eastern Mexico: tobacco, chenopod, and grain amaranth. While tobacco as a ritual plant was grown throughout the farming area of the East, the two edible seed plants were limited to Arkansas for reasons still to be explained. Again, however, none of these plants reached the Southwest from the East and it was not until the arrival of the Spanish that domesticated tobacco from Mexico (as well as chiles) was introduced to the Southwest.

It would be a mistake to look solely to archaeobotany for examples of processes of food production. They are practiced today with both the devil's claw and the European weed mustard (Bye 1979) undergoing domestication. North America remains an active laboratory for understanding plant production, and with the rapid pace of discovery by paleoethnobotanists, we should expect exciting information about additional indigenous plant domestication and equally enlightening insight into changing subsistence technology required to propogate both newly recognized and the familiar food plants discussed by contributors to this volume.

Bibliography

Adair, Mary J.
 1977 Subsistence Exploitation at the Young Site. M.A. thesis, Department of Anthropology, University of Kansas.
 1984 Prehistoric Cultivation in the Central Plains: Its Development and Importance. Ph.D. dissertation, University of Kansas, Lawrence.

Adams, Karen R.
 1984 Barley (Hordeum) as a Possible Domesticate in the Prehistoric American Southwest. Paper presented at the twenty-fifth annual meeting of The Society for Economic Botany, College Station.

Adovasio, J.M., and W.C. Johnson
 1980 The Appearance of Cultigens in the Upper Ohio Valley: A View From Meadowcroft Rockshelter. *Pennsylvania Archaeologist* 51:63-80.

Aellen, Paul, and Theodor Just
 1943 Key and Synopsis of the American Species of the Genus Chenopodium L. *American Midland Naturalist* 30:47-76.

Aginsky, Burt W.
 1939 Population Control in the Shanel (Pomo) Tribe. *American Sociological Review* 10(2):209-10.

Aguirre-González, Carlos D.
 1977 Competencia entre el Polen de Maiz y de Teocintle durante la Fecundación. Tesis de Maestro en Ciencias. Escuela Nacional de Agricultura, Chapingo, Mexico.

Albert, Lois E.
 1981 *Ferndale Bog and Natural Lake: Five Thousand Years of Environmental Change in Southeastern Oklahoma.* Oklahoma Archeological Survey, Studies in Oklahoma's Past 7.

Alexander, Hubert G., and Paul Reiter
 1935 Report on the Excavation of Jemez Cave, New Mexico. *University of New Mexico Bulletin* No. 278.

Alexander, Robert Kirk
 1974 The Archaeology of Conejo Shelter: A Study of Cultural Stability at an Archaic Rockshelter Site in Southwestern Texas. Ph.D. dissertation, Department of Anthropology, The University of Texas at Austin.

Allen, Harry
    1974   The Bagundji of the Darling Basin; Cereal Gatherers in an Uncertain
            Environment. *World Archaeology* 5:309-22.
Ames, Oakes
    1939   *Economic Annuals and Human Cultures.* Cambridge:Botanical Museum of
            Harvard University.
Amsden, Charles Avery
    1949   *Prehistoric Southwesterners from Basketmaker to Pueblo.* Los An-
            geles:Southwest Museum.
Anderson, Edgar
    1948   Racial Identity of the Corn from Castle Park. *The Archeology of Castle Park,
            Dinosaur National Monument.* University of Colorado Studies, Series in
            Anthropology 2:91-92.
    1952   *Plants, Man and Life.* Boston:Little, Brown.
Anderson, Edgar, and W.L. Brown
    1948   A Morphological Analysis of Row Number in Maize. *Annals of the Missouri
            Botanical Gardens* 35:323-36.
    1952   Origin of Corn Belt Maize and Its Genetic Significance. *Heterosis*, edited
            by John W. Gowen, pp. 124-28. New York:Hafner Publishing Company.
Anderson, Edgar, and Hugh C. Cutler
    1942   Races of *Zea mays*: I, Their Recognition and Classification. *Annals of the
            Missouri Botanical Garden* 29:69-86.
Anderson, Harry G.
    1959   Food Habits of Migrating Ducks in Illinois. *Illinois Natural History Survey
            Bulletin* 27(4):289-344.
Andreas, Lyter and Co.
    1873   Atlas Map, Pike County, Illiois. Davenport, Iowa:Andreas, Lyter & Co.
Antevs, Ernst
    1955   Geologic-Climatic Dating in the West. *American Antiquity* 20(4):317-35.
Applegarth, J.D.
    1977   Macrofloral Remains. *Excavation at Sparks Rockshelter (15JO19), Johnson
            County, Kentucky,* by P. Fitzgibbons, J. Adovasio, J. Donahue. *Pennsylvania
            Archaeologist* 47(5).
Arbingast, Stanley A., Lorrin G. Kennamer, Robert H. Ryan, James R. Buchanan,
William L. Hezlap, L. Tuffly Ellis, Terry G. Jordan, Charles T. Granger, and Charles P.
Zlatkovich
    1973   *Atlas of Texas.* The University of Texas at Austin, Bureau of Business
            Research.
Arnold, James R., and Willard F. Libby
    1950   *Radiocarbon Dates.* University of Chicago Institute of Nuclear Studies.
Asch, David L., and Nancy B. Asch
    1977   Chenopod as Cultigen: A Re-evaluation of Some Prehistoric Collections
            from Eastern North America. *Midcontinental Journal of Archaeology*
            2(1):3-45.
    1978   The Economic Potential of *Iva annua* and Its Prehistoric Importance in
            the Lower Illinois Valley. *The Nature and Status of Ethnobotany*, edited by
            Richard I. Ford, pp. 301-41. University of Michigan, Museum of An-
            thropology, Anthropological Papers, 67.
    1982   A Chronology of the Development of Prehistoric Horticulture in West
            Central Illinois. Paper presented at the 47th annual meeting of the Soci-
            ety for American Archaeology, Minneapolis.
    1983   Archeobotany. *Excavations at the Smiling Dan Site: Delineation of Site Struc-
            ture and Function During the Middle Woodland Period*, edited by Barbara D.
            Stafford and Mark B. Sant. Center for American Archeology, Contract
            Archeology Program Report of Investigations 137.
    1984   *Archeobotany of Campbell Hollow: The Archaic Occupations.* Center for Amer-
            ican Archeology Archeobotanical Laboratory Report 64.

Asch, David L., Kenneth B. Farnsworth, and Nancy B. Asch
1979   Woodland Subsistence and Settlement in West Central Illinois. *Hopewell Archaeology: The Chillicothe Conference*, edited by David S. Brose and N'omi Greber, pp. 80-85. Ohio:Kent State University Press.
Asch, Nancy B., and David L. Asch
1979   *Plant Remains from Deer Track, A Late Woodland Site in Adams County, Illinois.* Northwestern University Archeological Program, Archeobotanical Laboratory, Report 27.
1979a   Archeobotany of the Koster Site: The Early and Middle Archaic Occupations. Paper presented at the 44th annual meeting of the Society for American Archaeology, Vancouver, British Columbia.
1980   The Dickson Camp and Pond Site. *Dickson Camp and Pond: Two Early Havana Tradition Sites in the Central Illinois Valley*, by Anne-Marie Cantwell. Illinois State Museum Reports of Investigations 36.
1981   Archeobotany of Newbridge, Carlin, and Weitzer Sites—the White Hall Components. *Faunal Exploitation and Resource Selection: Early Late Woodland Subsistence in the Lower Illinois Valley*, by Bonnie Whatley Styles. Northwestern University Archeological Program Scientific Papers 3.
1982   Analysis of the Plant Remains. *Cypress Land, a Late Archaic/Early Woodland Site in the Lower Illinois River Floodplain, Greene County, Illinois*, by Michael D. Conner, Center for American Archeology Contract Archeology Program Report of Investigation 118.
1983   *Archeobotany of the Napolean Hollow Site, Pike County, Westcentral Illinois: The Woodland Period Occupation.* Center for American Archeology, Archeobotanical Laboratory, Report 50.
1984   Archeobotany. *Archeological Testing Along FAS 603 in Pike County, Illinois.* Part II: *The Hill Creek Site*, edited by Michael D. Conner, Center for American Archeology Contract Archeology Program Report of Investigation 151.
Asch, Nancy B., Richard I. Ford, and David L. Asch
1972   *Paleoethnobotany of the Koster Site: The Archaic Horizons.* Illinois State Museum, Reports of Investigations, 24.
Aten, Lawrence E.
1972   *An Assessment of the Archaeological Resources to be Affected by the Taylors Bayou Drainage and Flood Control Project, Texas.* The University of Texas at Austin, Texas Archaeological Salvage Project, Research Report 7.
1979   Indians of the Upper Texas Coast: Ethnohistoric and Archeological Frameworks. Ph.D. dissertation, Department of Anthropology, The University of Texas at Austin.
1981   Determining Seasonality of *Rangia cuneata* from Gulf Coast Shell Middens. *Bulletin of the Texas Archeological Society* 52:179-200.
1983   *Indians of the Upper Texas Coast.* New York: Academic Press.
Aten, Lawrence E., C.K. Chandler, Al B. Wesolowsky, and R.M. Malina
1976   *Excavations at the Harris County Boys' School Cemetery: Analysis of Galveston Bay Area Mortuary Practices.* Texas Archaeological Society Special Publication 3.
Bailey, Liberty H.
1930   Three Discussions in Cucurbitaceae. *Gentes Herbarum* 2:175-86.
1943   Species of *Cucurbita*. *Gentes Herbarum* 6:267-322.
1944   *Manual of Cultivated Plants.* New York:Macmillan.
Baker, Victor R., and Margarida Marie Penteado-Orellana
1977   Adjustment to Quaternary Climatic Change by the Colorado River in Central Texas. *Journal of Geology* 85:395-422.
Bandelier, Fanny
1904   *The Journey of Alvar Nuñez Cabeza de Vaca.* New York:Allerton.
Barbour, Roger
1973   Vertebrates of the Red River Area, Kentucky. In: Environmental Impact

Statement, Red River Lake, Kentucky, Kentucky River Basin. Draft of a report prepared by the U.S. Army Corps of Engineers, Louisville, Kentucky.

Barrett, Samuel A.
1952   Material Aspects of Pomo Culture. *Bulletin, Public Museum of the City of Milwaukee* 20 (Pts. 1,2).

Bartlett, Alexandra S., E.S. Barghoorn, and R. Berger
1969   Fossil Maize from Panama. *Science* 165:389-90.

Bartram, William
1958   *The Travels of William Bartram.* Naturalist's edition, edited by Francis Harper. New Haven: Yale University Press.

Baumhoff, Martin
1963   Ecological Determinants of Aboriginal California Populations. *University of California Publications in American Archaeology and Ethnology* 49(2):155-236.

Beadle, George W.
1972   The Mystery of Maize. *Field Museum of Natural History Bulletin* 43:1-11.
1980   The Ancestry of Corn. *Scientific American* 242(1):112-119.

Bean, Lowell B., and Katherine S. Saubel
1972   *Temalpakh.* Morongo Indian Reservation:Malki Museum Press.

Beardsley, Gretchen
1939   The Groundnut as Used by the Indians of Eastern North America. *Papers of the Michigan Academy of Science, Arts and Letters* 25:507-15.

Bell, Robert E., ed.
1984   *Prehistory of Oklahoma.* New York:Academic Press.

Bemis, William P., J.W. Berry, C.W. Weber, and Thomas W. Whitaker
1978   The Buffalo Gourd: A New Potential Horticultural Crop. *HortScience* 13(3):235-40.

Bemis, William P., L.D. Curtis, C.W. Weber, and J. Berry
1978   The Feral Buffalo Gourd, *Cucurbita foetidissima. Economic Botany* 32(1):87-95.

Bemis, William P., A.M. Rhodes, Thomas W. Whitaker, and S.G. Carmer
1970   Numerical Taxonomy Applied to *Cucurbita* Relationships. *American Journal of Botany* 57(4):404-12.

Bender, Margaret M.
1968   Mass Spectometric Studies of Carbon 13 Variations in Corn and Other Grasses. *Radiocarbon* 10:468-72.

Bender, Margaret M., David A. Baerreis, and Raymond L. Steventon
1981   Further Light on Carbon Isotopes and Hopewell Agriculture. *American Antiquity* 46:346-53.

Benedict, James B.
1973   Chronology of Cirque Glaciation, Colorado Front Range. *Journal of Quarternary Research* 3(4).
1979   Getting Away From It All: A Study of Man, Mountains, and the Two-Drought Altithermal. *Southwestern Lore* 45(3):1-12.

Benfer, Alice, and Bob Benfer
1962   A Vertical Cave Burial in Uvalde County, Texas. *The Texas Caver* 7(4):41-42.

Benn, David W.
1974   Seed Analysis and Its Implications for an Initial Middle Missouri Site in South Dakota. *Plains Anthropologist* 19(63):55-72.

Benn, David W., ed.
1981   *Archaeological Investigations at the Rainbow Site, Plymouth County, Iowa.* Archaeological Research Center, Luther College, Decorah, Iowa. Submitted to Interagency Archeological Services, Denver.

Benson, Lyman
1962   *Plant Taxonomy* New York:Ronald Press.

Berry, Claudia F.
    1980   Regional Overview. *Cultural Resources Overview: The Middle Gila Basin*, by Claudia F. Berry and William S. Marmaduke, pp. 101-97. 2 Vols. Draft submitted to Water and Power Resources Service, Arizona Project Office by Northland Anthropological Research, Inc., Flagstaff.

Berry, Michael S.
    1980   Time, Space and Transition in Anasazi Prehistory. Ph.D. dissertation, Department of Anthropology, University of Utah.
    1982   *Time, Space, and Transition. Anasazi Prehistory.* Salt Lake City: University of Utah Press.

Binford, Lewis R.
    1968   Post-Pleistocene Adaptations. *New Perspectives in Archaeology*, edited by Lewis Binford and Sally Binford, pp. 313-41. New York: Academic Press.

Black, M. Jean
    1978   Plant Dispersal by Native North Americans in the Canadian Subarctic. *The Nature and Status of Ethnobotany*, edited by Richard I. Ford, pp. 255-62. Anthropological Papers, Museum of Anthropology, University of Michigan.

Black, Meredith
    1963   The Distribution and Archeological Significance of the Marsh Elder, *Iva annua* L. *Papers of the Michigan Academy of Science, Arts, and Letters* 48:541-47.

Blair, Frank W.
    1950   The Biotic Provinces of Texas. *The Texas Journal of Science* 2(1):93-117.
    1952   Mammals of the Tamaulipan Biotic Province in Texas. *The Texas Journal of Science* 4(2):230-50.

Blake, Leonard W.
    1981   Early Acceptance of Watermelon by Indians of the United States. *Journal of Ethnobiology* 1(2):193- 99.

Blake, S.F.
    1939   A New Variety of *Iva ciliata* from Indian Rock Shelters in the South-Central United States. *Rhodora* 41:81-86.

Bohrer, Vorsila L.
    1962   Nature and Interpretation of Ethnobotanical Materials from Tonto National Monument, edited by Louis R. Caywood. Archeological Studies at Tonto National Monument, Arizona. *Southwestern Monuments Association Technical Series* 2:75-114.
    1966   *Pollen Analysis of the Hay Hollow Site East of Snowflake, Arizona.* Geochronology Laboratories, University of Arizona, Tucson, Interim Research Report 12.
    1970   Ethnobotanical Aspects of Snaketown, A Hohokam Village in Southern Arizona. *American Antiquity* 35(4):413-30.
    1972   Paleoecology of the Hay Hollow Site, Arizona. *Fieldiana: Anthropology* (1).
    1975   The Prehistoric and Historic Role of the Cool-Season Grasses in the Southwest. *Economic Botany* 29(3):199-207.
    1982   Former Dietary Patterns of People as Determined from Archaic-Age Plant Remains from Fresnal Shelter, Southcentral New Mexico. *The Artifact* 19 (3-4):41-50.
    1983   New Life from Ashes: The Tale of the Burnt Bush (Rhus trilobata). *Desert Plants* 5:122-24.
    n.d.   Some Speculation Bearing on Domesticated and Wild Crops Harvested from the Marginal Agricultural Land Surveyed by the Central Arizona Ecotone Project. Ms. on file at Southern University, Center for Archaeological Investigations, Carbondale, Illinois.

Bohrer, Vorsila L., Hugh C. Cutler, and Jonathan D. Sauer
    1969   Carbonized Plant Remains from Two Hohokam Sites, Arizona BB:13:41 and Arizona BB:13:50. *The Kiva* 35(1):1-10.

Bohrer, Vorsila L., and Gloria J. Fenner
    1974   Cotton, Squashes, Gourds, Uncultivated Plants. *Casas Grandes, A Fallen Trading Center of the Gran Chichimeca*, by Charles C. DiPeso, John B. Rinaldo, and Gloria J. Fenner, Vol. 8, pp. 314-17. Flagstaff:Northland Press.
Bonnie, Michael E., K.R. Holz, C.C. Gill, J.P. Weiler, and Stanley A. Arbingast
    1970   *Atlas of Mexico*. Austin:The University of Texas, Bureau of Business Research.
Boserup, Ester
    1963   *The Conditions of Agricultural Growth: The Economics of Agrarian Change Under Population Pressure*. Chicago:Aldine.
Bourne, Edward G., ed.
    1904   *Narratives of the Career of Hernando De Soto*. Vols. 1 and 2. New York:A.S. Barnes.
Bowen, William R.
    1979   The Late Archaic in the Upper Duck Valley. *Tennessee Anthropologist* 4:140-59.
Braidwood, Robert J.
    1960   The Agricultural Revolution. *Scientific American* 203:130-41.
Braun, E. Lucy
    1950   *The Deciduous Forest of Eastern North America*. Philadelphia:Blakiston Company.
Bray, Warwick
    1977   From Foraging to Farming in Early Mexico. *Hunters, Gatherers and First Farmers beyond Europe: An Archaeological Survey*, edited by J.V.S. Megaw. Leicestershire University Press.
Brenckle, J.F.
    1946   Notes on the Avicularia. II. *Phytologia* 2(5):169-71.
Brendel, Frederick
    1870   Distribution of Immigrant Plants. *American Entomologist and Botanist* 2(12):378-79.
Breternitz, David A.
    1969   Radiocarbon Dates: Eastern Colorado. *Plains Anthropologist* 14(44, Pt. 1).
    1970   *Archeological Excavations in Dinosaur National Monument, Colorado-Utah, 1964-1965*. University of Colorado Studies, Series in Anthropology, 17.
Bretting, P.K.
    1982   Morphological Differentiation of *Proboscidea parviflora* ssp. *parviflora* (Martyniacca) Under Domestication. *American Journal of Botany* 69:1531-37.
Brewbaker, J.L.
    1964   *Agricultural Genetics*. New York:Prentice-Hall.
Brewer, Andrea J.
    1973   Analysis of Floral Remains from the Higgs Site (40Lo45). *Excavation of the Higgs and Doughty Sites: I-75 Salvage Archaeology*, edited by Major C. R. McCollough and C. H. Faulkner, pp. 141-44. Tennessee Archaeological Society, Miscellaneous Papers, No. 12.
Briuer, Frederick L.
    1977   Plant and Animal Remains from Caves and Rock Shelters of the Chevelon Canyon, Arizona: Methods for Isolating Cultural Depositional Processes. Ph.D. dissertation, Department of Anthropology, University of California, Los Angeles.
Broida, Mary
    1983   Maize in Kentucky Fort Ancient Diets; An Analysis of Carbon Isotope Ratios in Human Bone. M.A. thesis, Department of Anthropology, University of Kentucky, Lexington.
Bronson, Bennet
    1977   The Earliest Farmers: Demography as Cause and Consequence. *Origins of Agriculture*, edited by Charles A. Reed, pp. 23-48. The Hague:Mouton.

Brooks, Richard H., Lawrence Kaplan, Hugh C. Cutler, and Thomas W. Whitaker
    1962   Plant Material from a Cave on the Rio Zape, Durango, Mexico. *American Antiquity* 27(3):356-369.

Brown, James A., and Robert K. Vierra
    1983   What Happened in the Middle Archaic? Introduction to an Ecological Approach to Koster Site Archaeology. *Archaic Hunters and Gatherers in the American Midwest,* edited by James Phillips and James A. Brown, pp. 165-95. New York:Academic Press.

Brown, William L., and Edgar Anderson
    1947   The Northern Flint Corns. *Annals of the Missouri Botanical Gardens* 34(1):1-28.

Broyles, Bettye J.
    1971   *Second Preliminary Report: The St. Albans Site, Kanawha County, West Virginia.* West Virginia Geological and Econonic Survey, Morgantown, Reports of Investigations 3.

Bryant, Vaughn M., Jr.
    1974   Pollen Analysis of Prehistoric Human Feces from Mammoth Cave. *Archeology of the Mammoth Cave Area,* edited by Patty Jo Watson, pp. 203-09. New York: Academic Press.
    1977   A 16,000 Year Pollen Record of Vegetational Change in Central Texas. *Palynology* 1:143-56.

Bryant, Vaughn M., Jr., and Harry J. Shafer
    1977   The Late Quaternary Paleoenvironment of Texas: A Model for the Archeologist. *Bulletin of the Texas Archeological Society* 48:1-25.

Bryd, K.M. and Robert W. Neuman
    1978   Archaeological Data Relative to Prehistoric Subsistence in the Lower Mississippi River Alluvial Valley. *Man and Environment in the Lower Mississippi Valley,* edited by S.B. Hilliard, pp. 9-21. Geoscience and Man, 19. Louisiana State University, Baton Rouge.

Bryson, Reid A., David A. Baerreis, and Wayne M. Wendland
    1970   The Character of Late-Glacial and Post-Glacial Climatic Changes. *Pleistocene and Recent Environments of the Central Great Plains,* edited by W. Dort, Jr., and J. Jones, Jr. pp. 53-74. University of Kansas, Department of Geology, Special Publication 3.

Buikstra, Jane E.
    1976   *Hopewell in the Lower Illinois Valley: A Regional Study of Human Biological Variability and Prehistoric Mortuary Behavior.* Northwestern University Archaeological Program Scientific Papers 2.

Bullard, William R.
    1962   *The Cerro Colorado Site and Pithouse Architecture in the Southwestern United States Prior to A.D. 900.* Papers of the Peabody Museum of Archeology and Ethnology, Harvard University 44(2).

Burkhill, I.H.
    1953   Habits of Man and the Origins of Cultivated Plants in the Old World. *Proc. Linn. Soc. London* 164:12- 42.

Buskirk, Winfred
    1949   Western Apache Subsistence Economy. Ph.D dissertation, Department of Anthropology, University of New Mexico.

Bye, Robert A., Jr.
    1979   Incipient Domestication of Mustards in Northwest Mexico. *The Kiva* 44(2-3):237-56.

Caldwell, Joseph R.
    1958   *Trend and Tradition in the Prehistory of the Eastern United States.* Memoirs of the American Anthropological Association, 88.
    1977   Cultural Evolution in the Old World and the New, Leading to the Beginnings and Spread of Agriculture. *Origins of Agriculture,* edited by C. Reed, pp. 77-88. The Hague:Mouton.

Campbell, Alastair H.
    1965   Elementary Food Production by the Australian Aborigines. *Mankind* 6(5):206-11.
Campbell, Thomas N.
    1948   The Merrell Site: Archaeological Remains Associated with Alluvial Terrace Deposits in Central Texas. *Bulletin of the Texas Archeological and Paleontological Society* 19:7-35.
    1960   Archeology of the Central and Southern Sections of the Texas Coast. *Bulletin of the Texas Archeological Society* 29: 145-175.
    1976   Archaeological Investigations at the Morhiss Site, Victoria County, Texas 1932-1940. *An Archaeological Survey of Coleto Creek, Victoria and Goliad Counties, Texas,* by Anne Fox and Thomas R. Hester, pp. 81-85. The University of Texas at San Antonio, Center for Archaeological Research, Archaeological Survey Report 18.
Campbell, Thomas N., and T.J. Campbell
    1981   *Historic Indian Groups of the Choke Canyon Reservoir and Surrounding Area, Southern Texas.* Choke Canyon Series: Vol. 1. The University of Texas at San Antonio, Center for Archaeological Research.
Carlson, J.B.
    1979   Bulldozers and Archeology: Can They Be Compatible? The Tellico Dam. *Early Man* (Summer 1978):3-11.
Carr, Christopher
    1982   *Handbook on Soil Resistivity Surveying: Interpretation of Data from Earthen Archeological Sites.* Evanston, Illinois:Center for American Archeology Press.
Carr, John T., Jr.
    1967   *The Climate and Physiography of Texas.* Texas Water Development Board, Report 53.
Carstens, Kenneth C.
    1974   Archeological Surface Reconnaissance of Mammoth Cave National Park, Kentucky. Master's thesis, Department of Anthropology, Washington University.
    1980   Archeology of the Central Kentucky Karst. Ph.D. dissertation, Department of Anthropology, Washington University, St. Louis.
Carter, George F.
    1945   *Plant Geography and Culture History in the American Southwest.* Viking Fund Publications in Anthropology 5.
Castetter, Edward F., and Willis H. Bell
    1941   *Pima and Papago Indian Agriculture.* Albuquerque:University of New Mexico Press.
Castetter, Edward F., and Morris E. Opler
    1936   The Ethnobiology of the Chiracahua and Mescalero Apache. *University of New Mexico Bulletin* 297.
Chapman, Carl H.
    1954   Preliminary Salvage Archaeology in the Pomme de Terre Reservoir, Missouri. *Missouri Archaeologist* 16(3-4).
    1974   *The Archaeology of Missouri,* I. Columbia:University of Missouri Press.
Chapman, Jefferson
    1973   *The Icehouse Bottom Site 40MR23.* Department of Anthropology, University of Tennessee, Report of Investigations 13.
    1975   *The Rose Island Site and the Bifurcate Point Tradition.* Department of Anthropology, University of Tennessee, Report of Investigations, 14.
    1977   *Archaic Period Research in the Lower Little Tennessee River Valley.* Department of Anthropology, University of Tennessee, Report of Investigations 18.
    1978   *The Bacon Farm Site and a Buried Site Reconnaissance.* Department of Anthropology, University of Tennessee, Report of Investigations 23.

Chapman, Jefferson, P.A. Delcourt, Patricia Cridlebaugh, Andrea Brewer Shea, and Hazel R. Delcourt
1982 Man-Land Interaction: 10,000 Years of American Indian Impact on Native Ecosystems in the Lower Little Tennessee River Valley, Eastern Tennessee. *Southeastern Archaeology* 1:115-21.

Chapman, Jefferson and Andrea Brewer Shea
1977 Paleoecological and Cultural Interpretations of Plant Remains Recovered from Archaic Period Sites in the Lower Little Tennessee River Valley. Paper presented at the 34th annual meeting of the Southeastern Archaeological Conference.
1980 The Archaeobotanical Record: Early Archaic to Contact in the Lower Little Tennessee River Valley. Paper presented at the 37th annual meeting of the Southeastern Archaeological Conference.
1981 The Archaeobotanical Record: Early Archaic to Contact in the Lower Little Tennessee River Valley. *Tennessee Anthropologist* VI:64-84.

Chapman, Jefferson, Robert B. Stewart, and Richard A. Yarnell
1974 Archeological Evidence for Precolumbian of *Portulaca oleracea* and *Mollugo verticillata* into Eastern North America. *Economic Botany* 28(4):411-12.

Childe, V. Gordon
1936 *Man Makes Himself*. London:Watts.
1952 *New Light on the Most Ancient East*. 4th ed. London:Routledge and Kegan Paul.

Chomko, Stephen A.
1976 The Phillips Spring Site, 23HI216: Harry S. Truman Reservoir, Missouri Archaeological Salvage Project. Illinois State Museum and University of Missouri; Contract CX-6000-4-0130. Columbia, Missouri.
1978 Phillips Spring, 23HI216, a Multicomponent Site in the Western Missouri Ozarks. *Plains Anthropologist* 23:235-55.

Chomko, Stephen A., and Gary W. Crawford
1978 Plant Husbandry in Prehistoric Eastern North America: New Evidence for its Development. *American Antiquity* 43(3):405-08.

Claassen, Cheryl
1983 Shellfishing Seasons in the Prehistoric Southeastern United States. Paper presented at the 40th annual meeting of the Southeastern Archaeological Conference, Columbia, South Carolina.

Cleland, Charles
1966 *The Prehistoric Animal Ecology and Ethnozoology of the Upper Great Lakes Region*. Museum of Anthropology, University of Michigan, Anthropological Papers 29.

Cobb, James E.
1978 The Middle Woodland Occupations of the Banks V Site, 40CF111. *Fifth Report of the Normandy Archaeological Project*, by Charles Faulkner and Major McCollough, Department of Anthropology. University of Tennessee, Report of Investigations 20.

Cobb, James E., and Andrea Brewer Shea
1977 The Identification of *Helianthus annuus* L. from the Owl Hollow Site, 40FR7, Franklin County, Tennessee. *Tennessee Anthropologist* 2:190-98.

Coe, Joffre Lanning
1964 The Formative Cultures of the Carolina Piedmont. *American Philosophical Society Transactions* 54(5).

Cohen, Mark N.
1977 Population Pressure and the Origins of Agriculture: An Archaeological Example from the Coast of Peru. *Origins of Agriculture*, edited by Charles Reed, pp. 135-77. The Hague:Mouton.

Collins, G.N.
    1914   A Drought-Resisting Adaptation in Seedlings of Hopi Maize. *Journal of Argicultural Research* 1:293-306.
    1921   Teosinte in Mexico. *Journal of Heredity* 12:338-50.
Collins, G.N., and J.H. Kempton
    1920   A Teosinte-Maize Hybrid. *Journal of Agricultural Research* 19:1-37.
Collins, Michael B., ed.
    1979   Excavations at Four Archaic Sites in the Lower Ohio Valley, Jefferson County, Kentucky. Occasional Papers in Anthropology, No. 1. Department of Anthropology, University of Kansas.
Colson, Elizabeth
    1979   In Good Years and in Bad: Food Strategies of Self-Reliant Societies. *Journal of Anthropological Research* 35(1):18-29.
Conard, Nicholas, David L. Asch, Nancy B. Asch, David Elmore, Harry E. Gove, Meyer Rubin, James A. Brown, Michael D. Wiant, Kenneth B. Farnsworth and Thomas G. Cook
    1983   *Prehistoric Horticulture in Illinois: Accelerator Radiocarbon Dating of the Evidence.* University of Rochester Nuclear Structure Research Laboratory, Report 257.
    1984   Accelerator Radiocarbon Dating of Evidence for Prehistoric Horticulture in Illinois. *Nature* 308:443-46.
Conklin, Harold C.
    1957   Hanunódo Agriculture: A Report on an Integral System of Shifting Cultivation in the Philippines. FAO Forestry Development Paper 12.
Conner, Michael D., ed.
    1984   *Archeological Testing Along FAS 603 in Pike County, Illinois.* Part II: *The Hill Creek Site.* Center for American Archeology Contract Archeology Program Report of Investigation 151.
Cook, Thomas G.
    1976   *Koster: An Artifact Analysis of Two Archaic Phases in Westcentral Illinois.* Northwestern Archeological Program Prehistoric Records 1.
    n.d.   Educational Archaeology and the Lagoon Site. Center for American Archeology, Studies in Educational Archeology, in press.
Corbin, James E.
    1974   A Model for Cultural Succession for the Coastal Bend Area of Texas. *Bulletin of the Texas Archeological Society* 45:29-54.
Correll, Donovan S., and M.C. Johnson
    1970   *Manual of Vascular Plants of Texas.* Renner, Texas: Contributions of the Texas Research Foundation.
Cosgrove, C.B.
    1947   Caves of the Upper Gila and Hueco Areas in New Mexico and Texas. *Papers of the Peabody Museum of American Archeology and Ethnology, Harvard University* 24(2):1-181.
Coulter, John M.
    1891-   *Botany of Western Texas.* Washington, D.C.:
    1894   Contributions from the National Herbarium.
Cowan, C. Wesley
    1975   An Archaeological Survey and Assessment of the Proposed Red River Reservoir in Powell, Wolf and Menifee Counties, Kentucky. Report submitted to the National Park Service Interagency Archaeological Services, Atlanta, Georgia, by the University of Kentucky, Museum of Anthropology.
    1976   Test Excavations in the Proposed Red River Lake, Kentucky: 1974 Season. Report submitted to the National Park Service Interagency Archaeological Services Office, Atlanta, Georgia, by the University of Kentucky, Museum of Anthropology.
    1978   The Prehistoric Use and Distribution of Maygrass in Eastern North

America: Cultural and Phytogeographical Implications. *The Nature and Status of Ethnobotany*, edited by Richard I. Ford, pp. 263-88. University of Michigan Museum of Anthropology, Anthropological Papers, 67.

1979   Excavations at the Haystack Rock Shelters, Powell County, Kentucky. *Midcontinental Journal of Archaeology* 4(2):1-33.

1979a   Prehistoric Plant Utilization at the Rogers Rockshelter, Powell County, Kentucky. Master's thesis, Department of Anthropology, The University of Kentucky.

Cowan, C. Wesley, H. Edwin Jackson, Katherine Moore, Andrew Nicklehoff, and Tristine L. Smart

1981   The Cloudsplitter Rockshelter, Menifee County, Kentucky: A Preliminary Report. *Southeastern Archaeological Conference Bulletin* 24:60-76.

Cowan, C. Wesley, and Frederick T. Wilson

1977   An Archaeological Survey of the Red River Gorge Area. Published and distributed by the Kentucky Heritage Commission, Frankfort, Kentucky.

Crane, H.R.

1956   University of Michigan Radiocarbon Dates I. *Science* 124(3224):664-72.

Crane, H.R. and James B. Griffin

1958a   University of Michigan Radiocarbon Dates II. *Science* 127(3306): 1098-1103.

1958b   University of Michigan Radiocarbon Dates III. *Science* 128(332):1117-22.

1960   University of Michigan Radiocarbon Dates V. Radiocarbon supplement of *American Journal of Science* 2:31-48.

Crawford, Daymond D.

1965   The Granite Beach Site, Llano County, Texas. *Bulletin of the Texas Archeological Society* 36:71- 97.

Crawford, Gary

1978   Analysis and Implications of Plant Remains from the Carlston Annis Site and Boules Site, Kentucky. Shell Mound Archaeological Project Report.

1982   Late Archaic Plant Remains from West-Central Kentucky: A Summary. *Midcontinental Journal of Archaeology* 7:205-24.

Crites, Gary D.

1978a   Paleoethnobotany of the Normandy Reservoir in the Upper Duck River Valley, Tennessee. M.A. thesis, Department of Anthropology, University of Tennessee.

1978b   Plant Food Utilization Patterns during the Middle Woodland Owl Hollow Phase in Tennessee: A Preliminary Report. *Tennessee Anthropologist* 3:79-92.

Crites, Gary D., and R. Dale Terry

1984   Nutritive Value of Maygrass, *Phalaris caroliniana*. *Economic Botany* 38:114-20.

Crook, Wilson W., Jr., and R.K. Harris

1952   Trinity Aspect of the Archaic Horizon: The Carrollton and Elam Foci. *Bulletin of the Texas Archeological and Paleontological Society* 23:7-38.

Cutler, Hugh C.

1952   A Preliminary Survey of Plant Remains of Tularosa Cave. *Mogollon Cultural Continuity and Change, the Stratigraphic Analysis of Tularosa and Cordova Caves*, by Paul Martin, J. Rinaldo, E. Bluhm, Hugh Cutler, and R. Grange, pp. 461-79. *Fieldiana: Anthropology* 40.

1956   Vegetable Material from the Site of San Cayetano. *The Upper Pima of San Cayetano del Tuacacori*, by Charles C. DiPeso. Amerind Foundation Publication 7:459-62.

1960   Cultivated Plant Remains from Waterfall Cave, Chihuahua. *American Antiquity* 26(2):277-79.

1965   Cultivated Plants. *The McGraw Site, A Study in Hopewellian Dynamics*, by Olaf H. Prufer. Scientific Publications of the Cleveland Museum of Natural History, New Series 4(1):107-09.

1966   *Corn, Cucurbits, and Cotton from Glen Canyon.* University of Utah Department of Anthropology Anthropological Papers 80.

1968   Origins of Agriculture in the Americas. *Latin American Research Review* 3(4):3-21.

Cutler, Hugh C., and Leonard W. Blake
    1969   Analysis of Corn from San Juan Capistrano. *The History and Archeology of Mission San Juan Capistrano, San Antonio, Texas.* State of Texas, State Building Commission, Archeological Program Report 11:107-09.

    1973   *Plants from Archeological Sites East of the Rockies.* St. Louis:Missouri Botanical Gardens.

    1976   Corn from Snaketown. *The Hohokam,* by Emil W. Haury, pp. 365-66. Tucson:University of Arizona Press.

Cutler, Hugh C. and Winson Meyer
    1965   Corn and Cucurbits from Wetherill Mesa. *Contributions of the Wetherill Mesa Archeological Project,* assembled by Douglas Osbourne. Memoirs of the Society for American Archaeology 19:136-52.

Cutler, Hugh C., and Thomas W. Whitaker
    1956   *Cucurbita mixta* pang, Its Classification and Relationship. *Bulletin of the Torrey Botanical Club* 83(4):253-60.

    1961   History and Distribution of the Cultivated Cucurbits in the Americas. *American Antiquity* 26:469-85.

    1967   Cucurbits from the Tehuacán Caves. *The Prehistory of the Tehuacán Valley,* Vol. I, *Environment and Subsistence,* edited by D.S. Byers, pp. 212-19. Austin:University of Texas Press.

Damon, P.E., and Austin Long
    1962   Arizona Radiocarbon Dates III. *Radiocarbon* 4:239-49.

Darlington, Charles D.
    1969   The Silent Millennia in the Origin of Agriculture. *Domestication and Exploitation of Plants,* edited by P. J. Ucko and G.W. Dimbleby. London: Gerald Duckworth & Co.

Darlington, Henry T.
    1922   The Introduced Weed Flora of Illinois. *Illinois State Academy of Science Transactions* 15:171-84.

Darwin, Charles
    1859   *The Origin of Species.* New York: The New American Library (Reprinted 1958).

    1868   *Animals and Plants Under Domestication.* London.

    1875   *The Variations of Animals and Plants Under Domestication.* London:Murray.

Deam, Charles C.
    1940   *Flora of Indiana.* Indianapolis:Indiana Department of Conservation.

Dean, Jeffrey S., Alexander J. Lindsay, Jr., and William J. Robinson
    1978   Prehistoric Settlement in Long House Valley, Northeastern Arizona. *Investigation of the Southwestern Anthropological Research Group,* edited by R. Euler and G. Gumerman, pp. 25-44. Flagstaff: Museum of Northern Arizona.

De Candolle, Alphonse
    1885   *Geógraphie botanique raisonnée.* Paris:V. Masson.

    1959   *Origin of Cultivated Plants.* New York:Hafner (Reprint 1886, 2nd edition).

Delcourt, Paul A., and Hazel R. Delcourt
    1978   *Late Pleistocene and Holocene Distributional History of the Deciduous Forest in the Southeastern United States.* Center for Quaternary Studies of the Southeastern United States, Contribution 12.

Dering, J. Philip
    1979   Pollen and Plant Macrofossil Vegetation Record Recovered from Hinds Cave, Val Verde County, Texas. M.A. thesis, Department of Botany, Texas A&M University.

Dering, J. Philip, and Harry J. Shafer
    1976   Analysis of Matrix Samples from Crockett County Shelter: A Test for Seasonality. *Bulletin of the Texas Archeological Society* 47:209-30.

Dibble, David S.
    1967   Excavations at Arenosa Shelter, 1965-66. Unpublished ms. dated 1967, on file at National Park Service, Lincoln, Nebraska.

Dibble, David S., and Dessamae Lorrain
    1968   *Bonfire Shelter: A Stratified Bison Kill Site, Val Verde County, Texas.* The University of Texas at Austin, Texas Memorial Museum, Miscellaneous Papers 1.

Dick, Herbert W.
    1952   Evidence of Early Man in Bat Cave and on the Plains of San Augustin, New Mexico, Vol. III, *Proceedings of the 29th International Congress of Americanists*, pp. 158-63.
    1954   The Bat Cave Pod Corn Complex: A Note on Its Distribution and Archeological Significance. *El Palacio* 61:138-44.
    1965   *Bat Cave.* The School of American Research, Monograph 27. Albuquerque:University of New Mexico Press.

Dickson, D. Bruce
    1979   Deduction on the Duck River: A Test of Some Hypotheses about Settlement Distribution Using Surface Site Survey Data from Middle Tennessee. *Midcontinental Journal of Archaeology* 4:113-31.

Dillehay, Tom D.
    1974   Late Quaternary Bison Population Changes on the Southern Plains. *Plains Anthropologist* 19(65):180-96.

Doebley, John F.
    1984   "Seeds" of Wild Grasses: A Major Food of Southwestern Indians. *Economic Botany* 38(1):52-64.

Doebley, John F., and Hugh H. Iltis
    1980   Taxonomy of *Zea* 1. Subgeneric Classification with Key to Taxa. *American Journal of Botany* 67:986-93.

Doehner, Karen and Richard E. Larson
    n.d.   Archaeological Research at the Proposed Cooper Lake, Northeast Texas, 1974-75. Final report submitted to the Interagency Archeological services Division, Office of Archeology and Historic Preservation, Heritage, Conservation and Recreation Service, Atlanta, by Southern Methodist Archaeology Research Program, in compliance with contracts CX7000-5-0238 and CX5880-6-0020.

Doggett, H., and B.N. Majisu
    1968   Disruptive Selection in Crop Development. *Heredity* 23:1-23.

Dolan, Robert, Bruce Haydon, and Harry Lins
    1980   Barrier Islands. *American Scientist* 68:14-25.

Driver, Harold E., and William C. Masey
    1957   Comparative Studies of North American Indians. *Transactions of the American Philosophical Society* 47(2).

Duffield, Lathel F.
    1963   The Strawn Creek Site: A Mixed Archaic and Neo-American Site at Navarro Mills Reservoir, Navarro County, Texas. Report submitted to the Naitonal Park Service by the Texas Archeological Salvage Project, The University of Texas, in accordance with the provisions of Contract 14-10-0333-812. Austin, Texas.

Duke, Paul L.
    1977   Lake Thunderbird Site (4lBP78), Bastrop, Texas. *La Tierra* 4(3):15-26.

Emerson, Rollins S., and H.H. Smith
    1950   *Inheritance of Number of Kernel Rows in Maize.* Cornell University Agricultural Experiment Station Memoir 296.

Epstein, Jeremiah F.
  1969   *The San Isidro Site, An Early Man Campsite in Nuevo Leon, Mexico.* The University of Texas at Austin, Department of Anthropology, Anthropology Series 7.
  1972   Some Implications of Recent Excavations and Surveys in Nuevo Leon and Coahuila. *The Texas Journal of Science* 24(1):45-56.
Erwin, Arthur T.
  1938   An Interesting Texas Cucurbit. *Iowa State College Journal of Science* 12:253-55.
Esau, Katherine
  1967   *Plant Anatomy.* 2nd ed. New York:John Wiley.
Fabac, Carol R.
  n.d.   Description and Analysis of the Human Skeletal Materials from the Prehistoric Cemetery 41WH39 at Wharton, Texas. Ms. dated 1983 and on file at the University of Texas at Austin, Texas Archeological Research Laboratory.
Falk, Carl R.
  1969   Archeological Salvage in the Kaysinger Bluff Reservoir, Missouri, 1966. Archeological salvage project for the National Park Service, University of Missouri, Columbia; contract 14-10-0232-1163.
Falk, Carl R., and Kerry A. Lippincott
  1974   Archeological Investigations in the Harry S. Truman Reservoir, Missouri: 1967-1968. Archeological salvage project for the NPS, University of Missouri, Columbia; contracts 14-10-2:920-6 and 49.
Farnsworth, Kenneth B., and David L. Asch
  n.d.   Early Woodland Chronology. Artifact Styles and Settlement Distribution in the Lower Illinois Valley Drainage. *Kampsville Conference on Early Woodland,* edited by Kenneth B. Farnsworth and Thomas E. Emerson. Kampsville, Illinois:Center for American Archeology. In press.
Farnsworth, Kenneth B., and John A. Walthall
  1983   In the Path of Progress: Development of Illinois Highway Archeology, and the FAP 408 Project. *American Archeology* 3(3):169-81.
Faulkner, Charles H.
  1977   The Winter House: An Early Southeast Tradition. *Midcontinental Journal of Archaeology* 2:142-59.
Faulkner, Charles H. and Major C.R. McCollough
  1973   *Introductory Report of the Normandy Reservoir Salvage Project: Environmental Setting, Typology, and Survey, Vol. 1, Normandy Archaeological Project.* Department of Anthropology, University of Tennessee, Report of Investigations 11.
  1974   *Excavations and Testing, Normandy Reservoir Salvage Project: 1972 Season, Vol. 2, Normandy Archaeological Project.* Department of Anthropology, University of Tennessee, *Report of Investigations 12.*
  1977   *Fourth Report of the Normandy Archaeological Project, Vol. 4, Normandy Archaeological Project.* Department of Anthropology, University of Tennessee, Report of Investigations 19.
  1978   *Fifth Report of the Normandy Archaeological Project, Vol. 5, Normandy Archaeological Project.* Department of Anthropology, University of Tennessee, Report of Investigations 20.
Fenneman, Nevin M.
  1938   *Physiography of Eastern United States.* New York: McGraw-Hill.
Ferguson, Leland G.
  1978   Southeast. Current Research, edited by Thomas P. Myers. *American Antiquity* 43(4):756-62.
Flannery, Kent V.
  1968   Archaeological Systems Theory and Early Mesoamerica. *Anthropological*

Archaeology in the Americas, edited by B. Meggars, pp. 67-87. Washington, D.C.:Anthropological Society of Washington.

1969 Origins and Ecological Effects of Early Domestication in Iran and the Near East. *The Domestication and Exploitation of Plants and Animals*, by P.J. Ucko and George W. Dimbleby, pp. 73-100. London:Duckworth.

1973 The Origins of Agriculture. *Annual Review of Anthropology* 2:271-310.

Ford, Richard I.

1968a Jemez Cave and Its Place in an Early Horticultural Settlement Pattern. Paper presented at the 33rd annual meeting of the Society for American Archaeology, Sante Fe.

1968b An Ecological Analysis Involving the Population of San Juan Pueblo, New Mexico. Ph.D. dissertation, Department of Anthropology, University of Michigan.

1973 Origins of Agriculture in Native North America. *Actes du VIIIe Congress International des Sciences Prehistoriques et Protohistoriques* Actes III:406-7.

1974 Northeastern Archaeology: Past and Future Directions. *Annual Review of Anthropology* 3:385-413.

1975 Re-excavation of Jemez Cave, New Mexico. *Awanyu* 3:13-27.

1977 Evolutionary Ecology and the Evolution of Human Ecosystems: A Case Study from the Midwestern U.S.A. *Explanation of Pre-historic Change*, edited by James N. Hill, pp. 153-84. Albuquerque: University of New Mexico Press.

1977a Archeobotany of the Fort Bliss Maneuver Area II, Texas. *Settlement Patterns of the Eastern Hueco Rolson*, by Michael E. Whalen. Centennial Museum Anthropological Paper 4:199-205.

1979 Gathering and Gardening: Trends and Consequences of Hopewell Subsistence Strategies. *Hopewell Archaeology: The Chillicothe Conference*, edited by D. Brose and N. Greber, pp. 234-38. Kent, Ohio: Kent State University Press.

1981 Gardening and Farming Before A.D. 1000: Patterns of Prehistoric Cultivation North of Mexico. *Journal of Ethnobiology* 1(1):6-27.

1984 Ecological Consequences of Early Agriculture in the Southwest. *Papers on the Archaeology of Black Mesa, Arizona* II:127-38, edited by Stephen Plog and Shirley Powell. Carbondale:Southern Illinois University Press.

Fowler, Melvin L.

1959 Modoc Rock Shelter: An Early Archaic Site in Southern Illinois. *American Antiquity* 24:257-70.

1971 The Origin of Plant Cultivation in the Central Mississippi Valley: A Hypothesis. *Prehistoric Agriculture*, edited by Stuart Streuver, pp. 122-28. Garden City:Natural History Press.

Fox, Daniel E., Robert J. Mallouf, N. O'Malley, and William M. Sorrow

1974 *Archeological Resources of the Proposed Cuero I Reservoir, Dewitt and Gonzales Counties, Texas*. Texas Historical Commission and Texas Water Development Board, Archeological Survey Report 12.

Fox, Anne A., and Thomas R. Hester

1976 *An Archaeological Survey of the Proposed Coleto Creek Project, Victoria and Goliad Counties, Texas*. The University of Texas at San Antonio, Center for Archaeological Research, Archaeological Survey Report 18.

Fox, Anne A., E.H. Schmiedlin, and J.L. Mitchell

1978 Preliminary Report on the J-2 Ranch Site (41VT6), Victoria County, Texas. *La Tierra* 5(3):2-14.

Fried, Morton H.

1967 *The Evolution of Political Society*. New York: Random House.

Fritz, Gayle J.

1984 Identification of Cultigen Amaranth and Chenopod from Rockshelter Sites in Northwest Arkansas. *American Antiquity* 49:558-72.

Fritz, John M.
  1974   The Hay Hollow Site Subsistence System, East- Central Arizona. Ph.D.
          dissertation, Department of Anthropology, University of Chicago.
Fryman, Frank B.
  1967   An Archaeological Survey of the Red River Reservoir in Wolfe, Powell,
          and Menifee Counties, Kentucky. Report submitted to the National Park
          Service Interagency Archaeological Services Office, Richmond, Virginia,
          by the University of Kentucky Museum of Anthropology.
Fulton, Robert L., and Clarence H. Webb
  1953   The Bellevue Mound: A Pre-Caddoan Site in Bossier Parish, Louisiana.
          Bulletin of the Texas Archeological Society 24:18-42.
Funkhouser, William D., and William S. Webb
  1929   The So-Called "Ash-Caves" in Lee County, Kentucky. *University of Ken-
          tucky, Reports in Anthropology and Archaeology* 1(2):37-112.
  1930   Rock Shelters of Wolfe and Powell Counties, Kentucky. *University of Ken-
          tucky, Reports in Anthropology and Archaeology* 1(4):239-306.
Gagliano, Sherwood M., and William G. Smith
  1977   Cultural Resources Evaluation of the Northern Gulf of Mexico Continen-
          tal Shelf, Vol. 1: Prehistoric Cultural Resource Potential. Report prepared
          for Interagency Archeological Series, Office of Archeology and Historic
          Preservation, National Park Service, U.S. Department of Interior by
          Coastal Environment, Inc.
Galinat, Walton C.
  1956   Evolution Leading to the Formation of the Cupulate Fruit-Case in the
          American Maydeae. *Botanical Museum Leaflets, Harvard University*
          17:217-39.
  1966   The Evolution of Glumeless Sweet Corn. *Economic Botany* 20:441-45.
  1970   The Cupule and its Role in the Origin and Evolution of Maize. *Mas-
          sachusetts Agricultural Experiment Station Bulletin* 585:1-22.
  1971   The Origin of Maize. *Annual Review of Genetics* 5:447-78.
  1973   Preserve Guatemalan Teosinte, a Relict Link in Corn's Evolution. *Science*
          180:323.
  1974   The Domestication and Genetic Erosion of Maize. *Economic Botany*
          28:31-37.
  1975   The Evolutionary Emergence of Maize. *Bulletin of the Torrey Botanical Club*
          102(6):313-24.
  1978   The Inheritance of Some Traits Essential to Maize and Teosinte. *Maize
          Breeding and Genetics* edited by D.B. Walden, pp. New York:John Wiley &
          Sons.
  1983   The Origin of Maize as Shown by Key Morphological Traits of its An-
          cestor, Teosinte. *Maydica* 28:121- 38.
Galinat, Walton C., and James H. Gunnerson
  1963   Spread of Eight-Rowed Maize from the Prehistoric Southwest. *Botanical
          Museum Leaflets, Harvard University* 20:117-60.
Galinat, Walton C., and Robert G. Campbell
  1967   The Diffusion of Eight-Rowed Maize from the Southwest to the Central
          Plains. *Massachusetts Agricultural Experiment Station, Monograph Series*
          1:1-16.
Galinat, Walton C., Paul C. Mangelsdorf, and Lloyd Pierson
  1956   Estimates of Teosinte Introgression in Archaeological Maize. *Botanical
          Museum Leaflets, Harvard University* 17:101-24.
Galinat, Walton C., Theodore R. Reinhart, and Theodore R. Frisbie
  1970   Early Eight-Rowed Maize from the Middle Rio Grand Valley, New Mex-
          ico. *Botanical Museum Leaflets, Harvard University* 22(9):313-31.
Galinat, Walton C., and Reynold J. Ruppé
  1961   Further Archaeological Evidence on the Effects of Teosinte Introgression

in the Evolution of Modern Maize. *Botanical Museum Leaflets, Harvard University* 19:163-81.

Gallagher, Marsha V.
  1977   *Contemporary Ethnobotany Among the Apache of the Clarkdale, Arizona, Area, Coconino and Prescott National Forest.* U.S. Forest Service Southwestern Region Archaeological Report 14.

Gasser, Robert E.
  1980   Exchange and the Hohokam Archaeobotanical Record. Current Issues in Hohokam Prehistory, edited by David Doyel and Fred Plog. *Arizona State University Anthropological Research Papers* 23:72- 77.
  1982   Hohokam Use of Desert Plant Foods. *Desert Plants* 3(4):216-34.

Gerstle, Andrea, Thomas C. Kelly, and Cristi Assad
  1978   *The Fort Sam Houston Project: An Archaeological and Historical Assessment.* The University of Texas at San Antonio, Center for Archaeological Research, Archaeological Survey Report 40.

Gifford, E.W.
  1932   The Southeastern Yavapai. *University of California Publications in American Archaeology and Ethnology* 29:177-252.

Gilles, A., and L.F. Randolph
  1951   Reduction of Quadrivalent Frequence in Autotetraploid Maize during a Period of 10 Years. *American Journal of Botany* 38:12-17.

Gilmore, Melvin R.
  1919   Uses of Plants by the Indians of the Missouri River Region. *Smithsonian Institution Bureau of American Ethnology 33rd Annual Report, 1911-1912,* pp. 42-154.
  1931   Vegetal Remains of the Ozark Bluff-Dweller Culture. *Papers of the Michigan Academy of Science, Arts, and Letters* 14:83-102.

Givens, R. Dale
  1968   A Preliminary Report on Excavations at Hitzfelder Cave. *Bulletin of the Texas Archeological Society* 38:47-50.

Gladwin, Harold S., Emil W. Haury, E.B. Sayles, and Nora Gladwin
  1937   *Excavations at Snaketown: Material Culture.* Medallion Papers 25. Gila Pueblo:Globe.

Glassow, Michael A.
  1972   Changes in the Adaptations of Southwestern Basketmakers: A Systems Perspective. *Contemporary Archaeology*, edited by M. Leone, pp. 289-302. Carbondale: Southern Illinois University Press.

Gleason, Henry A.
  1952   *The New Britton and Brown Illustrated Flora of the Northeastern United States and Adjacent Canada.* Vol. 3. New York:New York Botanical Garden.

Goad, Sharon I.
  1978   Exchange Networks in the Prehistoric Southeastern United States. Ph.D. dissertation, Department of Anthropology, University of Georgia.

Goldschmidt, Walter R.
  1951   Ethics and the Structure of Society: An Ethnological Contribution to the Sociology of Knowledge. *American Anthropologist* 54(4):444-56.

Goodspeed, Thomas Harper
  1954   *The Genus Nicotiana: Origins, Relationships and Evolution of Its Species in the Light of Their Distribution, Morphology and Cytogenetics.* Waltham, Massachusetts:Chronica Botanica Company.

Goodwin, Grenville
  1935   The Social Divisions and Economic Life of the Western Apache. *American Anthropologist* 37:55-65.

Gorski, Linda
  1979   Microstratigraphy at the Carlston Annis Site. Paper presented in symposium, Natural and Cultural Processes in the Formation of an Archaic

Shell Midden on the Green River, Kentucky. 36th annual meeting of the Southeastern Archaeological Conference, Atlanta, Georgia.

1980   Microstratigraphic Analysis at the Carlston Annis Site, 15BT5, Butler County, Kentucky. Master's thesis, Department of Anthropology, University of Missouri, Columbia.

Gould, Frank W.
1962   Texas Plants—A Checklist and Ecological Summary. The Agricultural and Mechanical College of Texas, Agricultural Experiment Station, Publication MP-585.

Gould, Stephen J.
1984   A Short Way to Corn. *Natural History* 93:12-20.

Gray, Asa
1850   In Plantae Lindheimereanae. *Boston Journal of Natural History* 6:141-240.
1857   Researches in the Specific Characters and the Varieties of the Genus *Cucurbita. American Journal of Science and Arts* 24:440-43.

Griffin, James B.
1952   Radiocarbon Dates for the Eastern United States. *Archeology of Eastern United States*, edited by James B. Griffin, pp. 365-70. University of Chicago Press.
1960   Climatic Change: A Contributary Cause of the Growth and Decline of Northern Hopewellian Culture. *Wisconsin Archeologist* 41(2):21-33.

Griffin, James B., and Richard G. Morgan (eds.)
1941   Contributions to the Archaeology of the Illinois River Valley. *American Philosophical Society Transactions* 32(1).

Grobman, Alexander, Wilfredo Salhuana, and Richard Sevilla with Paul C. Mangelsdorf
1961   *Races of Maize in Peru*. Natural Academy of Science, Natural Res. Count. Publication 915, pp. 374. Washington, D.C.

Guffey, Stanley Z.
1977   A Review and Analysis of the Effects of Pre-Columbian Man on the Eastern North American Forests. *Tennessee Anthropologist* 2(2):121-37.

Gumerman, George J., and R.C. Euler
1976   *Papers on the Archeology of Black Mesa, Arizona*. Carbondale: Southern Illinois University Press.

Gunn, Charles R., and John V. Dennis
1976   *World Guide to Tropical Drift Seeds and Fruits*. New York: New York Times Book Co.

Gunn, Charles R., and Frederick B. Gaffney
1974   Seed Characteristics of 42 Economically Important Species of Solanaceae in the United States. *U.S. Department of Agriculture Technical Bulletin* 1471.

Gunn, Joel
1979   Occupation Frequency Simulation on a Broad Ecotone. *Transformations: Mathmatical Approaches to Culture Change*, edited by Colin Renfrew and Kenneth L. Cooke, pp. 257-74. New York: Academic Press.

Gunn, Joel, and Frank Weir
1976   Tool Kit Hypotheses: A Case of Numerical Induction. *Lithic Technology* 5(3):131-35.

Gunn, Joel, and Royce Mahula
1977   *Hop Hill: Culture and Climatic Change in Central Texas*. The University of Texas at San Antonio, Center for Archaeological Research, Special Report 5.

Haag, William G.
1974   The Adena Culture. *Archaeological Researches in Retrospect*, edited by Gordon R. Willey. Winthrop Publishers.

Haberman, Thomas W.
1984   Evidence for Aboriginal Tobaccos in Eastern North America. *American Antiquity* 49(2):269-87.

Hack, John T.
  1942   The Changing Physical Environment of the Hopi Indians of Arizona. *Reports of the Awatovi Expedition, No. 1.* Papers of the Peabody Museum of American Archeology and Ethnology (35)1.
Hajic, Edwin
  1982   *Radiocarbon Addendum to the Shallow Subsurface Geology and Geomorphology of the Nutwood and Hartwell Drainage and Levee Districts, Greene and Jersey County, Illinois.* Center for American Archeology. Submitted to the U.S. Army Corps of Engineers, St. Louis District.
Hahn, Edward
  1909   *Die Entstehung der Pflugkultur.* Heidelberg:C. Winter.
Hall, Grant D.
  1981   *Allens Creek: A Study in the Cultural Prehistory of the Lower Brazos River Valley, Texas.* University of Texas at Austin, Texas Archeological Survey Report 61.
Hall, Stephen A.
  1977   Late Quaternary Sedimentation and Paleoecologic History of Chaco Canyon, New Mexico. *Geological Society of America Bulletin* 88:1593-1618.
Harlan, Jack R.
  1971   Agricultural Origins: Centers and Noncenters. *Science* 174:468-73.
Harlan, Jack R., and Jan M. de Wet
  1965   Some Thoughts on Weeds. *Economic Botany* 18(1):16-24.
  1973   On the Quality of Evidence for Origin and Dispersal of Cultivated Plants. *Current Anthropology* 14:51-55.
Harlan, Jack R., and Daniel Zohary
  1966   Distribution of Wild Wheats and Barley. *Science* 153:1074-80.
Harper, Francis, ed.
  1958   *The Travels of William Bartram.* Naturalist's edition. New Haven:Yale University Press.
Harper, John L.
  1965   A Comment on: Sunflowers, Weeds, and Cultivated Plants, by Charles B. Heiser, Jr. *The Genetics of Colonizing Species,* edited by H.G. Baker and G. Ledyard Stebbins, pp. 399. New York:Academic Press.
  1977   *Population Biology of Plants.* London:Academic Press.
Harper, John L., P.H. Lovell, and K.G. Moore
  1970   The Shape and Sizes of Seeds. *Annual Review of Ecology and Systematics* 1:327-56.
Harrington, Mark R.
  1920   Certain Caddo Sites in Arkansas. *Museum of the American Indian, Heye Foundation, Indian Notes and Monographs.* New York.
Harris, David R.
  1969   Agricultural Systems, Ecosystems on the Origins of Agriculture. *The Domestication and Exploitation of Plants and Animals,* edited by P. J. Ucko and G. W. Dimbleby, pp. 3-15. London:Duckworth.
  1977a   Alternative Pathways Toward Agriculture. *Origins of Agriculture,* edited by Charles A. Reed, pp. 179-244. The Hague: Mouton.
  1977b   Subsistence Strategies Across the Torres Strait. *Sunda and Sahul: Prehistoric Studies in Southeast Asia, Melanesia and Australia,* edited by Jim Allen, Jack Golson and Rhys Jones, pp. 421-63. New York: Academic Press.
Harshberger, John W.
  1896   The Purposes of Ethnobotany. *American Antiquarian* 17:33-81.
Harvard, V.
  1895   Food Plants of the North American Indians. *Bulletin of the Torrey Botanical Club* 22:98-123.
Hastings, James R., and Raymond M. Turner
  1965   *The Changing Mile.* Tucson: University of Arizona Press.

Haury, E.W.
    1957   An Alluvial Site on the San Carlos Indian Reservation, Arizona. *American Antiquity* 23:2-27.
    1962   The Greater American Southwest. *Courses Toward Urban Life*, edited by Robert J. Braidwood and Gordon R. Willey, pp. 106-31. Chicago:Aldine.
    1976   *The Hohokam, Desert Farmers and Craftsmen: Excavations at Snaketown, 1964-1965.* Tucson: University of Arizona Press.
Hawkes, James G.
    1969   The Ecological Background of Plant Domestication. *The Domestication of Plants and Animals*, edited by P.J. Ucko and G.W. Dimbleby, pp. 17-29. London.
    1977   The Importance of Wild Germplasm in Plant Breeding. *Euphytica* 26:615-21.
Haynes, C. Vance
    1968   Geochronology of Late Quaternary Alluvium. *Means of Correlation of Quaternary Successions*, edited by R.B. Morrison and H.E. Wright, pp. 591-631. *Proceedings of the VII Congress of the International Association of Quaternary Research.* Salt Lake City:South University of Utah Press.
    1976   Late Quaternary Geology of the Lower Pomme de Terre Valley. *Prehistoric Man and His Environments: A Case Study in the Ozark Highland*, edited by R. Wood and B. McMillan, pp. 47-61. New York: Academic Press.
Haynes, C. Vance, and Austin Long
    1976   Radiocarbon Dating at Snaketown. *The Hohokam: Desert Farmers and Craftsmen*, edited by E. Haury. Tucson:Unversity of Arizona Press.
Hays, Thomas R. (comp. and ed.)
    1982   *Archaeological Investigations at the San Gabriel Reservoir Districts, Central Texas.* Vols. 1-4. North Texas State University, Institute of Applied Sciences.
Heer, O.
    1865   Die Pflanzen der Pfahlbauten. *Neujahrsblatt fur Naturforsch Gesellschaft* 68:1-54.
Heiser, Charles B.
    1951   The Sunflower among the North American Indians. *Proceedings of the American Philosophical Society* 95:432-48.
    1951a   Hybridization in the Annual Sunflowers: *Helianthus annuus* x *H. debilis* var. *cucumeri folius. Evolution* 5(1):42-51.
    1954   Variation and Subspecification in the Common Sunflower, *Helianthus annuus. American Midland Naturalist* 51:287-305.
    1955   The Origin and Development of the Cultivated Sunflower. *American Biology Teacher* 17:161-67.
    1965   Cultivated Plants and Cultural Diffusion in Nuclear America. *American Anthropologist* 67:930-49.
    1965a   Sunflowers, Weeds, and Cultivated Plants. *The Genetics of Colonizing Species*, edited by H.G. Baker and G. Ledyard Stebbins, pp. 391-401. New York:Academic Press.
    1969   Some Considerations of Early Plant Domestication. *BioScience* 19(3):228-31.
    1976   *The Sunflower.* Norman:University of Oklahoma Press.
    1978   Taxonomy of *Helianthus* and Origin of Domesticated Sunflower. *Sunflower Science and Technology*, edited by Jack F. Carter. Madison, Wisconsin:Agronomy 19.
    1979a   *The Gourd Book.* Norman:University of Oklahoma Press.
    1979b   Origins of Some Cultivated New World Plants. *Annual Review of Ecology and Systematics* 10:309-26.
Heiser, Charles B., Jr., and David C. Nelson
    1974   On the Origin of the Cultivated Chenopods (Chenopodium). *Genetics* 78:503-05.

Heiser, Charles B., Jr., Dale M. Smith, Sarah B. Clevenger, and William C. Martin, Jr.
    1969   The North American Sunflowers (*Helianthus*). *Memoirs of the Torrey Botanical Club* 22(3):1-218.
Heizer, Robert F., ed.
    1978   *Handbook of North American Indians*, Vol. 8: *California*. Washington: Smithsonian Institution Press.
Henderson, Jerry
    1979   *The Mothershed Spring Site*. Texas State Department of Highways and Public Transportation, Highway Design Division, Publications in Archaeology, Report 12.
Hester, Thomas R.
    1969a   The Floyd Morris and Ayala Sites: A Discussion of Burial Practices in the Rio Grande Valley and the Lower Texas Coast. *Bulletin of the Texas Archeological Society* 40:157-66.
    1969b   *Archaeological Investigations in Kleberg and Kenedy Counties, Texas, in August, 1967*. Texas State Building Commission, Archeological Program Report 15.
    1971   Archeological Investigations at the La Jita Site, Uvalde County, Texas. *Bulletin of the Texas Archeological Society* 42:51-148.
    1976   The Archaic of Southern Texas. *The Texas Archaic: A Symposium*, edited by Thomas R. Hester, pp. 83-90. The University of Texas at San Antonio, Center for Archaeological Research, Special Report 2.
    1979   Early Populations in Prehistoric Texas. *Archaeology* 32(6): 26-33.
    1980   A Chronological Overview of Prehistoric Southern and South-Central Texas. *Papers on the Prehistory of Northern Mexico and Adjacent Texas*, edited by J.F. Epstein, T.R. Hester, and C. Graves, pp. 119- 138. The University of Texas at San Antonio, Center for Archaeological Research, Special Report 9.
    1981   Tradition and Diversity Among the Prehistoric Hunters and Gatherers of Southern Texas. *Plains Anthropologist* 26(92):119-28.
Hester, Thomas R., and James E. Corbin
    1975   Two Burial Sites on the Central Texas Coast. *The Texas Journal of Science* 26(3 and 4):519-28.
Hester, Thomas R., and H. Kohnitz
    1975   The Chronological Placement of "Guadalupe" Tools. *La Tierra* 2(Pt. 2):22-25.
Higgins, Paul D.
    1970   A Preliminary Survey of the Vascular Flora of the Red River Gorge, Kentucky. Master's thesis, University of Louisville, Louisville, Kentucky.
Hitchcock, A.S.
    1950   *Manual of the Grasses of the United States*. 2nd ed., rev. by Agnes Chase. U.S. Department of Agriculture, Miscellaneous Publication 200.
Hitchcock, R.K.
    1978   The Traditional Responses to Drought in Botswana. *Proceedings of the Symposium on Drought in Botswana*, edited by M. Hinchey, pp. 91-97. Worchester, Mass.:Clark University Press.
Hoffman, Michael A.
    1965   The Ashby Site: A Late Woodland Occupation in the Lower Green River Valley. Ms., University of Kentucky, Museum of Anthropology, Lexington.
Hoffman, Michael P.
    1969   Prehistoric Developments in Southwest Arkansas. *Bulletin of the Arkansas Archeological Society* 10(1):37-49.
    1970   Archaeological and Historical Assessment of the Red River Basin in Arkansas. *Archeological and Historical Resources of the Red River Basin*, edited by Hester A. Davis, pp. 135-94. University of Arkansas Museum,

Arkansas Archeological Survey Publications on Archeology, Research Series 1.

Holmberg, Alan
1950   *Nomads of the Long Bow: The Siriono of Eastern Bolivia.* Smithsonian Institution Publications of the Institute of Social Anthropology 10.

Hudson, Charles M., Editor
1979   *Black Drink, A Native American Tea.* Athens:University of Georgia Press.

Hughes, Jack T.
1947   An Archeological Reconnaissance in Tamaulipas, Mexico. *American Antiquity* 13:33-39.

Human Systems Research, Inc.
1973   *Technical Manual, 1973 Survey of the Tularosa Basin.* Tularosa:Human Systems Research.

Hurst, C.T.
1940   Preliminary Work in Tabeguache Cave—1939. *Southwestern Lore* 6:48-62.
1941   The Second Season in Tabeguache Cave. *Southwestern Lore* 7:48-62.
1942   Completion of Work in Tabaguashe Cave. *Southwestern Lore* 8:7-16.

Hurst, C.T., and Edgar Anderson
1949   A Corn Cache from Western Colorado. *American Antiquity* 14:161-67.

Hutchinson, Sir Joseph, ed.
1965   *Crop Plant Evolution.* Cambridge University Press.

Iltis, Hugh H.
1972   The Taxonomy of *Zea mays* (Graminae). *Phytologia* 23:248-49.
1973   The Maize Mystique: A Taxonomic-Geographic Interpretation of the Origin of Corn. Symposium on Origin of *Zea mays* and Its Relatives. Botanical Museum, Harvard University.
1983   From Teosinte to Maize: The Catastrophic Sexual Transmutation. *Science* 222:886-94.

Iltis, Hugh H., and John F. Doebley
1980   Taxonomy of *Zea.* II. Subspecific Categories in the *Zea mays* Complex and a Generic Synopsis. *American Journal of Botany* 67:994-1004.

Iltis, Hugh H., John F. Doebley, Rafael M. Guzman, and B. Pazy
1979   *Zea diploperennis* (Gramineae): A New Teosinte from Mexico. *Science* 203:186-88.

Irving, Robert S.
1966   A Preliminary Analysis of Plant Remains from Six Amistad Reservoir Sites. *A Preliminary Study of the Paleoecology of the Amistad Reservoir Area,* assembled by Dee Ann Story and Vaughn M. Bryant, Jr., pp. 61-110. Report submitted to the National Science Foundation.

Irwin, Henry J., and Cynthia C. Irwin
1959   Excavations at the LoDaisKa Site. *Proceedings of the Denver Museum of Natural History* 8.
1961   Radiocarbon Dates from the LoDaisKa Site, Colorado. *American Antiquity* 27:114-17.

Irwin-Williams, Cynthia
1967   Picosa: The Elementary Southwestern Culture. *American Antiquity* 32:441-52.
1973   *The Oshara Tradition: Origins of Anasazi Culture.* Eastern New Mexico University Contributions in Anthropology 5, No. 1.

Irwin-Williams, Cynthia, and C. Vance Haynes
1970   Climatic Change and Early Population Dynamics in the Southwestern United States. *Quaternary Research* 1:59-71.

Irwin-Williams, Cynthia and S. Tompkins
1968   *Excavations at En Medio Rock Shelter, New Mexico.* Eastern New Mexico University Contributions in Anthropology 1(2).

Janzen, Donald E.
1977   An Examination of Late Archaic Development in the Falls of the Ohio

River Area. *For the Director: Research Essays in Honor of James B. Griffin*, edited by Charles E. Cleland, pp. 123-43. University of Michigan Museum of Anthropology, Anthropological Papers 61.

Jelinek, Arthur J.
  1965   Radiocarbon Dating in the Southwest United States. Paper presented at the Sixth International Conference on Radiocarbon and Tritium Dating, Pullman.

Jelks, Edward B.
  1965   The Archeology of McGee Bend Reservoir, Texas. Ph.D. dissertation, Department of Anthropology, University of Texas at Austin.

Jennings, Jesse D.
  1967   Review of "Bat Cave." The School of American Research, Monograph 27. *American Antiquity* 32:123.
  1974   *Prehistory of North America*. Second ed. New York: McGraw-Hill.
  1975   Preliminary Report: Excavation of Cowboy Caves, June 3-July 26, 1975. Department of Anthropology, University of Utah, Salt Lake.

Jensen, Harold P.
  1968   Coral Snake Mound (X16SA48). *Bulletin of the Texas Archeological Society* 39:9-44.

Johannessen, Sissel
  1981   Plant Remains from the Julien Site (11-S-63). *The Julien Site (11-S-63): An Early Bluff and Mississippian Multicomponent Site*, by George R. Milner and Joyce A. Williams. University of Illinois, Champaign-Urbana, FAI-270 Archeological Mitigation Project Report 31:267-99.
  1982   Paleoethnobotanical Trends in the American Bottom: Late Archaic through Mississippian. Paper presented at 47th annual meeting, Society for American Archaeology, Minneapolis, Minnesota.
  1984   Paleoethnobotany. *American Bottom Archaeology*, edited by Charles J. Bareis and James W. Porter, pp. 197-214. Urbana:University of Illinois Press.
  1984a   Plant Remains. The Fish Lake Site (11-MO-608). *American Bottom Archaeology, FAI-270 Site Reports* 8:189-99.

Johnson, Alfred E.
  1976   A Model of the Kansas City Hopewell Subsistence-Settlement System. *Hopewellian Archaeology in the Lower Missouri Valley*, edited by Alfred E. Johnson. University of Kansas Publications in Anthropology 8:7-15.
  1979   Kansas City Hopewell. *Hopewell Archaeology: The Chillicothe Conference*, edited by D. Brose and N. Greber. Kent, Ohio:Kent State University Press.

Johnson, Elmer H.
  1931   *The Natural Regions of Texas*. The University of Texas at Austin, Bureau of Business Research, Monograph 8.

Johnson, F., ed.
  1951   *Radiocarbon Dating*. Society for American Archaeology, Memoir 8.

Johnson, LeRoy, Jr.
  1962   The Yarbrough and Miller Sites of Northeastern Texas, with a Preliminary Definition of the LaHarpe Aspect. *Bulletin of the Texas Archeological Society* 32:141-284.1964 *The Devil's Mouth Site: A Stratified Campsite at Amistad Reservoir, Val Verde County, Texas*. The University of Texas at Austin, Department of Anthropology, Archaeology Series 6.

Jones, George Neville, and George Damon Fuller
  1955   *Vascular Plants of Illinois*. Illinois State Museum Scientific Series 6.

Jones, Rhys
  1969   Fire Stick Farming. *Australian Natural History* 16:224-28.

Jones, Volney
  1936   The Vegetal Remains of Newt Kash Hollow Shelter. *Rockshelters in Menifee County, Kentucky*, edited by William S. Webb and William D. Funkhouser,

pp. 147- 65. University of Kentucky Reports in Anthropology and Archaeology 3(4).

1949   Maize from the Davis Site: Its Nature and Interpretation. The George C. Davis Site, Cherokee County, Texas, by H. Perry Newell and Alex D. Krieger. *Memoirs of the Society for American Archaeology* 5:239-49.

1951   Plant Materials from the Babocomari Village Site. *The Babocomari Village Site on the Babocomari River, Southeastern Arizona.* Amarind Foundation Publication 5:15-19.

1968   Corn from the McKees Rocks Village Site. *Pennsylvania Archeologist* 38(1-4):81-86.

Jones, Volney H., and Robert L. Fonner
1954   Plant Remains from Sites in the Durango and LaPlata Areas, Colorado. *Basketmaker II Sites Near Durango, Colorado,* by E. Morris and R. Burgh, pp. 93-115. Carnegie Institution of Washington Publication 604.

Jones, Volney H., and Elizabeth Ann Morris
1960   A Seventh-Century Record of Tobacco Utilization in Arizona. *El Palacio* 64(4):115-17.

Kaemlein, Wilma
1963   A Prehistoric Twined-Woven Bag from the Trigo Mountains, Arizona. *The Kiva* 28:1-13.

Kaplan, Lawrence
1956   The Cultivated Beans of the Prehistoric Southwest. *Annals of the Missouri Botanical Garden* 43:189-227.

1963   Archeoethnobotany of Cordova Cave, New Mexico. *Economic Botany* 17:350-59.

1963a   Beans. *Basket Maker III Sites near Durango, Colorado,* by Roy Carlson. University of Colorado Studies, Series in Anthropology 8:47.

1965a   Archeology and Domestication in American *Phaseolus* (beans). *Economica Botany* 19:358-68.

1965b   Beans of Wetherill Mesa. *Contributions of the Wetherill Mesa Archeological Project,* assembled by Douglas Osborne. Memoirs of the Society for American Archeology 19:153-55.

1970   Plant Remains from the Blain Site. *Blain Village and the Fort Ancient Tradition in Ohio,* by Olaf H. Prufer and Orrin C. Shane III, pp. 227-31. Kent, Ohio:Kent State University Press.

1971   Archeology and Domestication in American *Phaseolus* (Beans). *Prehistoric Agriculture,* edited by Stuart Struever, pp. 516-34. Garden City:Natural History Press.

1971a   *Phaseolus*: Diffusion and Centers of Origin. *Man Across the Sea,* edited by C.L. Riley, J. Charles Kelley, C.W. Pennington, and R.C. Rands, pp. 416-27. Austin:University of Texas Press.

1981   What is the Origin of the Common Bean? *Economic Botany* 35(2):240-54.

Kaplan, Lawrence, and Shirley L. Maina
1977   Archeological Botany of the Apple Creek Site, Illinois. *Journal of Seed Technology* 2:40-53.

Kato-Y, Takeo A.
1975   Cytological Studies of Maize and Teosinte in Relation to their Origin and Evolution. Ph.D. dissertation, University of Massachusetts, Amherst.

Kaufman, Barbara E.
1977   Preliminary Analysis of Seeds from the Shawnee-Minisink Site: The Paleo-Indian Levels. Senior Honor's thesis, Department of Anthropology, The American University.

Kay, Marvin
1979   Phillips Springs, Missouri: Report of the 1978 Investigations. Report to the U.S. Army Corps of Engineers, Kansas City District.

Kay, Marvin, Frances B. King, and Christine K. Robinson
    1980   Cucurbits from Phillips Spring: New Evidence and Interpretations. *American Antiquity* 45(4):806-22.
Keene, Arthur S.
    1979   Prehistoric Hunter-Gatherers of the Deciduous Forest: A Linear Programming Approach to Late Archaic Subsistence in the Saginaw Valley (Michigan). Ph.D. dissertation, Department of Anthropology, University of Michigan.
Kehoe, T.F.
    1966   The Small Side-Notched Point System of the Northern Plains. *American Antiquity*, 31:827-41.
    1973   The Gull Lake Site: A Prehistoric Bison Drive Site in Southwestern Saskatchewan. *Milwaukee Public Museum Publications in Anthropology and History 1*.
Kelley, J. Charles
    1952   Some Geographic and Cultural Factors Involved in Mexican-Southeastern Contacts. *Indian Tribes and Aboriginal America: Selected Papers of the 29th International Congress of Americanists*, edited by Sol Tax, Vol. 3, pp. 139-44. Chicago.
Kelly, Frank G., Jr.
    1971   Archeologist Unearths Indian Campside. *Texas Highways* 18(4):2-7.
Kelly, Thomas C., and Thomas R. Hester
    1976   *Archaeological Investigations at Sites in the Upper Cibolo Creek Watershed, Kendall County, Texas.* The University of Texas at San Antonio, Center for Archaeological Research, Archaeological Survey Report 17.
Kidder, Alfred V.
    1924   *An Introduction to the Study of Southwestern Archaeology.* Phillips Academy, Department of Archaeology No. 1.
Kidder, Alfred V., and Samuel F. Guernsey
    1919   *Archeological Exploration in Northeastern Arizona.* Bureau of American Ethnology Bulletin 65.
Kindall, Sheldon M.
    1980   Piekert Site. *Houston Archeological Society Newsletter* 66:5-9.
King, Frances B.
    1976   Forest Density and Nut Production Potential for the Rodgers Shelter Area, Appendix B. *Prehistoric Man and His Environments: A Case Study in the Ozark Highland*, edited by W. Raymond Wood and R. Bruce McMillan, pp. 261-64, New York:Academic Press.
    1980   Plant Remains from Phillips Spring, a Multicomponent Site in the Western Ozark Highland of Missouri. *Plains Anthropologist* 25(89):217-22.
    1982   Plant Remains from the Yeo Site (23CL199). *Plains Anthropologist* 27(95):54-56.
    n.d.   Early Cultivated Cucurbits in Eastern North America. Paper prepared for School of American Research Advanced Seminar, The Origins of Plant Husbandry in North America.
King, Frances B., and R. Bruce McMillan
    1975   Plant remains from Woodland Storage Pit, Boney Spring, Missouri, *Plains Anthropologist* 20 (68):111-15.
King, James E.
    1981   Late Quaternary Vegetational History of Illinois. *Ecological Monographs* 51:43-62.
King, James E., and E.H. Lindsay
    1976   Late Quaternary Biotic Records from Spring Deposits in Western Missouri. *Prehistoric Man and His Environments: A Case Study in the Ozark Highlands*, edited by W. Raymond Wood and R. Bruce McMillan, pp. 63-78. New York: Academic Press.

Klein, William M., Richard H. Daley, and Joanne Wedum
  1975   *Environmental Inventory and Assessment of Navigation Pools 24, 25, and 26,*
          Upper Mississippi and Lower Illinois Rivers: A Vegetational Study. St.
          Louis:Missouri Botanical Garden.
Kline, Gerald W., and Gary D. Crites
  1979   Paleoethnobotany of the Ducks Nest Site: Early Mississippi Plant Utiliza-
          tion in the Eastern Highland Rim. *Tennessee Anthropologist* 4:82-100.
Klippel, Walter E.
  1972   An Early Woodland Period Manifestation in the Prairie Peninsula. *Jour-*
          nal of the Iowa Archeological Society 19.
Klippel, Walter E., Gail Celmer, and James R. Purdue
  1978   The Holocene Naiad Record at Rodgers Shelter in the Western Ozark
          Highland of Missouri. *Plains Anthropologist* 23(82):257-71.
Krieger, Alex D.
  1948   Importance of the "Gilmore Corridor" in Culture Contacts Between Mid-
          dle American and the Eastern United States. *Bulletin of the Texas Arch-*
          eological and Paleontological Society 19:155-78.
  1961   The Travels of Alvar Nuñez Cabeza de Vaca in Texas and Mexico,
          1534-1536, pp. 459-74. *Homenaja a Pablo Martinez del Rio . . . .* Mex-
          ico:Instituto Nacional de Antropologia e Historia.
Kroeber, Alfred
  1925   Handbook of the Indians of California. *Bureau of American Ethnology,*
          Bulletin 78.
Lawton, Harry W., Phillip J. Wilke, Mary DeDecker, and William M. Mason
  1976   Agriculture Among the Paiute of Owens Valley. *Journal of California An-*
          thropology 3:13-50.
LeBlanc, Steven A.
  1982   The Advent of Pottery in the Southwest. *Southwestern Ceramics A Com-*
          parative Review, edited by A. Schroeder, pp. 27-52. The Arizona Archae-
          ologist 15.
Lee, Richard B.
  1968   What Hunters Do for a Living, or, How to Make Out on Scarce Re-
          sources. *Man the Hunter*, edited by R. Lee and I. DeVore, pp. 30-48.
          Chicago:Aldine.
  1973   Mongongo: The Ethnography of a Major Wild Food Resource. *Ecology of*
          Food and Nutrition 2:307-21.
  1979   *The Kung San: Men, Women, and Work in a Foraging Society.* Cambridge:
          Cambridge University Press.
Lee, Richard B., and Irvin DeVore, eds.
  1968   *Man the Hunter.* Chicago:Aldine Press.
Lewis, Henry T.
  1972   The Role of Fire In the Domestication of Plants and Animals in South-
          west Asia: A Hypothesis. *Man* 7(2):195-222.
  1973   *Patterns of Indian Burning in California: Ecology and Ethnohistory.* Ballena
          Press Anthropological Papers 1:1-101.
Lewontin, Richard C., and L.C. Birch
  1966   Hybridization as a Source of Variation for Adaptation to New Environ-
          ments. *Evolution* 20:315- 36.
Libby, Willard
  1951   Radiocarbon Dates II. *Science*, 114.
  1952   Radiocarbon Dates III. *Science* 116:673-681.
  1955   *Radiocarbon Dating.* University of Chicago Press (2nd edition).
Lindsay, Alexander J., Jr., J. Richard Ambler, Mary Ann Stein, and Philip M. Hobler
  1968   Survey and Excavation North and East of Navajo Mountain, Utah,
          1959-1962. *Museum of Northern Arizona Bulletin* 45.
Linton, Ralph
  1924   North American Maize Culture. *American Anthropologist* 26:345-59.

Lintz, Christopher, and Leon George Zabawa
1984   The Kenton Caves of Western Oklahoma. *Prehistory of Oklahoma*, edited by Robert Bell, pp. 161-74. New York: Academic Press.

Lipe, William D.
1978   The Southwest. *Ancient Native Americans*, edited by Jesse D. Jennings, pp. 327-99. San Francisco: W.H. Freeman and Company.
1955   *Radiocarbon Dating*. Second ed., Chicago: University of Chicago Press.

Loeb, Edwin M.
1936   The Distribution and Function of Money in Early Societies. *Essays in Anthropology Presented to A.L. Kroeber*, edited by R. H. Lowie: pp. 153-168. Berkeley:University of California Press.

Long, Austin, and Bruce Rippeteau
1974   Testing Contemporaneity and Averaging Radiocarbon Dates. *American Antiquity* 39:205-15.

Lopinot, Neal H.
1983   Analysis of Flotation Sample Materials from the Late Archaic Horizon. *The 1982 Excavations at the Cahokia Interpretive Center Tract, St. Clair County, Illinois*, by Michael S. Nassaney, Neal H. Lopinot, Brian M. Butler, and Richard W. Jefferies. Southern Illinois University at Carbondale. Center for Archaeological Investigations Research Paper 37.

Lorenzo, José Luis, and L. Gonzalez-Quintero
1970   The Oldest Teosinte. *Boletín del Instituto Nacional de Antropología e Historia*, pp. 1-3.

Lowden, J.A.
1969   Isotopic Fractionation in Corn. *Radiocarbon*, 11:391-93.

Luke, Clive J.
1980   *Continuing Archaeology on State Highway 16: The Excavations of the Shep Site (41KR109) and the Wounded Eye Site (41KR107)*. State Department of Highways and Public Transportation, Highway Design Division, Publications in Archaeology, Report 16.

Lumholtz, Carl
1902   *Unknown Mexico*. New York:Scribners.

Lundelius, Ernest L., Jr.
1967   Late-Pleistocene and Holocene Faunal History of Central Texas. *Pleistocene Extinctions, The Search for a Cause*, edited by Paul S. Martin and Herbert E. Wright, Jr., pp 287-319. New Haven:Yale University Press.

Lynott, Mark J.
1979   Prehistoric Bison Populations of Northcentral Texas. *Bulletin of the Texas Archeological Society* 50:89-101.
1981   Prehistoric Adaptive Patterns in Northern Texas. *Plains Anthropologist* 26(92):93-110.

Lynott, Mark J., and Duane E. Peter
1977   *1975 Archaeological Investigations at Aquilla Lake, Texas*. Southern Methodist University, Department of Anthropology, Archaeology Research Program, Archaeology Research Report 100.

McClintock, Barbara, Takeo A. Kato-Y., and A. Blumenschein
1981   *Chromosome Constitution of Races of Maize, Its Significance in the Interpretation of Relationships between Races and Varieties in the Americas*. Mexico:Colegio de Postgraduados Chapingo.

McClurkan, Burney B., William T. Field, and J. Ned Woodall
1966   *Excavations in Toledo Bend Reservoir, 1964-65*. University of Texas at Austin, Papers of the Texas Archeological Salvage Project, No. 8.

McClurkan, Burney B., Edward B. Jelks, and Harald P. Jensen
1980   Jonas Short and Coral Snake Mounds: A Comparision. *Louisiana Archaeology* 6:173-206.

McCollough, Major C.R., and Charles H. Faulkner
1973   Excavation of the Higgs and Doughty Sites; I-75 Salvage Archaeology.

Tennessee Archaeological Society Miscellaneous Paper 12.

1976 *Third Report of the Normandy Reservoir Salvage Project*, Vol. 3, *Normandy Archaeological Project*. Department of Anthropology, University of Tennessee, Report of Investigations 16.

1978 Sixth Report of the Normandy Archaeological Project, Vol. 6, *Normandy Archaeological Project*. Department of Anthropology, University of Tennessee, Report of Investigations 21.

McFarlan, Arthur C.
1943 *Geology of Kentucky*. Lexington:University of Kentucky Press.

McGraw, A. Joachim, and Fred Valdez, Jr.
1978 *Investigation of Prehistoric Rockshelter and Terrace Sites Along Portions of the Salado Creek Drainage, Northern Bexar County, Texas*. The University of Texas at San Antonio, Center for Archaeological Research, Archeological Survey Report 55.

McGregor, John C.
1958 *The Pool and Irving Villages: A Study of Hopewell Occupation in the Illinois River Valley*. Urbana:University of Illinois Press.

McGuff, Paul R.
1978 *Prehistoric Archeological Investigations at Palmetto Bend Reservoir: Phase I, Jackson County, Texas*. The University of Texas at Austin, Texas Archeological Survey, Research Report 58.

Mackenzie, Kenneth K.
1902 *Manual of the Flora of Jackson County, Missouri*. Kansas City, Missori.

McKinney, Wilson W.
1981 Early Holocene Adaptations in Central and Southwestern Texas: The Problem of the Paleoindian-Archaic Transition. *Bulletin of the Texas Archeological Society* 52:91-120.

McMillan, R. Bruce
1971 Biophysical Change and Cultural Adaptation at Rodgers Shelter, Missouri. Ph.D. dissertation, Department of Anthropology, University of Colorado.

1976 The Pomme de Terre Study Locality: Its Setting. *Prehistoric Man and His Environments*, edited by W. Raymond Wood and R. Bruce McMillan, pp. 13-44. New York:Academic Press.

MacNeish, Richard S.
1965 The Origins of American Agriculture. *American Antiquity* 39:87-94.
1947 A Preliminary Report on Coastal Tamaulipas, Mexico. *American Antiquity* 13:1-14.
1958 Preliminary Archaeological Investigations in the Sierra de Tamaulipas, Mexico. *Transactions of the American Philosophical Society* New Series, 48 (Pt. 6).
1964 The Food-Gathering and Incipient Agriculture Stage of Prehistoric Middle American. *Handbook of Middle American Indians*, edited by Robert Wauchope, Vol. 1 of *Natural Environment and Early Cultures*, edited by Robert C. West, pp. 413-26. Austin: University of Texas Press.

MacNeish, Richard S., Antoinette Nelken-Terner, and Irmgard W. Johnson
1967 *The Prehistory of the Tehuacan Valley*, Vol. 2, *Nonceramic Artifacts*. Austin:The University of Texas Press.

Magers, Pamela C.
1975 The Cotton Industry at Antelope House. *The Kiva* 41(1):39-47.

Maina, Shirley L.
1967 Ethnobotany of the Prehistoric Newbridge Site, Lower Illinois River Valley. Unpublished Master's thesis, Department of Botany, University of Chicago.

Mallouf, Michael G.
1979 *Archeological Investigations at Lake Limestone*. The University of Texas at Austin, Texas Archeological Survey, Texas Research Report 71.

Mallouf, Robert J., Barbara J. Baskin, and Kay L. Killen
    1977   *A Predictive Assessment of Cultural Resources in Hidalgo and Willacy Counties, Texas.* Texas Historical Commission, Archeological Survey Report 23.

Mangelsdorf, Paul C.
    1952   Evolution Under Domestication. *American Naturalist* 86:65-77.
    1954   New Evidence on the Origin and Ancestry of Maize. *American Antiquity* 19:409-10.
    1958   The Mutagenic Effect of Hybridizing Maize and Teosinte. *Cold Spring Harbor Symposium on Quantitative Biology* 23:409-21.
    1974   *Corn: Its Origin, Evolution, and Improvement.* Cambridge:Harvard University Press.
    1983   The Mystery of Corn: New Perspectives. *Proceedings of the American Philosophical Society* 127:215-47.

Mangelsdorf, Paul C., E.S. Barghoorn, and U.C. Banerjee
    1978   Fossil Pollen and the Origin of Corn. *Botanical Museum Leaflet, Harvard University* 26:237-55.

Mangelsdorf, Paul C., Herbert W. Dick, and Julián Cámara-Hernández
    1967   Bat Cave Revisited. *Botanical Museum Leaflets, Harvard University* 22:1-31.

Mangelsdorf, Paul. C., and Robert H. Lister
    1956   Archaeological Evidence on the Evolution of Maize in Northwestern Mexico. *Botanical Museum Leaflets, Harvard Univesity* 17(6).

Mangelsdorf, Paul C., Richard S. MacNeish and Walton C. Galinat
    1956   Archaeological Evidence on the Diffusion and Evolution of Maize in Northeastern Mexico. *Botanical Museum Leaflets, Harvard University* 17:125-50.
    1967a   Prehistoric Wild and Cultivated Maize. *The Prehistory of the Tehuacan Valley,* Vol. 1: *Environment and Subsistence,* edited by Douglas S. Byers, pp. 178-200. Austin: University of Texas Press.
    1967b   Prehistoric Maize, Teosinte, and *Tripsacum* from Tamaulipas, Mexico. *Botanical Museum Leaflets, Harvard University* 22:33-63.

Mangelsdorf, Paul C., Richard S. MacNeish, and Gordon R. Willey
    1964   Origins of Agriculture in Middle America. Natural Environments and Early Cultures, edited by Robert C. West. *Handbook of Middle American Indians* 1:427-445.

Mangelsdorf, Paul C., and R.G. Reeves
    1939   The Origin of Indian Corn and Its Relatives. *Texas Agricultural Experiment Station Bulletin* 574:1-315.

Mangelsdorf, Paul C., and C. Earle Smith, Jr.
    1949   New Archaeological Evidence on Evolution in Maize. *Botanical Museum Leaflets, Harvard Unversity* 13:213-47.

Marquardt, William H.
    1971   The Prehistory of the Western Coal Field Region. Ms. Seminar in Regional Archaeology. University of Kentucky, Department of Anthropology.
    1974   A Statistical Analysis of Constituents in Human Paleofecal Specimens from Mammoth Cave. *Archeology of the Mammoth Cave Area,* edited by Patty Jo Watson, pp. 193-202. New York:Academic Press.

Marquardt, William H., and Patty Jo Watson
    1976   Excavation and Recovery of Biological Remains from Two Archaic Shell Mounds in Western Kentucky. Paper presented at the 33rd annual meeting of the Southeastern Archaeological Conference.
    1983a   Excavation and Recovery of Biological Remains from Two Archaic Shell Middens in Western Kentucky. *Bulletin of the Southeastern Archaeological Conference* Volume 20:112-129.
    1983b   The Shell Mound Archaic of Western Kentucky. *Archaic Hunters and Gatherers in the American Midwest,* edited by James L. Phillips and James A. Brown, pp. 323-339. New York:Academic Press.

Martin, Paul S.
　　1963　*The Last 10,000 Years*. Tucson:University of Arizona Press.
Martin, Paul S., John B. Rinaldo, and Elaine Bluhm
　　1954　Caves of the Reserve Area. *Fieldiana: Anthropology* 42.
Martin, Paul S., John R. Rinaldo, Elaine Bluhm, Hugh C. Cutler, and R. Grange, Jr.
　　1952　Mogollan Cultural Continuity and Change: The Stratigraphic Analysis of Tularosa and Cordova Caves. *Fieldiana: Anthropology*, Vol. 40.
Martin, Paul S., and James Schoenwetter
　　1960　Arizona's Oldest Cornfield. *Science* 133:33-34.
Martin, Paul S.
　　1967　*Hay Hollow Site (200 B.C.-A.D. 200)*. Field Museum of Natural History Bulletin 38(5).
　　1972　Foreward to "Paleoecology of the Hay Hollow Site, Arizona." *Fieldiana: Anthropology* 63(1):1-5.
Martin, Paul S. and Fred Plog
　　1973　*The Archeology of Arizona: A Study of the Southwest Region*. Garden City, New York:Doubleday/Natural History Press.
Mathews, T.W., and E.H. Neller
　　1979　Atlatl Cave: Archaic–Basket-Maker II Investigations in Chaco Canyon National Monument. *Proceedings of the First Conference on Scientific Research in the National Parks*, Vol. II, edited by R. Linn, pp. 873. National Park Service Transactions and Proceedings Series 5.
Matson, R.G., and William D. Lipe
　　1978　Settlement Patterns on Cedar Mesa: Boom and Bust on Northern Periphery. *Investigations of the Southwestern Anthropological Group*, edited by R. Euler and G. Gumerman, pp. 1-12. Flagstaff: Museum of Northern Arizona.
Mayer-Oakes, William J.
　　1955　*The Prehistory of the Upper Ohio Valley: An Introductory Archaeological Study*. Annals of the Carnegie Museum 34.
Mayr, Ernst
　　1942　*Populations, Species, and Evolution*. Cambridge:Harvard University Press.
Mehringer, Peter J., Jr.
　　1967　Pollen Analysis and the Alluvial Chronology. *The Kiva* 32(3):96-101.
Mellars, Paul
　　1976　Fire Ecology, Animal Populations and Man: A Study of Some Ecological Relationships in Prehistory. *Proceedings of the Prehistoric Society* 42:15-45.
Mertens, Thomas R., and Peter H. Raven
　　1965　Taxonomy of *Polygonum*, Section *Polygonum* (Avicularia) in North America. *Madroño* 18:85-92.
Meyers, J. Thomas
　　1973　The Origins of Agriculture. An Evaluation of Three Hypotheses. *Prehistoric Agriculture*, edited by Stuart Streuver, pp. 101-21. Garden City:Natural History Press.
Mills, W.C.
　　1901　Plant Remains from the Baum Village Site. *Ohio Naturalist* 1(5):70-71.
Minnis, Paul E.
　　1981　Economic and Organizational Responses to Food Stress by Non-Stratified Societies: A Prehistoric Example. Ph.D. dissertation, Department of Anthropology, University of Michigan.
Minnis, Paul E., and Richard I. Ford
　　1976　Analysis of Plant Remains from Chimney Rock Mesa. *Archaeological Investigation at Chimney Rock Mesa: 1970-1972*, by F. Eddy, pp. 81-91. Memoirs of the Colorado Archaeological Society 1.
Minnis, Paul E., and Stephen E. Plog
　　1976　A Study of the Site Specific Distribution of *Agave parryi* in East Central Arizona. *The Kiva* 41(3-4):299-308.

Mohlenbrock, Robert H.
    1972   *The Illustrated Flora of Illinois. Grasses: Bromus to Paspalum*. Carbondale:Southern Illinois University Press.
    1975   *Guide to the Vascular Flora of Illinois*. Carbondale:Southern Illinois University Press.
    1978   *The Illustrated Flora of Illinois: Flowering Plants, Hollies to Loasas*. Carbondale: Southern Illinois University Press.
Morenon, E. Pierre, and Thomas R. Hays
    1978   New Evidence from the Jornada Branch: Excavations in the Placitas Arroyo. Paper presented at the annual meeting of the Society for American Archaeology, Tucson.
Morgan, David T., David L. Asch, Charles R. McGimsey, and Nancy B. Asch
    1982   Ambrose Flick and the Bushmeyer: Excavations at Two Early Woodland Sites in the Mississippi River Floodplain, Pike County, Illinois. Paper presented at Kampsville Conference on Early Woodland, Center for American Archeology, Kampsville, Illinois. October 1982.
Morgan, Lewis H.
    1877   *Ancient Society*. Chicago:Charles H. Kerr.
Morris, Earl H., and Robert F. Burgh
    1954   Basketmaker II Sites Near Durango, Colorado. *Carnegie Institution of Washington Publication*, 604.
Mosher, Edna
    1918   The Grasses of Illinois. *University of Illinois Agricultural Experiment Station Bulletin* 205.
Munson, Patrick J.
    1966   An Annotated Bibliography of Archaeological Maize in Eastern North America. *Pennsylvania Archaeologist* 36:50-65.
    1973   The Origins and Antiquity of Maize-Beans-Squash Agriculture in Eastern North America: Some Linguistic Implications. *Variation in Anthropology: Essays in Honor of John C. McGregor*, by Donald W. Lathrap and Jody Douglas, pp. 107-35. Urbana:Illinois Archaeological Survey.
    n.d.   Censuses of Weedy Plants on Disturbed Areas in the Central Illinois River Valley. Unpublished ms.
Murphy, James L.
    1971   Maize from an Adena Mound in Athens County, Ohio. *Science* 171(3974): 897-98.
Murray, Priscilla M., and Mark C. Sheehan
    1984   Prehistoric *Polygonum* Use in the Midwestern United States. *Experiments and Observations on Aboriginal Wild Plant Food Utilization in Eastern North America*, edited by Patrick J. Munson. Indiana Historical Society Prehistory Research Series 6(2).
Nabhan, Gary Paul
    1977   Viable Seeds from Prehistoric Caches Archaeobotanical Remains in Southwestern Folklore. *The Kiva* 43(2):143-59.
Nabhan, Gary P., and Richard S. Felger
    1978   Teparies in Southwestern North America—A Biogeographical and Ethnohistorical Study of *Phaseolus acutifolius*. *Economic Botany* 32(1):2-19.
Nabhan, Gary P., and Jan M. J. de Wet
    1984   *Panicum sonorum* in Sonoran Desert Agriculture. *Economic Botany* 38 (1):65-82.
Nabhan, Gary P., Alfred Whiting, Henry Dobyns, Richard Hevly, and Robert Euler
    1981   Devil's Claw Domestication: Evidence from Southwestern Indian Field. *Journal of Ethnobiology* 1(1):135-64.
Nance, Charles Roger
    1971   The Archaeology of La Calsada: A Stratified Rock Shelter Site, Sierra Madre Oriental, Nuevo Leon, Mexico. Ph.D. dissertation, Department of Anthropology, The University of Texas at Austin.

1972   Cultural Evidence for the Altithermal in Texas and Mexico. *Southwestern Journal of Anthropology* 28:169-92.

1980   La Calsada and the Prehistoric Sequence in Northeast Mexico. *Papers on the Prehistory of Northern Mexico and Adjacent Texas*, edited by J. F. Epstein, T.R. Hester, and C. Graves, pp. 41-57. The University of Texas at San Antonio, Center for Archaeological Research, Special Report 9.

Nelson, Charles E.
1967   The Archeology of Hall-Woodland Cave. *Southwestern Lore* 33:1-13.

Nelson, N.C.
1917   Contributions to the Archaeology of Mammoth Cave and Vicinity, Kentucky. *Anthropological Papers of the American Museum of Natural History* 22(1):1-73.

Newell, H. Perry, and Alex D. Krieger
1949   Maize from the Davis Site: It's Nature and Interpretation. *The George C. Davis Site, Cherokee County, Texas*. Memoirs for the Society for American Archaeology, 5.

Niederberger, Christine
1979   Early Sedentary Economy in the Basin of Mexico. *Science* 203:131-42.

Nichols, Robert F., and David G. Smith
1965   Evidence of Prehistoric Cultivation of Douglas-Fir at Mesa Verde. *Contributions of the Wetherill Mesa Project*, edited by D. Osborne, pp. 57-64. Society for American Archaeology Memoir 19.

Nickel, Robert K.
1974   Plant Resource Utilization at a Late Prehistoric Site in North-Central South Dakota. M.A. thesis, Department of Anthropology, University of Nebraska, Lincoln.

Nunley, Parker, and Thomas Roy Hester
1966   Preliminary Archeological Investigations in Dimmit County, Texas. *The Texas Journal of Science* 18(3):233-53.

Nuttall, Thomas
1818   *The Genera of North America Plants, and Catalogue of the Species to the Year 1817*. Vol. 2. Philadelphia:D. Heartt.

O'Brien, Patricia
1982   The Yeo Site (23CL199): A Kansas City Hopewell Limited Activity Site in Northwestern Missouri. *Plains Anthropologist* 27(95):37-54.

Olsson, Ingrid U., ed.
1970   Radiocarbon Variations and Absolute Chronology. *Proceedings of the 12th Nobel Symposium, Uppsala, 1969*.

Ozker, Doreen
1982   *An Early Woodland Community at the Schultz Site 20SA2 in the Saginaw Valley and the Nature of the Early Woodland Adaptation in the Great Lakes Region*. Anthropological Papers, Museum of Anthropology, University of Michigan 70.

Pammel, L.H., Carleton R. Bell, and F. Lamson-Scribner
1904   *The Grasses of Iowa*. Iowa Geological Survey Supplementary Report (1903), Part II.

Parker, Robert H.
1960   Ecology and Distributional Patterns of Macro-Invertebrates, Northern Gulf of Mexico. *Recent Sediments, Northwest Gulf of Mexico*, edited by Frances P. Shepard, Fred B. Phleger, and Tjeerd H. Van Andel, pp. 302-37. Tulsa:The American Association of Petroleum Geologists.

Parmalee, Paul W., R. Bruce McMillan, and James King
1976   Changing Subsistence Patterns at Rodgers Shelter. *Prehistoric Man and His Environments: A Case Study in the Ozark Highland*, edited by W.R. Wood and R. Bruce McMillan, pp. 141-61. New York:Academic Press.

Passmore, Sara F.
1930   Microsporogenesis in the Cucurbitacae. *Botanical Gazette* 90:213-23.

Patch, Diana
    1976   An Analysis of the Archaeological Shell of Fresh Water Mollusks from the Carlston Annis Shellmound, West Central Kentucky. Senior honor's thesis, Department of Anthropology, Washington University, St. Louis.

Patterson, Leland W., and J. Hudgins
    1981   Site 41WH19, A Long Occupation Period in Wharton County, Texas. *Houston Archeological Society Newsletter* 70:4-13.
    1983   Additional Artifacts from 41WH19, Wharton County, Texas. *Journal of the Houston Archeological Society* 76:7-11.

Payne, Willard W., and Volney H. Jones
    1962   The Taxonomic Status and Archaeological Significance of a Giant Ragweed from Prehistoric Bluff Shelters in the Ozark Plateau Region. *Papers of the Michigan Academy of Science, Arts and Letters* 47:147-63.

Pearsall, Deborah M.
    1978   Phytolith Analysis of Archaeological Soils: Evidence for Maize Cultivation in Formative Ecuador. *Science* 199:177.

Perino, Gregory H.
    1964   The Peisker Site, Calhoun County, Illinois. *Oklahoma Anthropological Society Newsletter* 12(2):6-9.

Perino, Gregory, and W.J. Bennett, Jr.
    1978   Archaeological Investigations at the Mahaffey Site, CH-1, Hugo Reservoir, Choctaw County, Oklahoma. Report submitted to the Army Corps of Engineers, Tulsa District, in compliance with Contract No. DACW56-77-C-0129. Museum of the Red River, Idabel, Oklahoma.

Pfahler, Paul L.
    1978   Biology of the Maize Male Gametophyte. *Maize Breeding and Genetics*, edited by D.B. Walden. New York:John Wiley & Sons.

Phillips Petroleum Co.
    1963   *Pasture and Range Plants*. Bartlesville, Oklahoma:Phillips Petroleum Co.

Pickersgill, Barbara
    1977   Taxonomy and the Origin and Evolution of Cultivated Plants in the New World. *Nature* 268:591-95.

Pickersgill, Barbara
    1977   Taxonomy and the Origin and Evolution of Cultivated Plants in the New World. *Nature* 268:591-95.

Pickersgill, Barbara B., and Charles B. Heiser
    1976   Cytogenetics and Evolutionary Change Under Domestication. *Phil. Transactions of the Royal Society of London* 275:55-69.
    1977   Origins and Distribution of Plants Domesticated in the New World Tropics. *Origins of Agriculture*, edited by C. Reed, pp. 803-35. The Hague:Mouton.

Plog, Fred
    1974   *The Study of Prehistoric Change*. New York: Academic Press.
    1978   The Nature of Hohokam Culture Change. Paper presented at the 43rd annual meeting of the Society for American Archaeology, Tucson.
    1980   Explaining Culture Change in the Hohokam Preclassic. *Current Issues in Hohokam Prehistory*, edited by David Doyle and Fred Plog, pp. 4-22. Arizona State University Anthropological Research Papers 23.

Preston, Nolan E.
    1969   The McCann Site. *Bulletin of the Texas Archeological Society* 40:167-92.

Prewitt, Elton R.
    1966   Preliminary Report on the Devil's Rockshelter Site, Val Verde County, Texas. *The Texas Journal of Science* 18:206-24.
    1974a   *Archeological Investigations at the Loeve-Fox Site, Williamson County, Texas*. The University of Texas at Austin, Texas Archeological Survey Research Report 49.
    1974b   *Upper Navasota Reservoir: An Archeological Assessment*. The University of

Texas at Austin, Texas Archeological Survey, Research Report 47.

1974c   Preliminary Archeological Investigations of the Rio Grande Delta of Texas. *Bulletin of the Texas Archeological Society* 45:55-66.

1981   Cultural Chronology in Central Texas. *Bulletin of the Texas Archeological Society* 52:65-89.

Prewitt, Elton R., and Michael G. Mallouf
1977   *Upper Navasota Reservoir: Test Excavations at Lake Limestone, Spring 1976.* The University of Texas at Austin, Texas Archeological Survey, Research Report 66.

Purrington, Burton L.
1966   The Jones Mound, HK 11: Hopewellian Influence in Western Kentucky. Ms. University of Kentucky, Museum of Anthropology, Lexington.

Putt, Eric D.
1964   Recessive Branching in Sunflowers. *Crop Science* 4:444-45.

Quimby, George L.
1946   The Possibility of an Independent Agricultural Complex in the Southeastern United States. Selected Readings Series, *Human Origins* No. 31:206-10.

Rackerby, Frank
1969   Preliminary Report on the Macoupin Site: A Lower Illinois Valley Middle Woodland Settlement. Paper presented at annual meeting of the Society for American Archaeology.

1982   Some Subsistence Settlement Insights from Macoupin: An Havana Hopewell Site in Jersey City, Illinois. Paper presented at 54th annual Midwest Archaeological Conference, Cleveland.

Ralph, Elizabeth K.
1971   Carbon-14 Dating. *Dating Techniques for the Archeologist*, edited by H.N. Michael and Elizabeth K. Ralph, pp. 1-48. Cambridge:The MIT Press.

Raun, Gerald G.
1966   Preliminary Report on the Herpetofauna of Val Verde County. *A Preliminary Study of the Paleoecology of the Amistad Reservoir Area*, assembled by Dee Ann Story and V.M. Bryant, Jr., pp. 209-26. Report submitted to the National Science Foundation.

Reagan, A. B.
1929   Plants Used by the White Mountain Apache Indians of Arizona. *Wisconsin Archaeologist* 8:143-61.

Reals, L.
1965   A Preliminary Report on the Country Road Site Artifact Distribution Analysis. Unpublished ms. on file with the Field Museum of Natural History, Chicago.

Reed, Charles A., ed.
1977   *Origins of Agriculture*. The Hague:Mouton.

Reed, Erik K.
1964   The Greater Southwest. *Prehistoric Man in the New World*, edited by Jesse D. Jennings and E.N. Norbeck, pp. 175-91. Chicago: The University of Chicago Press.

Reeves, Brian O.
1973   The Concept of the Altithermal Cultural Hiatus in Northern Plains Prehistory. *American Anthropologist* 75:1221-53.

Renaud, Etienne B.
1929   Archaeological Research in Northeastern New Mexico and Western Oklahoma. *Colorado Scientific Society Proceeding* 12:113-50.

Rhodes, Ashby M., William P. Bemis, Thomas W. Whitaker, and Samuel G. Cramer
1968   A Numerical Taxonomić Study of *Cucurbita*. *Brittonia* 20: 251-66.

Richardson, James B. III
1972   The Pre-Columbian Distribution of the Bottle Gourd (Lagenaria siceraria): A Re-evaluation. *Economic Botany* 26:265-73.

Robinson, Ralph L.
    1979   Biosilica and Climatic Change at 41GD21 and 41GD21A. *Archeological Investigations of Two Prehistoric Sites on Coleto Creek Drainage, Goliad County, Texas*, by D. Fox, pp. 102-113. The University of Texas at San Antonio, Center for Archaeological Research, Archaeological Survey Report 69.

Robinson, Sara
    1976   An Analysis of Charred Seeds from a Middle Woodland Occupation Site in Central Missouri. *Hopewellian Archaeology in the Lower Missouri River Valley*, edited by A. Johnson, pp. 100-09. University of Kansas Publications in Anthropology 8. Lawrence, Kansas.

Robison, Neil D.
    1978   *A Zooarchaeological Analysis of the Mississippian Faunal Remains from the Normandy Reservoir. Fifth Report of the Normandy Archaeological Project*, edited by C. Faulkner and M. McCollough, pp. 498- 595. Department of Anthropology, University of Tennessee.

Rodden, R.J.
    1959   Mechanical and Chemical Analyses of the Deposits of the LoDaisKa Site. *Excavations at the LoDaisKa Site*, by Henry J. Irwin and Cynthia C. Irwin, pp. 91-99. Proceedings of the Denver Museum of Natural History, No. 6.

Rohrbaugh, Charles L., Robert J. Burton, Susan S. Burton,
and Lura J. Rosewitz
    1971   Hugo Reservoir 1: The Description of the Archaeological Sites Excavated During the 1970 Field Season Including Ch-1, Ch-43, Ch-70, Ch-75, Pu-82 and Ch-90. *University of Oklahoma Research Institute, Oklahoma River Basin Survey, Archaeological Site Report 22*.

Rolingson, Martha
    1967   Temporal Perspective on the Archaic Cultures of the Middle Green River Region, Kentucky. Ph.D. dissertation, University of Michigan, Department of Anthropology.

Root, Matthew J.
    1979   The Paleoethnobotany of the Nebo Hill Site. *Plains Anthropologist* 24:239-47.

Ross, Richard E.
    1965   *The Archeology of Eagle Cave*. The University of Texas at Austin, Papers of the Texas Archeological Salvage Project 7.

Rubey, William W.
    1952   *Geology and Mineral Resources of the Hardin and Brussels Quadrangles (in Illinois)*. U.S. Geological Survey Professional Paper 218.

Sahlins, Marshall
    1972   *Stone Age Economics*. Chicago:Aldine.

Sahlins, Marshall D., and Elman R. Service
    1960   *Evolution and Culture*. Ann Arbor:University of Michigan Press.

Salaman, Redcliffe N.
    1940   Why "Jerusalem" Artichoke? *Journal of the Royal Horticultural Society* 65:338-48, 376-83.

Sauer, Carl O.
    1952   *Agricultural Origins and Dispersals*. Bowman Memorial Lectures Series 2. New York:American Geographical Society.
    1963   The Barrens of Kentucky. *Land and Life. A Selection of the Writings of Carl Ortwin Sauer*, edited by John Leighly, pp. 23-31. Berkeley: University of California Press.

Sauer, Jonathan D.
    1969   Identity of Archaeological Grain Amaranths from the Valley of Tehuacan, Puebla, Mexico. *American Antiquity* 34(10:80-81.

Sauer, Jonathan D., and Lawrence Kaplan
    1969   *Canavalia* beans in American Prehistory. *American Antiquity* 34(4):417-24.

Savage, Argyle D., and Thomas R. Mertens
     1968   A Taxonomic Study of Genus *Polygonum*, Section *Polygonum* (Avicularia)
              in Indiana and Wisconsin. *Indiana Academy of Science Proceedings*
              77:357-69.
Saxe, Arthur A.
     1971   Social Dimension of Mortuary Practices in the Mesolithic Population
              from Wadi Halfa, Sudan. *Approaches to the Social Dimensions of Mortuary
              Practices*, organized and edited by James A. Brown, pp. 39-57. Society for
              American Archaeology Memoir 25.
Sayles, E.B. and Ernst Antevs
     1941   *The Cochise Culture*. Medallion Papers No. 29. Gila Pueblo:Globe.
Schambach, Frank F.
     1970   Pre-Caddoan Cultures in the Trans-Mississippi South: A Beginning Se-
              quence. Ph.D. dissertation, Department of Anthropology, Harvard
              University.
     1982   An Outline of Fourche Maline Culture in Southwest Arkansas. *Arkansas
              Archeology in Review*, edited by Neal L. Trubowitz and Marvin D. Jeter, pp.
              132-97. Arkansas Archeological Survey Research Series 15.
Schambach, Frank F., and Ann M. Early
     1982   Southwest Arkansas. *A State Plan for the Conservation of Archeological Re-
              sources in Arkansas*, edited by Hester A. Davis. Fayetteville: Arkansas Arch-
              eological Survey, Research Series 21.
Schiffer, Michael B.
     1982   Hohokam Chronology: An Essay on History and Method. *Hohokam and
              Patayan: Prehistory of Southwestern Arizona*, edited by Randall H. McGuire
              and Michael B. Schiffer, pp. 299-344. New York:Academic Press.
Schmits, Larry J.
     1978   The Coffey Site: Environment and Cultural Adaptation at a Prairie Plains
              Archaic Site. *Mid-Continental Journal of Archaeology* 3:63-185.
Schock, Jack M.
     1984a   An Archaeological Survey for a Proposed 130 Acre Coal Mining Permit
              in Western Butler County, Kentucky. Report for Derek Mining, Inc. sub-
              mitted to Ted A. Norris, Vaughn Engineering, 1002 N. Main St.,
              Madisonville, Kentucky 42431.
     1984b   An Archaeological Survey for a Proposed 30 Acre Coal Mining Permit in
              Western Butler County, Kentucky. Report for Hoke Company, Inc. sub-
              mitted to Richard LeGrand, Vaughn Engineering, 1002 N. Main St.,
              Madisonville, Kentucky 42431.
Schock, Jack M. and T.W. Langford
     1979   An Archaeological Shoreline Reconnaissance of Barren River Lake, Al-
              len, Barren, and Monroe Counties. Kentucky Report to the Louisville
              Corps of Engineers, Contract #DAWC 27-77-M-0873. Bowling
              Green:Western Kentucky University.
Schroedl, Gerald F.
     1978   *The Patrick Site (40Mr40), Tellico Reservoir, Tennessee*. University of Ten-
              nessee, Department of Anthropology, Report of Investigations 25.
Schwanitz, Franz
     1966   *The Origin of Cultivated Plants* (Gerd von Wahlert, trans.). Cambridge:
              Harvard University Press.
Schwartz, Douglas W.
     1960   An Archaeological Survey of the Nolin River Reservoir. Ms. on file at the
              Department of Anthropology, University of Kentucky, Lexington.
Schwartz, Douglas W., Tacoma G. Sloan, and John Walker
     1958   Survey of the Archaeological Resources of the Rough River Basin;
              Hardin, Breckinridge, and Grayson Counties, Kentucky. Ms. on file at
              Department of Anthropology, University of Kentucky, Lexington.

Sears, Paul B.
    1982   Fossil Maize Pollen in Mexico. *Science* 216:932-34.
Sehgal, Surrinder M.
    1963   *Effects of Teosinte and "Tripsacum" Introgression in Maize.* Cambridge:Bussey
            Institution, Harvard University.
Service, Elman R.
    1962   *Primitive Social Organization: An Evolutionary Perspective.* New York:Ran-
            dom House.
Shafer, Harry J.
    1963   Test Excavations at the Youngsport Site: A Stratified Terrace Site in Bell
            County, Texas. *Bulletin of the Texas Archeological Society,* 34:57- 81.
    1973   Lithic Technology at the George C. Davis Site, Cherokee County, Texas.
            Ph.D. dissertation, Department of Anthropology, The University of Texas
            at Austin.
    1977   Early Lithic Assemblages in Eastern Texas. *The Museum Journal* (Texas
            Tech University, West Texas Museum Association) 27:187-97.
    1981   The Adaptive Technology of the Prehistoric Inhabitants of Southwest
            Texas. *Plains Anthropologist* 26(92):129-38.
Shafer, Harry J., Edward P. Baxter, Thomas B. Stearns, and
James Phil Dering
    1975   *An Archeological Assessment of the Big Thicket National Preserve.* Texas A&M
            University, Anthropology Laboratory Report 19.
Shafer, Harry J., and Thomas B. Stearns
    1975   *Archeological Investigations at the Scotts Ridge Site (41MQ41), Montgomery
            County, Texas.* Texas A&M University, Anthropology Laboratory Report
            17.
Shafer, Harry J., and Vaughn M. Bryant, Jr.
    1977   *Archeological and Botanical Studies at Hinds Cave, Val Verde County, Texas.*
            Texas A&M University, Anthropology Laboratory, Special Series 1.
Shafer, J., Phil Dering, and Edward P. Baxter
    1975   *Richland Creek Watershed, Hill County, Texas.* Texas A&M University, An-
            thropology Laboratory Report 14.
Shane, Orin
    1967   The Leimbach Site. *Studies in Ohio Archaeology,* edited by Olaf H. Prufer
            and Doublas H. MacKenzie, pp. 98-120. Cleveland:Western Reserve Uni-
            versity Press.
Shea, Andrea Brewer
    1978   An Analysis of Plant Remains from the Middle Woodland and Mississip-
            pian Components on the Banks V Site and a Paleoethnobotanical Study
            of the Native Flora of the Upper Duck Valley. *Fifth Report of the Normandy
            Archaeological Project,* edited by Charles Faulkner and Major McCollough,
            pp. 596-699. Department of Anthropology, University of Tennessee, Re-
            ports of Investigations 20.
Simmons, Alan H.
    1981   Paleo-subsistence and Technology in the San Juan Basin Archaic: A
            Comparative Study from Northwestern New Mexico. Paper presented at
            the 46th annual meeting of the Society for American Archeology, San
            Diego.
    1984   Chronical Implications. *Archaic Prehistory and Paleoenvironments in the San
            Juan Basin, New Mexico: The Chaco Shelters Project,* edited by Alan H.
            Simmons. University of Kansas, Museum of Anthropology, Project Re-
            port Series 53:210-16.
Simpson, George G., Anne Roe, and Roger C. Lewontin
    1960   *Quantitative Zoology.* Harcourt, Brace and Company, New York.
Skelton, Duford W.
    1977   *Archeological Investigations at the Fayette Power Project, Fayette County, Texas.*

The University of Texas at Austin, Texas Archeological Survey, Research Report 60.

1978   The Seasonal Factor of R. Cuneata Clam Collecting. Appendix in *Prehistoric Archeological Investigations at Palmetto Bend Reservoir: Phase I, Jackson County, Texas*, by Paul R. McGuff, pp. 263-74. The University of Texas at Austin, Texas Archeological Survey Research Report 58.

Skinner, S. Alan
1981   Aboriginal Demographic Changes in Central Texas. *Plains Anthropologist* 26(92):111-18.

Smith, Bruce D.
1984   *Chenopodium* as a Prehistoric Domesticate in Eastern North America: Evidence from Russell Cave, Alabama. *Science* 226(4671):165-67.

In   The Role of *Chenopodium* as a Domesticate in Pre-maize Garden Systems
press   of the Eastern United States. *Southeastern Archaeology.*

Smith, Buckingham
1871   *Relation of Alvar Nuñez Cabeza de Vaca.* Ann Arbor, Michigan:University Microfilms (Reprint, 1966).

Smith, C. Earle, Jr.
1950   Prehistoric Plant Remains from Bat Cave. *Botanical Museum Leaflets, Harvard University* 14:157-80.

1969   From Vavilov to the Present—A Review. *Economic Botany* 23(1):2-19.

Sollberger, J.B., and Thomas Roy Hester
1972   The Strohacker Site: A Review of Pre-Archaic Manifestations in Texas. *Plains Anthropologist* 17(58):326-44.

Sorrow, William M.
1966   *The Pecan Springs Site: Bardwell Reservoir, Texas.* The University of Texas at Austin, Papers of the Texas Archeological Salvage Project 10.

1968   *The Devil's Mouth Site: The Third Season—1967.* The University of Texas at Austin, Papers of the Texas Archeological Salvage Project 14.

Sorrow, William M., Harry J. Shafer, and Richard E. Ross
1967   *Excavations at Stillhouse Hollow Reservoir.* The University of Texas at Austin, Papers of the Texas Archeological Salvage Project 11.

Speck, Frank G.
1941   *Gourds of the Southeastern Indians.* Boston:New England Gourd Society.

Spinden, H.J.
1917   The Origin and Distribution of Agriculture in America. *Proceedings of the XIX Inter-Congress of Americanists.* Washington, D.C.

Spooner, Brian, ed.
1972   *Population Growth: Anthropological Implications.* Cambridge:MIT Press.

Stafford, Barbara D., and Mark B. Sant, eds.
1983   Excavations at the Smiling Dan Site: Delineation of Site Structure and Function during the Middle Woodland Period. Center for American Archeology Contract Archeology Program Report of Investigations 137. Submitted to Illinois Department of Transportation.

Stains, Donna
1972   Seed Analysis: The Brewster Site (13 CK 15), Western Iowa. M.A. thesis, Department of Anthropology, University of Wisconsin, Madison.

Stein, Julie
1978   Augering Archaeological Sites. *Southeastern Archaeological Conference Newsletter* 20:11-18.

1979   Geological Analysis of the Green River Shell Middens. Paper presented in the symposium, Natural and Cultural Processes in the Formation of an Archaic Shell Midden on the Green River, Kentucky. Southeastern Archaeological Conference 36th annual meeting, Atlanta, Georgia.

1980   Geoarcheology of the Green River Shell Mounds. Ph.D. dissertation, Center for Ancient Studies, University of Minnesota, Minneapolis.

1983   Earthworm Activity: A Source of Potential Disturbance of Archaeological
        Sediments. *American Antiquity* 48:277-289.
Stein, Julie K., Patty Jo Watson, and William B. White
1981   Geoarcheology of the Flint Mammoth Cave System and the Green River,
        Western Kentucky. *Geological Society of America Cincinnati '81 Field Trip
        Guidebooks III*, edited by T. Roberts.
Stephens, Alexander M.
1936   *Hopi Journal*, edited by E.C. Parsons. Columbia University Contributions
        to Anthropology 23(1 and 2).
Steward, Julian H.
1929   Irrigation without Agriculture. *Papers of the Michigan Academy of Science,
        Arts, and Letters* 22:149-56.
1938   *Basin-Plateau Aboriginal Socio-Political Groups*. Smithsonian Institution
        Bureau of American Ethnology Bulletin 120.
1949   Cultural Causality and Law: A Trial Formulation of the Development of
        Early Civilizations. *American Anthropologist* 51(10):1-27.
Stewart, Omer
1956   Fire as the First Great Force Employed by Man. *Man's Role in Changing the
        Face of the Earth*, edited by W.L. Thomas, Jr., pp. 115-33. Chicago: The
        University of Chicago Press.
Stewart, Robert B.
1974   Identification and Quantification of Components in Salts Cave Paleofeces
        1970-1972. *Archaeology of the Mammoth Cave Area*, edited by Patty Jo Wat-
        son, pp. 41-47. New York:Academic Press.
Steyermark, Julian A.
1963   *Flora of Missouri*. Ames:Iowa State University Press.
Stiger, Mark A.
1977   Anasazi Diet: The Coprolite Evidence. M.A. thesis, Department of An-
        thropology, University of Colorado.
Story, Dee Ann
1968   *Archeological Investigations at Two Central Texas Gulf Coast Sites*. Texas State
        Building Commission, Archeological Program Report 13.
1976   The East Texas Archaic. *The Texas Archaic: A Symposium*, edited by
        Thomas R. Hester, pp. 46-59. The University of Texas at San Antonio,
        Center for Archaeological Research Special Report 2.
1981   An Overview of the Archeology of East Texas. *Plains Anthropologist*
        26(92):139-56.
Story, Dee Ann, and Harry J. Shafer
1965   *1964 Excavations at Waco Reservoir, McLennan County, Texas: The Baylor and
        Britton Sites*. The University of Texas at Austin, Texas Archeological Sal-
        vage Project Miscellaneous Papers 6.
Struever, Stuart
1962   Implications of Vegetal Remains from an Illinois Hopewell Site. *American
        Antiquity* 27:584-87.
1964   The Hopewell Interaction Sphere in Riverine-Western Great Lakes
        Culture History. *Hopewellian Studies*, edited by Joseph R. Caldwell and
        Robert L. Hall. Illinois State Museum Scientific Papers 12.
1968a   Flotation Techniques for the Recovery of Small-Scale Archaeological Re-
        mains. *American Antiquity* 33(3):353-62.
1968b   A Re-examination of Hopewell in Eastern North America. Ph.D. disserta-
        tion, Department of Anthropology, University of Chicago.
1968c   Woodland Subsistence-Settlement Systems in the Lower Illinois Valley.
        New Perspectives in Archeology, edited by Sally R. Binford and Lewis R.
        Binford, pp. 285-312. Chicago:Aldine.
Struever, Stuart, and Kent D. Vickery
1973   The Beginnings of Cultivation in the Midwest-Riverine Area of the

United States. *American Anthropologist* 75(5):1197-220.

Stuart, Laurence C.
 1964 Fauna of Middle America. *Handbook of Middle American Indians*, edited by R. Wauchope, Vol. 1:316-62. *Archaeological Frontiers and External Conditions*, edited by Gordon F. Ekholm and Gordon R. Willey, pp. 59-94. Austin: The University of Texas Press.

Swanton, John R.
 1946 The Indians of the Southeastern United States. *Bureau of American Ethnology Bulletin* 137:602-08.

Symms, E. Leigh
 1977 Cultural Ecology and Ecological Dynamics of the Ceramic Period in Southwestern Manitoba. *Plains Anthropologist* 22(76):Pt. 2.

Tapley, W.T., W.D. Enzie, and G.P. Van Eseltine
 1937 The Vegetables of New York, Part IV: The Cucurbits. *Report of the New York State Agricultural Experiment Station* for 1935. Albany.

Taylor, Walter W.
 1966 Archaic Cultures Adjacent to the Northeastern Frontiers of Meso-America. *Handbook of Middle American Indians*, edited by Robert Wauchope, Vol. 4: *Archaeological Frontiers and External Conditions*, edited by Gordon F. Ekholm and Gordon R. Willey, pp. 59-94. Austin: The University of Texas Press.

Thomas, Alfred B.
 1932 *Forgotten Frontiers*. Norman: University of Oklahoma Press.

Thomas, D.H.
 1976 *Figuring Anthropology*. Holt, Rinehart and Winston.

Thone, Frank
 1935 Nature Ramblings. *Science News Letter* 27:419.

Traylor, Diane, Nancy Wood, Lyndi Hubbel, Robert Scaife, and Sue Weber
 1977 Bandelier: Excavations in the Flood Pool of Cochiti Lake, New Mexico. Unpublished ms. on file with the National Park Service Southwestern Cultural Resource Center, Santa Fe.

Tuan, Yi-fu, Cyril E. Everard, G. Widdison, and Iven Bennett
 1973 *The Climate of New Mexico*. Santa Fe:New Mexico State Planting Office.

Turnbow, Christopher, and Lathel F. Duffield
 1977 An Archaeological Survey of the Red River Gorge Area of the Daniel Boone National Forest in Powell, Wolfe, and Menifee Counties, Kentucky. Report submitted to the United States Forest Service, Daniel Boone National Forest, Winchester, Kentucky, by the University of Kentucky, Museum of Anthropology.

USDA
 1965 Silvics of the Forest Trees of the United States. United States Department of Agriculture Handbook No. 271.

Van Devender, Thomas R. Spaulding, and W. Geoffrey Spaulding
 1979 Development of Vegetation and Climate in the Southwestern United States. *Science* 204:701-10.

van der Merwe, Nikolaas J., and J.C. Vogel
 1978 ^{13}C Content of Human Collagen as a Measure of Prehistoric Diet in Woodland North America. *Nature* 276:815-16.

Vaughan, J.G.
 1970 *The Structure and Utilization of Oil Seeds*. London:Chapman and Hall.

Vavilov, N.I.
 1926 Studies on the Origins of Cultivated Plants. *Bulletin of Applied Botany, Genetics and Breeding* 16:139-248.

 1949- The Origin, Variation, Immunity, and Breeding of Cultivated Plants.
 1950 *Bulletin of Chronica Botanica* 13.

Vayda, Andrew
 1966 Pomo Trade Feasts. *Tribal and Peasant Economies*, edited by George

Dalton, pp. 494-500. Garden City, New York: Natural History Press.

Vehik, Rain
1974   Archaeological Investigations in the Harry S Truman Reservoir Area: 1970 Archaeological salvage project, National Park Service and University of Missouri: contract #14-0-2:920-191,
1977   A Multivariate Analysis of the Fristoe Burial Complex in Southwestern Missouri. *Plains Anthropologist* 22(76):123-32.
1978   An Analysis of Cultural Variability During the Late Woodland Period in the Ozark Highland of Southwest Missouri. Ph.D. dissertation, University of Missouri, Department of Anthropology.

Vivó, Jorge A. Escoto
1964   Weather and Climate of Mexico and Central America. *Handbook of Middle American Indians*, edited by Robert Wauchope, Vol. 1: *Natural Environment and Early Cultures*, edited by Robert C. West, pp. 187- 215. Austin: The University of Texas Press.

Vogel, J.C., and Nikolaas J. van der Merwe
1977   Isotopic Evidence for Early Maize Cultivation in New York State. *American Antiquity* 42:238-242.

Wagner, Gail E.
1978   An Archeobotanical Analysis of Five Sites in the Mammoth Cave Area. Master's essay, Department of Anthropology, Washington University, St. Louis, Missouri.
1979   The Green River Archaic: A Botanical Reconstruction. Paper presented in the symposium, Natural and Cultural Processes in the Formation of an Archaic Shell Midden on the Green River, Kentucky. 36th annual meeting of the Southeastern Archaeological Conference, Atlanta, Georgia.
1983   Fort Ancient Subsistence: The Botanical Record. *West Virginia Archeologist* 35:27-39.

Wahl, Herbert A.
1952-   A Preliminary Study of the Genus *Chenopodium* in North America.
1953   *Bartonia* 27:1-46.

Wallace, Henry A., and William L. Brown
1956   Corn and Its Early Fathers. Chicago:The Michigan State University Press and The Lakeside Press.

Walley, Raymond
1955   A Preliminary Report on the Albert George Site in Fort Bend County. *Bulletin of the Texas Archeological Society* 26:218-34.

Watkins, T., ed.
1975   *Radiocarbon: Calibration and Prehistory*. Edinburgh:Edinburgh University Press.

Watson, Patty Jo
1976   In Pursuit of Prehistoric Subsistence: A Comparative Account of Some Contemporary Flotation Techniques. *Mid-Continental Journal of Archaeology* 1:77-100.

Watson, Patty Jo, and Kenneth C. Carstens
1979   Cave Research Foundation Archeological Project and Shellmound Archeological Project, 1978. *Cave Research Foundation, 1978 Annual Report*, edited by S. Wells and B. Wells, pp. 46-49. Yellow Springs, Ohio.

Watson, Patty Jo, ed.
1974   *Archeology of the Mammoth Cave Area*. New York:Academic Press.

Watson, Patty Jo, et al.
1969   *The Prehistory of Salts Cave, Kentucky*. Illinois State Museum, Reports of Investigations 16. Springfield.

Watt, Bernice K. and Annabel L. Merrill
1963   *Composition of Foods*. United States Department of Agriculture. Handbook No. 8.

Watt, Frank H.
    1938   The Waco Sinker. *Central Texas Archeologist* 4:21- 70.
Watt, Frank H., and George A. Agogino
    1968   First Citizens of Central Texas. *Texana* 5(4):293- 316.
Waugh, F.W.
    1916   Iroquois Foods and Food Preparation. *Canada Department of Mines, Geological Survey, Anthropological Series,* 12.
Weatherwax, Paul
    1935   The Phylogeny of *Zea mays. American Midland Naturalist* 16:1-71.
Webb, Clarence H.
    1977   *The Poverty Point Culture.* Geoscience and Man, Vol. 17. Louisiana State University, Baton Rouge.
Webb, Clarence H., and Hiram F. Gregory
    1978   *The Caddo Indians of Louisiana.* Louisiana Archaeological Survey and Antiquities Commission Anthropology Study 2.
Webb, Clarence H., Forrest E. Murphey, Wesley G. Ellis, and
H. Roland Green
    1969   The Resch Site 41HS16, Harrison County, Texas. *Bulletin of the Texas Archeological Society* 40:3- 106.
Webb, William S.
    1940   The Wright Mounds: Sites 6 and 7, Montgomery County, Kentucky. *University of Kentucky Reports in Anthropology and Archaeology* 5(1).
    1950   *The Carlson Annis Mound; Site 5, Butler County, Kentucky.* University of Kentucky Reports in Anthropology 7.
    1951   Radiocarbon Dating of Samples from the Southeast. *Radiocarbon Dating,* edited by F. Johnson, pp. 30. Society for American Archaeology, Memoir 8.
Webb, William S., and Raymond S. Baby
    1957   *The Adena People, No. 2.* Columbus:Ohio State University.
Webb, William S., and William D. Funkhouser
    1929   The So-Called "Hominy-holes" of Kentucky. *American Anthropologist* 31(4):701-09.
    1936   Rockshelters in Menifee County, Kentucky. *University of Kentucky Reports in Archaeology and Anthropology* 3(4):101-67.
Weinland, Marcia K., and Thomas N. Sanders
    1977   A Reconnaissance and Evaluation of Archaeological Sites in Powell County, Kentucky. *Kentucky Heritage Commission, Archaeological Survery Reports* 3., Frankfort.
Weintrub, Nancy
    n.d.   Plant Communities in the Red River Gorge, Kentucky. Report prepared for the Red River Gorge Archaeological Project.
Weir, Frank A.
    1976a   The Central Texas Archaic. Ph.D. dissertation, Department of Anthropology, Washington State University.
    1976b   The Central Texas Archaic Reconsidered. *The Texas Archaic: A Symposium,* edited by T.R. Hester, pp. 60-66. The University of Texas at San Antonio, Center for Archeological Research, Special Report 2.
    1979   Greenhaw: An Archaic Site in Central Texas. *Bulletin of the Texas Archeological Society* 50:5- 68.
Wellhausen, Edward J., L.M. Roberts, and E. Hernandez-X., with Paul C. Mangelsdorf.
    1952   *Races of Maize in Mexico, Their Origin, Characteristics and Distribution.* Cambridge: Bussey Institution, Harvard University.
Wendland, Wayne M.
    1978   Holocene Man in North America: The Ecological Setting and Climatic Background. *Plains Anthropolgist* 23(82):273-87.
Wendland, Wayne M., and Reid A. Bryson
    1974   Dating Climatic Episodes of the Holocene. *Quaternary Research* 4:9-24.

Wesolowsky, Al B., Thomas R. Hester, and Douglas R. Brown
    1976   Archeological Investigations at the Jetta Court Site (41TV151), Travis
            County, Texas. *Bulletin of the Texas Archeological Society* 47:25-88.
West, Robert C.
    1964a   Surface Configurations and Associated Geology of Middle America.
            Handbook of Middle American Indians, edited by Robert Wauchope, Vol. 1:
            Natural Environment and Early Cultures, edited by Robert C. West, pp.
            33-83. Austin:The University of Texas Press.
    1964b   The Natural Regions of Middle America. *Handbook of Middle American
            Indians*, edited by Robert Wauchope, Vol. 1: *Natural Environment and Early
            Cultures*, edited by Robert C. West, pp. 363-83. Austin:The University of
            Texas Press.
Wettersten, Vernon H.
    1983   A Study of Late Woodland Cultural Change in the Lower Illinois River
            Valley. Unpublished Ph.D. dissertation, Department of Anthropology,
            Northwestern University, Evanston, Illinois.
Wetterstrom, Wilma
    1978   Cognitive Systems, Food Patterns, and Paleoethnobotany. *The Nature and
            Status of Ethnobotany*, edited by Richard I. Ford, pp. 81-95. University of
            Michigan Museum of Anthropology, Anthropological Papers 67.
Whalen, Norman M.
    1971   Cochise Culture Sites in the Central San Pedro Drainage. Ph.D. disserta-
            tion, Department of Anthropology, Arizona State University.
    1973   Agriculture and the Cochise. *The Kiva* 39:89-96.
Wheat, Joe Ben
    1953   The Addicks Dam Site: An Archeological Survey of the Addicks Dam
            Basin, Southeast Texas. River Basin Survey Papers No. 4: Smithsonian
            Institution, *Bureau of American Ethnology Bulletin* 154:143-252.
Whitaker, Thomas W.
    1981   Archaeological Cucurbits. *Economic Botany* 35:460-66.
Whitaker, Thomas W., and William P. Bemis
    1964   Evolution in the Genus *Cucurbita*. *Evolution* 18:553-59.
    1975   Origin and Evolution of the Cultivated *Cucurbita*, *Bulletin of the Torrey
            Botanical Club* 102:362-68.
Whitaker, Thomas W. and G.W. Bohn
    1950   The Taxonomy, Genetics, Production and Uses of the Cultivated Species
            of *Cucurbita*. *Economic Botany* 4(1):52-81.
Whitaker, Thomas W., and George F. Carter
    1946   Critical Notes on the Origin and Domestication of the Cultivated Species
            of *Cucurbita*. *American Journal of Botany* 33:10-15.
    1954   Oceanic Drift of Gourds: Experimental Observations. *American Journal of
            Botany* 4(1):52-81.
    1961   A Note on the Longevity of Seed of *Lagenaria siceraria* (Mol.) Standl. after
            Floating in Sea Water. *Bulletin of the Torrey Botanical Club* 88:104-06.
Whitaker, Thomas W., and Hugh C. Cutler
    1965   Cucurbits and Cultures in the Americas. *Economic Botany* 19:344-49.
    1971   Prehistoric Cucurbits from the Valley of Oaxaca. *Economic Botany*
            25(2):123-27.
Whitaker, Thomas W., Hugh C. Cutler, and Richard S. MacNeish
    1957   Cucurbit Materials from Three Caves Near Ocampo, Tamaulipas. *Ameri-
            can Antiquity* 22(4):352-58.
Whitaker, Thomas W. and Glen N. Davis
    1962   *Cucurbits: Botany, Cultivation, and Utilization.* New York:Interscience
            Publishers.
Wiant, Michael D., Edwin R. Hajic, and Thomas N. Styles
    1983   Napolean Hollow and Koster Site Stratigraphy: Implications for Holo-
            cene Landscape Evolution and Studies of Archaic Period Settlement Pat-

terns in the Lower Illinois River Valley. *Archaic Hunters and Gatherers in the American Midwest*, edited by James Phillips and James A. Brown, pp. 147-64. New York:Academic Press.

Wilcox, David
    1979   The Hohokam Regional System. *An Archeological Test of Sites in the Gila Butte-Santan Region, South-Central Arizona*, by G. Rice, D. Wilcox, K. Rafferty and J. Schoenwetter. Arizona State University Anthropological Research Papers 18.

Wilkes, H. Garrison
    1967   Teosinte: The Closest Relative of Maize. Cambridge:Bussey Institution, Harvard University.
    1972   Maize and Its Wild Relatives. *Science* 177:1071-77.

Will, George F., and George E. Hyde
    1917   *Corn Among the Indians of the Upper Missouri* (1964 reprint by the University of Nebraska Press, Lincoln).

Willey, Gordon R. and Philip Phillips
    1958   *Methods and Theory in American Archeology*. Chicago:University of Chicago Press.

Williams, J.T., and J.L. Harper
    1965   Seed Polymorphism and Germination. I. The Influence of Nitrates and Low Temperatures on the Germination of *C. album. Weed Research* 5(2):141-50.

Williams-Dean, Glenna Joyce
    1978   Ethnobotany and Cultural Ecology of Prehistoric Man in Southwest Texas. Ph.D. dissertation, Department of Botany, Texas A&M University.

Wilson, Hugh D.
    1976   A Biosystematic Study of Cultivated Chenopods and Related Species. Ph.D. dissertation, Indiana University.
    1976a   Identification of Archeological *Chenopodium* Material from Eastern North America. The Botanical Society of America, *Abstracts of Papers* 64.
    1980   Artificial Hybridization among Species of *Chenopodium* Sect. *Chenopodium. Systematic Botany* 5:263-73.
    1981   Domesticated *Chenopodium* of the Ozark Bluff Dwellers. *Economic Botany* 35:233-39.

Wilson, Hugh D. and Charles B. Heiser
    1979   The Origin and Evolutionary Relationships of 'Huauzontle' (*Chenopodium nuttalliae* Safford), Domesticated Chenopod of Mexico. *American Journal of Botany* 66:198-206.

Wilson, Roger E., and Leroy L. Rice
    1968   Alleopathy as Expressed by *Helianthus annuus* and Its Role in Old Field Succession. *Bulletin of the Torrey Botanical Club* 95:432-48.

Wilson, Ronald
    n.d.   A Catalog of Squash and Gourd Remains from Salts Cave and Mammoth Cave, Kentucky. Ms. on file, Shell Mound Archaeological Project, Department of Anthropology, Washington University, St. Louis.

Winter, Joseph C.
    1973   The Distribution and Development of Frement Maize Agriculture: Some Preliminary Interpretations. *American Antiquity* 38(4):439-51.
    1976   The Processes of Farming Diffusion in the Southwest and Great Basin. *American Antiquity* 41:421-29.

Winter, Joseph C., and Henry G. Wylie
    1974   Paleoecology and Diet at Clyde's Cavern. *American Antiquity* 39:303-15.

Winterhalder, Bruce P.
    1977   Foraging Strategies of the Boreal Forest Cree: An Evaluation of Theory and Models from Evolutionary Ecology. Ph.D. dissertation, Department of Anthropology, Cornell University.

Winters, Howard D.
    1963   *An Archaeological Survey of the Wabash Valley in Illinois.* Illinois State Museum, Reports of Investigations 10.
    1968   Value Systems and Trade Cycles of the Late Archaic in the Midwest. *New Perspectives in Archeology,* edited by Sally R. Binford and Lewis R. Binford, pp. 175-222. Chicago:Aldine Publishing Co.
    1969   *The Riverton Culture: A Second Millennium Occupation in the Central Wabash Valley.* Illinois State Museum Reports of Investigations 13.
    1974   Introduction to the New Edition. In a reprinting of William S. Webb's *Indian Knoll,* pp. v-xxvii. Knoxville:University of Tennessee Press.
Wise, Edward N., and Dick Shutler
    1958   University of Arizona Radiocarbon Dates. *Science* 127(3289):72-74.
Woermann, J.W.
    1905   Map of the Illinois and Des Plaines Rivers from Lockport, Illinois, to the Mouth of the Illinois River, in 58 sheets including an index map. U.S. Army Corps of Engineers.
Wood, John J.
    1967   Archeological Investigations in Northeastern Colorado. Ph.D. dissertation, Department of Anthropology, University of Colorado.
Wood, W. Raymond
    1961   The Pomme de Terre Reservoir in Western Missouri Prehistory, *The Missouri Archaeologist* 23.
    1967   The Fristoe Burial Complex of Southwestern Missouri, *Plains Anthropologist* 29.
    1976   Archaeological Investigations at the Pomme de Terre Springs. *Prehistoric Man and His Environments: A Case Study in the Ozark Highland,* edited by W. Wood and R. McMillan, pp. 97-107. New York:Academic Press.
Wood, W. Raymond, and R. Bruce McMillan, eds.
    1976   *Prehistoric Man and His Environments: A Case Study in the Ozark Highland.* New York: Academic Press.
Word, James H., and Charles L. Douglas
    1970   *Excavations at Baker Cave, Val Verde County, Texas.* The University of Texas at Austin, Texas Memorial Museum Bulletin 16.
Woosley, Anne I., and Ruth L. Baker
    1984   Evidence for the Prehistoric Cultivation of Grain Amaranth from Pot Creek Pueblo, Taos District, New Mexico. Paper presented at the Seventh Annual Ethnobiology Conference, Seattle.
Wright, Henry A., and Arthur W. Bailey
    1983   *Fire Ecology.* New York:John Wiley - Interscience Publication.
Wright, Herbert E., Jr.
    1977   Environmental Change and the Origin of Agriculture in the Old and New Worlds. *Origins of Agriculture,* edited by Charles A. Reed, pp. 281-320. The Hague:Mouton.
Wright, Sewall
    1931   Evolution in Mendelian Populations. *Genetics* 16:97-159.
Wyckoff, Don G.
    1965a   *The Biggham Creek Site of McCurtain County, Oklahoma.* University of Oklahoma, Oklahoma River Basin Survey Project, Archeological Site Report 3.
    1965b   *The Hughes, Lamas Branch, and Callahan Sites, McCurtain County, Southeast Oklahoma.* University of Oklahoma, Oklahoma River Basin Survey Project, Archeological Site Report 4.
    1967a   *The Archaeological Sequence in the Broken Bow Reservoir Area, McCurtain County, Oklahoma.* University of Oklahoma, Stovall Museum of Natural History and Oklahoma River Basin Survey Project. Norman:University of Oklahoma Research Institute.

1967b   *The E. Johnson Site and Prehistory in Southeastern Oklahoma.* University of
         Oklahoma, Oklahoma River Basin Surveys, Archaeological Site Report 6.

1967c   Woods Mound Group: A Prehistoric Mound Complex in McCurtain
         County, Oklahoma. *Bulletin of the Oklahoma Anthropological Society* 15:1-76.

1968   *The Bell and Gregory Sites: Archeological Chronicles of Prehistory in the Pine
         Creek Reservoir Area, Southeast Oklahoma.* University of Oklahoma Re-
         search Institute, Oklahoma River Basin Survey, Archeological Site Report
         11.

1970   Archeological and Historical Assessment of the Red River Basin in
         Oklahoma. *Archeological and Historical Resources of the Red River Basin,*
         edited by Hester A. Davis, pp. 69-134. University of Arkansas Museum,
         Arkansas Archeological Survey Publications on Archeology Research Se-
         ries 1.

1984   The Foragers: Eastern Oklahoma. *Prehistory of Oklahoma,* edited by R.E.
         Bell, pp. 119-60. New York:Academic Press.

Wymer, Dee Anne
1983   A Preliminary Analysis of the Zencor/Scioto Trails Site (33FE8) Archae-
         obotanical Assemblage. Ms. Prehistory Laboratory, Department of An-
         thropology, Ohio State University, Columbus, Ohio.

Wyss, James D., and Sandra K. Wyss
1977   An Archaeological Assessment of Portions of the Red River Gorge,
         Daniel Boone National Forest, Kentucky. Report prepared for Depart-
         ment of Agriculture, U.S. Forest Service, and Ohio Valley Archaeological
         Research Associates, Lexington, Kentucky.

Yarnell, Richard A.
1964   *Aboriginal Relationships Between Culture and Plant Life in the Upper Great
         Lakes Region.* Museum of Anthropology, University of Michigan, An-
         thropological Paper 23.

1969   Contents of Human Paleofeces. *The Prehistory of Salts Cave, Kentucky,* by
         Patty Jo Watson et al., pp. 41-54. Illinois State Museum, Reports of Inves-
         tigations 16.

1972   *Iva annua* var. *macrocarpa*: Extinct American Cultigen? *American An-
         thropologist* 74:335-41.

1974a   Plant Food and Cultivation of the Salts Caves. *Archeology of the Mammoth
         Cave Area,* edited by Patty Jo Watson, pp. 113-22. New York:Academic
         Press.

1974b   Intestinal Contents of the Salts Cave Mummy and Analysis of the Initial
         Salts Cave Flotation Series. *Archeology of the Mammoth Cave Area,* edited by
         Patty Jo Watson, pp. 109-12. New York: Academic Press.

1976   Early Plant Husbandry in Eastern North America. *Cultural Change and
         Continuity,* edited by Charles E. Cleland, pp. 265-73. New York:Academic
         Press.

1977   Native Plant Husbandry North of Mexico. *Origins of Agriculture,* edited by
         Charles A. Reed, pp. 861-75. The Hague:Mouton.

1978   Domestication of Sunflower and Sumpweed in Eastern North America.
         The Nature and Status of Ethnobotany, edited by Richard I. Ford, pp.
         289-99. Anthropological Papers, Museum of Anthropology, University of
         Michigan 67.

1981   Inferred Dating of Ozark Bluff Dweller Occupations Based on Achene
         Size of Sunflower and Sumpweed. *Journal of Ethnobiology* 1(1):55-60.

1983   Prehistory of Plant Foods and Husbandry in North America. Paper pre-
         sented at the 48th annual meeting, Society for American Archaeology,
         Pittsburgh.

Yen, Doug E.
1974   Arboriculture in the Subsistence of Santa Cruz, Solomon Islands. *Eco-
         nomic Botany* 28:247-84.

York, John C., and William A. Dick-Peddie
    1969   Vegetational Changes in Southern New Mexico During the Past Hundred Years. *Arid Lands in Perspective*, edited by W. McGinnies and B. Goldman, pp. 157-66. Tucson:University of Arizona Press.

Young, Jon Nathan
    1962   Annis Mound: A Late Prehistoric Site on the Green River. M.A. thesis, Department of Anthropology, University of Kentucky, Lexington.

Zevallos, Carlos M., Walton C. Galinat, Donald W. Lathrap, Earl R. Leng, Jorge G. Marcos, and Kathleen M. Klumpp
    1977   The San Pablo Corn Kernel and Its Friends. *Science* 196:385-89.